I'll Take
HYPNOSIS
with a Side of
MEDIUMSHIP:
A Journey from Atheism to Spirituality

Garry Gewant

BALBOA.
PRESS
A DIVISION OF HAY HOUSE

Balboa Press books may be ordered through booksellers or by contacting:

Balboa Press
A Division of Hay House
1663 Liberty Drive
Bloomington, IN 47403
www.balboapress.com
1 (877) 407-4847

Because of the dynamic nature of the Internet, any web addresses or links contained in this book may have changed since publication and may no longer be valid. The views expressed in this work are solely those of the author and do not necessarily reflect the views of the publisher, and the publisher hereby disclaims any responsibility for them.

The author of this book does not dispense medical advice or prescribe the use of any technique as a form of treatment for physical, emotional, or medical problems without the advice of a physician, either directly or indirectly. The intent of the author is only to offer information of a general nature to help you in your quest for emotional and spiritual well-being. In the event you use any of the information in this book for yourself, which is your constitutional right, the author and the publisher assume no responsibility for your actions.

Any people depicted in stock imagery provided by Thinkstock are models, and such images are being used for illustrative purposes only.
Certain stock imagery © Thinkstock.

Print information available on the last page.

ISBN: 978-1-5043-9152-8 (sc)
ISBN: 978-1-5043-9153-5 (hc)
ISBN: 978-1-5043-9154-2 (e)

Library of Congress Control Number: 2017917739

Balboa Press rev. date: 12/18/2017

PREFACE

As I prepared to submit the final draft of this book to the publisher, I was still struggling over the title.

I had been writing my book, on and off, for the past 13 years. I was comfortable with the title that I'd imagined from the beginning. Spiritual Evolution: A Journey from Atheism to Spirituality, felt right to me, and was a very descriptive and accurate title. But when I shared parts of my book with friends and family, I was told that although they loved the parts they'd read, the title made it seem like a boring New Age text book and had to go. I soon realized that they were right, so I began 'trying on' different titles, in search of the 'perfect fit'.

As the new title suggests, my book does belong in the New Age section. I think it's amusing how I eventually found its present title. My website, HYP4LIFE.com, had been up and running for over ten years by the time I'd finished the final draft, and it had become the best source of new hypnosis clients I could have imagined.

By now, the choice of a perfect title had become a huge priority. I had my manuscript complete and ready for publishing and it was open on my computer as I sat staring at the original title. But I couldn't conceive of a new and catchy title; I needed help.

So, as I usually do, I leaned back at my desk, looked up and asked for guidance in making that important decision... just as my business phone rang.

"Hi Garry, I was on your site and have a bunch of questions. There is so much there, and I was wondering if you could help me?" I asked which topics interested her most, and she said with a chuckle, "Well... I'll take hypnosis with a side of mediumship!"

I quietly laughed, and as I always do, looked up and thought, *Thanks guys! You just gave me the answer to my search. Oh, and thank-you for that synchronicity."*

To know whom I'd just thanked, you'll have to read on.

I'LL TAKE HYPNOSIS WITH A SIDE OF MEDIUMSHIP: A JOURNEY FROM ATHEISM TO SPIRITUALITY

On My Journey: Finding My Road
- A Life Lesson I learned on the Road - (The first of many) -

Lao Tzu the Chinese philosopher said,
"The journey of a thousand miles begins with one step."
I have learned that for a journey to begin,
it is necessary to realize that you are, in fact, on a journey.
Without that realization, you are merely taking a long stroll.

INTRODUCTION

My journey began in steps, starting at the point where I accepted that there are things that can't be proven: things that can't be explained easily, nor denied. My journey started when I began to question my own cynicism.

Along the way, I began to see and learn from what I describe as *Life Lessons*: those events that, after they have been experienced, profoundly change your life, and always for the better. A Life Lesson is a signpost placed in front of us, to suggest a direction that will prove helpful for our growth. I view these Life Lessons as a fortune cookie: a short and sweet statement that helps us understand this moment on our earthly journey. Who or what placed that sign post in front of us and why... Well, that takes a little longer to explain.

However, Signposts and Life Lessons are merely cosmic suggestions. It's always up to us to decide to acknowledge or ignore them. It is our Free Will, which Captain Kirk would call *The Universe's Prime Directive.*

This book is about my experiences, which are shaded by my perceptions and biases. It is also about my view of the world and the Universe. It is my **opinion** and please accept it as such.

RELIGION

One of the struggles I have with organized religion is that it limits the inner truths of its followers. When children are not allowed to question their teachers, when they are being taught as incredibly complex a concept as God, their natural curiosity may be restricted and they can, as I did, reject the concept entirely.

You know that a discussion concerning either religion or politics always brings with it an incredible amount of passion. If the person or people with whom you are conversing are of like mind, there are only pleasantries and agreement. If you are in disagreement but can remain civil with one another, the conversation may end with, "Let's just agree to disagree."

If you are reading this, I would guess that you are someone who is civil with people no matter their views. The expression, "I may not agree with what you say, but I will defend your right to say it," may resonate with you as much as with me. Unfortunately, in our world today, a theoretical discussion of politics - or religion - in specific places on this planet will not end so civilly. It could end in one murdering the other. How sad is it that God's children kill each other in His name... Over an opinion that is presented as truth. As fact.

This book is not written to convince you that my belief is better than yours or to convince, persuade, or change your views about religion or life. That would be the opposite of what I believe, and the last thing that I would want.

The purpose of this book is to suggest to you how my beliefs - my truths - have evolved over the past 65+ years. The purpose of this book is to suggest to you, as I have learned through these experiences, that life is more than just a physical journey.

This book is about my journey, my Spiritual Evolution: my journey from atheism to spirituality.

Along the way, I hope I can inform, entertain, and stimulate your imagination and curiosity. And if you resonate or identify with the words in this book, then I have succeeded. After all, that is the purpose and goal of a teacher. My life, I'm sure, is not all that different than yours, but because I am a teacher, I have an overwhelming desire to impart my experiences, my Life Lessons, to you.

THE PHYSICAL WORLD

Life is perceived by some to begin at conception and by some at birth, when you take your first breath. It would seem that, over the past years, this debate has turned into a political question as opposed to a spiritual one.

It is my belief that the **physical** journey begins when a child takes its first breath. Suddenly, in an explosion of frightening lights and sounds, no longer muffled, now a deafening cacophony of strange, frightening and powerful energy, accompanied by an instant temperature drop of thirty degrees...

It is born. The child then first perceives, through its senses, that there is something out there: at first shades in black, white and gray. Through the five senses it becomes acclimated to its new environment. The smell and taste of a warm bottle or its mother's milk, the feel of her gentle embrace and being swathed in a soft cozy blanket. Each new moment in this life, its neurons are sending messages to its open and receptive brain. Making connections between sounds, sights, smells, tastes and touch, it begins to learn and grow.

I have also come to believe that included in our physical world is another sense that is even more powerful and important than all the others: Our easily ignored and often maligned sixth sense.

I believe that this is how our **physical** journey begins. The words 'I believe' are the most important part of the previous sentence. Those words, along with 'in my opinion', are absolutely necessary in beginning a conversation on the topics of religion and/or Spirituality, which are two very different terms and philosophies. Unfortunately these two statements, 'I believe' and 'in my opinion', are rarely heard in a conversation regarding religion. Or politics, for that matter.

WHAT ABOUT THE *META*-PHYSICAL WORLD?

We have all heard the word *metaphysical*. But what does it mean?

The University of Sedona - and if you want to learn about Metaphysics, could there be a better place to learn about it, than Sedona? - defines Metaphysics as a major branch of philosophy which concerns existence and the nature of things that exist. It is a theory of reality.

Traditionally, the word Metaphysics means over and beyond physics. In the definition found in most dictionaries, Metaphysics is referred to as a branch of philosophy that deals with the nature of being. When one expresses an interest in Metaphysics, that interest may be in any one or a combination of the following subjects: Philosophy, Religion, Parapsychology, Mysticism, Yoga, ESP, Dreams, Jungian Psychology, Transpersonal and Theocentric Psychology, Astrology, Meditation, Self-Help Studies, Hypnosis, Positive Thinking, Life After Death, Transcendentalism, Mysticism, Reincarnation and more.

OK... I think I just confused myself with that convoluted definition, but I think you get the point. There are many people on this planet who agree: There is more to life than the physical. Thus we can include the metaphysical in a discussion of life on Earth. Just to make it easier, I find that the terms *metaphysical* and *spiritual* are interchangeable.

We have all been on this journey since birth, but the awareness of the journey is the point at which it accelerates. I can tell you that my spiritual journey was not planned.

I've been aware of my journey since the age of 50, and I know that I will follow it for the rest of this life. The path has been there, waiting for me to become conscious of it. But, that is my experience. We are all on our own journeys down our own path of experiential learning.

If what I share with you feels real and resonates with you, I hope you'll accept and embrace it. If you disagree with my view, let's agree to disagree and accept that a person's beliefs can and often do change with time.

Whether you are in elementary school, high school, college, on a job, unemployed, the CEO of a Fortune 500 corporation, or the President of the United States, you are and always will be in school, until you take your last breath. This school is called Earth and it is an Ivy League university. The course of study you and I are enrolled in is called... **Humanity.**

> *As a side note... I am neither a psychologist, social worker nor a mental health practitioner; I am an educator and hypnotherapist, and although I am nationally certified, in New Jersey I am considered a* hypnocounselor.

Sometimes your eyes tell you one thing and the world tells you that you must be blind!

THE MOVE TO EAST 26ᵀᴴ ST

My metaphysical journey actually began in Brooklyn, NY on a warm June evening of 1955. I was six and between kindergarten and First Grade. You may question how I can pinpoint that moment so precisely? That's because it was the evening when I first saw a ghost. And that experience frightened me so, that very quickly I shut down my ability to perceive spirits at all.

A moving day is exciting for anyone, but moving into a new house in a new neighborhood was more than exciting for this little six-year-old kid. Built in the late 1930's, our large brick house was located in a neighborhood of young families. And it was all ours.

Finally, we came to the end of that very busy move-in day. Furniture and boxes were everywhere, but my exhausted parents said we would clean up tomorrow. Time for bed: three words that were magic to that six-year-old's ears.

I flopped down in my bed and pulled the sheets up under my chin. The windows in my new room were open, and a gentle early summer's breeze made the curtains sway back and forth. I liked the feeling of the warmth from that breeze against my legs, so I kicked the sheet off. I was tired but still excited about finally being in my new house. I wanted to go to sleep, but my mind was so busy thinking of the day's events and what tomorrow had in store for me that I found sleep was not going to happen.

I tried to force my eyes to close, but knew it was a losing battle. The only thoughts on my mind were if there were any kids my age nearby? How would I meet them? And what would First Grade be like in a new school?

THE MAN IN MY ROOM

I couldn't sleep, so I got out of bed and began to explore. My father heard me. He came up behind me and before I knew it, I was on his shoulders headed back to my room. He tossed me on the bed and smiling down at me said, "Ga, time for sleep. It's been a long day for all of us. We'll have plenty of time to wander around tomorrow." He turned, shut the light, and I heard his footsteps going down the stairs.

The sounds in the house began to diminish as the minutes clicked by. My parents came upstairs to their bedroom, where my baby sister was fast asleep. The only sounds in the house were my grandfather's snoring and the sound of the TV in my parents' bedroom. The snoring was something I was so used to that if it wasn't there through the entire night

I would probably stay up wondering what was missing. The sound of a click and silence told me that my parents had decided to go to sleep.

This was my first night in my new bedroom. Although my room was dark and quiet, there were still a lot of things happening. The traffic on East 26th Street was much less than in my old neighborhood, and I watched the lights dance on the ceiling from the headlights of the few cars going by. I was busy noticing the differences between my new room and my old bedroom as sleep began to take those thoughts away.

It was that pre-sleep time, a gentle buzz in the back of my head, heaviness in my body and the feeling of my eyes rolling up to the back of my head all by themselves. As I lay there, I felt a presence at the foot of my bed.

It started as the feeling you get when you think someone is looking at you, and turn to see them look away. I did not want to look but felt compelled to. I was trying so hard to keep my eyes closed, yet knowing that they were going to open. No matter how hard I tried to keep them closed, no matter how hard I squeezed them shut, my eyes would not comply. Slowly, they opened.

Standing at the foot of my bed was an old man! Dressed in an old fashioned grey suit, holding his Hamburg hat in his hands, he was simply there. He wasn't threatening; he wasn't even looking at me. He was simply there, standing at the foot of my bed, staring at the door!

I screamed as loud as I could, but realized no sound was coming from my mouth. I jumped out of bed and raced for the door, but realized that I was still under the sheets, frozen stiff. These were actions that I wanted to do but was totally incapable of accomplishing. All I was able to do was close my eyes. Tight! I did, and when I opened them again, he was gone.

Now, with my heart pounding like a jackhammer and my breathing more like panting, I allowed my eyes to search the room... Nothing.

No one was there.

I started to calm down. *That must have been a dream*, I thought and began to rest again. After a few moments, I felt sleepy again. *Ga, go back to sleep!* I pleaded. *There can't be anybody in the room. You know it had to be a dream.*

And then, to reassure myself that I was truly alone, I allowed one eye to open...

And to my horror, he was back. Not threatening. Not even looking at me; just standing there.

But this time I found my voice. And did I ever use it... screaming at the top of my lungs!

I could only imagine the scene in my parents' bedroom. Both of them jumping straight out of bed and bumping into each other as they tried to get to my room. Now with my baby sister crying and my grandfather snoring, my parents came bursting in, expecting to find… Well, I don't know what they thought they'd find.

What they found was their son, sitting straight up in bed, frozen, pointing to the closet at the foot of the bed and saying, "There's an old man standing there. Don't you see him?"

I'm not sure how to describe the expression on my father's face, sort of a combination of concern and exhaustion. He opened the closet, searched through it, looked under my bed and had me look all over the room, too. He sat on the bed and lifted me up, put me on his lap and said, "Ga, you had a real busy, exciting day and you just had a dream." Then he tossed me in bed, pulled my sheet up and said, "G'night."

He smiled at my mother and the two of them went back into their room. I wish the story ended there, but unfortunately for my parents and me, it didn't.

I continued having these visions for the next few weeks. Each time my father's patience became more strained. He finally looked at me and said, "Garry! You are having that same dream again, that's all. There is no one in your room or in the house! Go to sleep!" He looked at my mother and said, "I give up! You take care of him. I gotta get some sleep! I have to be up at 5 am! You stay with him," and went to bed.

I felt tears welling up in my eyes. I knew the old man wasn't in my room. I knew there was no one in my room, yet I also knew what I saw. But it was the look on my father's face that made me feel so hopeless. I was confused and so sad, as my mother sat beside me, stroking my arm. "Shhh honey, just close your eyes. You were just having the same dream again."

"But Mommy, I saw the man. He was in a grey suit with a hat like grandpa wears. He has a long beard and he was wearing a *tallis*." She looked at me with more curiosity than confusion.

"You saw him wearing a *tallis*?" my mother asked. A tallis is a Jewish prayer shawl.

"Yes Mommy," I said. "He was wearing the same type of *tallis* that grandpa wears on Saturday mornings."

My mother's expression changed from comforting to curiosity. "Tell me more about him," my mother said, and the more I described the vision of this old man the more my mother seemed to believe me, which made me feel much better.

"You know your daddy works very hard, Honey," my mother said, "and he's also very tired. He's not mad at you, he just needs to sleep. Roll over and close your eyes. I'll stay here until you fall asleep." And as I rolled over with my mother sitting at the side of the bed with her hand on my back, I felt my fears fading away.

But I still knew what I'd seen. I knew it wasn't my imagination. I didn't want to upset my father, and I didn't want to have my parents fighting over me. My mother sat in my room for weeks, stroking my back until I fell asleep. Finally, I convinced myself that there was no old man in my room after all, and when I told that to my mother, she was able to get some well-deserved sleep of her own.

I fell asleep from that night and for many nights afterwards with my head under the pillow, repeating what my father had said: "It's just a dream... Just a dream... Just a dream," and eventually he did leave.

The experience of that old man's ghost frightened me so much that I eventually decided to disallow anything that could not be proven by the five senses. I shut down anything that could bring that man's ghost back to my awareness. I denied even the implication of anything that could not be explained scientifically. If it was not seen, felt, heard, smelled or tasted, it was simply not there. It did not exist!

~ ~ ~

But you can't prove that God exists...

You can't prove there is a heaven or hell...

You can't prove anything but things that come through your five senses.

We call this situation *veiling over*: the denial of any and all extra sensory perception. And at the age of six, I was about to veil over completely. Along with denying the existence of the old ghost in my room, it soon seemed logical that I, by necessity, must deny the existence of God. And I threw the baby out with the bath water.

Over the next few weeks I saw him again, but each time I used my own personal denial mantra, and soon I was no longer aware of him at all. By high school, I became a hard core cynic with regard to so-called psychics. And that denial continued for many years, but the price I paid was the denial of my own intuitive abilities.

In retrospect, I believe that the prior owners of our new home must have had their orthodox Jewish father living with them, just as we had our grandfather living with us. I believe that he lived in the room that had been my bedroom, and had probably died there.

It took over forty-five years for me to understand what I had been sensing and why. I now know that all children have a special ability to sense spirits.

Depending on the family and society, children who are told that what they are seeing, hearing, feeling and sensing is only a dream, or their imagination, will quickly veil over as I did. And all too often they will never access that natural human ability again. Thereafter, like any unused muscle, their ability to access extra sensory perceptions will atrophy and wither away.

PSYCHIC KIDS

Let's try an exercise in imagination…

- What if - there were no such thing as an ear? No human organ which can perceive sound, no section of the brain designed to decipher sound. What if there were no such experience in all of human awareness as a sense of hearing? How would you be able to describe to someone who has no concept of this thing that we know as sound, that you hear something?

Let's make a comparison to the anatomy of a shark, which has a sense organ called the Ampullae of Lorenzini. This is an organ that has evolved over millions of years. It stretches around a shark's body to detect the electrical impulses of its prey.

Unfortunately, in the world of a four-sense human, we would have neither the Ampullae of Lorenzini, nor ears. Imagine a world where that situation is true. We have four senses: sight, touch, smell and taste… period.

But - What if - a child were born with invisible, internal ears? No one, not his parents, his friends, his teachers or his doctors… no one knows he has this amazing ability, and he grows up blissfully unaware that he hears things that no other human on the planet can.

Of course, he is human, and should only have four senses. For him, the perception of sound is normal, but he has no word for it. He cannot know any different, and assumes that this sense he is experiencing is normal to everyone.

When something falls near him, he reacts by turning toward it, not knowing why. People around him see this reaction to… What? Nothing! He becomes aware that he is different from others around him, including his family. He becomes withdrawn.

Very soon, this *sensitive* child realizes he needs to control his reaction to what he is sensing, because it makes those around him uncomfortable. If he continues to react to things they cannot sense, his family may think he's crazy. They may want to institutionalize him or put him on drugs to control his delusions. Doctors may even diagnose him as schizophrenic or worse!

Soon, the child learns to shut it down completely, in order to survive. He cannot stand out; he must be like everyone else. He no longer reacts, and very soon he becomes so desensitized, he no longer notices sounds at all. He veils over; he must in order to survive and fit into his four-sense society.

Of course, his is a hypothetical 4-sense world. In reality, we know that there are precisely 5 senses because we recognize our 5 sensory organs: the eyes, ears, nose, tongue and skin.

However, I am a firm believer that we in the western world have been raised to deny the existence of a very important sensory organ: our sixth sense. All humans possess the ability for extra sensory perception (ESP), and this has always been accepted in many eastern cultures. Unfortunately, western society does not recognize it as such.

The sixth sense organ is located in the middle of the forehead, and is attached to the most amazing and complicated structure on the planet: the human brain. It is even referred to as an organ, and is called our *Third Eye*. Through this organ we can perceive so much more than the standard five senses would allow.

Now, let's assume that some of us have a more developed extra sensory ability. We assume that these individuals are in some way more advanced, enlightened or *special* than we are. They are viewed in different ways, from being *gifted* to being weird. In the past, people who shared their ESP were feared, called witches, and put to death. Even now, they may be shunned by their family due to religious dogma. But I believe that all humans are born with the same sensing abilities.

Children are born with their third eye wide open. They go through their early lives (birth through about three) with the ability to sense spirit easily and naturally. It is usually the society (and family in particular) that makes children feel as if it is abnormal to communicate with spirit.

> *For you parents out there: If your child says he or she is seeing a ghost, don't automatically assume it is their imagination. There are many strongly psychic children in the world. Ask them questions about what they perceived. Ask open ended questions, like, "What was this man wearing?" or "What do you think he was trying to tell you?" or "How did you feel when you were with him?" Show support, concern and acceptance instead of annoyance, fear or apathy. Just because **you** don't see the spirit your child is seeing, doesn't mean your child is imagining it. More than likely he is truly psychic, as we all are.*

~ ~ ~

In our modern, five-sense western society, the scenario of minimizing the perceptions of young children is, unfortunately, still the norm. People ask, "What's the point of encouraging a child to believe in these supernatural musings?" The answer is that eventually, human society will realize that we have never been just five-sense humans. We are, in fact, six-sense humans - veiled over and in denial for a very, very long time.

You may have heard that some young children are unaware of the difference between the living and the spirits of those who have passed. This is true. I shut down my own psychic abilities at the age of 6, and I can tell you that I was desperate to be free of them. I did not want to see spirits any longer, and my desire to no longer see them - along with the spirit's acceptance of my desire - stopped the visions from recurring.

I was very happy, from the age of 6 until my early 50's, to be a cynic. I laughed at anyone who even mentioned the existence of a soul. I was content in my Darwinian view: that there is nothing after we die but blackness, and our bodies simply return to the dust they came from.

Then there came a time when I became curious about ESP.

Now, you may ask, after totally shutting off my innate psychic abilities as a child, and becoming completely contemptuous of anything New Age or metaphysical, how did I rediscover them? The answer to that question lies in the type of person I am. I am very curious, and everything that I question I need to explore. For forty years I was able to keep my curiosity about ESP in check because my cynicism of all New Age concepts was driven by fear: the subconscious fear of ever seeing that old man again. But in my early 50's, a talented medium was able to arouse my curiosity about ESP, and I found that I could no longer cynically discard what had become clearly possible.

Now, with my curiosity piqued, I began to explore ESP with an open mind, and a time came when I took a basic psychic development class and was amazed with the images and feelings I was receiving. I found I was able to *read* perfect strangers with an accuracy that actually shocked me. I was hooked! The more I explored psychic phenomenon the more questions it raised and the more I was driven to learn. And the person who had me question my cynicism and eventually accept ESP, as a truth, was a man named John Edward.

CROSSING OVER WITH JOHN EDWARD

It was the early 2000's and mediums like James Van Praagh, John Edward, George Anderson and John Holland became more accepted by the public due to television shows like *Medium, Ghost Whisper*er, *Psychic Detective* and *Crossing Over with John Edward*. As public acceptance of psychics and mediums became more popular, my curiosity of psychic phenomenon grew.

Again, when my natural curiosity comes into play, the cynic within me becomes a healthy skeptic and I begin to explore the things that, in the past, I would have dismissed out of hand (or out of fear). I look at the difference between cynics and skeptics as: a skeptic needs strong proof to believe, while a cynic believes that no proof is **ever** good enough.

At that time, I became aware of an unusual coincidence. It seemed that each time I turned on my television, the same show was there - *Crossing Over with John Edward* - and, over time, I began to watch it with a much less cynical attitude. The more I watched the show, the more curious I became about its authenticity.

At first I thought it was staged and edited, fabricated for television. But as I viewed the show, I found that the audience was made almost entirely of New Yorkers, like me. These were normal, everyday men and women who were touched very deeply by this man, John Edward. They truly believed he was able to communicate with their dead loved ones. But these were hardened New Yorkers; certainly not the type of people who were gullible, and certainly not the type who would cry on television.

There was something very real to me about this show, and I was now on the verge of becoming a believer. John would frequently use terms like "the continuation of consciousness." He would explain to his audience that our souls are immortal and never die; a concept that I was not prepared to accept, until I began to watch his show in earnest.

As I will explain later, my father passed away when I was 23 years old. Soon afterwards I began to hear him talking to me. Although I always felt comforted, I also knew it wasn't him, it couldn't be him; he had died. However, the results of his communications began to impact my life in ways that caused me to question my own cynicism.

I began to reevaluate my old atheistic thoughts and beliefs. If the continuation of consciousness could be proven to me, it would lift the depression I felt that once the body dies, it turns into dust, along with any evidence of its existence. Except upon a tombstone, or in the minds of the people we had loved.

As I continued to watch *Crossing Over*, inside my head, a lively debate was raging between two diametrically opposing parts. One part that I could no longer deny was intrigued by John Edward's ability to communicate with the dead. This was the same part that took comfort in hearing from my deceased father. I laughingly called this my Psychic Part. The other was that ingrained, resolute cynic, who was becoming considerably less ingrained and resolute.

If someone like John Edward could convince me of the continuation of consciousness the same way he proved it to everyone on his show, I could no longer deny the existence of psychic abilities, mediumship, the soul and yes, even the existence of, dare I say… God?

If there could be actual, credible evidence of communication with the dead, then our souls actually do continue! Our life's knowledge, all the wealth of experience, insight and maturity, all our Life Lessons, if you will, would not be lost when the body ceases to function.

Watching *Crossing Over* convinced me that it was indeed possible that my deceased father **had** been communicating with me, although at times I still had doubts. But skeptical doubt is much better than the cynical contempt I'd had. I began to doubt my own doubts! But, I needed to really believe. I needed to be convinced beyond any shadow of doubt. I wanted to be as convinced as the New Yorkers I watched on *Crossing Over*. I wanted to be brought to tears, not from sadness but from the knowledge that comes with an amazing mediumship reading. I needed to eliminate every shred of doubt, in my heart, that my father was still watching over, helping and supporting me.

I decided at that point to seek out a real medium, equal to the talents of John Edward. What better way to prove the continuity of the soul's existence? Those tears of closure shed by all those grieving families on *Crossing Over* finally convinced me to look at spiritual matters with a more open and accepting mind. And healthy skepticism trumps hard core cynicism, every time.

I began to research John and other mediums, and the more I explored, the more I became convinced that what I had been so very cynical of - Life After Death - may very well be factual. I also observed a fascinating change happening within me. The total cynic of all New Age concepts that I had been, where I would not even consider ESP as a remote possibility, began to wither as I questioned why I had been so adamantly negative about these beliefs. I realized how wrong I had been to view life through those cynical eyes. I was becoming a healthy skeptic.

Meeting a determined spirit can be a great learning experience,
even for a teacher.

GLORIA & NANA

Years later I would become an established medium, reading for clients in my hypnosis office. But I will never forget the first time that I became aware of a spirit requesting my assistance to connect with their loved one in a different setting. And the place this spirit chose was in the classroom where I was teaching US History.

Gloria and I were co-teachers in a US History I class. We had known each other for over 15 years, but this was the first time we were working together in the same classroom, she as the History content area teacher and I as the Special Education support teacher. It had been some years since my introduction to Metaphysics, and I had expanded my hypnosis practice to include Past Life Regression Therapy, Reiki healing and, eventually, mediumship.

One Monday, on a perfect spring morning, Gloria and I were in our US History I class. The windows in the classroom were open and the unmistakable smell of honeysuckle came through the window, reminding me that summer would be arriving soon. The students were atypically quiet and had their textbooks out reviewing the lesson on US slavery. It was about five or ten minutes before the end of the period.

Gloria was sitting at her desk as I walked up and down the rows, checking the students' progress and answering any questions they had. Looking up, I noticed that Gloria was drawing on a small piece of memo paper. She folded it and put it in her purse, as the bell rang and the kids jumped up to get to their next class.

I stood at the door, saying goodbye to them. Suddenly, the hair on the back of my neck stood up and an electric tingling ran down my spine. This had become the unmistakable sign of a spirit being close to me. By that point in my psychic and mediumship development, I was comfortable with that feeling, but I had never experienced it in a situation like this: a classroom in my school.

I had also become quite knowledgeable regarding the process of connecting with the energy of people who had passed away and were in spirit, but it had always been under specific and controlled situations. Usually I would meditate, in my hypnosis office, while waiting for my next client. As incense burned, I would enter a meditative state called *Sitting in the Power*, where I would focus my intention to connect with the spirits of my scheduled mediumship client. Then I would feel them: the tingling, the hair standing up. But I had never before felt a spirit anywhere other than in a controlled environment; least of all, in a classroom of high schoolers. And this spirit was communicating powerfully!

Over the previous five years, I had taken many psychic development classes. As a psychic, I knew that something was about to happen in that classroom that would strongly impact my growth as a medium. I felt that I was going to be a student in my own classroom and that I should pay close attention to what was about to happen. But who was communicating this to me was another story.

In my early mediumship classes I had learned many things, including how spirits communicate. For me, the two primary ways are Clairaudience, or clear-hearing, when I hear a spirit talking to me, and Clairsentience, or clear-knowing, when I simply know something about that person or spirit that I could not have known on my own. The one thing I knew at that moment was that I was connecting with a spirit, right there in my classroom.

I took a deep breath and sat in my chair as the last student waved goodbye and the door closed. With the click of the door, I could sense this spirit even stronger. The silence in the room was palpable as I looked over to Gloria, who was writing at her desk. I began to communicate with this spirit, and asked her to come closer and talk to me.

Immediately I felt her presence even stronger than before. She felt like a grandmother to me and told me to call her Nana. She asked me to say hello to her granddaughter, Gloria.

I acknowledged, through my thoughts, that I was aware of her. However, I also communicated that I felt that there are times and places that a medium should work and give a person a reading, and there are those times and places where they shouldn't.

So here I was, in a classroom with a teacher whom I'd known for a long time, but had never discussed metaphysical topics with. I felt that this was clearly an inappropriate time and I relayed my concerns to the spirit. How could I tell Gloria that her grandmother, who had passed years ago, was now whispering in my ear?

I knew that Gloria was a religious Roman Catholic, and I didn't know how she might feel about mediumship. How would she react if I raised the subject of having a conversation with her Nana in the middle of a classroom? Probably not the right thing to do!

That's why I decided not to broach this with Gloria. But her Nana was very persistent and did not want to take 'no' for an answer. An excellent spirit communicator, Nana brought to my mind's eye a pivotal memory from my own past: when I received an impromptu and unsolicited reading from Millie, our school secretary…

I was shown how wonderful it felt to hear from my own deceased dad during that first mediumship reading. In retrospect, Millie's timing had been perfect, and that spontaneous connection with my father became the most beautiful gift I have ever received. I am eternally grateful to Millie for changing my view of the permanence of death. Since Millie's reading was the experience that opened me to my present belief in Spirituality, by reminding me of this, Nana completely resolved my reticence to inform Gloria of her grandmother's presence in the room.

It would seem that my role had now changed, and I was the medium as Millie had been for me. Gloria would be the sitter (the person receiving a reading) whose life was about to be irrevocably changed, as mine had been.

I also knew that this spirit, Gloria's Nana, heard my thoughts. As I directed my thoughts to her, I conveyed that I felt it would be inappropriate of me to push my beliefs onto Gloria. I knew her granddaughter was religious and I feared she would not be open to the subject of mediumship.

I felt her Nana smile at me with acceptance, and instantly I could no longer sense her. (In retrospect, the timing of this communication also couldn't have been more perfect. Gloria and I both had a prep period and had forty minutes with nothing to do and no place to be.)

At the same instant that I stopped sensing her Nana - and almost on cue - Gloria called to me.

"Hey Garry, have you ever seen the TV show with Lisa Williams, the medium? She's a woman from England who walks around Los Angeles and connects people with their loved ones who died."

Lisa Williams was as popular on TV at that time as Teresa Caputo, *The Long Island Medium*, is today. I had to hold back the laugh and simply smiled, knowing that her Nana had whispered to Gloria, without her knowledge, to raise that question at that exact time. If a spirit is that determined to communicate with her loved one, it would be wrong, in my opinion, to ignore her at this point, considering how perfectly she timed this connection.

"I watch her every week," I said. "Not only have I seen her on TV, but I'm going to see her next month in New York City with John Holland, another world renowned medium."

After we discussed Lisa's abilities to connect with loved ones who had passed, Gloria said it would be wonderful to talk to some of her family members who'd passed away.

And in a snap, her Nana was back in my mind, communicating to me – she actually smiled - to say that she had checked in with Gloria and her granddaughter would love to hear from her. Again, my thoughts went to my first mediumship reading with Millie, and how my father had been that strong and persistent to get a message to me.

I smiled, accepting the transition I had just made: from a sitter to a reader in almost the same scenario I'd had with Millie. I said to Nana in my mind, '*OK Nana. You win.*' Now looking at Gloria, I pulled up a chair and said with a smile, "Gloria, did you know that along with my hypnosis practice, I am also a medium?"

She looked at me with disbelief, saying, "Come on... you're kidding. Right?"

As we sat, I briefly explained how I became interested in Metaphysics; about my father's spirit talking to me; my experience with Millie; my change from cynic to skeptic to medium; and even about reincarnation. I went on to explain my current belief in the continuity of consciousness: that we never die, but shed our bodies and return to our true home.

I described what I was doing with my Development Circle. "Every Tuesday evening, I get together with two mediums named Bill and Jill," I explained. "We bring family members into my office where we relay information to them from their passed love ones." She seemed even more curious about that and asked me about how a reading works with three mediums working together.

I explained that I called our development circle 'Connecting with Loved Ones in Spirit' and described how Bill, Jill and I each brought a different type of energy to a reading. Bill was predominantly clairvoyant, having the ability to 'see' loved ones, while Jill and I were predominantly clairaudient and clairsentient, meaning we heard and felt the loved ones who had passed away.

Gloria seemed very interested in what I was saying. "What a coincidence!" she exclaimed. "My sisters and I have been talking about finding a medium. Isn't that weird?"

Then as naturally as our conversation was flowing, I said to her, "Actually, Gloria, I've been feeling your Nana here for the past 10 minutes!" I asked Nana to give me some information that only Gloria could know and that I could not just guess. I started describing her grandmother to her, while she validated everything I said with a tear welling in her eyes.

"TICKLED PINK"

Gloria was able to validate all the information that Nana relayed to me, and we continued our discussion about Metaphysics a little longer. She was absolutely thrilled to have heard from her grandmother and curious about the process. But what was confusing me was that I hadn't yet received an actual message from Nana.

I am almost always aware of a specific message early in a reading. A spirit that comes through as forcefully as Nana almost always has a message that would be important to communicate to her loved one. It's the reason why a spirit would connect with me in the first place. Her grandmother was a wonderful communicator, but I hadn't heard the message at all, unless the purpose for her grandmother's visitation was to simply let Gloria know that Nana loved her. I was about to tell Gloria that I was losing my connection with her grandmother when I once again felt her Nana... strongly! This time I just heard two words, 'Tickled Pink.'

I hesitated to mention it for a moment and then again I heard: 'Tickled Pink... say Tickled Pink!' I looked questioningly at Gloria, who looked back at me knowing that I was sensing something new from her Nana. Now smiling at me, she said, "What?"

I nodded both to Gloria and Nana as I realized that this phrase was the message. Again looking at Gloria, I said, "Your Nana is now telling me to say 'Tickled Pink'?" Her expression changed, and she gasped as the tear that formed in her eye ran down her cheek. I had no idea what 'Tickled Pink' meant; it meant nothing to me. But the message was, after all, not for me. And it clearly meant a lot to Gloria!

She took a tissue from the box on her desk, took a breath and began, "My son and daughter-in-law are expecting their first child. It's going to be a girl. My first grandchild! And I'm just starting to plan the baby shower."

Gloria paused. "Garry, we were just talking about the baby shower this weekend, the plans, the guest list, the menu, where we were going to hold it. It's such a wonderful time and I was even thinking how much my Nana would love these times and how she was always so involved with our family. When my son was born, she arranged for **my** baby shower. I have been thinking of her so much lately and how much I miss her. Now I am going to be a 'Nana' to my first granddaughter."

She continued earnestly, "One thing that I am responsible for is getting the baby announcement card done, and I was just sitting here before class today thinking of my Nana and what I wanted to put on the baby shower announcement." She took a deep breath as she opened her purse and pulled out the piece of folded memo paper that I had seen her working on.

Now I could see that it was a card. She looked at it, shook her head and turned it around so I could read it. And there on the very top of the card, in bright hot pink letters were the words,

*'We are **TICKLED PINK** to announce...'*

I felt her grandmother's energy pulling back, which I told Gloria, but before Nana left, she thanked me. After talking for the rest of our prep period about what we'd both experienced, Gloria made an appointment to bring her sisters for a full reading with my development circle, Connecting with Loved Ones in Spirit.

OUR METAPHYSICAL SCHOOL TRIP TO NEW BRUNSWICK, NJ

A month after a wonderful reading with Gloria and her sisters, Gloria and I were the chaperones on a school trip. Along with US History, I was also teaching Tenth Grade English and had the opportunity to take my class to see a theater performance of Romeo and Juliet in New Brunswick, NJ. Gloria volunteered to go as a chaperone with my class, which would give us an opportunity to discuss our new mutual interest in Metaphysics. However, I was unprepared for what would occur on this ordinary school trip: another spontaneous mediumship experience arranged by spirit.

The students were so well behaved that after the play, we told them they could choose a Main Street restaurant and return to our rendezvous point in an hour and a half.

They immediately scattered, while Gloria and I tried to decide where we would eat. As we stood there, I suddenly felt that same familiar chill again... the unmistakable feeling of the presence of a spirit. I knew that this spirit was not related to Gloria but to someone nearby; I also knew that Gloria would have a part in what was about to unfold.

The way Gloria's grandmother had let her presence be known to me - in a quiet classroom - was quite different than what was happening now. I was surprised at the strength and persistence of this spirit. I was standing on a very busy street in the middle of urban New Brunswick with traffic and students and lots of noise, and yet I felt his presence as strongly as if I were meditating in my office.

I knew it was a male, and young, who was strongly pushing me toward a small deli across the street. It was the type of restaurant that I would never have chosen. And if it were not for the pull from this spirit, I'm sure Gloria and I would have chosen the Chinese restaurant instead. I asked Gloria if the deli looked good to her and she agreed. We crossed the street and I held the door open for her as we walked in. There were tables and chairs to the right and I chose one by the large picture window in the front, to keep an eye out for our students. We put our jackets on the chairs, got our food, and walked back to our table for four. There were small round tables for one or two people between our table and the window.

I knew I would be giving one of my business cards to someone in that restaurant, so I took one from my wallet and slipped it into my shirt pocket. I still had no idea who I would be talking to or what the conversation would be about. All I knew was that there was a young man who was in spirit, and I would be talking to someone about hypnosis and/or mediumship. It was certainly going to be an interesting lunch! All this time I never said anything to Gloria about whom or what I was feeling.

At that point in my psychic development, I still carried some doubt. I questioned if it was my imagination: had I imagined feeling this spirit, or was it a real presence? I knew he'd pushed me to enter this deli, but now I didn't feel him at all. So, I shrugged and asked myself what I would do if this spirit told me to give a message to someone? Interrupt their lunch by asking them if they knew a kid who died in his twenties? Ask some poor woman if her son had died and see the woman scream, call her son to make sure he was still breathing, and then immediately call the cops... on me!

No way. Now I was about to accept the fact that I needed to stop being so obsessed with this psychic and mediumship stuff.

And then it happened...

Once again, I felt this young man. Gloria had put her jacket over the back of the seat directly opposite me. She placed her food on the table, but then moved to her right with her dish. Looking at me, she laughed, "Why did I just move over?" The answer to that question would come quite soon and was something we could not have guessed at the time.

At the same time, a woman was walking behind me with her lunch. The spirit touched my shoulder and moved my face to follow her, as she sat directly between me and the window. Had Gloria not moved, I would not have even noticed the woman.

In my left ear I heard, *Talk to my mother... Please!*

I quickly began to receive more information from the boy. I knew he died in his 20's; in a car accident with a driver who was DWI; his car caught on fire. I knew his mother was devastated by the thought that he died painfully in that fire.

My name is Michael. Please talk to my mother. Again, I was communicating with him in my mind, the same way I had spoken with Nana.

To say that I **talk** to these spirits would be inaccurate; it is simply thinking. I simply **thought** to him, *Have your mother open the door, Michael. I can't just approach her like this. She needs to open the door and then I'll tell her anything you want me to.*

I knew that he was aware of everything in my mind, including how Gloria's Nana had led Gloria to open the door. Immediately, Michael left my mind and I no longer felt his presence.

Now, with Gloria sitting across from me, once again the timing was perfect. We both started to eat, but it would be impolite to talk with our mouths full. We ate quietly, knowing that the conversation would turn to Metaphysics after we finished our lunch. This was the perfect opportunity to communicate with spirit.

As we ate, I wondered how this Life Lesson was going to pan out, not only for me, but for Michael, his mother, and even for Gloria. I realized that I could present the door to his mom: the door that I needed her to open before I could proceed.

A thought just popped into my mind: *Talk about hypnotic intervention to eliminate a dental phobia. That will open the door.* As I had become accustomed, the thoughts came to me and I just followed their lead.

I began to discuss hypnosis with Gloria, specifically about how I work with people who have phobias. Then I directed the discussion to dental phobia. I knew the woman needed to hear me, so I raised my voice just a bit. As I described my technique, I noticed that she began to lean into the conversation like the old E. F. Hutton commercials.

Although I was talking to Gloria about hypnosis, I kept looking at Michael's mother. At one point Gloria actually turned around to look at her, too. I couldn't believe it when I noticed the woman making eye contact with me. She had a perplexed look about her, as if she found what I was saying fascinating.

And then it actually happened! I had told Michael that I couldn't broach the subject of his death with his mom unless she was the one to open the door. And I heard the unmistakable sound of a door creaking open. Metaphorically speaking, of course.

Clearly this woman was listening intently to our conversation. She looked as if she were conflicted, and I sensed that she wanted to talk to us but was hesitant to intrude. I saw the internal conversation she was having with herself conclude. She nodded to herself as if she had just come to an important conclusion, and turned to Gloria.

"Excuse me..." the woman said, speaking directly to Gloria. "I never eavesdrop into conversations, but I just had to tell you that what this man is saying," pointing to me, "is absolutely true."

She moved her chair a bit closer to our table and lowered her voice. "It's just so interesting, because what he is saying is exactly what happened to me. I had a dental phobia and my daughter, who went to a hypnotherapist, scheduled an appointment for me. And the hypnotherapist did exactly what your friend is describing! I just found this such an interesting coincidence. I'm really sorry for interrupting. Please excuse me, but I couldn't help telling you that hypnosis really works." She seemed embarrassed by her interruption. It probably felt completely out of character for her; however, I knew it was because she was actually being influenced by her son. But what happened next I could never have guessed.

As Michael's mother reached for her coat and prepared to leave, Gloria said, "Well, he's not only a hypnotherapist. He's also a psychic medium!" I couldn't believe it. I could have given her a kiss! Without even realizing it, Gloria not only presented the door to this woman, but even opened it wide for her. I had to sit back with an air of amazement on my face.

I looked at Gloria, shaking my head as the events unfolded in front of me. What Gloria was unaware of was that she, Gloria, had very strong psychic and mediumship abilities. Her presence there was not an accident or coincidence. It was a *synchronicity*: a purposeful coincidence. One that blows my mind every time I think about it. (But more about synchronicities later.)

"Really..." The woman said as her jaw dropped. She sat and now, looking at me, said, "I have been looking for one!" Once again the timing was perfect, and in my mind I thought to the spirit of her son, *Good job, Mike*, I thought. *I need you to connect with me and tell me what happened.*

"You lost your son, didn't you?" I said to her quietly.

Her reaction was immediate and powerful. "Yes, yes! Oh my God Yes! How could you know?" she said to me with her hands covering her mouth, as Gloria almost fell off her chair!

OK, kid. You did good! I thought to him as I stood and walked around the table. Pulling up a chair next to his mom, I held her hands and looked into her eyes as tears ran down her cheeks. I said, "He says that his name is Michael, and that he passed in his 20's from

21

a car accident. Is that true?" His mother couldn't speak. She just nodded as Gloria handed her a pile of napkins to dry her eyes.

Gloria seemed to be observing what was unfolding with a combination of excitement, questioning, empathy and perhaps a little awe. I know I was awed by what was happening: I was about to give a reading to this woman, who was devastated by the loss of her child. As a medium, I could give her the information she needed to move on with her life. And to this day this experience has stayed with me and will for the rest of my life. I think 'Awe-Some" would be an appropriate adjective to use here.

Still holding her hands, I felt her son Michael come closer to me again as I began relating to her exactly what I was hearing, feeling and seeing from her son.

"He tells me that he died in a car accident with a driver who was drunk. He is telling me, it happened so fast that he didn't even realize he was involved in an accident. He wants you to know he didn't feel the flames. He's telling me he passed before the car exploded and that he knows that the thought of him dying in the car alone has been plaguing you since that terrible day. He says he was with you when the police called saying that there had been an accident and asked you if you had a son named Michael. He says he saw you drop the phone and walk to the couch and sit down."

As his mother regained her composure, there were still tears in her eyes. She was totally involved in the reading and wanted to hear everything I was saying. Staring deeply into my eyes, she nodded in affirmation and validated everything I was relating to her. She said there was no doubt that this truly was her son communicating with us. Her tears stopped and her energy changed as she took a deep breath. But Michael was still not finished.

More information was coming to me, which I happily relayed to her. "He says that his father couldn't handle the news of his death, that he was aware of the cancer that his father had before the accident and that the news of Michael's death triggered the cancer to become more aggressive. He is telling me that along with your son you lost your husband within six months of each other." She nodded with tears in her eyes.

I heard and relayed, "Mom, I was there when dad passed. I saw you holding his hands. When he took his last breath I was there to cross him over."

At that point I saw his mother smile for the first time. Her whole energy seemed to change, as Michael told me to tell her that her husband, his father, is happy that she is seeing 'John'.

Her smile became even broader and a hint of a blush came to her face. She said to me that she had recently been seeing her husband's best friend John, who had lost his wife Mary three years prior. She confided in me that she didn't want to betray the memory of her husband or their friend Mary by having a relationship with his best friend. I needed at that point to stop her from confiding anymore, saying that I needed to tell her what Mike was telling me.

Although I was still aware that Mike had not pulled his energy back, I became aware of a different energy stepping in: older and related to both Michael and his mother. I knew her husband was now talking with me.

When I told her who was now coming through, she began to smile and laugh. The entire energy in the restaurant seemed to change.

"Your husband is telling me that his best friend John was devastated with the loss of his wife years ago, the way your life has been devastated by the loss of your son and then him. He's telling me, to remind you of the difficulty you both had in trying to find a 'good woman' for John." She was now laughing, nodding and smiling. "He just told me that the reason why you never found a good woman for John was because you are that woman!"

As her eyes reflected and registered what she'd just heard, I said, "Your husband is now saying that you will all be together again: you, Michael, John, Mary and him. And until then, Mikey, Mary and he will be watching over you and John."

I started to feel the connection to both spirits begin to fade. I told his mother that they were both pulling back, but that they will always be with her and that she should never doubt that.

At that point, I did lose contact with the two souls. And after explaining a little more of how connecting with spirit works, she stood and put her arms around me. Hugging me tightly, she whispered in my ear, "Thank you so much! You have no idea what you have done for me. Thank you so, so very much."

Although I gave her my business card, I never heard from her, which was fine because Michael and his father had given her everything they needed to tell her. And she had heard everything she needed to finish the grieving process, and continue her life with John.

Spirit Helpers are not only here to help you.
They are also here to help other spirits help <u>their</u> own loved ones
who are still here on Earth.

THE BUS RIDE BACK TO SCHOOL

As we left the deli, we were eager to review what we had shared, which had been a Life Lesson for both of us. I was now aware of how a strong spirit can get through to me, even on a crowed city street, despite my responsibilities as a teacher with thirty active students. And Gloria learned that the process of communication is much more than just language.

But there was no time to talk as all the students started gathering at our meeting place. We saw the bus pull up, had all our students seated, did our headcount and returned to the front of the bus. We knew that with traffic, we had a good forty minute trip ahead of us, so we jumped right in.

Gloria couldn't wait to share her excitement. "That was AMAZING! Does this type of thing happen to you all the time?" she asked.

"No, Gloria. That communication with your Nana was the first time I ever gave a spontaneous reading. I guess, because she's such a skilled communicator?" I wondered. "I didn't tell you, but I felt her with us as soon as we left the theater. You know, Nana is always around you, and I've become used to sensing her whenever we're together." As Gloria smiled, a realization hit me.

"And you want me to really blow your mind? Nana wasn't even here for **you** this time. She was actually here to help another soul in spirit - Michael - connect with his grieving mom."

Gloria looked shocked!

"Do you know why Michael needed your Nana's help? Remember when she wanted to communicate with you, that day in school, and wouldn't take 'no' for an answer? That's when your Nana learned how to open the door, when she whispered to you to mention Lisa Williams."

Gloria jumped in. "Do you remember when I moved my seat over and questioned why I had done that? I heard her! But I didn't recognize it was my Nana in my thoughts. She asked me to move over."

"And if you hadn't listened to her, and stayed in that chair and not moved, I never would have noticed Michael's mother. That poor grief stricken mother would never have had the closure she needed so badly. And that is how mediumship works, and why I love doing this work."

I continued, "Michael had to do the same thing that Nana did - open the door. He just wasn't experienced enough to know how. Your Nana is always around you, but today she was really here for Michael and his mother." Gloria was listening intently.

"Isn't it amazing how spirit works?" I marveled. "Sure, Nana had to bring us to that deli. Obviously, I was needed as the medium. But you had a very special role also. You informed his mom that I was a medium. Gloria, **you** opened the door and got the whole thing started." I took a breath. "And do you know what **this** is called?" As I indicated in the conversation we were having: "A synchronicity."

Suddenly, there was a commotion going on in the back of the bus, as there often is. I stood up, went back and settled the students down, and as I returned to my seat, Gloria seemed deep in thought.

She asked, "Garry, I do have a question about what you said to that woman about hypnosis..." she paused. "You said that hypnosis can help with pain management for a dentist visit. Did you make that up, just to open the door?"

"No way," I replied. "I would never just make something up. A medium always works with the truth. Honesty is integral to mediumship. But you know," I confided, "a few years ago I actually had a root canal done using self-hypnosis instead of Novocain."

She looked at me questioningly, raised her eyebrow and said, "You're kidding, right?"

I laughed and said, "Hey, that's exactly what my dentist said when I told him my plan!"

She took a deep breath, shook her head, and said, "You must be crazy! But now you've got to tell me all about it." The rest of the bus ride was spent describing that memorable root canal.

Pain can be a large part of any journey.
Finding different ways to cope with that pain
opens you to new learnings and growth.

THE NOVOCAIN FREE ROOT CANAL

I told Gloria that I had known our family dentist, Dr. Howard Goodkin, for over ten years. We had a lot in common, and had become friends. Howard is a very caring person who, I feel, would prefer to inflict pain on himself rather than his patients. That's why I knew I was in for a long discussion and a lot of convincing before I could actually put my plan into action.

Gloria interrupted, "He must have thought you lost your mind. Why inflict unnecessary pain on yourself?"

And to be honest, I'd been thinking pretty much the same thing on that spring morning of 2000 as I entered Dr. Goodkin's office.

I continued, telling her that I'm not insane, not a Mr. Macho I-Can-Take-a-Lot-of-Pain-Kinda-Guy, nor a masochist. I simply needed to know that I could believe in and rely upon the hypnosis training I had just completed.

I went on to explain, "If the tutor who had instructed me in the art of hypnosis says that he undergoes root canals without Novocain and that there is no difference between a little pain and a lot of pain, and if I have believed in everything else I'd learned in his classes, I still needed to test my own ability to control pain using hypnosis."

I continued, "Gloria, this was the time to test! To test myself; to test my training; to test my faith in hypnosis… To reaffirm that if I tell someone that hypnosis can eliminate the pain of a root canal, I am stating a fact. Confirmed by firsthand information and not just, 'what my teacher told me'."

Gloria nodded. "Yeah, Garry. I understand how important it was for you to be sure."

"Exactly. Doing this crazy experiment would prove to me that hypnosis could have a powerful effect on the perception of pain. After all, I tried to stop smoking by myself for over a year. But it only took one hypnosis session to permanently quit. And that's the reason I became a hypnotherapist. I was confident in using hypnosis for smoking and phobia clients, but I never attempted hypnosis for pain management. Because, what if I was wrong?"

"But Garry, weren't you really scared to go through with it?"

"I know how crazy it seems, but I had to experience hypnotic pain management, on myself, before I could offer it to my hypnosis clients."

"But Ga," Gloria questioned, "were you really willing to sit in your dentist's chair and have a root canal with no anesthesia, just to prove to yourself that hypnosis can really work on pain? You were that confident?"

"To say I was completely confident that do it may not be quite honest. I was really a nervous wreck!"

I paused. "What's funny is that I had recently seen *The Oprah Winfrey Show*, where she interviewed James Frey, the author of A Million Little Pieces. That was his autobiography about his experiences with drug addiction, and included his description of having a root canal without Novocain. It turned out he'd been lying. Oprah and her audience were outraged that they'd been lied to: No one can have a root canal without some sort of drug!"

"Wow! I absolutely remember that episode," Gloria exclaimed.

"Listen, I didn't come to this decision lightly. First, I had a filling drilled with no anesthesia. Dr. Goodkin was hesitant but pleasantly surprised that it worked so well."

"So it worked?" Gloria exclaimed.

"Yeah, but, using hypnosis for a filling was nowhere near as extreme as my next experiment: drilling through a tooth, out the bottom of its root… and then having the live nerve ripped out of my jaw! Now **that** would certainly convince me of how truly effective hypnosis can be."

I used the rest of our trip back to school describing to Gloria what an anesthesia-free root canal entailed.

*It's interesting to observe how things go through your mind;
how one thought leads to another seemingly different thought,
until you realize there is a bigger picture behind these
seemingly random thoughts that eventually makes perfect sense.*

DOUBTS OVER A NOVOCAIN FREE ROOT CANAL

I did have a certain amount of doubt in my ability to control pain, which began to increase as my resolve to have this procedure began to diminish. But as I was driving to Dr. Goodkin's office, I tried to shake myself out of the dark cloud of negativity and doubt that was creeping up on me, and smiled to myself. *Get a grip there Ga,* I thought to myself, *this won't be that hard.*

As I stopped at a light, I took a breath as I had been trained to do, and found a truth: taking a deep breath is the most effective way to reduce stress and allow your mind to focus. As my mind began to quiet, I found that all those doubting voices began to quiet also. The light finally changed green, and as I accelerated, my mind started to relax. I had a ten mile drive to the dentist's office and decided that I would sit in the car and de-stress in the office parking lot, considering I would be half an hour early.

I was aware of the dangers of driving while under the influence of alcohol and had joked with people that I had a problem with DWH: Driving While Hypnotized. I knew I needed to begin the relaxation process as soon as possible, but behind the wheel was certainly not the best place to begin a hypnotic session. Although I wasn't actively beginning self-hypnosis behind the wheel, I did start to relax. I allowed other memories from my subconscious to slowly flow into my conscious awareness, if only to distract my concerns over the sanity of an anesthetic-free root canal.

~ ~ ~

It's interesting to observe the functioning of your own mind: the voices; the conflicts; the connections; the associations; the past; the future. However, the one thing that is usually not that obvious to your consciousness is the Now. The now is where that observer of your mind is. This is an excellent description of what I was going through. Although I was not allowing the voices in my head the opportunity to share their concerns with the people around me, they sure were letting me know their concerns!

Becoming and staying proactive on the journey is a necessity.
But be careful of what you wish for. You
just might get it, and then what?

TIME TO PUT UP OR SHUT UP

The time for questions and concerns was over as I snapped myself out of those negative thoughts. And the time had come to focus on getting through the next two hours, get this root canal done, and at the same time prove an important lesson to myself.

Sitting in my car at the end of the parking lot, I became aware of the fragrance of the trees and flowers in bloom, bringing back memories of my youth. But reminiscing time was done, hypnosis time was here, so I closed the windows, got out, locked the doors and walked into my dentist's office determined to challenge myself. And that is exactly what I did.

Okay gang, it's put up or shut up time. It's time to put our money where our mouth is. Literally! It's time to put our hypnosis training to the test. Now, once again, I found myself talking to the voices in my head. As a hypnotherapist, I recognize these voices as Parts: We each have them, the inner voices representing individual aspects of our personality.

I wasn't exactly speaking to my Parts as much as I was asking them for help. Yet I knew that the only help I was going to receive was from either a large shot of Novocain, or from my own subconscious, and I decided that I was going to test my new found hypnotic skills, in a possibly very painful way.

Just then a relatively new Part took over. *Shut up, all of you!* This new take-charge Part demanded from all the other voices chattering away in my head. To my relief, I heard them all stop. *If we're going to do this, he needs you all working together. Stop distracting him and let's start helping him instead.* I understood instantly exactly who this Part was - my Hypnotherapist Part.

I checked in with the receptionist and had a seat in the waiting room. I hadn't been awfully confident that I could get myself into a hypnotic state deeply enough for pain management. So a week before my appointment, I'd made a cassette tape using my karaoke machine specifically for this purpose. On the cassette tape, I described my safe place, a beautiful beach in Hawaii. I also incorporated into the tape some happy childhood memories. When I listened to it at home, I was pleasantly surprised at the depth of trance I achieved, along with the speed in which I entered that very deep state of relaxation.

Now with my Sony Walkman cassette player and hypnosis cassette tape in hand, I sat and waited to be called in. Finally, the door to the waiting room opened and Dr. Goodkin's assistant, Margie, directed me to the dentist's chair. And there, on the counter, sat a rather large hypodermic needle next to a small bottle that I assumed to be the Novocain.

If I were ever going to change my mind, this was the time.

I had thought it all out and, from the comfort and safety of my car, it hadn't seemed as frightening, misguided and… well… stupid, as it did from the dentist's chair. As I looked at the needle, it seemed to grow before my eyes! But my opportunity faded as Dr. Goodkin entered the room. I was determined and committed to do this and I was about to learn, perhaps the hard way, whether a root canal can be performed without anything for the pain except for the much underutilized power of the mind.

Dr. Goodkin entered the room with his normal broad, bright smile. "How are you?" he asked, briskly shaking my hand. We talked about kids and family. Dr. Goodkin has the best bedside manner of any doctor you could ever meet. We enjoyed small talk about kids, school and vacations.

As he and Margie prepared for the root canal, the topic came up about my new business venture. "So Ga, how is your hypnotherapy practice doing?" Dr. Goodkin asked, as Margie said that she found hypnosis fascinating, and asked me for a HYP4LIFE business card.

I took that opportunity to mention to Dr. Goodkin that I once again had a proposal that he might find a little uncomfortable.

As he looked at me quizzically, I began, "I always need to prove to myself, through personal experience, that hypnosis will work. I know it works for smokers, because I was able to quit through hypnotherapy myself. And it worked well for my last cavity, didn't it?" He nodded that he recalled, so I continued. "But now I have to challenge myself to prove that hypnosis will work for extreme pain management, too." Howard looked nervous. I took a breath and prepared for what was to come. "I need to prove to myself that hypnosis blocks all pain. So I want to have this root canal without Novocain."

Dr. Goodkin reacted as I knew he would, with a loud laugh, as if I had just told him a good joke. Then he looked at me and noticed I wasn't laughing. "You are kidding, right? We're not talking about simple dentistry now. We're talking about a root canal. Garry, I really can't let you do this."

"Okay, how about this? Fill up the needle," I said with a smile, "and if I scream you can use it."

Margie's eyes were as wide as saucers. When she realized what was coming, she shook her head and said sarcastically, "Oh, this is gonna be fun."

"There's no way I can change your mind about this?" Dr. Goodkin asked, almost pleading. But I was adamant.

"It'll be fine. You can stop and numb me up if I can't block the pain." Finally, he agreed and discreetly began to fill the needle. My look prompted him to say that he liked to be prepared, just in case. My heart rate was probably 120 bpm when I took out the cassette recorder and headphones and began to focus on the tape.

I immediately felt my heart rate slow. I took a few deep breaths as I heard Dr. Goodkin and his assistant moving around the room. My eyes were closed, but I was very aware of what was happening around me. Then I realized that I hadn't described the way I would communicate with them and how they could communicate with me. Although I didn't want to, I opened my eyes.

Dr. Goodkin took a deep breath and smiled with relief. "So you've changed your mind. Thank God! It'll take a few minutes for the Novocain to take effect," as he picked up the large hypodermic. His smile disappeared when I told him that I just needed to explain how to communicate while I was under hypnosis.

I began to describe ideomotor responses: a thumbs-up meant yes or good; a thumbs-down was no; and if I raised my hand, it meant to stop. I told Margie that when the procedure was finished, she should lift up my headphones, tell me that it was over, and I would bring myself out of the trance. Now, with my headphones in place once more, and the tape playing, I fell quickly into a deep state of hypnosis, despite knowing that the drilling was about to start.

Before turning on the drill, Dr. Goodkin asked again if I was sure. My response? One thumbs-up.

The familiar buzz, the feeling of my heart rate slowing…

As my tape directed me, I went to a beach in Hawaii…

Cobalt blue sky…

Transparent pastel turquoise blue water…

Floating on a raft…

Drifting deeper…

HYPNOSIS AND THE ROOT CANAL

Although I thought I was thoroughly prepared for this experiment in pain management, my subconscious mind had its own plans. My self-made hypnosis cassette successfully brought me from the dentist's chair to a raft off the Hawaiian beach, looking up at the most beautiful blue sky. The clouds were more than puffy and cotton-like. They seemed to be in HD, with a texture I had never noticed before. As I began to visualize the scene presenting itself, in my own words and voice, I began to feel distracted - not by what was happening in my mouth, but by my own very active subconscious.

The beach began to darken as I was drawn away from the images of Hawaii, and brought to the familiar classroom in the school where I had learned hypnosis. The images on the tape, that had worked so well at home, started to change and morph. I was unconcerned and knew to just go along with the thoughts that were entering my mind. I also knew that if I focused strongly on this vivid memory, I could not focus on my current situation.

I soon found myself at The Institute of Hypnotherapy in Edison NJ. Remarkably, my subconscious knew the best way to get my focus away from the pain I was about to endure. It knew exactly what I wanted to accomplish here, and how to achieve my goal. So, as Dr. Goodkin began to drill the tooth, my subconscious brought me back to my hypnosis training with a different doctor.

Memories of that pain management class came flooding back. The vividness and clarity was normal for me while under hypnosis. I saw Dr. Jaime Feldman, the school's director, standing in front of the class. I felt as though I was not experiencing a memory at all. It felt as if I were back in the class once again. Dr. Feldman was there in front of me, explaining how the functioning of the mind works while in hypnosis, explaining that pain could be masked or completely eliminated. As he continued his lecture, he quite nonchalantly mentioned that he had undergone root canals using hypnosis, without the use of Novocain.

I looked around to see if anyone really believed this story. *Yeah, hypnosis is a powerful tool, but really... a root canal? No one can do that,* I thought. As I looked at the other students in the class, there were expressions of doubt on some faces, but I suppose mine was the one that showed the most disbelief. Perhaps he saw the smirk on my face as I looked at my fellow students, because Dr. Feldman chose me as his guinea pig.

"Garry," Dr. Feldman said, looking at me. "Would you like to 'volunteer' to experience pain management in front of the class?" Dr. Feldman preferred to introduce new hypnotic techniques by using a hands-on demonstration. I did not know at that time, just how 'hands-on' this demonstration was about to get.

So here I was, in front of the classroom, going deeply into hypnosis so he could demonstrate how to administer pain reduction. But I would soon learn that, to administer pain management, there has to be pain that needs to be managed!

"Take a deep breath..." His standard hypnotic induction began. By this time in my training, I didn't need much direction to enter a very deep trance state. The more often someone is hypnotized, the more proficient he becomes at being in *The Altered State*, which is the traditional description of hypnosis.

Although the expression 'Altered State' may sound far out, it is really a quite accurate description of hypnosis. While in hypnosis, you are neither conscious nor asleep; you are somewhere in between the two, as in an Altered State of Consciousness. Perhaps a better description of hypnosis should be the 'Altering' State of Consciousness: the state of moving from consciousness to sleep and visa versa. So as I allowed myself to sink deeper into that deepest of all states of hypnosis, I experienced the tingling and the feeling of floating, at the same time that my body felt heavy.

"Do you see the smile on his face?" Dr. Feldman asked the class, as I sank even more deeply into hypnosis. "Ten percent of a given population go into hypnosis almost instantly. They are the ones that a stage hypnotist will look for. The reason I asked Garry to volunteer for this demonstration is because he is a 'somnambulant': a person who easily enters somnambulism, which is the most efficient state of hypnosis that you as a hypnotist can direct someone into."

I remained aware that the class was continuing. Questions, answers, and conversations between Dr. Feldman and the other students went on around me, as if I were a high school science project. Although the class was continuing in real time, my own sense of time changed. Minutes felt like seconds as my perception of time seemed to slow down as I entered somnambulism.

Off in the distance, I became aware of a high-pitched sound. At this point, I was not even aware that I was in Dr. Goodkin's office. Rather, I was back in my hypnosis class, years earlier, being hypnotized in front of my classmates to experience pain management. Pretty interesting, huh? I find it amazing how the subconscious knows just what you need, when you need it, and it is always working for you.

"You all see the signs of hypnosis. He is already very deep, but let's get him deeper before we introduce the pain aspect..." the class continued, as I pictured him smiling in anticipation of causing me great pain. I wondered how the pain was going to be administered and then a moment later, I just did not care. I was already enjoying the beneficial feelings and positive effects of being a somnambulant.

Dr. Feldman lifted my left hand which he described as "feeling like a dish rag... limp." I felt my hand lift up, seemingly by itself and moving in a circular motion. He began demonstrating this new technique to the class. He had lifted my hand. Now he was moving it in a clockwise movement, but I did not feel his touch. To me, it felt like my hand had a mind of its own.

"The more your hand moves, the more you relax... and now as I touch the back of your hand, you will notice a very nice numb feeling spreading over the back of that hand." I felt the touch and at the same time, my hand became numb.

"With each touch to the back of that hand, it gets more and more numb, until you cannot feel my touch at all. When you no longer feel the back of your hand, you can nod." He continued moving and tapping the back of my hand. Then the tapping stopped.

I nodded.

As he was suggesting that the back of my hand was cool and completely numb, without my knowledge, he was fanning the back of my hand until I was not even aware that I had a hand any longer. The whole procedure felt as if it lasted for two minutes. I would later learn it was closer to twenty.

Soon, he brought me back to a conscious state, although I really didn't want to come back. "On the count of five, you will open your eyes…" Dr. Feldman began his de-hypnosis procedure and I felt even more reluctant to become conscious again. I wanted to stay in that wonderful altered state. However, with each number he counted, I felt the awareness of my surroundings becoming more activated. Dr. Feldman continued his slow de-hypnosis count.

"On the count of five, you'll find your eyes will open and you will feel completely alert and happy to be back. One - starting to emerge from hypnosis." I knew I was about to awaken and I was actually resentful that it was ending so soon. I was also being distracted by what I felt was a fly buzzing around my ear. "Two - Feeling wonderful in every way." He continued to five as my eyes responded on their own.

My eyes slowly opened and began to focus. I gradually became more aware of the people in the room. Coming out of hypnosis is a process in itself, and can take five to ten minutes. I became very aware of the expressions on the faces of the other students.

In the past, the experience of coming out of hypnosis after participating in a demonstration had always been a comforting feeling, particularly seeing the faces of my classmates. They would always be excited and totally involved with the procedure, and curious about my perspective of the hypnotic experience. They were always smiling and animated. However, as I opened my eyes, the faces I saw around me reflected feelings ranging from empathy to concern, which immediately confused me. And that annoying fly was still buzzing around my head!

"What?" I asked the students in the front row, as if I had done something wrong.

"How is your hand feeling?" one student asked. There was so much empathy in her voice that I was taken aback. If I didn't know better, I would have thought that I'd just had my hand amputated. I raised my left hand, clenching and unclenching it, noticing how strange it felt. I was quite confused, but I had just come out of hypnosis and, as I've said, it can take as much as ten minutes to become fully conscious again. I was still in a type of twilight sleep, feeling as if I had just woken up.

Still confused by the students' reaction, I looked toward Dr. Feldman for an explanation, but he just smiled at me. As my awareness fully returned, I suddenly felt like the back of my hand was on fire! I could not help but rub it, which seemed to make Dr. Feldman smile even more.

"Did Garry show any signs of pain, while he was hypnotized?" he asked the class, and in unison, the class replied negatively. "He was completely pain free, wouldn't you say?" nodding to them as they nodded back in agreement. "How does your hand feel now, Garry?" he asked me with a smile like the Cheshire cat from Alice in Wonderland.

My answer was, "It hurts like hell!" which seemed to tickle him even more.

"GREAT! This is a perfect demonstration of how the mind works while in hypnosis. Wonderful! Thanks, Garry. Have a seat. How about some applause for our subject?"

As I stood to walk back to my seat, I once again became aware of that annoying sound. That same high pitched buzzing sound, like the sound of a fly on steroids, off in the distance. Interestingly, the buzz changed to the sounds of applause, as I went to the table in the back of the room. The drinks were located there, and I put some ice in a napkin to apply to my swollen hand.

The others in the class were still offering me sympathetic looks as I found out what had happened. Dr. Feldman was describing how my mind had preferred to ignore the pain. The ice was helping, but the back of my hand was red, swollen, and had crescent-shaped depressions in the skin at the site where Dr. Feldman's fingernails had been digging into it.

Just as, in real time, Dr. Goodkin's drill was digging into my tooth.

"Do you all remember," Dr. Feldman asked the class, as my awareness returned totally to the classroom scene once again, "what I did to Garry's hand? And again I apologize if it hurts now, Garry. The ice will help." (The apology was accepted, but my hand still hurt a lot.) "As you see, as I moved his hand in a circle, he was focused only on the motion and the numbness; he wasn't even aware that I was digging my nails into the back of his hand. Does anyone think that I was NOT hurting him? Garry, do you think I could have done that to you and you would just calmly sit there and accept the pain, if you weren't hypnotized?"

"No… and thanks a lot for another wonderful demonstration of the power of the human mind. Next time I 'volunteer', someone please remind me how great I feel right now."

In retrospect, I realize that my subconscious mind gave me the memory of a pain management class instead of a generic Hawaiian vacation. It knew what I wanted to accomplish and it knew that the memory of that class would work much better during the root canal. It also fascinates me that as I was being 'de-hypnotized' in the memory, I began to come slightly out of hypnosis in real time.

The image of the class faded a little as I once again became aware of that annoying high-pitched buzz. It was becoming louder and I found myself coming slightly out of hypnosis. This may be very normal but not something you want to happen midway through a root canal. My awareness of that sound was bringing me out of hypnosis. I became aware that the buzz I had been hearing off in the distance was actually much closer, and sounded very much like a dentist's drill.

When you prove to yourself that you have an obvious skill, you become your own best teacher.

DEEPENING DURING THE ROOT CANAL

Two of the many important lessons I have learned at the Institute covered the physiology and brainwave activity of the human brain. When we are awake, our brains produce activity that can be measured in the Beta range. Studies show that a brain producing Beta waves is alert, conscious and awake. The brain goes through a different brainwave pattern when it is transitioning from conscious to sleep or from sleep to being awake; that pattern is called Alpha brainwaves and it is in the Alpha range that hypnosis takes place.

Although every human being experiences Alpha brainwaves daily and every human being can experience hypnosis, the level in which they experience hypnosis may vary greatly.

There are ten levels of hypnosis. Level 1 is simply closing your eyes. Level 10 is so deeply into the experience of hypnosis that at a level 11, the person would be asleep and ignore the words of the hypnotherapist. Level 1 is not nearly deep enough for any therapeutic use of hypnosis, and level 10 is too deep. A somnambulant will go very quickly to a level of 8, which is the most productive level of trance for hypnotherapy.

~ ~ ~

Back in Dr. Goodkin's chair, I was now aware that the fly buzzing around my head was really Dr. Goodkin's drill, which was almost half way through my root as I was becoming more conscious. I needed to get deeper… Back into the Alpha state, and quick!

My hand gently and slowly rose from my chest to indicate that I needed a minute. Instantly, Dr. Goodkin stopped drilling, and as my mouth closed, I took a few deep breaths. Dr. Goodkin asked, "Are you okay, Ga?" My response was another thumbs-up as I started to deep breathe. Without coming out of hypnosis, with my eyes closed, I calmly reset my cassette player.

Clicking my Walkman back on, hearing my voice describing the beach in Hawaii did the trick. I gave another thumbs-up signal and opened my mouth. The conversation between Howard and Margie quickly faded away into the background, as I found myself back on that pristine beach, all by myself in paradise. But my subconscious knew better and the beach, once again, morphed as I found myself back at the Institute of Hypnotherapy.

Again I saw Dr. Feldman in front of a class, as I sat in the rear of the room, observing. "Ladies and gentlemen," he addressed the new students, "how long do you think it would take to hypnotize a subject?" I knew what he was about to do, but this time, I was actually looking forward to participating. I allowed myself to be ready.

"5 minutes," an older man said from the row in front of me. I took a deep breath and began to relax.

"10 minutes," called out a young college student. She was a psychology major at Rutgers and wanted to learn another tool for her trade. I always enjoyed speaking with her, and frequently told her about the value hypnosis can be for a therapist.

"Would you believe I could hypnotize someone, as quickly as this?" Raising up his hand and snapping his fingers, once. The sound of that familiar snap began the process for me. I felt the noise in the room subside. I also heard some of the students say that they doubted a snap of a finger could hypnotize a person. Little did they know that I was already hypnotized, and at a level 2.

A student to my right said that he had seen a hypnosis show where the hypnotist did that 'snapping thing,' but all the people on stage had already been hypnotized, and he doubted that anyone not recently hypnotized could be hypnotized by the snap of a finger.

I saw the smile on Dr. Feldman's face and knew what he was about to do. "Garry?" he said as he looked directly into my eyes… All heads in the room turned to look at whom he was addressing.

Earlier, I had been introduced to all the students who knew me as an Institute graduate and a professional hypnotherapist. Although I was quite aware of the attention I was getting from the entire class, I was also anticipating and looking forward to what was about to happen.

"SLEEP!" Dr. Feldman said firmly, looking squarely in my eyes as he snapped his fingers once.

The room went dark. My eyes rolled up, my eyelids fluttered and closed. I felt as if they were glued shut. The familiar feelings of deep relaxation swept through my body, from my scalp that began to tingle to my toes that began to feel comfortably warm. All sounds in the room, from the voices saying "Oh my God!" to the sounds of chairs being turned, to the hum of the air conditioner and the sounds of people standing and conversing, all began to feel as if they were on a volume control that was being turned down. At the same time, I was aware that his voice was becoming louder and closer as he walked from the front of the class to where I was seated.

He touched my forehead and said, "Sleep," another hypnosis deepening technique, and I was out.

"Ladies and gentlemen, this is a demonstration of how fast someone can be hypnotized." His hand went to my shoulder and I felt my depth of hypnosis increase even more. "Does anyone have an idea of the contributing factors that would allow a person to instantly be hypnotized?"

The answers came flooding in:

"Your training?"

"Maybe, he was tired?"

"Has he been hypnotized often… before?"

"Trust?"

"There's an old hypnosis joke," Dr. Feldman said, as I proceeded into an even deeper state (both in the memory, and in Dr. Goodkin's chair). "How many hypnotists does it take to screw in a light bulb? The answer: One, but only if that light bulb REALLY wants to be screwed in!"

The class laughed politely.

"What I'm saying is," he continued, "perhaps the most important contributing factor in the process of hypnotizing someone is their willingness to be hypnotized, along with the rapport you have with them. Although I have hypnotized Garry dozens of times, he would never allow himself to be this deep…" as he spoke he lifted and dropped my hand into my lap, "… if he were the least bit concerned with my ethics or if he simply didn't want to be in a hypnotic state. Remember, your hypnosis client, or subject, is always in control."

I needed to go back to a very deep state, and again my subconscious had given me that perfect memory to put me instantly and deeply back to where I needed to be, yet I was not even aware that I had done it. I had proved to myself that not only could I ignore the pain of a root canal, but even more, I unexpectedly found that the subconscious, by itself, can determine and implement the states of consciousness that you immediately need to experience. Once again, I became aware of that high-pitched buzzing and as I did, it suddenly stopped; the sudden quiet almost made me open my eyes.

~ ~ ~

Back in the dentist's chair, I felt my headphones being moved and realized that Margie was speaking to me. It took a concerted effort on my part to focus on her words. "We're just about done," she said. "We should be through in like five minutes. Do you need anything? It was amazing! You didn't even flinch. I'm impressed!" I gave her another thumbs-up sign, not even opening my eyes.

I fell back into hypnosis quickly, but this time I was no longer at the Institute. I was quite relieved that it was over and for the first time that day, it hit me: I'd actually done it - a Novocain free root canal!

Now, with the stress gone and with the knowledge that I'd succeeded in using hypnosis for pain management, I found myself back on the raft, floating in the Pacific Ocean in Hawaii as I allowed myself to slowly come back to full consciousness. There are people who are resistant to awaken, because being hypnotized just feels so good. After the stress of proving to myself the effectiveness of hypnosis, I wanted to come out to discuss the experience we had all shared.

It took about five minutes to return to full consciousness as Dr. Goodkin and I discussed the experience. He mentioned how impressed he was, and extended an invitation to me to give a presentation on the benefits of hypnosis to the Men's Club in his synagogue, which I gladly accepted.

Driving home from Dr. Goodkin's office, I understood why he suggested that I take some Advil as soon as possible. One of the benefits for Novocain, he told me, was the long lasting effect of the numbness. When I came back to full consciousness, I became fully aware of the procedure that I had just gone through, and a dose of Advil was an effective way of dealing with the resulting pain.

I had proved to Dr. Goodkin - but more importantly to myself - that hypnosis works for pain management. I had used my new found skills to stop extreme pain. And now I was ready to get my company 'HYP4LIFE- Improving your Life through Hypnotherapy' off the ground and up and running.

For over 20 years I'd known that I would be practicing hypnotherapy, ever since the day a hypnotherapist was able to end my addiction to tobacco. At that time I didn't know how, but I knew that one day I would be using hypnosis to help people the way he had helped me. And now everything was set... except for having clients.

~ ~ ~

Of course I had told Gloria the shorter version, but by the time we entered the school's parking lot, I could tell she had heard enough, just by the expression on her face.

I was very comfortable telling people that I was a medium and in fact, I had to control myself during conversations. In retrospect, when you are passionate about a subject you tend to talk about it extensively and perhaps relentlessly, which can turn people off. My wife, Chris, would often tell me that when I saw people's eyes start to glaze over, it meant that they'd had enough and I should chill out for a while.

Because I was so passionate about my metaphysical pursuits, I would happily talk with anyone who was curious, and I would jokingly warn them what Chris always said.

But, Gloria and I would continue our metaphysical discussions for years to come.

She and I said our goodbyes as we walked to our cars. All the buses had cleared the parking lot as I got in my car and followed the last bus to the light, smiling at the sight of 45 arms hanging out the windows. I made the right on red and accelerated my Mazda 6 home.

~ ~ ~

I get more from driving than just traveling from point A to point B. And getting from Point A: School to Point B: Home, always gave me a lot of quiet time to think. Considering that I had just given the most powerful mediumship reading of my career, to a complete stranger in a deli on a school trip, you can imagine the questions swirling through my mind.

The experience in New Brunswick really had me thinking. I had been working on my abilities to connect with the energies of discarnate people for the past six years, and had been asking for my skills to improve. Now, I knew they had. But who had I been asking? God? Spirits? Archangels? Spirit Guides?

Perhaps.

The light at the firehouse had just turned red and I took a deep breath waiting for it to turn green again. At this point in my life, I had gotten very comfortable feeling the energy of my deceased father near me. I have often felt him close to me, especially when I'm alone in my car. And on the drive home that afternoon, I felt as if he were sitting next to me. Images and memories filled my thoughts, not centered on the day's events, but on my father. Thoughts and feelings of how much I missed him and the last year I had with him, filled my mind.

ASKING DAD TO QUIT SMOKING

By the spring of 1970, I was twenty-one and in my junior year at Brooklyn College. Each night, the family tradition was to sit and talk during dinner about what was happening in all our lives. Then, after my mother cleared the table and served my father and herself coffee, dad would light up his first cigarette. There were times in my father's life when he was under stress that he would even smoke during meals.

As usual, I watched him inhale so deeply that half the cigarette turned into ash. As we spoke, I noticed the smoke come out of his nose and mouth for a full minute. I would tell him that smoking must be hurting him and he would simply say, "I'm as healthy as a horse and strong as an ox. Look at me, fifty eight and I look like I'm forty!"

Unfortunately, neither of us realized how correct I was. How in two short years, my strong as an ox, healthy as a horse, chain smoking father would be fighting for breath, slowly dying of a self-inflicted slow suicide known as cigarettes.

I had been dating Christine for almost three years, which bothered my father because of the Jewish/Catholic situation. He was honest in his view of the world and when I asked my parents if I could invite Chris to our home for a dinner as her family had frequently invited me, he said that he would prefer not to. When pressed for a better answer than what I had received, he was again brutally honest.

"Ga, if I meet her I know I will accept her and love her, but, she's not Jewish... I can't. It'll be better not to meet her... Why can't you find a nice Jewish girl?"

My answer should have been, "No, because I love her." But instead I answered by simply accepting his reasoning with a nod. I looked down as he lit up another cigarette, coughed a few times and went up to bed. That moment in time solidified two thoughts in my mind.

One... All organized religions put huge walls between people who, given the opportunity, could love and accept one another.

And

Two... Physically, there was something very wrong with my father.

~ ~ ~

By the next winter, Chris and I were beginning to plan our marriage, something we shared joyfully with her family, but had not yet addressed with mine. Chris had come to my house a few times for dinner and it would be an understatement to say it was uncomfortable. I had become accustomed to the arguments I was having with my father over Chris or his smoking, but I had noticed a change in him that really concerned me.

He was sleeping more than ever before. After dinner, when the family would normally sit around speaking of politics or television shows or the day's events, he excused himself and went to bed. He was also losing weight, which had always been something that had been an issue in the past. Weighing 230 pounds for most of his adult life, he was always on a diet. A few years earlier, he had joined Weight Watchers and was so proud that he had gotten his weight down to 200. But he wasn't dieting any longer and it seemed that he just didn't have the appetite he once had. He was thinner and frailer than I had ever remembered him. But it was his coughing that was my main concern.

After dinner one evening, he leaned back and decided to have that first, after-dinner smoke for the night. We were now arguing much more, mainly over his health. I was insisting that he see a doctor and as he usually did, he waved me off, saying he was fine and he just had a little cold. As he lit up, I felt my eyes roll and anger begin to burn inside me.

Can't he see that his smoking is killing him? I thought to myself.

As he took that first drag, I could hear the rattling in his chest. The sound was from the thick mucus deep in his lungs being agitated by the introduction of unfiltered tobacco smoke. What I didn't know at that time, what no one knew, was that cancer had already spread from a malignant mass in his lung to other parts of his body.

He took another drag and, whether it was because he was conscious of our fighting over his addiction or because he didn't want to acknowledge his illness to himself, he stubbornly held the cough back.

Stifling the cough made his body need to expel the mucus in his lungs more strongly. With his face turning red, the veins bulging in his forehead and throat, he still obstinately tried to take another drag. But he had no more strength to repress his coughing and he started to cough so hard that his whole body began to shudder. Finally, after what seemed to be an eternity, his coughing ceased while my concern and anger grew.

He sat with his cigarette still in his hand, although it was no longer straight and cylindrical, as his coughing fit had caused his hand to twist and bend the cigarette. As its smoldering head began to fall off, he still attempted to take another drag!

Rage at my father's stubbornness, at his inability to admit he had to quit smoking, along with my concern for his health, formed a combination of feelings that welled up inside me, producing an eruption of emotions that neither I nor anyone in my family had ever seen in me before.

I angrily took the smoldering cigarette from his hand and firmly crushed it out in his ashtray as my family looked at me, in shock. I felt control slipping away as my vision became blurred. I realized tears were now running down my cheeks.

"What the hell is wrong with you?" I screamed, probably for the first time in my life. I found myself leaning on the table, inches from his face. "Don't you know this is killing you?" I grabbed the pack of cigarettes from his hand, showing them to him as I crushed them in my fist. "I have been asking you for years to stop this Goddamn habit." First, I shook them in his face and then threw the crushed ball of tobacco across the kitchen. The Chesterfields ricocheted off the kitchen cabinets and into the sink. "Christ! Dad, you gotta know that it's the damn cigarettes that are making you cough, not just some little cold!"

"GARRY! Such language! In front of your sister and me," my enabling mother shouted, trying to get me to calm down and change the subject while taking a drag from her own cigarette. I was not going to calm down. I couldn't, not now. I had to finish venting or I would explode.

I wanted to grab him and shake him.

I wanted to shake the desire to smoke out of him.

I wanted to shake out the mucus that rattled in his lungs.

I wanted to tell him how frightened I was that he was going to die.

I wanted to shake the Smoker Part out of him, step on it, and crush it like the cigarettes that caused his illness and his inevitable death.

I wanted him to listen to me when I asked him to stop smoking, but I knew he wouldn't. I knew that the decision to quit smoking was up to him. And I also knew that he couldn't quit.

I had never spoken to my father like that before and he and my family were taken by surprise, not knowing what to do or say. After I took a breath to calm down, I pulled my chair close to him, and whispered.

"Dad, I'm not just bustin' your balls…" I said.

"GARRY!" my mother protested once again, hand to her chest. I ignored her. She was rolling her eyes, with a look of both irritation and shame on her face. But I'd like to think that, in reality, she was happy that, at least, I was stating the obvious: that Dad had a serious health issue.

Again ignoring my mother's complaints, I continued, "Dad, the only reason I'm saying this is that there are all these reports coming out on TV about how cigarettes can kill you. Look at you, you're losing weight, you can't play 9 holes without a golf cart, you cough constantly and can't catch your breath! Yeah, I'm bustin' your balls but it's 'cause I love you! And I just want you to be healthy."

**When walls form between people who love each other,
which seem to form instantly and feel impenetrable,
you may find that they can crumble from
something as innocuous as a tear.**

THE SMOKER'S WALL

I thoroughly expected his wall to form as it always did. *The Wall* is a strong part of a smoker's addiction. The smoker, realizing that he has to defend his indefensible decision to smoke, will form a wall of denial.

I picture this wall as being made of brick and mortar, ten feet thick, solid and unshakable, as long and solid as the Great Wall of China. Sometimes I would picture it as a thick curtain, like the curtains in a theater: dusty, thick, heavy and blocking all sound from the other side. The sounds from the other side of that wall are the tears, cries and pleas of the smoker's loved ones, who know that their addiction is deadly. These words of concern which are sent to the smoker, in many different forms, are often unheeded until it is too late.

Words aren't very effective when trying to convince a smoker to quit. It's like snowballs being thrown against a brick wall, in an attempt to break it down. I threw an awful lot of snowballs and words at my father's wall that night; they were thrown with anger, fear, and concern, but most importantly, with love.

And it is the love that a family member has for their smoker that is hurt so often. If there was no love, there would be no concern. "Let him smoke himself to death, I don't care!" No walls come up to a statement like that. There is no threat to the Smoker Part of the subconscious. However, as soon as you, with tears in your eyes, go to your loved one and say, "I love you and I am afraid that your smoking is going to kill you," watch out for raising walls and dropping curtains.

Dad's wall shot up as soon as the topic of quitting was mentioned. Even if he thought that he should quit, his wall grew between him and the thought of stopping. That's how strong his addiction was. No non-smoker (someone who has never smoked) can imagine the difficulty of quitting a habit like smoking. They also cannot comprehend what a Smoker's Wall is, although they experience dealing with it every time they ask their smoker to quit. I had no idea of the difficulty - almost the impossibility - of the task I was asking him to do.

"Just throw them away," I would say, with no concept of the enormity of the undertaking. There would come a time, later in my life, when I would learn just how strong and imposing an obstacle a Smoker's Wall could be.

So as I looked at my father, red faced and weak from coughing, I asked him again to please quit, or at least go to the doctor.

I expected my father's wall to rise as it usually did.

I expected him to get up and go to his room.

I expected to be ignored.

I expected to hear once again: "Ga… it's just a cold." But what he did do surprised me.

He was never an affectionate father. He always had trouble showing emotions, particularly love. He pushed his chair back and stood up, looking down at me as his thumb wiped away a tear that was running down my cheek. The expression on his face was one that I was unprepared for and will always remember. The look on his face was a combination of love and fatherly pride, reflected in a gentle smile.

He put his two large hands on my cheeks, lifting my face up, and looked into my eyes. His hands were hard and calloused from years of working in the laundry, yet there was softness to that touch. "I had no idea how strongly you felt about me going to the doctor, Ga." His expression reflected a sad resignation to what he knew was happening to his body.

"OK, I'll call the doctor tomorrow." I saw his resistance disappear. I had gotten through his defenses, his wall. "Will that make you happy?" he asked, looking into my eyes in a way that I was not used to. His expression was not the expression of my strict father. His response told me that he was going to go to the doctor for me, simply because I wanted him to. I had convinced him!

Wow! I thought to myself, *he listened!* However, my euphoria was short lived, and there was a profound sadness in his expression. He had always been a very proud man. He would not accept weakness in himself and going to the doctor was always something he avoided - an admission of weakness. It was also an admission to himself that there really was something very wrong with his health.

As he waited for a response to his question, I simply nodded, trying to keep my chin from quivering and any more tears from running down my face. With that, he bent over and, for the first time in many years, kissed the top of my head. Then he said goodnight to us, turned, and went upstairs to bed.

I used my sleeve to wipe the remaining tears from my eyes as I tried to smile at my mother, who had her own tears falling.

Two years later, seven months before Chris and I married, on March 15, 1972, when I was 23, my father, the strongest man I had ever known, passed away.

Why do they say 'passed away'?

That sounds so comforting...

Passed away... sounds almost easy.

It wasn't.

He died.

Painfully, from metastasized lung cancer. For a year he was irradiated and shot full of poison called chemotherapy, all to no avail. I would sit with my mother in the doctor's office, but the oncologist seemed to be intentionally evasive with his responses to our questions.

"Doctor, what is the prognosis?" we asked... And we received nothing but a shrug as a response.

"Doctor, what can we do?" ...And again, nothing from the doctor.

"What can **you** do?" ...And with a shrug he would say, "We'll just have to see," as he stood to shake my hand and end the consultation.

What do you mean, we have to wait and see? I thought as I left the office. I had lost all faith and respect for the man. *See about WHAT?* I screamed in my mind. *Why can't we get an answer from anyone here?* I felt hopelessly frustrated and annoyed with the lack of responsiveness of the medical community. I wanted something to be done to save my father's life!

Something... anything... But what could we do?

My mother was raised to view doctors as demigods. "They know what they are doing, Garry. Don't be disrespectful," my mother scolded me, with an expression of grief and frustration on her face. But I didn't care. I wanted answers. I was getting lip service, yes. But not answers.

What we were totally unaware of was that my father had instructed the doctors to shelter his family from the truth. The truth was that my father had advanced, inoperable, stage-4 lung cancer. His cancer had already metastasized throughout his body. So, my family was unprepared for what was to come.

You see, in our family everyone tried to shelter everyone else from everything, to the point that no one knew what the hell was going on with anyone!

Dad told us that his doctors wanted him to be admitted into the hospital for more testing. It was true that the doctors wanted him admitted, but not for testing. He was in fact admitted into the hospital for hospice care. He had sworn the doctors to secrecy about the seriousness of his health. He wanted to shelter us from the truth: that he was dying.

So on a cold, dreary, rainy, mid-March morning…

In a cold, lonely, sterile, room in Maimonides Hospital in Brooklyn…

With no one there…

My father died.

There was no bedside vigil, no one there to tell him it was okay to let go and not fight the darkness he must have felt surrounding him. No one to comfort him or ease **his** fears, no one to hold his hand as he took his last painful, labored breath… No one… I never had the chance to say good-bye or I love you.

We had no closure.

That morning the phone rang. Sensing bad news, I stood at her door. From her bed, my mother answered it, said hello and listened for a moment. I saw a chill envelop her. "He's gone," was all she said, as she turned and sobbed quietly into her pillow.

What I did not know or believe at that time, was that my father had gone home. Not to East 26th Street, but to his true home, where he would never be alone again. Where there was no longer any pain, and from where he could see all his children and their children grow.

I was also unaware that, from that moment in time, my father began to help me on **my** journey. On that cold morning, March fifteenth, the Ides of March, 1972.

Change can be viewed at times as good or bad,
but the fact of the matter is that change is neither good nor bad.
It is as inevitable as the sun rising in the
morning and setting at night.
It is not good or bad. It simply IS.
It is our perceptions of the changes in our lives
that make change feel 'good' or 'bad'.

JOB SAMPLING AND QUESTIONING A SPIRITUAL COMMUNICATION

All throughout my early years in school, I loved art. I was a very imaginative child but I had difficulty reading, and when I was tested in Second Grade, the results showed that I was dyslexic. Yet despite my reading disability, I went to college, where I found that there was something I loved as much as I loved art. I loved imparting the information and knowledge that I'd learned, to others. I also learned that teaching was something I seemed to be good at.

During my summer breaks at college, I worked at a day camp as an art teacher, sharing what I was learning in school with the campers enrolled there. I knew that I would be happy as a teacher, and so I minored in Education at Brooklyn College, where I was an Art major.

I was excited to be accepted into the Masters of Fine Arts program at the State University of New York majoring in photography and sculpture. But I was engaged to be married, and although I loved being a photographer and an artist, being a 'starving artist' was not in my future.

1972 was a year of great change for me. In January I graduated from Brooklyn College with a Bachelor's Degree. In March dad passed. And in October, Chris and I were married, bought our first car and moved into our first apartment.

As I said, 1972 was a year of great change and - oh by the way - I forgot to tell you... I hate change!

So, in January 1973, with my BA and teaching certification in my pocket, New York City experienced its first fiscal crisis. Mayor Abe Beame instituted an immediate hiring freeze in all schools. Thanks a lot, Abe. All my plans to teach went down the tubes with the NYC economy.

As I applied for teaching positions throughout the NYC school bureaucracy, Chris was the bread winner, working full time as a teacher's aide to support us. We had a small apartment in Brooklyn, and fortunately the rent was only $100 a month. It wasn't too long before I realized I wasn't going to be a teacher, and I better get a job that would pay a living wage.

During the first five years of our marriage, I was doing what some people might call job sampling. Unfortunately, every new job just didn't work out. During this five year period I found myself working in a supermarket, as a photographer, an exterminator, an auto glass installer, a UPS driver, a parking lot attendant and as an assistant restaurant manager at the World Trade Center in Manhattan.

My first job after graduation was in a print shop in NJ as an off-set cameraman. At my father's funeral, a friend of his had offered me the job. I was trying to convince myself that it would be a good fit for me, but the more I tried, the more I knew it wasn't. What I wanted to do was teach.

MY FATHER'S FIRST COMMUNICATION

On a Friday early in 1973, while I was still working at the print shop, I was asked to work some overtime. I agreed to work till 6:30, and when my shift was over, I got into my 1972 blue Volkswagen Superbeetle for the long trip home. That drive home began like every other. However, what I experienced during that drive home would be anything but ordinary.

If you are familiar with a 1972 VW Superbeetle, you know that you should avoid an accident at all costs. There were no airbags, disc breaks or crumple zones to absorb a head-on impact. The VW Superbeetles of those days were built with one thing in mind: economy.

The car cost a whole twenty two hundred dollars! That's right, 22 HUNDRED, not thousand... BRAND NEW! Because the engine was in the rear, all the support structure in the chassis was back there, too. In the front was the empty trunk, a steering wheel, a little sheet metal, a couple of headlights, lots of air and you... the driver. And it was you the driver who became as damaged as the front of the car in a serious accident.

When I say serious accident, I'm not talking about a head-on with a Mack truck. I am talking about an accident with another small car. Heck, that VW bug would get totaled in an accident with a bicycle! Now don't get me wrong, I loved that car and was very aware of the precautions needed when driving it. I was then, and still am, a very defensive driver.

My daily drive home took me past the World Trade Center and through a short connecting tunnel to the FDR Drive on my way to the Brooklyn Bridge and home.

It was 7:00 pm that Friday night and, surprisingly, there was very little traffic. So, with no one in front of me, I decided to get through the tunnel as quickly as possible. It was late, I was hungry and I just wanted to be home. I stepped down on the clutch, dropped the stick into forth gear and kicked my little blue bug up to sixty-five MPH.

I had WABC on the radio at full volume and as expected when entering a tunnel, the AM radio's reception completely stopped. There was a noticeable difference in the car. When the radio's reception went dead, I could actually *feel* the silence in the car. I had been so intent on singing along with the radio, that when the car went silent, my mind became eerily still as well.

I'm sure you know the feeling, when you make the same trip day after day. You go into autopilot mode. You let your subconscious drive, while you daydream, listening to the radio. This is called highway hypnosis and is very common, but definitely limits the driver's attention. Well, I was very familiar with the drive through that connecting tunnel, having driven through it countless times.

The very sharp turn allowed visibility of only twenty feet ahead. It seemed that every ten feet was a sign saying 'DO NOT CHANGE LANES', along with frequent 20 MPH speed limit signs. But there was no traffic, I was anxious to get home, and so I decided to accelerate through the blind turn.

As I made that decision, in the silence of the car I became aware of a familiar voice there with me. It is difficult to explain exactly how I became aware of him, but his presence was as real and tangible as if he were in the seat next to me. I heard my father warn me, urgently, *"SLOW DOWN AND PULL OVER!"*

I was doing 45 MPH in the left lane. There was no time to analyze the situation or question why, out of the clear blue, I felt his presence. I simply complied and reacted by breaking and immediately crossing the double yellow line into the right lane in a split second.

As I crossed into the right lane, I narrowly missed hitting a 55 gallon steel drum that was sitting in the center of the left lane: the lane I had just been driving in a second earlier!

I was driving on a blind turn. I could not have possibly known that drum was right there at the instant I made the illegal lane switch. Without a doubt, I would have hit that drum at full speed in my tiny VW bug!

As I approached the end of the tunnel, the radio came back to life at full volume. As if the experience of hearing my father in my mind and missing a fatal accident by mere inches wasn't enough, the song that came on the radio at the very first note, as if on cue, was You've Made Me So Very Happy, by Blood, Sweat and Tears. Which was our wedding song!

I could not absorb everything that had just happened. A coincidence? It was much too powerful to be coincidental. Perhaps a synchronicity? But at that point in my life, I was not even aware of the concept of a synchronicity. The volume on the radio was the same, the song was the same one we had danced to at our wedding, and the FDR Drive in front of me was the same. But I had changed.

As I exited the tunnel, I was terribly perplexed. I hadn't been thinking of my father at all prior to entering that tunnel. Then why was he suddenly and so powerfully on my mind? But the warning I heard was not my own thought. It was a powerful command, with such urgency that I didn't question it. How could I know that there was a steel drum in the road? I could not have known! And yet I did. It had to be my father's warning that allowed me to avoid the inevitable accident that would have taken my life. And yet, I still couldn't help doubting it was him…

~ ~ ~

I drove the rest of the way home, much slower and to be honest, I don't know if the radio was on or not. I didn't hear it if it were. When I got my wits together, in my mind I said, *Thanks Dad*, and I heard or felt my father say, *You're welcome, son.*

I would struggle with that experience for decades, trying to rationalize what happened. *That's what he would have said if he were here*, was my main rationalization then. However, that rationalization could never explain how I knew that that 55 gallon drum would be on the roadway.

Many times over the coming years, I would hear his voice in those far reaches of my awareness. At the birth of my son Aaron, I felt him say, *Congratulations son, he's beautiful,* and again at the birth of my daughter Amy. When I was in my teens, we played golf together often and he would celebrate my good shots more than his own. As an adult, when I would get a birdie (which was rare), I would feel him say, *Good shot, Ga* and as I had become accustomed to, I'd say, *Thanks Dad. Wish you were here with me.* But the question always lingered: Was that really him or was it from my own thoughts, driven by my missing him?

It would be almost thirty years before I would have my question answered. But from that moment onward, I became very comfortable with talking to my father and it would not be the last time I felt his presence, heeded his warnings, accepted his assistance, or felt his love.

Recently, I was driving on Rt. 287 in northwest New Jersey. The traffic was relatively light, just before rush hour, and I was cruising along at about 70 MPH in the left lane, singing along with the radio, just day dreaming, when once again the hair on the back of my neck stood up and I heard him powerfully warn me to slow down.

By this time there was no denying or even questioning, and once again the timing was perfect. Quickly looking into my rearview mirror, there was no one in the middle or right lanes. I didn't signal. I just moved right while decelerating.

Then directly in front of me grey smoke began to bellow out from the rear wheels of a truck in the right lane. His rear tires for some reason had locked. The screeching of truck tires leaving thick black parallel lines on the road snapped me out of my daydreaming as

I braked hard. The truck began to fishtail and cross the center and left lanes, hitting the steel girder exactly where I would have been. I passed him on the right as if in slow motion.

Again that old doubt crawled back into my mind: *How did I know?* Once again I simply thanked my father and felt his acknowledgment. I understood that it wasn't important how it happened, just that it did. I was ready to accept that my father was still watching out for me after all these years, from wherever he was currently 'living'.

When you go for the money instead of your passion,
sometimes you can get a second or even a third chance at happiness.

MY FIRST REAL JOB

In 1973, I was having a frustrating time working at that printing job while hoping for an art teaching position to become available. I received a call from my cousin who was a Store Manager in a supermarket chain that was expanding. His call could not have come at a better time.

"Hey Ga," Howie said. "I have an opening for an Assistant Customer Service Manager, on second shift. There'll be plenty of overtime and lots of opportunity for promotion. I could start you at $20,000 a year. Whaddaya think?"

I couldn't say yes fast enough. That salary was twice as much as I would be making as a teacher, and teachers don't even get overtime. So, after giving my two week notice to the printing company, I began working for my cousin at his supermarket.

My decision was based solely (or should I say soullessly) on finance and not on passion for what I wanted to do with my life. Probably because at that time it was impossible to follow my dream.

Anyone who works in retail can attest to the pressure involved on a job where you are required to deal with the public. I was scheduled to work the second shift, from 3:30 to 11 pm, and the word stressful does not nearly come close to describing the work. If you couldn't multi-task, you could not function, and I hope you will have an appreciation for the people in that position the next time you complain at your supermarket.

One evening, I was the only one behind the Courtesy Counter during the busiest time of the shift. The customers were becoming irate waiting on the long lines, while the alcoholic Assistant Store Manager was berating me on the phone. This was a typical crazy Saturday night. However, this particular crazy night was important in my life, because on **this** night, I became a smoker.

There was hardly enough time to breath let alone take a break, so when it did slow down, I escaped into the claustrophobic Bookkeeper's Office in the back section of the Courtesy Counter.

When I entered, the bookkeeper smiled and decided to take his break too. In those days smoking was allowed everywhere, so Kevin lit up a Marlboro and blew the smoke leisurely into the air. The smoke filled the tiny space like the smell of pot at a Grateful Dead concert, and a strange melancholy overtook me.

My wife Chris was only 12 years old when she lost her dad to a massive heart attack caused by his two-pack a day habit. She hated cigarettes and assumed that, considering how hard I'd fought to try to save my father's life, I would never ever smoke. Unfortunately, that night, a combination of situations contributed to this healthy non-smoker becoming one.

SMOKING BRINGS BACK MEMORIES

It had been a year since my father died of lung cancer, and the smell of that cigarette smoke brought back memories of my Dad. I could close my eyes and be back at the kitchen table, having finished dinner. Dad would light up a Chesterfield and sit back, blowing smoke up in the air the same way Kevin was doing now.

"Give me one of those," I suddenly demanded of Kevin, who responded by saying that I wasn't a smoker and shouldn't start.

All I knew was that the smell of that cigarette brought back good memories of my father. I missed him and if smoking made me feel closer to him, *Then screw it*, I thought, *I'm gonna smoke and the hell with it **and** this job.*

It didn't occur to me until many years later how stupid I was to allow my emotions - my sadness over losing my father - to direct me into the same addiction that killed him.

The smell of cigarette smoke didn't remind me of the antiseptic used in the corridors in the hospital as my father took his last breath. It reminded me of the smell of his large hand as he jokingly messed up my hair that my mother had just spent fifteen minutes combing.

The smell of cigarette smoke didn't bring back memories of him dying. It brought back memories of, when I was sixteen, I saw the pride in his eyes when I was finally able to do more push-ups than he could.

The smell of cigarette tobacco didn't remind me of his coughing. It reminded me of younger, happier times with my family.

There is a reason and a lesson for everything
that happens to you in your life,
good or bad.
However, the experiences that are the most horrid
may also be the most enlightening
if you have the strength and courage to allow them to be.

SMOKING IN THE 50'S

When I was a child growing up in the Fifties, it was expected that everyone smoked. Cigarettes were everywhere. From signs on the subway to billboards on the highway, from television and radio to newspapers and magazines, cigarette advertising bombarded the American psyche with the idea that tobacco smoking = being cool. 'LSMFT' stood for 'Lucky Strike Means Fine Tobacco'. Whether it was a Marlboro Country TV ad showing cowboys on horseback overlooking a winter wonderland, or a huge billboard featuring a young Tom Selleck enjoying a pack of Salems, every teenager wanted to become a smoker.

It was the thing to do. And if the government approved all that advertising, it couldn't possibly be bad for you?

Right?

BECOMING A SMOKER

When I do something, I like to throw myself into it completely. As an employee of this supermarket, I truly believed it was the best supermarket chain in the world. As a new smoker, I wanted to be the best smoker I could be. So I smoked Marlboro 100 Lights and smoked them down to the nub, much as my dad had done with his unfiltered ones. Kevin gave me my first cigarette when I was twenty three, and that was the beginning of an eleven - year addiction.

Meanwhile, at work, my cousin was transferred to a different location and a new Store Manager replaced him. Unfortunately, my new boss, Tony, took an instant dislike to me (and enjoyed demonstrating this by busting my chops every opportunity he had).

I didn't know what I wanted to do with my life, but I knew it wasn't getting a daily beating from Tony. So I did the most logical thing… I quit. Which was exactly what Tony wanted me to do. And which marked the beginning of a horrendous five-year job sampling period which caused Chris and me so many arguments in our early married life.

During this five year period, I was anxious to find a job that I could enjoy that would bring in an adequate salary, but each new job was just not right, and I went through almost a dozen. The one career I desperately wanted more than any other was teaching, but I had just about given up on that dream.

I worked as a baby photographer, a photographer for an insurance company, a parking lot attendant, an exterminator, and an auto glass installer, just to name a few. My latest not quite right job was in the World Trade Center as an assistant cafeteria manager. Sadly, I knew I would have to leave this position as well, and I was becoming increasingly pessimistic about finding a position that could allow me to support Chris and the baby we were now expecting.

In April of 1977 we welcomed our son Aaron to the world. Unfortunately, I was about to leave my latest job as an assistant manager at McDonalds. Now with an additional mouth to feed, Chris was increasingly frustrated with me, which led to some heated discussions.

One night while watching TV, Chris and I had a calm conversation about our future. "Garry, I know you're anything but lazy. You've been working really hard ever since we've been married. But you need to accept the fact that being a teacher is just not going to happen for you."

Looking down, I sighed and shook my head. "Yeah, I know you're right Hon. I'm just so upset with myself that every single job I've tried doesn't work out."

"You know we have lots of bills now, Ga, and with the baby, we need more money. And health insurance."

"I know. The only job I ever had with health insurance was at Howie's store… And you know why I had to leave there."

"Yeah. The guy who replaced Howie was a real jerk. But you really liked working there. You were making really good money, with lots of overtime." At that very moment a commercial for that supermarket came on, announcing yet another new Grand Opening. I wasn't aware of synchronicities at that time, but Chris and I looked at each other and laughed. "Look! It must be a sign!" she said. "Why don't you just give them a call?"

That night we went to sleep much more hopeful and positive about our future, and the next morning I went to their district office where I was interviewed by the very person who had hired me five years earlier.

BACK TO THE SUPERMARKET, AGAIN

I was placed in one of the newer stores, and life was wonderful. My salary had almost tripled. I was guaranteed ten hours of overtime, and whenever I worked on a Sunday I was paid double time and a half. Even though it was an exhausting six day week, I had a year-old son and lots of bills to pay. And finally, I had a job I could love.

Five years later, I had a six-year-old son, a three-year-old daughter, and (thanks to my first round in the supermarket business,) a nine year, two pack a day smoking addiction.

I was promoted from Assistant to Customer Service Manager, went through the Store Management Training Program, and became an Assistant Store Manager. My life was now dramatically better than I could ever have dreamed. Best of all, I was finally earning a salary that allowed Chris to leave her job and stay at home with our babies. I was simply ecstatic.

Not to say the job was a walk in the park. If you've worked in the retail business, you know how difficult it can be. If you worked as an Assistant Manager, you know how impossibly stressful it is. Not only do you have to deal with customers who are always right, even when they are wrong, you have to be able to handle all the challenges that arise from dealing with unions, payroll, expenses, profit and loss, Department Managers, the other Assistant Store Managers, good and bad Store Managers, District Managers, Area Supervisors, shoplifters, police, and last but never least… Tony.

Yes, the exact same Tony whom I'd had the pleasure of meeting eleven years prior in Staten Island. The same Tony who'd taken pleasure in constantly berating me. And whom I'd had the pleasure of telling that I was quitting. Yep, I was transferred from a store I loved, and deposited into a store 30 miles further from my apartment. And, I was back with Tony again.

But now, Tony wasn't just a Store Manager any longer. Nope. He'd been promoted to a District Manager in charge of six stores. And I was not nearly as ecstatic as I had been, when I found myself transferred to one of his stores.

TONY T-BONE

Five years later, when I finally left the industry for the second and final time, I had worked for that supermarket for twelve years, and during that time I was sent to eleven different stores. Considering that each store had well over 300 employees, I got to meet a lot of people. Some I missed after I was transferred, and some I thanked God I would never see again.

Tony T-bone was one who definitely fell into the second group. His real name was never used. He was called a lot of things: 'T', 'Mr. T', 'Tony', 'Boss' and some others that I won't mention and couldn't mention to his face, or else.

Tony ran his stores as if they belonged to him, personally. He also ran the supermarkets as his idol, Don Vito Corleone would: with an iron fist. He proudly saw himself as a miracle worker to be put into the most poorly run districts, in order to turn them around and make them profitable. At the expense of a lot of overworked and underpaid employees. Including yours truly.

He was one of those supervisors whom the owners of the corporation loved and the majority of the employees feared tremendously. The owners loved Tony because he was ruthless in his desire to make money for them. If he had to fire you, you were gone. Period. It didn't matter if the union was defending you. It didn't matter if your mother was dying or your kid had cancer. It didn't matter if the reason for your problem was not even your own fault. You were a number, a body, completely replaceable, and you could and would be replaced easily. The reason? 'The Bottom Line.'

*When the pursuit of money supersedes the pursuit of happiness,
a change becomes necessary and hopefully inevitable.*

THE BOTTOM LINE

The bottom line was the P&L Report we received, that told us if we'd made a profit or a loss that week. The former was good, and the higher the profit the better. The latter, a loss, was not good at all. As a Store Manager, Tony was sent to any store that was losing money and he would fix it, one way or another. But always his way… or the highway. And now as a District Manager, he was put in charge of the worst districts to perform even larger miracles. And amazingly, he did.

Working with Tony, you learned really quickly, exactly what was important in his world. And it wasn't people. It was numbers. Low numbers in the expense column and high numbers in the sales column made the owners and Tony happy. Anything else and heads would roll. When the numbers came back bad, you could feel the tension in the store. Starting from the Store Manager down to the cart boys, everyone was on edge, waiting for the moment that Tony would arrive.

"TONERIZATION"

I would get the call, usually from an Assistant Manager in another store, who'd just had the pleasure of being 'Tonerized'. Tonerization was a very unpleasant experience, to say the least. It was a term that didn't need any explanation. To be Tonerized meant that you'd been put through a process of, well, let's just say grown men have been seen weeping when it was over.

It would begin when I heard the announcement over the PA system calling me to the phone. "Garry… It's Pete from Lyons Avenue. Tony just left and is he ever on the warpath. I just got Tonerized and he's on the way to you. Good luck buddy. You'll need it!"

I would let the Store Manager know that Tony was on the way, which was immediately followed by him informing me that he was just leaving, as he put on his coat while running to the exit.

"See ya," was all he would say as I saw his back flying down the stairs. Too bad he didn't turn to see me wave a special good-bye, as I hit the inside of my left elbow with my right hand, while raising my left forearm up in that infamous Brooklyn salute.

As always, I lit a cigarette, hoping I would have a heart attack and avoid what was coming. So, as the Store Manager high tailed it to his car, I dropped my cigarette on the floor, crushed it into dust under my shoe, lit another, and proceeded to chain smoke. I smiled, reflecting that this was probably the only time I ever saw that man move. He usually sat on his butt and delegated all his responsibilities to others (which was mainly me).

It was nice of him to let me know he was leaving, I would think to myself. *Thanks a lot, asshole. Leave me to swing in the wind while you wing it home... Great! Another opportunity to experience Tonerization.*

Waiting for the arrival of The Boss, as he liked to be called, was a lot like anticipating a root canal without Novocain: something that I would find out about some years later. And in retrospect, the real root canal was actually much easier, and considerably less painful.

I do believe Tony enjoyed inflicting pain, and the more people witnessing his pain delivery abilities, the more fun he seemed to have. One afternoon, Tony was screaming so loudly at someone on the phone that he could be heard from his back office, all the way to the front end of the store. The bus from the local senior citizen apartments had dropped their residents off to shop and the store was pretty full, mostly with seniors. They were all looking around to see who was being so loud and crass. The words coming from that office would embarrass a truck driver, let alone fifteen elderly church goers.

One little gray haired grandmother came over to me, as I stood at the Courtesy Counter. Her normal smile was replaced with a scowl. She told me that whoever was hollering so loudly, and using such profanity, should have his mouth washed out with soap. Then she proceeded to tell me, "And I'm just the one who could do it, too!" It took all my will power to keep from walking her down the soap aisle, handing her a bar of Ivory, and escorting her to Tony's office.

TIE-LINE

"Mr. Gewant... tie-line," one of the girls at the Courtesy Counter would announce. If she were in sight, she would cup the receiver and, with a facial expression somewhere between horror and deep sympathy, mouth the name, "Tony!"

I would slowly walk to my office, light up a Marlboro, take a deep drag, and answer the multi-store line. "Belleville... Gewant speaking." There was a tie-line protocol, the store name first, then who you were, so the person on the other end didn't rip into some poor part-time employee. There would be no point in venting all that wonderful venom on a peon. Better to save it for an unfortunate Assistant Manager, like me, who just wanted to make enough money to survive and get through the day without putting the barrel of a gun in his mouth and pulling the trigger.

Before I answered the phone, I took a deep breath and allowed the song from Annie to enter my head:

'The sun'll come out... tomorrow...

Bet your bottom dollar that, tomorrow...

There'll be sun...'

But it didn't really help; I felt that there would never be sun for me again, tomorrow or ever.

"Howyadoin." Tony started every phone call with that nicety, so you didn't know if you were actually in trouble or not. But it usually only took a nanosecond to find out. "Good, Tony. How are you?" I knew small talk was not going to save me.

"How am I...? How am I...? Is that what you asked me? Huh...?"

I could hear the anger starting to build. I responded with a simple gulp, saying to myself... *Ok Ga, here it comes,* and taking another deep drag from my cigarette.

"Well, you fucken piece of shit, I'll tell you 'How I'm doin'... I'm fucken pissed that I have a bunch of waste of fucken life managers working for me that don't know their fucken assholes from a hole in the fucken wall. I swear that if I could, I'd fire all you fucks and replace you with somebody who can follow directions. Hopefully they would know how to fucken run a fucken supermarket, better than you fucken idiots! Is the fucken idiot, piece of shit, Store Manager there?"

With a gulp, I simply answered, "No."

"Tell that fuck that I want him to call me first thing in the fucken morning! Can you fucken handle that?"

"Yes..."

Click

You can see that Tony was a man of few words.

The one word that he did like using more than any other was "Fuck."

He used it as a noun, such as "Gewant, you are a stupid Fuck."

He used it as an adjective, such as "Get out of my fucken store," or "Are you out of your fucken mind?"

He used it as an adverb, such as "Are you fucken kiddin' me?"

And of course, the compound word that he was renowned for... "Underfuckenstand?"

He would boggle my mind with the incredible variety of uses he could get out of a simple four letter word.

T'S MEETINGS

Tony would schedule monthly Managers Meetings in his flagship store. All six Store Managers and six Assistant Managers were required to be present. And although his conference room was large, with thirteen men, most of whom smoked, we certainly could have used a room twice as large.

During those meetings, some Assistant Managers and I would play "The Tonerize Game." The game would involve Tony, an unfortunate manager (who was in the hot seat in front of the group) and a score sheet for each player. The game worked like this: at the start of the meeting, each Assistant would count all the 'Fucks' uttered by Tony. Now, remember, these 'Fucks' could be nouns, adjectives, adverbs, or any combination, contraction or compound of the word. At one meeting I lost count at 253 when my pen ran out of ink.

There were times when his meetings would be scheduled in one of Tony's other stores. And you can imagine how overjoyed I was whenever I received the call from his secretary Carol, that our store would be hosting this month's Managers Meeting. Every store had a meeting room, but ours was smaller and much dirtier than the one in Tony's home store. I now had to have the room thoroughly cleaned. But amazingly, everything fell into place. By the scheduled time for the meeting, I - and the store - were ready.

In the center of the meeting room ceiling was a speaker that piped in Muzak and store announcements. The girl at the Courtesy Counter that afternoon was Agnes, who'd moved to New Jersey from Brooklyn. She was a cute but quite naïve high school senior who, when she spoke, seemed to be doing an impression of Fran Drescher from the TV show *The Nanny*.

You could clearly hear her chewing and cracking her gum as she nasally announced, "Mista Gawan (chew, chew, crack, crack) ya gotta call on 91, Mista Gewan pick up on line 9...1..." My conversations with Aggie always made me smile. Her accent and personality reminded me of so many people I grew up with, and although I was now living in Staten Island, talking with Aggie always brought the Brooklyn out in me.

When I say that Aggie was naïve, I mean that you could convince her about anything, and she would believe you: space aliens, urban legends, the reason why Tony was so mean was due to the fact that his wife put too much starch in his underwear. She would believe it all.

Her gullibility had often made her the brunt of a lot of jokes in the store that I would go out of my way to stop. Perhaps I didn't like to see anyone used as a scapegoat, or I just wanted her to keep her sweetness a little longer, before becoming hardened and cynical like the rest of us. In any case, I liked to keep her at the Courtesy Counter, if only to hear her pronounce, "Courtesy Counter" as the Brooklyn version: "KOYDUHSEE COWNNA."

Back in our meeting, you could barely breathe. Tony and twelve managers, all of us heavy smokers, were filling up that windowless office with cigarette smoke so thick our eyes were burning. Tony was just getting to an important point, when the shrill beep of the

PA system broke his train of thought. As he always did when interrupted, his expression showed a combination of emotions that clearly implied frustration, annoyance and anger. He would let out a deep breath, shake his head, look directly at the speaker in the ceiling (as if trying to intimidate it into silence) and grudgingly wait for the announcement to end. If he wasn't already smoking, it would remind him to light up, as the rest of us did, too.

"Attention Shoppas," Agnes announced in her NY accent, "If dairs a Dick Weed in da store, please come to da Koyduhsee Cownna for a phone call... DICK WEED please come to da Koyduhsee Cownna." Someone in the store had called her, knowing that Tony was at the meeting, and knowing that Agnes would repeat whatever she heard, verbatim, over the PA system. I should have been upset, but I actually appreciated the joke.

SILENCE...

No one made a sound.

No one knew exactly what to do.

Everyone knew not to look at anyone else.

Eventually, all eyes went to Tony. I fought the smile forming on my face and without looking at any of the other managers, I knew what was going on in their minds, too. It's that feeling you have in a serious situation, like a funeral, where laughter would be totally inappropriate but nonetheless, you feel like bursting out loud. It was one of those situations where you need the release that a great laugh can give, but you absolutely cannot give into it.

We all looked straight at Tony, who was staring down at the table, trying to figure out if the announcement could be real. His expression, knotted up eyebrows and a questioning stare as if he smelled something bad, started a serious battle inside my gut to resist the urge to laugh. I knew better than to look at anyone else, as they knew not to look at me. Then the announcement came on again, but this time Agnes was annoyed as she repeated in her thick Brooklynese:

"Attention Shoppas," she yelled, "If dairs a Dick Weed in da store, please come to da Koyduhsee Cownna for a phone call... DICK WEED ya gotta phone call... Please come to da Koyduhsee right now!"

The silence was finally broken. By me. I was trying to control it but a sort of snort came out of my nose. I could not control it. It controlled me.

And that one snort started a flood of screams, snorts and hysteria exploding all over the meeting room.

It was wonderful!

The pent up frustration of a miserable job, the anger of being accused of mismanagement, the disgusting taste in my mouth of being forced to eat 'crow', the pain of trying to control a natural response to laugh, all exploded in a joyous uncontrollable fit of hysteria. Even Tony was laughing - the first time I'd ever seen the man laugh. I didn't think he had the capacity for a good laugh. But as all good things in the supermarket, the laughter was short lived.

"Gewant," Tony sneered, looking directly at me. "She's yours, right? Stop her before I get a letter from one of your pain in the ass senior citizens, complaining about four letter words coming over the PA!"

~ ~ ~

When the meeting was over, Tony called me to the office. I reached into my pocket, popped another cigarette into my mouth, lit it and walked slowly through the store toward my office. I wasn't sure why, but it didn't matter then and it doesn't matter now. Only that as usual, I was going to be beaten up, and as I walked up the stairs like a convict walking up the steps to the gallows, I reassessed my life. I had a loving wife and two great kids. I should be thankful. But at that time, jumping on the first freight train out of town was looking like a viable option.

Tony was sitting at a desk when I entered. "Sit the fuck down," was his introduction, as he kicked a rolling chair toward me. My eye squinted as the smoke from my cigarette drifted into it, making it seem like I was going to cry. I didn't want to cry as much as I wanted to quit that job, right then and there.

I crushed my cigarette into the disgusting butt-filled ashtray. And as I sat, my hand went to the store keys dangling from my belt clip. I wanted to unclip them and toss the keys at him, telling him, "I quit!" However, Tony, perceptive manager that he was, read me like a book.

"You wanna quit?" he asked snidely. "Go 'head, I'll replace you in a heartbeat." He looked over to my desk, nodding toward the pictures of Aaron and Amy and our family portraits. "Nice family," he sneered, and ended with the question he knew would work. "Who's going to pay the bills if you quit?"

He said the one and only thing that I couldn't fight. He was good at what he did and he knew it. My family was the only thing that was worth what he put me through, and he knew that too. As I said, he was good at what he did. So I just sat there, despondent, clicking my store keys back onto my belt. I took a deep breath and lit another cigarette, preparing myself for the beating I knew was coming.

He began as he had numerous times before. "When I tell you to do something do you underfuckenstand me? When I say I want to talk to you AND that asshole, piece of shit Store Manager I unfortunately got saddled with in this fucken store, do you underfuckenstand that I want to talk to both of your sorry asses?"

Perhaps my answer was not thought out too clearly, but at the time, clear thinking was not on the agenda. I was sick to death of being the scapegoat for all the problems in the store. I was tired of having to cover up for the incompetence of a Store Manager whose management style was to throw everyone in the store under the first available bus. If I had thought about it, I would have realized that Tony was more upset with the Store Manager than with me. But, as I said, clarity was not my strong suite at the time.

"Underfuckenstand? Yeah Tony, I 'underfuckenstand' you." Obviously, this was not the response he was looking for.

"Are you intentionally trying to piss me off more than I am right now? I will be here tomorrow at 8 am. You better be here. And tell your fucken waste of life Store Manager that if he likes his job, his ass better be in this fucken chair at 7 am. Do you 'underfuckenstand' THAT?"

I decided to use my brain for a change and not give him a wise answer this time. And simply replied, "Yeah."

It was a late spring evening as I began my commute to my apartment in Staten Island. I didn't notice the beauty of spring or the atypically sweet smell in the air. All I was aware of was the particularly horrendous day that I'd just had. I didn't notice the attractive woman walking her poodle in the street, nor the way the breeze lifted her dress, showing a hint of thigh. All I saw was another obnoxious customer. All I could think of was how I hated everything at work, from the people who shopped in the store to the shoplifters who stole from it. I couldn't enjoy that beautiful spring day during that perfect season of new life and new possibilities. Not after having experienced my daily dose of Tonerization.

BECOMING AN EX-SMOKER

All I wanted to do was get home to my family: my wife, son and daughter. All I wanted to do was to de-stress. Driving home, I opened my third pack for that day. I took a deep drag and suddenly began coughing so hard I almost caused an accident.

I knew I couldn't physically smoke another cigarette. My lungs were on fire, and as my coughing subsided, I began to think about my dad. Perhaps he came into my thoughts because I was coughing as he had coughed years earlier. The thought of quitting crossed my mind, which reminded me of how badly I'd wanted him to quit. I knew he died due to the damage caused by smoking, but I was in no mood to think about quitting at that point. Even though I had a smoker's cough, even though my lungs burned, cigarette smoking did relax me, and I really needed to relax.

That evening after dinner, I was ready for an after dinner smoke. 'Do as I say, not as I do' never works, so I was determined that my children would never see me smoke. As was my habit, I took my smokes, lighter and ashtray into the hallway of the apartment, and sat on the top step of the landing. With my ashtray next to me, I lit my first one. Just as I took that first deep drag, I heard the doorknob move and the door open behind me.

Hearing Aaron open the door, I quickly tried to hide my smoke by my left leg. Aaron sat next to me in a huff. "Daddy, how come some of my friends have two granddaddies and I don't have any?" he asked, questioningly tilting his head up at me and looking a little mad.

I have always been truthful with my children, so when he asked me a question, my response was always sincere. "Well, Aa," I said to him, "both mommy's daddy and daddy's daddy died."

"Why did they die, Daddy?" he asked, looking deeply into my eyes as his expression turned from anger to curiosity. I considered a white lie, but I had never lied to him before and I was not going to start. I had made the ridiculous decision to begin a habit that killed my father, and I would not lie to cover the absurdity of that decision.

Looking down at my feet, I tried to avoid eye contact, "Well, Aa, both your granddaddies smoked, and that made them sick..." I felt Aaron's gaze burning into the side of my face, but I still couldn't look at him. "Both your grandfathers smoked, and that's what caused them to get sick and die."

I began to rationalize to him and myself about addictions, and how self-destructive they can be. How they cause children to lose their parents, and how grandchildren can grow up never knowing their grandfathers.

The more I explained how he became grandfather-less, the more I realized that I needed to quit smoking. The more I tried to rationalize my addiction, the less the argument held any validity for me. The more I avoided eye contact with my son, the joy of my life, the reason for me to smile, the more my defenses fell. I slowly turned to look at my son, his eyes darting from the cigarette burning in my cupped hand, to my eyes, and back again.

"But you smoke, Daddy," he said, "and if you get cancer and die, I won't have anybody to play with!" He put his small, soft hands on my cheeks, and with tears welling up in his eyes, he looked into my eyes, shook his head and pleaded, "Please, Daddy, don't smoke anymore."

MY SMOKER'S WALL

Walls form between people when one is doing something that the other can't accept. In my case I had the same Smoker's Wall as my father did. I'd been able to break his down, years ago. Unfortunately for him and everyone who loved him, it was too late. Now that I was confronting my own Smoker's Wall, I understood how difficult a task I'd asked of my father.

My wall had been reinforced with each argument I had with Chris over the subject of quitting. My Smoker Part was so strong, that no matter who spoke to me about quitting - Chris, my mother (who'd quit smoking after my father died), my sister, even my own thoughts about quitting - the wall went up immediately. That wall was as strong, immovable, and impenetrable as my father's had been. But in one unscripted moment, my young son was able to make it all come crumbling down.

That wall tried to re-form, but it was not nearly as solid as it had been before. That wall seemed porous now. Aaron wanted me to quit and be healthy because he loved me. It was the same pure love I'd had for my father when I begged him to quit.

MY SMOKER'S WALL CRUMPLES

There are moments in your life that become etched in your mind. Life-changing events, whether good or bad, become memories that you can never forget. That moment with Aaron in the hallway of my apartment became one of those moments for me.

That emotional exchange with my son caused memories from twelve short years earlier to come flooding back. But now I was the father who smoked, and it was my son who took over the role of *wall buster*. His job was to simply get through my defenses, which he did with perfection. What Aaron didn't know was how he was able to get through those reinforced walls. He opened my eyes to the fact that I was unwittingly going to cause the same pain to him that my father had caused me.

If my father had stopped smoking when I'd first asked him to, the conversation I was now having with Aaron would never have been necessary. If my dad had only realized that he would die if he continued smoking, and never be able to experience the joy of being a grandfather - denying my son and daughter the joy and love of having a grandpa - he would have thrown away his cigarettes and in the process change the lives of three generations.

I did not want a conversation between my son and his child to be like the one I was now having with Aaron. I knew I needed to quit smoking and do what had been impossible for my own dad. I knew that I needed to quit, and for the first time in all the years I had been a smoker, I actually **wanted** to stop smoking… and I wanted to quit immediately.

Promises are easily made and at times impossible to honor.
But the lying and the covering up of these broken promises
can make the guilt unbearable.
Especially when the deceptions are directed
toward those who are the most important people in your life.

MY FINAL STRAW

I had found my *Final Straw*. I stubbed out the cigarette I was smoking, took my pack of cigarettes out of my pocket and crushed them into a ball, the same way I had crushed my father's cigarettes 12 years before.

I showed them to him and said, "For you Aaron, I'm gonna quit. 'Cause I love you." A smile came across his little face as he took my hand and pulled me up, dragging me back into our apartment.

"Mommy!" he shouted enthusiastically to my wife, who had just finished washing the dishes. "Guess what? Daddy is going to quit smoking! He promised!"

Chris dried her hands on a dish rag and picked up the baby, who was joining in on the excitement and gave me the smile that always made me beam. The whole family was jubilant with my decision to quit. Although, to be honest, I thought I saw a bit of skepticism reflected back to me in the eyes of my wife.

Before Aaron went to sleep that night, he came over to my recliner and jumped up on my lap, throwing his arms around my neck. There was a glow about him. I could see the satisfaction he felt because he was able to present his point of view, intelligently and rationally. His words had gotten through my defenses and he knew it. I knew it as well and was (and am) indebted to my little seven-year-old.

It was late, so I followed him into his room. Amy was already asleep. I tossed him on his bed and as was our tradition, I tickled him before tucking him in. He was laughing before his body even landed on the blanket.

It was one of those body laughs that you can't fake.

One of those contagious laughs that parents live for.

One of those laughs that say,

"I love you Daddy…"

"Thank you Daddy..."

"You're my best friend, Daddy..."

And no matter how much he protested about being tickled, his laughter always said, 'more'.

Chris called from the living room, "Ga, stop. He's got school tomorrow and it's getting late." I stopped tickling him as he held his breath and looked at me in the way every father is so familiar with. The anticipation in his eyes, the smile on his face. He wanted to play more.

"No more, Kiddo... time for sleep."

His pout turned into a smile as he put his arms up for his goodnight kiss. And as I leaned over him to kiss him on the forehead, he threw his arms around my neck and said, "I love you, Daddy... Remember, you promised ...no more smoking... Right?"

With a kiss to his forehead, I said, "Promise!" And I meant it. I closed his door half way and walked quietly into Amy's room. Her stuffed animals seemed to be smiling at me as I quietly kissed my baby girl goodnight. She was sleeping with her thumb in her mouth as I stood looking down at her.

The Protector Part of me had made that commitment, that promise I'd just given my son. I would not love my cigarettes more than my kids; I could never abandon them. I looked once again at my daughter, who rolled over, eyes half closed. As if on cue, Amy smiled at me and closed her eyes again, safe knowing her Daddy would always be there to protect her.

I thought of not being there for her as she got older. Who would protect them and Chris? How would Chris provide for them as a widow with two kids? As I pulled the covers up over my daughter, I told myself that there would be no further thoughts about smoking.

I Quit. Period.

Trying to go to sleep that night was not easy. So many things were going through my mind.

I really HAVE to quit...

I really WANT to quit...

I CAN do it...

I will never smoke again!

This determination, internal strength and commitment lasted about 8 hours. Until I was in my car driving to work.

MY YEAR FROM HELL

My commute the next morning seemed very different than normal. I couldn't understand why I was so angry. Everything and everyone seemed to be intentionally pissing me off. All the lights were red and all the drivers were driving extremely slowly, and the reason didn't hit until I was on the Outerbridge Crossing, leaving Staten Island.

I GOTTA HAVE A SMOKE! I screamed to myself. I felt like pulling out all my hair! Although the driver in front of me was already 20 miles over the speed limit, I found myself cursing at him as I sat on my horn. I wanted to pull out all his hair too! I wanted to run this poor guy off the road, take out a tire iron and smack him with it a few times. I had been driving for less than 15 minutes, and had not thought of one single thing, except for the need to smoke.

Then I thought of the coming 12 hour day... WITH NO CIGARETTES. It felt like a punch to my solar plexus. "I can't do this..." I said out loud. *But what about the promise you made to Aaron?* I thought. "What the hell am I going to do?" I said out loud, behind the wheel, speeding at 85 mph on Rt. 440.

This was Day One of 'My Year from Hell'.

I'd finally decided to quit smoking, but I hadn't a clue as to how I would be able to succeed. At that time, 'cold turkey' was the only option. And if the first eight hours of my smoking sobriety was a taste of what was in store for me, I was up a long, rough creek without a paddle.

As I got off the highway on that first day as an ex-smoker, I was planning out my day. But more importantly, I was planning how to score my first cigarette. *Let's see,* I thought, *Phil, Tom, Mike and Nick smoke. I'll hit them up first.* This became my all-consuming and only priority.

As I pulled into the parking lot, the conditions of the store were not on my mind. The number of cashiers scheduled for the day was not on my mind. Deliveries? Orders? Nope. Nothing was on my mind except how I was going to get my first cigarette.

This was in the early 1980's and smoking was everywhere. Now, suffering from nicotine withdrawal, it seemed that EVERYONE in the store had a cigarette hanging from their mouth. I swear, I saw a five-year-old kid walking with his mother, stop, take his pacifier out of his mouth, put it in his pocket, pull out a pack of Marlboro 100 Lights and light up. *Great,* I thought, *now I'm hallucinating! Look what quitting does to you!* I was almost ready to quit, quitting.

That year I became a professional quitter. I must have quit smoking a thousand times, which meant that I went back to smoking a thousand and one. The life of a professional quitter is, mildly stated, a misery. I wasn't smoking my Marlboro 100 Lights - I was smoking whatever cigarette I could grub from anyone with a pack.

When I was not smoking, I hated everyone and everything. The crazy thing about it was that I held my loved ones responsible for my misery. I knew that blaming them was ridiculous, but I was now not only miserable at work, but also at home. My one place of comfort and happiness was home, and now I didn't even have that. I was short tempered and antsy because when I needed to smoke a cigarette, there were none to be had.

When I was smoking, I hated myself, because I was so weak. But the absolute worst part was that I also became a professional liar. I was now lying to everyone whom I loved and who loved me. I would sneak away whenever I had a chance to light up a cigarette, which I had stashed all over the house and my car. Can you imagine how I felt, when my son looked at me with love and respect in his eyes and said, "Thank you Daddy, for not smoking anymore."

I was despondent and I thought that my despair would never end.

I was now no longer a smoker. I was now one of those annoying, pain in the ass smokers who can't admit to themselves that they cannot stop smoking. Instead, they grub from every other smoker around them. I wanted to quit smoking, but it was obvious to everyone in the store that the only thing I quit doing, was buying cigarettes. So as to not annoy the entire smoking population of the store, I decided to buy a pack of cigarettes for everyone I was grubbing from.

And my misery continued. But you know what they say about misery?

It loves company!

- Another Life Lesson - # 15

When the quote: <u>"There is no such thing as a coincidence,"</u>
stops being a silly New Age cliché, and you think
that the 'weird' happenstances in your life are,
as Carl Sagan described,
"Too coincidental to be accidental,"
your life just may begin to get a whole lot weirder.

NICK, COINCIDENCES AND HYPNOSIS

Nick was the Produce Manager, married with two kids and as addicted to smoking as I was. We shared an interesting, if not somewhat annoying, smoking routine. I would quit, sometimes for a week, sometimes for two minutes. He would notice my commitment to a healthier lifestyle and would literally blow smoke in my face and offer me a cigarette. With a devilish smile, he would say, "Come on Ga... you know you want one." And of course, I did. And when I took it, I went right back to smoking.

I would quit, Nick would get me hooked again. Nick would quit and I would blow smoke in his face, so that he would start again. Repeatedly, for a year, we would quit, start and quit again. I was depressed, angry and frustrated. We were your typical smokers who want to quit but couldn't. Every time Nick quit, I would feel weak and went out of my way to re-hook him. And visa-versa.

On one fateful day, I noticed Nick in the break room. I realized that I hadn't seen him smoking for a while. "Hey Nicky, got a smoke?" I asked, one eyebrow raised, anticipating our normal interaction.

"Nope. I finally quit, a week ago. Haven't had one and don't want one."

"Yeah. Right," I said as I removed my cigarette pack from my pocket. *Here we go again*, I thought. *One drag and he'll be back on the smoking bandwagon.*

I flipped open the pack and popped a cigarette in my mouth, all the time looking at him. Taking my lighter, I lit the end, and as I dropped the lighter back in my pocket, I took a very long, slow drag. I leaned my head back in the euphoria of satisfying my craving, while rubbing his nose in his futile attempt to quit. As I exhaled, lowering my head and raising my eyes, I looked through the smoke to monitor Nick's reaction and resolve. I took another deep drag. The end of my cigarette crackled as the head of the cigarette got red hot, but instead of doing the politically correct thing and turn my head away to exhale, I blew the smoke directly into Nick's face.

In retrospect, I can't believe what a nasty smoker I was. This was our little 'I don't want you to quit before I do because I'm stronger than you' routine. I knew from past experience, he would be smoking as soon as I offered him one.

As the smoke cleared away from Nick's face, he opened his eyes and said, "Ga... not only don't I want a cigarette, but your breath really stinks!"

My mouth dropped open. I couldn't believe what I was hearing. "I can't believe it. You really quit? How?" Nick merely smiled and shrugged. "Wait. You really don't want one? Get the hell outa here! How did you do it? Come on, tell me."

I could not believe it. Nick, my smoking partner, my rock of smoking Gibraltar; the guy who would always have an extra smoke; the guy who I would go to first when I decided that I couldn't stand quitting any longer and who would be there for me with a cigarette. *Nick, Nick, Nick! How could you do this to us?* I screamed in my mind.

"Nick, really, how'd you do it?" I asked with the cigarette hanging on my lower lip, its smoke rising, causing my right eye to squint.

Nick looked at me and with a shrug and quietly said, "Hypnosis."

And with that one word at that moment in time, in the break room of the store, my life was about to change completely.

"WHAT THE HELL IS HYPNOSIS?"

"My cousin," Nick began, "lives in Long Island. He smoked for 25 years and like you and me has been trying to quit for years. He heard about this guy in Long Island who uses hypnosis to help people quit smoking. Anyway, he went to him and quit smoking in only one session. I waited a month to see if he'd go back, like you and me do all the time, but he hadn't smoked in over a month and he even says that he'll never smoke again. So I got this guy's number and got hypnotized. And Ga, I swear to God, I don't even miss it. I haven't smoked in almost two weeks. But the crazy thing is that I really believe I'll never smoke again!"

Nick smiled, stood up, and told me that his break was over. As he walked by me, he stopped and took the cigarette from my hand. I thought, *Wow, he almost convinced me. He's going to smoke my cigarette and we are back to square one.* Honestly, the thought that he'd been lying to me saddened me somehow. I had thought, *If he quit I can quit.* But when he took that cigarette from my hand, I lost all hope. However, instead of smoking it, he dropped it on the floor and stepped on it.

Walking to the door, he stopped and said with a grin, "Oh, by the way, Ga. Your breath... It really does stink!"

When I got home that night, over dinner, Chris surprised me too. She started by saying, "Ga, I know you're still smoking. I can smell it on you. I've known it all along, but I felt if I didn't say anything, at least you would be cutting back." At that moment I didn't know what to say. Defend myself? Lie? Or admit I had been lying for a year?

"But," she continued, "I was speaking to my niece Melissa today. You know she's been struggling with smoking just like you? But she told me that she's going to try something new. It's called hypnosis. She found a hypnotist in Long Island who is going to help her quit."

If I didn't know what to say before, I absolutely did not know what to say now. *First Nick and now my niece Melissa?* I thought. *Wow, now that's an interesting coincidence.* Of course, I had not yet heard of synchronicity.

The next day on my lunch break, I went to the pizzeria next door for a Coke and a slice and to look at the magazines Louie, the owner, had behind the counter. While waiting for my slice to heat up, I was flipping through an old Playboy when my attention was drawn to a quarter page ad which read:

"Learn Hypnosis and get all the girls you want!"

I wasn't interested in 'all the girls' - I had my hands full enough with my wife and three-year-old daughter. But what was really curious to me was that the word **HYPNOSIS** seemed to be twice as large as the other words on the page.

I could not believe my eyes. This was the third time in as many days that I had been hit in the head by this hypnosis stuff. Now I may be a little thick headed sometimes, but even I had to acknowledge that something I didn't quite understand was going on.

When I asked Nick, the next day, he told me it cost $350 to be hypnotized, which was an awful lot of money. Considering cigarettes were 75 cents a pack, it would take an awfully long time to pay it back. Driving home I wondered how I could ever get my hands on that much money. I really wanted to do this. I really believed that hypnosis was the only way I would be able to quit. Although I didn't believe in God, driving home I prayed in my own way, *"Please God, help me with this. I have to quit smoking."*

Unbeknownst to me, at that exact moment, Chris was talking to my mother, who'd called to inform her of some wonderful news. My mom had won a small NY lotto; her ticket had 5 out of the 6 winning numbers and paid $2000. During that conversation, Chris mentioned to her that I was interested in hypnosis to quit smoking.

Over dinner that evening, the phone rang. "Garry, Honey, Chris told you about the Lotto? So, I insist that you make that appointment to be hypnotized. It would be a blessing. Dad would want it too. And I will pay for it. It'll be my belated birthday gift to you." Reluctantly, I accepted her generous gift.

Chris called Melissa for the name and number of the hypnotist. And when she told me his name, I almost fell off my chair, realizing that Nick, his cousin, and Melissa, all went to the same man! It was also the fourth 'coincidence', and I was blown away by the weirdness of it all.

After discussing his experience with Nick, I had a basic understanding that hypnosis works with the part of your mind that makes you smoke. Although I saw the amazing results with Nick, I couldn't foresee how my hypnosis experience would so profoundly change my life. And I am not just referring to becoming an ex-smoker.

When coincidences become synchronicities
and are so profound and frequent, you have
to question if they are purposeful.
And if they are, who or what designed them, and why?
Finding those answers will make you question your cynicism.

MY LAST CIGARETTE

My last cigarette was smoked on February 8, 1984 at 1:30 pm, in front of a three story office building in Long Island, almost twelve years after my first cigarette.

I had driven from Staten Island and had smoked three quarters of a pack in that hour and a half drive. Although I was determined to never smoke another cigarette again, a part of me was still resistant to that healthy decision.

I parked the car and got out. It was 1:25 and my hypnosis appointment with Al was at 2:00. The chill of that February wind was cutting right through my parka as I paced, smoked another cigarette and thought how nice it would be not to have to hide outside to smoke these cursed things any longer. However, 'till then, I was going to smoke the hell out of them. I chain smoked two more cigarettes and by the time I took my last drag, I felt dizzy, nauseous, and my lungs felt like they were on fire.

I was surprised by the conflicting emotions flowing through my mind. I was definitely nervous, but sadness was a feeling that I really hadn't expected. As strange as it may seem, the thought of never smoking again felt as if I were losing my best friend.

Cigarettes had always been there for me. They were consistent in a very inconsistent world. They always looked the same; they always smelled the same; they tasted the same and I could always rely on them. When I was nervous, they calmed me down. When I was hungry, they took the edge off my hunger. When I was stressed, they relaxed me. And they gave me something to do with my hands when I was bored.

Of course, I knew that this 'friend' had killed my father, and he would kill me too. Already, I couldn't walk up a flight of stairs without wheezing. And like my father, I started each day coughing, until I could get out the crap that was stuck in my lungs. I knew that this past year had been the worst year in my life, and it was all because of my best friend, Mr. Marlboro Light 100's.

But, worst of all, I knew that I'd made a promise to my son that I had broken again and again. I had visions of those tears in his eyes. Similar tears had welled in my own eyes, as I'd seen my father slowly die of lung cancer. I could envision Aaron in front of my coffin, the same way I'd stood in front of my father's. I could feel his pain, his anger! His fury that

76

I'd secretly continued to smoke, despite my promise. The same anger and helplessness I'd felt toward my father for never listening to me, when I pleaded with him to quit.

I decided at that moment that this hypnosis stuff **would** work. I said to myself that when I drove home to Staten Island later that day, it would be as an ex-smoker. I would **not** put my son through what I'd gone through. I would quit right then and there. I exhaled the smoke from my lungs, looked at the filter of my best friend, dropped him on the concrete sidewalk in front of that office building, and crushed him under my foot.

~ ~ ~

By the time I got to the third floor, I was wheezing. Fortunately, the door to the hypnotist's office was open, so I walked in and hung up my parka next to a fur coat on the coatrack, which I assumed belonged to his current client. The office waiting room had a few chairs and a few coffee tables with magazines on them. As I walked around the office, I noticed that the walls were covered with thank-you letters. Some were type written, some hand written, all describing the results of their hypnotic experience. It seemed that Al did more than help people quit smoking. Although the majority of the thank-you letters were from ex-smokers, there were many others from professional golf players, nail biters, stutterers, along with articles about hypnosis.

I was about half an hour early and decided to sit and read a magazine. As soon as I sat down, I noticed that the coffee table to my right had a mountain of cigarette packs on it. Marlboros, Parliaments, Kools, Salems, Kents. Probably every cigarette made was there, along with a variety of lighters, from disposable Bics to gold plated. I scratched my head, wondering what was up with all those cigarettes, when a woman from an adjoining office walked in, looked over the pile of butts, took a pack of Kools and left. I just laughed. *Like I might ever put my cigarettes in that pile for her to take*, I thought.

As I opened an old copy of <u>The Inquirer</u>, I glanced at my watch. *It's 1:55, Great. I've got five minutes to have one last smoke.* But just then, the door to the waiting room opened, and in walked a woman, with Al. *Damn*, I thought. *Too late for another smoke.* So I sat back and observed what happens after this thing called hypnosis.

MEETING AL THE HYPNOTHERAPIST

The woman, who had just been hypnotized, thanked Al. Rummaging through her purse, she threw her Parliaments on the top of the pile, along with her gold cigarette lighter. Then she took out her check, handed it to Al, said goodbye, and walked out of the office.

This was the first time I'd met Al. He was about 5' 9" with a ZZ Top type of a scraggly beard. He was also about 80 pounds overweight with a large beer belly, and wore a Harvard sweatshirt that had a pizza stain on it.

Not a very professional entrance there, Guy, I thought. But it was the perfect opportunity for the part of my subconscious, involved with smoking, to make his presence known.

77

MY SMOKER PART AND MY DRIVER PART

There is a part of the subconscious mind of a smoker that deals only with smoking. Let's call this separate functioning portion of the subconscious his *Smoker Part*.

The Smoker Part is just one of the many Parts that reside in the subconscious realm of the mind. We use these different Parts, like wearing different hats. You know that you act (consciously) one way at work and another at play. You act one way with friends, which is different from the way you are with your mother and another way with your child, etc. If this concept seems simplistic, that's because it is.

These Parts are created automatically at the point when you perform a particular action continually. It is the way habits are formed. Whether it is a Smoking Part, Exercise Part, Overeating Part or Driving Part, your conscious mind does not want to be bothered having to remember to do the same, specific, repeated action over and over again. Relieving your conscious mind of these repetitious actions is one of the many functions of your subconscious mind. It allows your conscious mind to do its job, which is analytical in nature. Interestingly, once a new Part is produced, it will take over the responsibility of that particular action for the rest of your life.

THE GOOD NEWS AND BAD NEWS ABOUT PARTS

To clarify this subconscious process, let's look at a Part that you certainly want to keep with you for the rest of your life: your Driver Part. As I said, once your subconscious forms a Part, it will stay with you for the rest of your life. I will be referring to this fact a lot because it is vitally important to understand in order to quit smoking or any other addiction.

So, think back to when you were first learning how to drive a car. For sixteen years you were aware of driving, and now it was finally your turn. You couldn't wait to get behind the wheel, but when the moment came, it was terrifying. It seemed so easy when it was someone else driving, when it was only an imaginary steering wheel in your hands. Now it was real, and you found out pretty quickly that driving was not going to be as easy as it had seemed.

There was so much to learn, do and remember. Not only the steering wheel, but the gas. The clutch. The stick. The signals. Not to mention the lights, mirrors, horn, wipers and the million and one other things, along with all those laws you needed to memorize. Now behind the wheel by yourself, for the first time, you question how on Earth you will ever become comfortable driving? Ugh! Your brain is about to explode… But after a while, you do become comfortable driving.

It is your Driver Part that allows you to take your right hand off the wheel and rest it on the back of the passenger seat, while singing along with the music, as you look around for friends on the street, switch CD's, and talk on your cell phone. Oh, and while we are

on the subject... NO TEXTING AND DRIVING. (But it's interesting that it is your Driver Part that allows your Texting Part to text. Get my point?)

All this and more is possible due to your Driver Part. You no longer have to consciously be aware of the light turning red; you find that your foot seems to go from the accelerator to brake by itself. It becomes a habit. All the habit patterns we form in our lives are still being thought about. Not by our conscious mind, but by the various Parts working 24/7 in our subconscious.

We take our Parts for granted, because the subconscious was designed to develop our habit patterns, and we would have a very hard time functioning without them. There is nothing complicated about allowing a different aspect of your personality to become dominant at different times. The subconscious works the same way, except that we are not aware of the existence of these Parts, what they are up to, or how to control them when they begin to cause problems.

Once again, when a Part is formed it is there for life. So your Driver Part will be there for you, allowing you to do all the things you are able to do when behind the wheel, for the rest of your life. As long as you are mentally and physically able to drive, it will be there waiting for you to turn the key. And that's a good thing, since driving allows us to be independent.

But, let's look at the bad news aspect of Parts. The bad news is that once a Part is formed, it will continue that behavior for the rest of your life. That's great for driving but not so great for a smoker who is ready to quit. Since the Smoker Part remains totally focused on the purpose it was designed for, it becomes necessary to introduce a new Part - a Healthy Part - to the subconscious. This new Healthy Part will cause internal conflict in the subconscious mind for the first time, and this is why smokers find themselves in such a state of hopelessness.

This is the root cause of the constant battle in the minds of smokers, which causes a powerful emotional upheaval not only for them, but for everyone in their lives. As a hypnotist, I have had many smokers tell me the same story. "I try to quit, but I become such an animal, even my wife says to go ahead and smoke, because she can't stand me any longer." They say, "I want to quit, but I guess I have no will power."

I tell these people that it was designed to be this way by the Tobacco Industry, not just through addictive chemicals, but by their pervasive advertising. It is my opinion that smokers are the victims of the tobacco companies' knowledge of the way the subconscious works, and the inability of the conscious and subconscious minds to communicate. I tell my hypnosis clients that it's as if the conscious mind speaks English but the subconscious mind speaks French. Eventually they can communicate to successfully stop smoking, but it takes a long time and a lot of effort.

~ ~ ~

Talk to anyone who has quit smoking and very few people say, "It was a breeze, I simply decided to quit and I just stopped." When I was quitting, those were the ex-smokers that I would love to have seen hanging off a cliff, holding on by their fingernails. I would have said to them, "What's the problem? Just pull yourself up… It's a breeze. Just decide to pull your big fat butt up and do it!"

Obviously, when someone is struggling with quitting a smoking addiction, laughter is the first thing to go. Followed closely by all the joy in their lives. They are angry and disappointed with themselves when they slip up and smoke, and they are angry and miserable with everyone and everything in their lives, when they are resisting cigarettes but still craves them. You can understand why the life of any smoker becomes such a misery when the decision to quit is made. As I have said, quitting smoking is a bear!

People I have helped quit, using Parts Therapy, realize that it isn't really hard at all. Once the smoker identifies and understands the role of his Smoker Part, there is a very good chance the majority can successfully quit smoking in one session, as I was about to learn.

~ ~ ~

So now, with my Smoker Part screaming in my ear, I stood to introduce myself to Allen the hypnotherapist, who gestured toward the door to his office, and we both walked in. He went behind his desk, littered with all sorts of papers and magazines, and directed me to sit in a large leather recliner.

*Hey! What are you doing? This guy is a threat to me! I want to smoke and there is nothing you, this fat jerk or this other Part of you that I am fighting with can do about it. I am **not** going to quit smoking.* This voice in my head was relentless and I could not stop these thoughts from echoing in my ears.

It continued yelling in my mind, *If this guy is such a good hypnotherapist, why doesn't he hypnotize himself to drop a few pounds? …Yeah, and if he is charging you $350.00, he sure could afford to buy himself a new sweatshirt. And for that matter, let's be a little more professional, here, guy. Why not trim that beard? What's the matter? Ever hear of a tie?*

These comments were going on nonstop in my head through our whole interview. It lasted almost an hour, and you cannot imagine how resistant I had become to the idea of being hypnotized. My Smoker Part was definitely winning this battle, the same as he'd won every battle over the past year.

TELLING THE VOICES IN YOUR HEAD TO SHUT UP!

Al continued to talk to me about how hypnosis can help me quit smoking, and yet all I could hear was the negative comments that no one heard but me. At the same time, my conscious mind was reminding me how much I truly wanted and needed to quit. And now I was sitting there with this man who had helped three people I knew to quit smoking, and was willing to help me. But I was throwing it all away because of a voice in my head.

I had had it. And to that voice in my head I screamed, *Shut up! Listen to this man. He will help you!* And amazingly the Smoker's voice ceased.

I began to listen to what Al was saying. He stated all the reasons why I should quit, and I was in total agreement with him. Somehow, Al had convinced the Smoker within me to help me quit.

So when Al asked me, "Are you ready to be hypnotized?" I said yes. And I really was.

Al started playing soft music in the background and asked me to close my eyes, which I did. He began to speak quietly to me, telling me to take some cleansing breaths and to relax all the muscles in my body. I did feel very relaxed and quite comfortable, but I didn't think I was hypnotized. I felt as if I could open my eyes at any time. It felt as if he were just talking to me with my eyes closed.

And before I knew it he was telling me that he was going to bring me out of hypnosis. I didn't want to be taken out. It felt really good! He said he would awaken me by counting from one to five, "And on the count of five you'll open your eyes." Although I definitely did not want to awaken, when he said "Five," I found that my eyes slowly opened.

It felt as if I had taken a nap, and it took a concerted effort on my part to focus. Al asked me how I was feeling, and I replied that I felt wonderful. And I wasn't lying. I had never felt that relaxed, but I thought that the session should have lasted longer. "Garry," Al asked, "how long do you think you were hypnotized for?" Considering it felt like ten minutes I thought that, since I was paying him $350, he could have worked on me a little longer. And when I said that it felt like ten minutes, a smile formed on his face as he pointed at the clock on the wall. I knew we had started at 2:00 pm and that we had spoken for an hour before he started the actual hypnosis. I was shocked to see the clock reading 3:55.

"One of the indications of deep hypnosis is time distortion," he said. What I sensed as ten minutes turned out to be almost an hour.

Al then explained what hypnosis is in greater detail: "Garry, your time distortion indicates that you were not only hypnotized, but that you were **very** deeply hypnotized. I believe that you are one of those people who, when hypnotized, goes into 'somnambulism': the deepest and most beneficial level of hypnosis that anyone can enter. You should use it to your best advantage. The ability to control the subconscious is something that can be incorporated into your daily life, which could be very helpful for you."

After discussing my experience a little longer, he stood up, shook my hand and said, "Garry, you're now an ex-smoker. Congratulations. I hope you'll use the knowledge of your battle with smoking and your use of hypnosis to conquer it, to help others." At that time I had no clue what he meant, but now it seems somewhat prophetic, in light of the fact that 15 years later I would become a hypnotherapist, helping other smokers quit their addiction.

I thanked him and handed him my check. He opened the door to the waiting room and we both walked out. As I was putting on my parka, a man sitting there, who was obviously his next client, smiled and nodded at me, and I nodded back.

I put my hand in the pocket of my shirt and removed my pack of Marlboro 100 Lights and my Bic lighter, and tossed them into the pile on the coffee table.

I smiled to myself as I looked at his expression. The smirk on his face was the same smirk that had been on my face two hours before, and I knew that in his mind he was saying the same thing I'd thought: *Like I might ever do that.*

I said thanks and goodbye to Al, zipped up my parka and closed the door to the office behind me.

As I stepped out into that cold February chill, I realized that my normal action would have been to light up a cigarette. I was pleasantly surprised that the urge to light up, after not having smoked in over two hours, was not there. That was the first inkling that just maybe it worked and I was now, in fact, an ex-smoker. Back in my car once again, heading toward the Belt Parkway and back to Staten Island, the *What-If's* began to fill my mind.

The *What-If's* are the doubts that any hypnosis client has after their hypnosis session, when they have time to contemplate what had just happened to them. I had my first What-If experience as soon as I left his office. Not needing a cigarette led to the '*what if this really worked*' thought. But of course my logical mind rationalized it and said that quitting smoking could not be that easy. After all, I had been trying to quit for well over a year, with no success, and to contemplate that a one hour hypnosis session could have been that effective was too much to hope for. It would be dishonest of me to say that I never had another urge for a cigarette, but they simply passed, unacknowledged. The power of that urge always faded within moments.

It was 4:30 by the time I was driving on the Belt Parkway. The sun was setting directly in front of me and between the sun glare and my dirty, nicotine stained windshield, I was just barely able to see beneath my visor. The traffic on the eastbound side was heavy with the beginnings of the evening's rush hour traffic. Fortunately for me I was westbound going against rush hour traffic and by 5:05 I saw the signs which said I was approaching the Verrazano Bridge to Staten Island.

Driving on the westbound lanes of the Belt Parkway in Brooklyn was something I was very used to. Considering I was born in Brooklyn and learned to drive on its streets, the Belt was a large part of the experience my Driver Part received in those early driving years.

There was only one exit lane to the Verrazano Bridge back then, and with my signal on, indicating I was going over the bridge, a brand-new bright red Camaro in the far left lane crossed three lanes of traffic and cut me off as if I were invisible.

A discourteous, aggressive driver like that always triggered my normal response which was, of course, major road rage. My immediate and automatic reaction was to accelerate to within 3 inches of the Camaro's rear fender, turning on my lights and high beams, driving with one hand on the horn, and flipping him off with the other.

I continued to tailgate the Camaro as he continued to cut off other cars that, of course, I also cut off so that I could continue tailgating him. I was wishing he would drive right over the guardrail of the bridge and die in a plunge into the Hudson River. Yes, road rage does crazy things to a usually calm and pleasant mind...

Finally, my intelligence and maturity came back and I allowed him to continue to cut everybody else off as I slowed down and was shocked to find myself laughing. The laugh was from my acknowledgement of another What-If, which had just changed from, 'What-If the hypnosis session **didn't** work?' to What-If it really **did** work?' The thought that I may really be an ex-smoker made me laugh.

The same way I would have automatically lit up a cigarette when leaving Al's office, I would have absolutely, positively, automatically lit up after experiencing road rage. It was my routine to relax with a cigarette after anything emotional. But my hand didn't even go to my shirt pocket. The desire was simply not there.

It wasn't that I didn't want a cigarette. I just wasn't thinking of a cigarette. My laughter was an indication that for the first time in my year from hell, I may have actually become the ex-smoker that I could only have dreamed of being. And it felt amazing.

For the first time in well over a year, I could feel comfortable looking into my son's eyes, knowing that I was truthful when I said to him I no longer smoked. It was the first time that I truly believed I could live the rest of my life without dependency on the cigarettes that had ruled my life for close to 12 years. I felt saved.

The rest of the drive home was uneventful, except for the thought that I had just changed my life. I parked my car in the same spot I always parked it. I opened the same door of the apartment house that I had been living in. I walked up the same two flights of stairs and looked at the same door to my apartment that I had lived in for four years. I passed the spot where I would smoke after dinner and where Aaron had changed and saved my life with a few questions that convinced me that I needed to quit smoking.

All the things that I had done countless times over many years became a different experience. I was seeing these things through different, new eyes.

Over that last year I would have been thinking: where I would hide my cigarettes; when could I get out to sneak one; did I need to get into my car to do an errand so I could have three or four smokes before reentering my apartment? But those concerns were not there any longer. Just the What-If it really did work, and the beginnings of new hope.

*When you start to believe that some coincidences
are actually synchronicities
and look for them as signposts
- in order to determine if the direction
you are headed is the right one -
you may find more signposts.
And then you realize how many you had missed along your journey.*

RENÉE

Some years after successfully becoming an ex-smoker, I was still working as an Assistant Store Manager in the supermarket, and was just as miserable. I was resigned to my fate of being an overworked, underpaid middle manager for the rest of my life. And although I was despondent, at least I could take comfort in the fact that I was no longer a smoker.

Throughout the 80's, I bounced from one store to another. I was used to being transferred every year and was not surprised when I received the call telling me I was moving again. But this call had me back in Tony's district for another session of my much-loved Tonerazation. As you can imagine, I was overjoyed to be back with Tony, and even more overjoyed when I found the new store was even further from my apartment in Staten Island. And if you read sarcasm in my words, it was intentional.

Once there, I recognized the need for more cashiers, so I helped the hiring coordinator organize a massive hiring blitz. I put a large 'Positions Available' sign in the front window, and every evening we reviewed the applications as the hiring wheels began to spin. As I walked around the store, I always made it my business to check in with the kids in the Courtesy Counter, who would call me over when an applicant looked good.

One Friday afternoon, it was the calm before the storm time. People were home making dinner, supervising their kids' homework, driving home from their jobs, making plans for their Friday night. And I was just hoping to leave by 11:00 pm.

Sandy waved at me from behind the Courtesy Counter, her thick, dark eyebrows raised up, head tilted in a questioning look, as I noticed a young woman filling out an application. Sandy gave me the 'I approve' nod and emphasized it with a strong thumbs-up.

Renée finished the application and handed it in, but as she turned to leave, she walked squarely into my chest, stepping with her full weight on my big toe. If I had been prepared for the pain exploding in my foot, I wouldn't have yelped so loudly. Unfortunately, my loud reaction contributed to her embarrassment. After turning a bright shade of crimson and profusely apologizing, she calmed herself down.

"I don't think this is a real good way to get a job," she laughed. "I hope I didn't hurt your foot too badly," she continued with a broad bright smile.

I thought to myself, *I disagree. This is the perfect way to get a job.* And with an assuring smile, I started my standard questioning of a prospective new cashier, knowing full well that if she was happy with the pay, she already had the job.

"So… why do you want to work here? Do you have any cashier experience? When are you available to work?" The questions came automatically. After ten years I had heard all the answers, and I usually just went with my gut feeling anyway. But this interview was going very differently.

As we were discussing the cashier position, she started talking about her true love, and I don't mean her fiancé. Renée was a full-time teacher in a local Catholic school. She needed a part time job, after school, to pay for her college loans and put a little money on the side for her wedding.

"The look in young children's eyes when they get it," her face positively glowed. "I love being able to be part of that little person's future. You know what I mean? You know how you remember your favorite elementary school teacher?" I nodded, thinking of Mrs. Murphy, my Second Grade teacher, who was so instrumental in my life. "Well, I'm one of my students' favorite teachers and when they're 60 and I'm gone, they will be remembering me and how I affected their life!"

She was just so very animated and passionate about her profession as a teacher, that the interview seemed to reverse itself. I was so impressed with her dedication that I started to discuss education with her instead of the job she was applying for. All the things that I had been missing and wanting, Renée was describing with such passion and devotion that I could not help but question myself as to why I was still working in a supermarket and not in a classroom.

I hired her on the spot and told her to come in Monday for orientation.

~ ~ ~

Four months later, I was near the end of another 11:00 am to 11:00 pm Sunday shift, which was enough to exhaust you even if you'd had a great day (and I never had a great day). I was sitting at my desk in the Manager's Office, looking through the narrow, horizontal windows that overlooked the store. If there were a relaxing, private place in the store, this would be it.

It was the best time of the day. Customers were coming in for last minute things, the employees of the store were cleaning up for the night crew and for the next day's business. It was a wind down time, a time for reflection and planning. I stood up, knowing I couldn't rest yet. It was time for my late evening walk through, making sure the myriad things that had to be done were finished before I could sit and relax.

As I always did, I went into the back of the Meat Department and put on a clean, white coat that the butchers use to keep their clothing clean, since I was really tired of ruining good shirts and pants. *Thank God,* I thought to myself, *the Sunday night rush is over.*

The last butcher had left hours ago, so I went into the cooler to pack out the sale items prepared earlier in the day. And as I pulled the rack that held eight trays of wrapped meat, a tray slipped from the shelf, hitting me in the chest and splattering me with a bit of blood that had accumulated on the tray. *Phew,* I thought. *Good thing I had this meat coat on. Chris would be as pissed off as I am, having to throw away another new shirt because of blood stains that won't come out.*

I finished my tour, and as I was walking back to the Meat Department to toss the soiled coat in the laundry, I looked down at the stain on my coat. I had a very strange feeling, similar to déjà vu, but I didn't feel like I had done this before. It was almost as if I were remembering a different time in the past, like being reminded of a similar scene that had happened to me long ago. Not déjà vu. What then? A memory?

I simply stopped in the aisle, looking down at the white coat with a splotch blood on it. Suddenly, a new image formed in my mind of a similar white coat. However, instead of a small stain, the entire coat was soaked with blood from my chest down!

I was stunned, and felt as if I were moving out of my body and seeing a scene that was certainly NOT my own memory. It wasn't a scene from a movie, either. I just stood there in a trance as images were hitting me one after another.

As I looked down at the gory coat, I noticed that I was wearing knee high black boots, and I was standing in thick, blood soaked mud. As I took a breath, I looked down and saw a metallic object around my neck. I recognized it and seemed to be comfortable with the fact that it was a stethoscope, although not like any I had ever seen.

As suddenly as those thoughts had come to me, they stopped. The strangeness of the images made me feel weird as I rushed into the back of the Meat Department. I couldn't wait to tear off the jacket and throw it into the basket with the other soiled coats, very happy to have removed it, and wishing I could remove the memories they had drawn out of me as easily.

As I threw the coat into the basket, I took a deep breath. The back of the Meat Department has a very distinctive smell. It is a combination of refrigerated air, cold raw meat, grease, fat and cleanser. I was very accustomed to that smell; I had been in meat departments for as long as I had been in the supermarket industry. But when I inhaled this time, I could not help but choke on the smell and the odd memories they stirred.

I could not get out of that Meat Department fast enough. It wasn't until I reentered the sales floor that I was finally able to take a comfortable breath.

Where the hell did that come from? I wondered, my head reeling. As I walked slowly to my office, trying to shake off the memories that still lingered, I saw Renée walking toward the employee lounge. I knew that the thoughts of those disturbing images would fade as soon as we could have our usual Sunday evening discussion.

Just focusing on Renée helped me calm down. I was always happy to have her work with me on Sundays because it gave us a chance to discuss teaching. Every Sunday, Renée would buy the Newark Star-Ledger, which had the largest classified ad section for available teaching positions in the state. She would take her break pouring over these classified ads, looking for a teaching position in a county school. Although she loved working at her current school, like most private schools, it paid considerably less than public schools, with few benefits and no pension.

Along with teaching, our conversations involved many topics including her upcoming wedding, my kids, and my desire to teach. As a teacher, she was probably earning a quarter of my salary. But she woke up each morning, happy to go to a job that she loved, even though it barely payed her bills. While I dreaded waking up, because it meant going to a job I hated, just to be able to pay my own bills.

I knew how happy I would be teaching, but I had a wife, two young kids and plenty of expenses, so I sadly accepted the fact that I wasn't going anywhere. I thought back to the day I had decided to work at my cousin's store instead of continuing to look for a teaching position and confirmed the truth: I had clearly made the wrong choice. And talking with Renée, seeing how happy she was with her decision to be a teacher, made me that much more frustrated with my own occupation.

What the hell am I doing with my life? I thought to myself. *Renée is contributing to the future of so many kids, and I am contributing to the happiness of people who, when they come into the store, like to have their cans of peas in nice straight rows with all the labels facing out.*

When I'm dead and gone, will I be remembered by anyone? Will I have contributed to anyone's life? I thought again of Mrs. Murphy, who had truly changed the direction of my life. Almost forty years later, I still thought of her.

I smiled to myself, thinking, *In forty years, someone might say to themselves, 'Boy, remember Garry, that Assistant Store Manager? Wasn't it so nice of him to have the cans of peas all packed out in those nice, neat rows? I loved the way he made sure all the labels of the cans were always facing up front. I'll never forget him.'*

I walked to the rear of the store, looking forward to a calm conversation with Renée. But as I approached the employee lounge, I was concerned to hear her raising her voice. She was calling some teenage cashiers to task for getting the lounge dirty, which she knew was a concern for the management.

"This room is disgusting! And don't tell me that it isn't your stuff. I sold this to you, Billy, and the receipt is still on it with the paid sticker that I put on. What's wrong with you guys? Do you live like this at home? Does your mother let you throw your stuff around her living room? NO! I think not. Come on guys. This is our lounge. Let's keep it clean. What do you say?"

Within a few seconds, the boys cleaned up the entire lounge and never even complained. She had a way of making the cashiers and cartboys do what was required of them without the objections normally associated with trying to get a teenager to do anything.

That is why I'd felt so confident and comfortable with my decision to hire and promote Renée. She had an ability to motivate cashiers who would complain to anyone else. Renée was a gift to every manager who worked with her. Which is why, when I heard her raise her voice to those kids, I planned to go in and give them my own version of 'Tonerization'.

I walked in there with every intention to rip into each one of them, until I saw Renée. With one look, she instantly knew my intent and by simply holding up her hand and calmly shaking her head, I knew she had it all under control. Instead of screaming at those kids and being upset; instead of having the kids in the break room calling me an asshole (or worse) behind my back; instead of having to drink half a bottle of Maalox, I simply smiled, winked at her and went back to the office. I sat in my chair, kicked my feet up on my desk, locked my fingers behind my head and thanked God for all the Renée's in this world.

A JOB THAT WAS MADE IN HEAVEN

I was glad to have the opportunity to close my eyes and try to get the bizarre experience of the bloody coat out of my mind, when the door to my office flew open. Renée rushed in from the lounge with the classified section of the Sunday Star-Ledger folded in half in her hands and a very excited look on her face.

"Garry, look at this!" she exclaimed as she ran up to my desk, holding the newspaper out in front of her as if it were on fire. I assumed she had found the perfect teaching job, probably in a school around the corner from her apartment. This new teaching position probably came with a substantial raise. Undoubtedly, this new teaching job would give her great pay and an excellent benefit packet.

I realized that I was so very envious it hurt, and I was ashamed of myself for not being overjoyed for her. I also realized to my dismay that this perfect teaching position would render her need for her part-time job at the store, unnecessary. I further assumed that this perfect job was going to take away my most valued employee.

"Garry, you are not going to believe this! This job is PERFECT! I couldn't believe my eyes when I read it!" I truly wanted to be happy for her. She was going to start her married life in the perfect job. However, in my mind she already had the perfect job: teaching. It didn't pay that well, but it was perfect. I also couldn't help feeling a little jealous, envious and yes, perhaps a little angry.

A little angry at my situation.

A little angry with myself for not following through with getting a teaching position in NY.

Even a little angry at my wife and kids (even though I loved them more than life itself) because without my concern for their wellbeing, I could quit this job and get an entry level teaching job, even if it meant sleeping in my car.

And of course I was always angry with my company for paying me more than a teacher but not nearly enough to compensate me for what I had to endure at Tony's hands daily.

With an expression on her face showing both excitement and wonder, she placed the want ads on my desk and pointed to a 2-column ad. At first I thought, *Thanks a lot Renée, I gave you a job, trained you, promoted you and now you are going to get some new teaching job and leave.* However, all I said was "So?"

She looked at me as if I weren't getting it. And I wasn't. "Well, what do you think?" she said, pointing at the want ad again, saying, "READ IT!"

Vocational Instructor Wanted

Bergen County Vocational Technical HS and Wakefern Corp. are looking for an individual for a new program planned for September of 1989.

- Supermarket experience required
- Teaching experience helpful but not required.

Apply at:

Department of Special Education
Bergen County Vocational Technical High School
275 Pascack Road, Paramus, NJ 07652

"I don't understand. I thought you're a math teacher. What would you want with a teaching job at a supermarket?" I replied.

She took a deep breath, sat in a chair next to me and gave me *The Look*. The Look is known by anyone who is in a relationship. My wife gives me The Look anytime I am being so dense that I can't see the obvious. You know The Look when you see it. It's a sort of knowing smirk. And the knowing is that she is aware of something that is clearly obvious to her, but oblivious to you.

I am very used to The Look from my wife and my daughter, but I had never seen it on the face of someone at work. Therefore, when Renée reacted with The Look I had to stop and make a quick mental check of exactly what was going on.

"Knucklehead!" she laughed. "I wasn't talking about this job for **me**. I was talking about it for **you**! I am a math teacher and that is what I love, but this teaching job looks like it was made for you! Look…" pointing at the want ad, "Supermarket experience is required, teaching experience is helpful. This job is perfect for you! You have always said that you regret the decision to work here and that you should have waited for a teaching position to open. Now here is a teaching job, where you don't even need teaching experience…Garry, if God made a job specifically for you, it would be this one: teaching supermarket skills to Special Ed students! Come on Ga, at least apply." So many things were going through my mind, I don't know if I answered her or not.

Yes, if God had designed a job specifically for me, as Renée said, it would be this one. But, my view of God was that He was non-existent. I would say that IF there were a God, Renée would be right. This job was custom made for me and after thinking about it for a second, I realized it was exactly what I would love to do.

When you believe that synchronicities
can guide you on your journey,
the path you need to take becomes brighter, clearer,
and you find dreams that you had given
up upon can actually come true.

A LIFE CHANGING JOB INTERVIEW
THAT WAS HEAVENLY MADE

I scheduled my job interview for the teaching position in August of 1989. As I parked my car and turned off the ignition, many thoughts were going through my mind. I knew I could not continue being a manager at the supermarket any longer. The job was draining everything from my life and now that the light at the end of the tunnel was shining so brightly, the thought of having to return to the store made my working life unbearable. I thought as I walked into the school, that if the decision was made to go with another applicant, I would jump off the Goethals Bridge instead of driving across it. I smiled to myself that joking about killing myself over not getting a job was a little over-reactive, but as Shakespeare wrote in 1605, "Many a true word hath been spoken in jest."

Going into a high school for the first time in well over twenty years was an interesting experience all by itself, but the reality of the situation hit me when a student in the hallway who was obviously new to the school said to me, "Excuse me sir, do you know where the Main Office is?" I smiled, telling him that I wasn't a teacher, but I may be one soon.

I was directed to have a seat in a room off the high school's Main Office and told that Jean, the person from ShopRite who had designed the program, would be right with me. I felt my anxiety starting to surge; this was my first job interview in 12 years. In those 12 years, I had been trained in the skills needed to conduct a job interview, and had interviewed hundreds of people, but now I was on the other side of the desk. I knew what to say and how to say it, and I knew what they were looking for. I also knew that this was an opportunity of a lifetime, and that this interview may be my one and only chance to change my life.

Not **too** much pressure.

While I sat in the waiting area, contemplating my past and what my future might be, the door opened to the Principal's Office and a man my own age walked out. As the door closed behind him, I assumed that we were both applying for the same teaching position.

A moment later, Jean came from the office, and introduced himself as the Supervisor at Wakefern Corporation who was involved with getting this new program off the ground.

After shaking his hand and introducing myself, I was told that the name of the program would be The Supermarket Careers Program.

He directed me into the Principal's Office, where three other men sat at the conference table. We spoke at length about the proposed program, and I was asked various questions about my background and my current position. They presented a few hypothetical situations that I could find myself involved with in the school and asked how I would deal with them. I tried to control my excitement when I saw them nodding through the entire interview and while reviewing my college transcript.

When the interview was over, Jean walked me out and said goodbye, telling me that I was the last applicant to be considered and that he would be calling soon with their decision. As I walked to my car, I reviewed how the interview had gone and felt that I had done the very best I possibly could have done. There was not a single thing about the interview that I would have changed.

I had never felt as confident, in my life, as I did at the end of that interview. I was ecstatic and when I got home, I gave Chris a huge kiss and said, "Say hello to the next Supermarket Careers Instructor at Bergen County Vocational Technical High School."

The look on her face reflected my own enthusiasm. "So they offered you the job?" she asked, and I responded with what I truly felt: that the interview went so well, I couldn't imagine that they would go with anyone else.

The following day Jean called me back to say that the decision was now between me and another applicant, a current ShopRite manager. The decision would be made by the following week.

The next day started the longest, slowest week of my entire life! There are so many clichés about waiting: 'A watched pot never boils' or 'If you want to see time slow down, watch the second hand on your clock.' Well my pot was not even close to boiling. It seemed to be turning to ice as the second hand of my clock began to move backwards. Or at least that's the way it seemed to me.

The next week I received the call from Jean, which started with classic 'good news/bad news'. I asked for the bad news first and was told that the school had decided to go with the ShopRite manager for the position. I felt my heart drop. I was so close to the perfect job and now that I didn't get it, my head began to spin. I was sick to my stomach and felt so bad that I almost missed the good news. "Garry, there are over 20 more schools just in the tri-state area who are on board with the Supermarket Careers Program and will be opening their own programs over the next two years! Garry, you are my number one choice for the next shop."

Two weeks after the good and bad news, I received another transfer; I had been in my current store for over a year and had anticipated being moved once again. I would miss all the people I worked with, especially Renée, but by then I was comfortable with being moved all over the company. When I heard what store I would be going to, my stomach dropped again. I would be an Assistant Store Manager in none other than Tony's flagship home store! I didn't look at it as a vote of confidence from Tony or as a wonderful opportunity for advancement; I viewed it as a free ticket to daily Tonerizations… Great!

- Another Life Lesson - # 19

***When you allow your guard to come down,
others may drop theirs
and you may be very pleasantly surprised
at what is on the other side of their guard-tower.***

THE SUPERMARKET CAREERS PROGRAM

True to his word, Jean and I spoke frequently over that year. And nine months after that initial interview, I received an important phone call from him. There were three Supermarket Career Programs scheduled to open that coming September, and the schools were now looking for instructors. Jean told me that I was his number one choice for all three. So on my day off I drove by them, and as soon as I glimpsed the last school, I knew I would be hired there. I didn't know how I knew it, I just did.

Although I felt that my first interview the prior year had gone perfectly, I had to admit that my interview at this school was even better. I had a feeling of confidence that was evident to the administrators conducting the interview. I described my visit to one of the current Supermarket Careers Programs and described how I would improve upon that design for the shop being proposed for their school.

This time I did not have to wait long. They asked me to have a seat in the outer office and in 10 minutes I was asked back in. All of the administrators had left except for the Director of Special Education who had some additional questions for me, and arranged to have a second interview with the school's Superintendent the very next day. When the second interview was concluded I was thanked and told that I would hear of their decision the next day.

And that next day I received the phone call that I had dreamed of for over twenty years.

I was offered the position starting in September 1990. All my dreams had finally come true with that one phone call. I was leaving a job that I hated, for the job I was now highly qualified for and wanted so desperately.

LEAVING THE SUPERMARKET BUSINESS FOR GOOD

It was late July when I was offered the teaching position. I had accrued three weeks of vacation and the timing couldn't have been more perfect (I would eventually believe that 'timing' is *always* perfect). And for the first time in my supermarket career I was eagerly looking forward to going to work that day. I was still an Assistant Manager in Tony's flagship store. And as I pulled into the parking lot I could not force the smile from my face, knowing that in a few short months, I would be doing what I had always dreamed of doing.

No more pressure, no more Tonerizations, no more dreading the alarm clock in the morning. I was going to tell Tony for the second and last time that I was leaving for a position that I knew, beyond a shadow of doubt, I was perfectly suited and qualified for... teaching.

I saw Tony enter the store from the parking lot. Instead of wanting to hide, I began to walk toward his office in the back of the store. I walked into his secretary's office with a different attitude. Perhaps for the first time, I had no concerns as she directed me in.

I was the only ex-smoker in his office and between Tony, his secretary and everyone else, there were times when the smoke was so thick that I found it hard to breathe. I had been an ex-smoker for almost seven years and as I walked in, I couldn't help but cough.

Tony was on the phone as I entered. He waved me in as if fanning his lit cigarette and had me sit across from his desk. Not a man to waste time, he got to the point immediately. "What's the problem?" he asked as he hung up the phone. I didn't want to go into any great explanation or detail. All I wanted to do was simply tell him that I was quitting and leave his office.

"Tony," I said, "I'm resigning. I'm giving you a month notice. I have three weeks of vacation coming to me. I'd like to take my vacation so that my last day will be August 31st."

It was the first time I'd ever seen him speechless. Tony didn't like to be surprised and I'd caught him off guard. "You're quitting? What are you doing? Where are you going?"

I explained that I was hired by a school as an instructor, teaching supermarket skills to kids with learning disabilities. He lit another cigarette, which was now making my eyes tear. Taking a deep drag, he just leaned back and stared at me through the smoke.

I didn't know how he was going to react and to my great relief and amazement, to quote him, 'I didn't give a fuck!' And that felt great!

I suppose that after so many years of expecting harsh treatment, sarcastic responses and being made to feel inadequate and incompetent, I really did not know what to expect. I thought that he would be happy to be getting rid of an Assistant Manager whom he constantly berated. I felt he would be angry, simply because he was always angry. I felt this conversation might be very brief, with him saying, "Fine. I'll replace you in a heartbeat." Which was something he said to me frequently. I really thought he would say, "You don't have to give me any notice. I'll pay you your three weeks' vacation. Have a nice life. Now get the fuck out of my office!" I felt he would turn his back, get on the phone and begin the process of finding my replacement without missing a beat.

But I never conceived of the conversation that did ensue.

He picked up his phone, buzzed his secretary and said, "Carol, hold my calls. And bring in a couple of cups of coffee. Call personnel and tell them I'll be interviewing for an Assistant position."

I was not prepared for this type of situation, sitting in the office quietly having a cup of coffee with Tony. It was something I had never experienced in my 12 years in the industry. He finished the cigarette he was smoking, slowly exhaling the smoke into the air. Again I couldn't help but cough. But instead of ignoring me, which was his normal reaction, he waved the smoke away and said he was sorry. He pushed his chair out from behind the desk and rolled it over to mine, sitting closer to me than I was comfortable with. "Are you leaving because I haven't made you a General Store Manager yet?" he asked in a tone that I was not used to. He seemed concerned.

Honestly, I never thought he was even considering me, and answered negatively. Carol walked in at that point with two cups of coffee, milk and sugar. She poured a cup for Tony and asked me how I liked mine. As she handed the coffees to each of us, I had to smile because he reached for another cigarette, looked at me, and put the pack down.

To my surprise, he began a conversation about the direction my life was going. His questions were pointed and specific, asking me about my plans for the future. This was a side of Tony I had never seen before and he became surprisingly human at that point.

We talked about my desire to teach before being hired, about Renée, whom he knew well, and how she had shown me the ad a year prior, which led to my new career opportunity. I became animated and, for the first time, showed Tony who I truly was. He began to share with me his challenges at work, dealing with incompetent people.

For the one and only time, he actually apologized for having vented his anger on me so often, explaining it was misplaced anger. He sputtered, "I was just so damned frustrated with that asshole you were working under. I was saddled with him, so I dumped it on you. And for that I am sorry."

In a matter of 15 minutes, the perception of Tony that I'd had for 12 years changed; not to the degree that I would even consider staying, but it felt good to allow the old animosity, frustration and anger to fade away, replaced with understanding. That was the first day of a new reality for me.

Tony looked at me and smiled, saying, "I think that this new position will be good for you. You always liked people more than the job. Good luck. I'll have Carol get all the paperwork together. You can go on vacation the last three weeks of August and we'll set it up so your last day will be August 31st."

He stood up and shook my hand saying, "I'm happy for you. Good luck, and if there is anything you need, please call me. Really." And we left his office together.

I was really surprised by his reaction. It was the very first time in all the years I had known him that he showed me his human side, and it was a little bittersweet that it took me quitting to see it. Nonetheless, our meeting couldn't have gone any better. I didn't know what I had done to deserve all the gifts I had just been given, but my life sure had turned around for the better!

~ ~ ~

So on the day after Labor Day of the 1990-1991 school year, I began my career as the instructor for the newly created SCP, the Supermarket Careers Program.

On that first day, I was told that my shop would be in the area that used to house the old heating and air-conditioning program. The Principal walked me up to the large building that housed the new supermarket along with some other vocational shops. He unlocked the door to my shop from the hallway and we walked in.

The room smelled of grease, and was covered in a thick coat of dirt and dust. Old pieces of air-conditioning and heating equipment were strewn all around the room that would soon be my supermarket. This was something I had not expected, and I looked at the Principal, who knew what I was thinking. He told me there was plenty of time to design and build the shop, because I wouldn't have any students until the second marking period at the beginning of November.

Two months flew by and the SCP was ready. It was a tall order, but with the help of Jean and other Wakefern people, we were able to install the cash registers, refrigeration cases, grocery shelving and all the other components that make a tiny supermarket. And with a $6000 donated grocery delivery from ShopRite scheduled to be delivered in a few days, I was ready to meet my first students.

- Another Life Lesson - # 20

Sometimes assumptions you make... make asses of you and me.
But there are times when an assumption that
causes you to feel like an ass, initially,
changes and you learn that you were right all along.

JOSHUA

The design and implementation of the store was done and now, on the first day of the second marking period, I was sitting in my recently painted office, anticipating what my first students would be like while reviewing the attendance sheet and class roster. Some of the students were classified with special needs and had an 'IEP', an Individualized Education Plan. An IEP is a legal document with an individualized, detailed educational plan, given to each teacher for each student. I felt comfortable that I could teach even severely handicapped students, entry level supermarket skills. I had familiarized myself with my students' names, reviewed all the available IEPs, and was now looking forward with eager anticipation to put faces to those names.

The name 'Joshua Miller' (not his real name) stood out to me, for some reason. I tried to picture this child, who was about to enter my perfect little supermarket. I pictured him physically, educationally and even emotionally, so I could be prepared to be the best teacher in the world. This job saved my life and I was going to give it my all. So I put myself completely into teaching. And Joshua was going to be my teacher's pet.

I pictured Joshua as a short, little Jewish kid with glasses. Probably this cute little kid had been picked on his whole life. No sports for little Joshua, oh no, his overprotective Jewish mother wouldn't want her little Joshua harming himself. He was probably into *Star Trek* and had an autographed picture of Captain Kirk, framed over his desk at home (I mean, with a name like 'Joshua Miller' could he be anything else?)

In the hallway the bell rang, signaling the start of the school day, and students started coming to the shops. I couldn't wait to finally meet Joshua and begin his (and my) education.

To tell you the truth, I was a little nervous about meeting these kids. My self-doubts started to pop up. *What if I can't reach them?* I thought. *What if they don't want to learn what I plan to show them? What if my supervisor doesn't think I have what it takes to be a Special Ed teacher? Damn, I'm not tenured, I could be fired... unemployed. How will I pay the bills? How will I be able to feed my kids?*

Self-doubts can be a real pain in the ass. Sometimes they can also become a self-fulfilling prophecy that can push you right into the situation you fear the most. But I had no time to

98

entertain self-doubts. I was a teacher now and I was meant to be one. I had what it takes and I was going to succeed. Period.

A new positive attitude took hold. I was about to meet my little friend Joshua and between the two of us I knew things were going to work out fine. I would be a great teacher and Joshua was going to lose his glasses, get contacts, grow six inches and in four years from now, upon graduation, be nominated Mr. Popularity of the school. *Okay, I'm ready now,* I thought. *Bring them on!*

~ ~ ~

The first student who entered the shop was a tall black kid with corn rows. His pants were worn in the 'sag' and he had on a pair of gold rimmed sunglasses. He carried a boom box in his left hand playing his favorite song - MC Hammer's <u>Can't Touch Dis</u> - while dribbling a basketball with his right. By now my other six students were arriving and began to sit at the desks I had set up for them.

Dribbling the ball right up to me, he landed a 3 pointer into the garbage can near the time clock. "Swish... nothin' but net. Or should I say, garbage can," he said, leaving his right hand up in the air, looking for a 'high five' from me. Which he was not going to get. Even if I wanted to, I couldn't reach that high anyway. I had to consciously close my mouth, because when he walked into the room, I found my jaw drop open.

"And who are you?" I questioned, in my most authoritarian voice.

He looked at me, leaning down with his face about six inches from mine, and with a scowl, tilted his head from left to right. Imitating my tone, he said, "I'm Joshua Miller. And who might **you** be?"

I began to think that working for Tony really wasn't that bad after all and perhaps I could take him up on his offer of a General Store Manager position!

"My name is Mr. Gewant," I said to his back, as he made a 180 degree turn that would have made James Brown proud, and slowly walked to the garbage can, retrieved his ball, walked to the back of the class and sat down.

I repeated, to him and the rest of the stunned students, "I'm your teacher, Mr. Gewant."

I realized that I needed to rethink my preconceived ideas about Joshua.

Obviously, I had been slightly mistaken. He stood up and began to walk slowly toward me as the last of my students took their seats. He looked around, knowing that he had an audience now, and was going to play it up. He walked directly in front of me. Staring down at me, he said, "Yo...You ain't the teacher... I'M THE TEACHER HERE!"

I felt all the students' eyes on us. Some were uncomfortable with the scene being played out, but most were enjoying seeing a teacher, on the first day of a new shop, in a confrontation with a student who was so big, bad, and oh so cool. Along with the feeling of being assessed by the students, I had another uncomfortable feeling as I realized a bead of sweat, which had just started to form at the top of my head, began to move toward my forehead. I projected its course and knew that it was going to be exiting my hairline about mid-forehead in around 30 seconds. And I was damned if I was going to let him - or them - see me sweat.

I am not aware of any college courses that can instruct a novice teacher on the correct procedure to handle a situation like the one I had found myself in. I don't know if a class could properly prepare new teachers for the plethora of thoughts that can speed through their mind, at the speed of light, when they find themselves being challenged for the control of their classroom on the very first day of school.

Do I begin my career as a teacher by screaming at this kid? I thought. *What does he want? How can I get him to sit down? What are the other kids going to do? Follow his lead? What if the Principal decides to observe me now and finds Joshua teaching the class? Where is my cute, shy, Jewish, little Joshua?*

WHAT... HAVE... YOU... DONE... WITH... MY... JOSHUA?! ! !

~ ~ ~

*Wait a minute…*I thought. *What WOULD happen if the tables were turned on this kid? What if the Principal walked in and Joshua WAS teaching the class?* It occurred to me what to do. Again, out of the blue, like so many other times, the answer simply popped into my head. From where, I didn't know…then.

"You ain't the teacher, I AM!" he had said to me, and my reaction seemed to him almost instantaneous, although for me it seemed an eternity. "You're the teacher?" I asked calmly, repeating his statement, as I walked to the last chair in the class. Flopping back into it, pulling another chair in front of me, I put my feet up on it, clasped my hands behind my head and said, "Okay, Teach… Go head 'n' school me!"

Teachers call the first two weeks of school the honeymoon period, when the students are on their best behavior. Well if this was the honeymoon, I'd hate to see what Joshua would be like when we were going through a divorce.

I feel fairly certain in saying that no other teacher Joshua had ever had did anything like that to him. At first, he simply looked dumbfounded, as did the rest of the class, who were ready for a new experience, but never imagined the scene that was now unfolding.

I had called his bluff, but with humor, in a way that we both could save face. I found myself in a situation where I could begin my school career by screaming at a student on the first day of class or allow the next move to be made by Joshua. I chose the latter. He had challenged me, and now had the choice to either escalate the confrontation or allow everything to calm down. Fortunately, he also chose the latter.

So there we were. I was sitting in the back of the room with my feet up on a desk, relaxing and requesting Joshua to 'school me' Joshua was now on the spot; he'd tried to be slick with me but I didn't take the bait. I refused to have the altercation he had planned for us and he seemed to be at a loss. As the other students waited for his response, I nonchalantly wiped the sweat that had begun in earnest, away from my face.

As he was standing in the front of the class, you could not help but keep your eyes on him. He was a strong, handsome, street wise young man, who probably had more adult experience in his sixteen years than I'd like to think about. But it was his eyes that drew your attention. His skin was darker than most of the other students, but his eyes were a beautiful light hazel and positively glowed with the turmoil he had begun in my class. I knew that he was not used to being in a position where he was not in control. I had turned the altercation around and the basketball was now on his side of the court.

He stared at me with a practiced angry look that I was very aware of from my supermarket days and I was not, nor would I ever be, intimidated by a student, even one as confrontational as Joshua. He glared *hard* at me for about twenty seconds (which felt much longer) and then something happened that I would always remember and appreciate.

Joshua's face changed from an angry snarl to a beautiful grin. His hazel eyes seemed to sparkle as his disposition changed and he revealed a broad smile. "You cool," he said, nodding his head and squinting one eye in the way you look when you're evaluating a situation.

His expression lightened even more, when I replied, "Thanks... I try."

"I'll let you teach us now," he said as he walked to the back of the class and sat in the chair next to me.

Now, what I did not know at that time was that Joshua would become the person I thought he'd be. The wrapper was different but the soul was the same. Instead of the quiet, introspective, shy little Jewish Joshua I had expected, I found myself teaching the tall, street wise, popular, athletic, all too often very angry Joshua. I would later notice that as I was teaching the class supermarket career skills, I was also teaching racial and religious tolerance, anger management and life skills.

The more I worked with at-risk kids, the more I liked their intensity. I was able to see through the outer angry shell to the child living in there. All I did was treat these kids with the respect that I demanded for myself, and I was always handsomely rewarded.

ABOUT THE SCP

School was exactly as I dreamt it would be. When you walked into the shop there was a classroom area to the right with 10 student desks, two cash registers, three grocery shelves, a frozen food case, a refrigerated dairy case and a bakery area. The school administration allowed students to come into the supermarket during their break time to purchase snacks. The shop became so popular that I soon learned the names and faces of almost every student enrolled in our school.

I now enjoyed waking up in the morning and, although I had an hour drive to school, I actually found it relaxing, as I planned out my day. My morning commute was now the opposite of the commutes I had become accustomed to. Every day I looked forward to school.

Along with becoming the most popular shop for students, the SCP became a popular place for faculty to visit. We made sure to keep a good supply of all the favorite food products for both the students and staff, and the only competitor we had was the cafeteria.

The administration was very supportive of my program, and on my third year as a teacher, I was offered tenure. I could not believe the change in my life - not only professionally but socially, emotionally and even spiritually. I had become so relaxed that my stress levels were nearly nonexistent; my road rage which had been the barometer of my stress level had all but disappeared. My home life had also dramatically improved. I was spending much more time at home with the family I loved instead of working sixty hours a week and being angry the rest of the time. I had the time to learn what being a father was supposed to be. At that point in my life I still was not accepting the existence of God, but nonetheless I thanked Him every day for how my life had changed.

DEALING WITH THE COMPETITION

By early spring of 1991, the first year we were open, the SCP was doing very well. But the students needed something new and exciting to keep them motivated, so I wrote a new lesson 1 called "Dealing with Your Competition." After a class discussion about which supermarket was ShopRite's biggest competitor, I made the analogy that our cafeteria was our own biggest competitor. I then directed the conversation to how we could take more business from them. The students recognized that we had already cornered the market on snacks and drinks. And that is how I came up with our *Lunch Special.*

I arranged to have pizza delivered fresh from a local pizzeria to my shop. Freezing the pies and reheating them by the slice in our convection ovens, I sold a package deal which we advertised throughout the school as our Lunch Special. I had my students hang our posters around the school, which read: "Come to our supermarket for a slice of fresh, hot, crispy pizza with a 12 oz. can of soda for the amazingly low, low price of only $2.00." Soon our Lunch Special became the lunch of choice in school, as I tied our Lunch Special into one of our most important lessons.

Our Lunch Special demonstrated quite effectively and explicitly the law of supply and demand, and how it works in the retail industry. Our shop was selling an average of ten pies a day, which was great for us, the local pizzeria and everyone in school who enjoyed a great, tasty, economical meal. The shop was also making a great profit, which I decided to give back to my students, as an incentive, in the form of a paycheck.

OUR 'STUDENT' PAYROLL

I ran the shop as close to a real world situation as I possibly could. I had a time clock installed and instructed the students to 'punch in' when they came to class/work. I soon realized that they followed my directions, simply because I told them to. However, they had no concept as to why they were being asked to punch a timecard. They also had no concept of paychecks, time cards, unions or taxes.

In another lesson, I took a blank check and stub and changed it to read Supermarket Careers Program - ShopRite Paycheck and told the students that I was going to pay them a dollar an hour! After the cheers had settled down, I explained that it wasn't real money, that it was ShopRite money which could be used to purchase anything in our store. After the initial letdown, they realized how beneficial it would be to get a paycheck. I explained to them how time cards worked. So instead of simply punching their time card because I told them to, they understood the point of punching in. When they received their first paycheck they were so excited over the check that it took them a few moments to realize that they could now use it to buy things in the shop... including our Lunch Special. It seemed to be a win-win situation for all involved.

In order to make the payroll program even more exciting for them, I described a bonus plan. I told them that if they did a particular job very well, doing things that had to be done without being told to do it, I would put a 'B' on their timecard. Each B meant a bonus of one dollar on their net paycheck. I also explained that they may also lose a dollar by not working well, which meant fighting, arguing, or by doing something that could get an employee fired at a real ShopRite. A 'D' on a timecard meant a deduction of one dollar from their net pay. I found that after I instituted this payroll bonus program, behaviors that would warrant a bonus increased, while negative behaviors that had been frequent were considerably reduced.

Our Lunch Special, in actuality, became a win-win-win situation. My students won by receiving their paychecks and the experience gleaned from the lesson, other students and faculty won by having a delicious, reasonably priced meal, and the pizzeria that delivered all those pizzas to our shop surely won, as well.

The only one who was a loser in this scenario was the cafeteria. I had effectively closed down the cafeteria's lunch program. I had undercut their price and gave a higher quality product. To add insult to injury, the students who bought my Lunch Specials were taking them back into the cafeteria to eat!

A few months after starting my Lunch Specials, the company that ran the cafeteria complained to the Principal. And although he loved what our kids were doing, he reluctantly asked me to be a little less competitive, at least during lunch time. Unfortunately, I learned that schools are also businesses, and that the contracts the school has with outside contractors, like a cafeteria management corporation, hold more weight than our Lunch Specials: a Life Lesson learned.

OUR 'DREAM' HOME

The year before I started teaching, Chris had also gone back to school and became a registered nurse. In one year with Chris working full-time as a nurse, we were finally able to save up enough money for a down payment for our first home. We had lived in various apartments our whole married life. That first year of teaching and nursing was spent looking for houses in NJ. We'd gone to look at houses in the past, not to buy, just for the fun of looking at new homes, but tinged with the sadness of knowing we could never afford to buy our own. We'd accepted the fact that we would be living in apartments forever, and now here we were, actually looking at houses to buy. Again, it was literally 'a-dream-come-true.'

My son was going into high school as a freshman and my daughter would be entering middle school. It was the perfect time to move. Our main concern was the school district that our kids would be enrolling into, and we found a school district that was rated highly. So after going to a bunch of open houses, we found the perfect bi-level and moved ourselves from our apartment in Staten Island to our new home in June of 1991. It was about 30 minutes northwest of my school, and Chris had no problem finding a new nursing position nearby.

Sometimes the challenges we face in our lives
can teach us lessons that can't be found in a book or at school.

LARRY

After spending the entire summer moving, painting, decorating and making our new home as perfect as we could, I was amazed at how quickly Labor Day came upon us. And before I knew it we were all back at school. I was surprisingly happy to be back and looking forward to meeting my incoming freshmen.

All the concerns that came with my first year of teaching had evaporated as I sat in the office of my shop, reviewing the new roster, the same as I had done the previous year. Now I had three separate shop periods, each two hours long. The students enrolled in the first class in the morning, like Joshua, had been in the shop last year. The second period held Freshman who were in the shop for the first time, while the afternoon group were graduating Seniors.

Larry Santamaria was in the middle shop. When I first met Larry, the students were all calling him 'Snaggletooth'. He had a wonderful attitude and was always happy and smiling, but you could not help but notice that he seemed to have entirely too many teeth in his mouth.

For a bully he was the perfect victim: a shy, skinny, Hispanic 14-year-old kid with a thick accent and a mouth full of way too many teeth. The bullies in the school were drawn to him like bees to honey. Which lasted in my class for about two seconds before I put a complete stop to it. I have never allowed any bullying in my classes, and it is something that I will never tolerate. I do believe that Larry had never been supported, in that respect, by his prior teachers. But that was before he met me.

LARRY'S DYSLEXIA

All the students in my classes were classified with various learning disabilities. But Larry was my first student who was also enrolled in the English as a Second Language (ESL) program. Considering he'd only been in the country for four years, I was impressed with his fluency in English.

My second lesson plan that year was the payroll program. We worked on our paychecks every Friday and it was one lesson that my students loved, for the obvious reasons. But they were also learning employability, math and writing skills. I always reviewed their paycheck for accuracy in arithmetic, handwriting, legibility, etc. A month after instituting our payroll lesson, I noticed that Larry's checks were always wrong, and always in the same curious way. His numbers and letters were frequently transposed. I looked over other projects that he had handed in and found the same transposed numbers and letters.

It was not uncommon to have the IEP's of incoming freshmen delayed from their middle school. So, I went to the office to see if Larry's IEP had arrived, and was pleasantly surprised to find that it had. I strongly suspected that he had dyslexia, but when I reviewed the document I was surprised that he had not been diagnosed with that learning disability. I also realized that he may not have been diagnosed, because he was not fluent in English. His dyslexia may have been masked due to his struggle with learning English as his second language.

I went to Larry's guidance counselor to voice my concerns and met his English teacher in the office who was just preparing to have him tested. Our observations were validated when his diagnostic tests revealed that he was indeed dyslexic. He was then scheduled to work with the learning consultant.

Larry was a quick learner and took to the retail business easily. He would always ask me in-depth and appropriate questions about the functioning of a supermarket. I knew he would do well and I thoroughly enjoyed his growth - not only intellectually, and vocationally, but physically as well. In four years he grew from a 105 pound, 5' 6" kid to a strapping six foot 190 pounds. When he graduated and I shook his hand, I smiled to myself, recognizing that I now had to look up at him.

In his senior year, I had gotten him a job at his local ShopRite, whose manager called to thank me for the referral and to ask if I had any other students like Larry, because he would hire them, sight unseen.

The school's graduation parties were always held in the cafeteria and I wanted to congratulate him and his family on winning the 'Student of the Year' award in my shop. He threw his arms around me and with a big hug, said to his mother, father and uncle that I was the man who taught him everything he knew. Of course, what normally happens in school is that you lose track of the students that you'd had, the good ones, the bad ones and the wonderful ones like Larry. But happily, in this case, I would one day meet him again.

~ ~ ~

The day before Christmas of my second year of teaching was a scheduled half day. Before the end of the school day, Larry came into my office, his normal smiling self. He was carrying a gift box which he had clearly wrapped himself, and the excitement he exhibited over the gift corroborated that assumption.

"Mr. G… I want to thank you for everything you do for me," he said with his face turning a little red. "I went to the store with my dad and we picked this out for you. We hope you like it." He awkwardly handed the box to me. I asked if he wanted me to open it, and he enthusiastically said, "Yes!"

I laughed as I tried to remove the half pound of scotch tape from the wrapping, and opened the box to reveal a tie. I took it out of the box and laughed even louder as Larry proudly beamed at my happiness over his gift. I quickly removed the tie I was wearing, folded it, and before I put my gift around my neck to tie it, I examined this precious gift thoroughly. In Christmas colors, my tie had a Santa Claus standing in front of a Christmas tree, with a bag full of toys, drinking a bottle of Coca-Cola. "I absolutely LOVE it!" I laughingly bellowed.

"I knew it!" Larry yelled. "*Mi Madre…* I mean, my mother said it's too silly and that I should get a better one, but I told her you would like it because you like to laugh." And he was so right.

"Larry, I don't like it. I LOVE it!" And while shaking his hand, I said, "*Gracias, mi amigo,*" as I walked him to his bus. What he didn't know was that I would wear that same tie, for the entire week before Christmas, over the next 25 years, until I retired in 2017.

DRIVING HOME WITH MY GIFT

As I left school that Christmas Eve afternoon, the sky was grey and gloomy. I knew that as soon as I got home and changed, we would be going to visit my in-laws in Brooklyn for our traditional and delicious Christmas Eve seafood dinner, *The Feast of the Seven Fishes.* And although it was overcast outside, in the car, I could not get the smile from my face. Of course I was happy to have a week's vacation, and was ready for all the fun that the holidays hold for us. But the smile was for so much more.

A few short years before, Christmas had been anything but joyous for me. I worked every single holiday at the supermarket, which made every holiday more draining than joyous. Just think about the people who work retail over the holidays… 'nuf said.

But now all the old negativity of years gone by had disappeared. After becoming a teacher, I was able to truly experience the joys of the holidays, and driving home I realized just how incredibly thankful I had become.

You don't need to be an educator
to understand the difference between good and bad teachers.
The good ones have to pick up the broken
pieces in the wake of the bad ones.

CHILDHOOD DYSLEXIA

The day after Labor Day, in September of 1955, I entered First Grade in a new school, PS 197. Being a very friendly kid, I made many new friends, and although it was somewhat disorienting for me, I just listened to the adults and went along with what we were told to do.

Later in the year, the school nurse came into our classroom for vision testing. A piece of tape was placed on the floor 20 feet from the eyechart she posted on the chalk board. The nurse announced that we would take turns reading the letters from the line.

From my desk in the very front of the room, I could read the letters clearly, but I knew that I needed to check if I could read them from a distance. On my own, I walked to the taped line causally, but when I turned and glanced at the chart, I realized that I could not even read the largest letter from that distance. Not wanting to embarrass myself, I formulated a plan. My seat was right in front of the eye chart, so I simply listened to and read along with the other children reciting the letters until I memorized the entire chart right down to the smallest line.

Again, not wanting to be embarrassed, I proceeded to read each line I had memorized and it was determined through that test that I had 20/20 vision, when in fact my vision was closer to 20/200. What my eyes saw at 20 feet, a normal eye could see at 200 feet. In other words, I desperately needed glasses. That year, I really struggled with reading but with my undiagnosed myopia, I was unsuccessful.

~ ~ ~

The next summer seemed to come and go quickly as I looked forward to seeing all my friends again after the summer break. And on that first day back at school, I ran to join them in the cafeteria. A teacher came over to me and redirected me to a group of students down the hall, away from all the other kids. Not wanting any undue negative attention and not wanting to be disrespectful, I simply followed her directions.

I had been transferred to the Slow Class.

In the 1950's, children who had learning disabilities were segregated from the 'normal' children, and placed in their own class away from the others. The schools also separated children into 'smart' and 'average' classes. We all knew who the 'smart kids' were simply by looking at which classroom they were assigned. We all knew where we stood in the intelligence hierarchy. The class I was placed into wasn't even given a class ranking. It would seem it was a case of, 'out of sight, out of mind.'

And so, I found myself in a new class in Second Grade. As my old friends were all together in their room, I found myself in a classroom in the back corner of the school with students whose disabilities ranged from mild cognitive impairment to autism and Downs syndrome. Unfortunately, at that time there was no such thing as Special Education, and children in those types of classes were basically warehoused until they were old enough to leave school.

My mother assumed that the school was run by professional educators and after driving me to school, kissing me goodbye and wishing me luck on my first day in Second Grade, she drove home, feeling that I was going to be fine. As a seven-year-old, all I knew was that I was suddenly in a new class with very 'different' kinds of kids.

~ ~ ~

Every Friday in our school we had assembly, which meant that the entire student body dressed for assembly appropriately and sat in the large auditorium to listen to various presentations. The dress code for the boys called for blue slacks (not jeans), white shirt, red tie, black shoes (no sneakers).

On that first Friday of Second Grade, my class, led by our teacher, Mrs. Murphy, walked into the packed auditorium as all the students turned to gawk at us.

Some students laughed and were chastised by their teachers, while some looked away, clearly uncomfortable looking at us. But when some of my old classmates saw me, they began to wave wildly for me to join them.

Now what does a second grader know about decorum in an assembly? I had not seen my friends all summer and as they were waving, smiling and gesturing for me to come over, I did what any seven-year-old would do: I ran over to where my old class was and joined them. I simply assumed that I had been put into the wrong class by mistake. And as we all patted each other on the back, I was asked where I had been, and as I was about to reply I felt a tug on my arm and their teacher - an angry, old, heavy, grey haired woman - grabbed me and forcefully pulled me out of the row.

Again I did what a child my age would do, when being dragged by a stranger: I pulled away from her and tried to get back to my friends. But this woman would have none of it. I was literally dragged down the center aisle of the auditorium, all the while trying to pull away from this woman.

With tears now pouring down my face and my nose running, the teacher angrily placed me on the aisle seat where my current class was sitting. She leaned over me and six inches from my face growled, "Listen to me young man," squeezing my arm tightly, "you will not make a scene in our auditorium again! **Everyone is looking at you!** And we will not hold the presentation up for you. Now you will sit there and be quiet or we will have to call your mother," as she glared at me again while squeezing my arm.

She said just the right thing to get me to comply. It was the *"everyone is looking at you,"* that got my attention. I looked around at the entire student body and realized they were all laughing - at me! I felt every eye on me and realized that I had made a fool of myself. I wanted to run out of the school, but that would have only made them laugh at me all the more. I stopped fighting, and put my head down, avoiding any eye contact with anyone.

So, as that teacher who was now sitting with my friends glared at me, I simply observed how a tear can hang onto the edge of your nose for a while, until another tear joins it and they both fall off to be absorbed by my shirt.

As I sat there avoiding the stare of my tormentor, I pulled inward. I went into my own little world where I was alone. I became that single tear slowly moving down from my eye to the tip of my nose. I would have liked a friend to sit with; to be with. I thought if I had a friend with me I wouldn't feel so alone. I felt that if I had someone to share the pain that I was feeling, it wouldn't hurt as much. Like my singular tear was joined by his friend, and they could both go to the edge of the cliff and jump off together.

But I had no friends near me in that assembly. They were ten rows in front of me, and I dared not even look up, lest that woman call my mother and embarrass me further.

Fortunately, my Second Grade teacher was a motivated, nurturing and dedicated professional who realized that I had been misdiagnosed.

Mrs. Murphy saw that whenever I would look at the chalkboard I squinted. Yet when she gave me her eye exam, using the same chart, I seemed to have 20/20 vision, easily reading the smallest letters. Until she realized that she was looking at the chart along with me as I read the letters. Suddenly she turned to me, asked me to read the chart again, and observed that, although I recited the letters accurately, I was not looking at the chart at all. It was then that she realized what I had done.

The chart was two sided. She had me stand there as she reversed the chart and asked me to read the letters now. I was unable to recognize even the largest letter and when I was 'found out' I couldn't help but cry; having the truth known to all was too humiliating.

My mother was called to school and was informed of my vision issues. No one in my family was aware of it, even though both parents wore glasses. I was tested and was found to not only be severely myopic, but also dyslexic.

After seeing an ophthalmologist and being prescribed a pair of thick glasses, my mother insisted that I must be reevaluated at school. And although I have struggled with dyslexia for my entire life, I was put back into the Second Grade class, with all my friends, and where I truly belonged.

I would love to say that being misdiagnosed had no long lasting negative impact on my life, but there was. I have learned various coping strategies which allow me to be the avid reader (although still, a slow reader) that I am now. They enabled me to graduate college as an art teacher and, years later, to earn a Master's Degree in Special Education from Rutgers University.

~ ~ ~

I am also aware of the irony of the profession I've chosen. I love teaching students with special needs. I see myself in each of them, and feel that this empathy is what makes me a good teacher.

Driving home from work that Christmas Eve 1991, I loosened Larry's Christmas tie and thought of Mrs. Murphy and where I would be now had she not gone out of her way to have me tested.

Half way home, it began to snow. *Wow, we are going to have a white Christmas*, I thought, *Perfect!* I pulled into the garage, shut down the engine, and smiled. *Hmmm*, I thought, *I did for Larry what Mrs. Murphy did for me*. I nodded to myself as I walked into the house and yelled to Chris: "Hey. It looks like we're gonna have a white Christmas! I'll change and be ready to leave in two minutes," and closed the door behind me.

When you realize that a dream you've had, has come to fruition, it's difficult not to put on a pair of 'Rose Colored Glasses'. Unfortunately, you can lose those glasses fairly quickly when reality hits you squarely in the nose.

FIGHTING WINDMILLS

My close connection with my students had contributed to the perception, by some administrators, that I had a tendency to 'rock the boat' entirely too much. I had been called 'Don Quixote' by faculty and administrators alike. If I felt that any student was being bullied or mistreated by anyone - another student, teacher, staff or administrator - I never hesitated, like my friend Don Quixote, to pull out my sword and attack!

Unfortunately, like old Mr. Quixote, I got the same results: attacking windmills and overstepping my job requirements caused me nothing but trouble. Still, if I became aware of a student being unjustly treated by a teacher, I could not help myself; I would pull out my metaphoric sword, and defend him. This idiosyncrasy, of confronting anyone that I believed was toxic to children, had caused me to have less than stellar evaluations, but still never stopped me from standing up for the kids.

TEACHERS WHO SHOULDN'T BE AROUND KIDS

As an educator, I realize the importance of knowing how to teach in the teaching/learning process. The quote, "Those who can, do. Those who can't, teach," really upsets me. Statements like that minimize the importance of great educators in the lives of those who make that declaration. My question to them would be, "Where would you be now, without the help and nurturing of those great instructors in your life?"

We've all experienced great teachers: people who have in depth knowledge of a particular subject, but choose to teach because that is what they truly love to do. We are also aware of those educators who may be equally knowledgeable, but so incompetent at teaching, that their students become resistant to the very subject their teacher loves. When this unfortunate situation arises, a student who could be passionate about a subject would likely be turned off to that subject, solely due to the instructor's inability to teach. But being an ineffectual teacher doesn't mean that this teacher is toxic to his students. Unfortunately, I have witnessed a few teachers who verbally abuse students or impart their biases, bigotry and falsehoods to their students. I would define a teacher like that as *toxic*.

As I have said, I am a teacher who will confront anyone who, in my opinion, does not hold their students' welfare as their prime concern. This has gotten me into trouble with some administrators who would have preferred if I were less confrontational with others.

MR. CONNARD

When I talk about toxic teachers, I don't use that term lightly. One day, one of the worst brought his entire class into my shop.

Mr. Connard was hired that year as a temporary, full-time replacement for a Phys-Ed teacher who left to have her first child. And fortunately for the school, the students, staff and administration, when her pregnancy leave was over, the administration wisely did not rehire him.

Connard was a man who thought that teasing and belittling students and staff was not only acceptable but appreciated by everyone within earshot, in the guise of "just having some fun." I believe he went through his life with a common but rarely diagnosed learning disability known by the acronym PPS or *Peter Pan Syndrome*, having never grown past the maturity level of a middle school adolescent. Although I can jest about him now, there came a time when I found his toxicity anything but funny.

One very warm spring day, in my tenure year, my supermarket shop was swamped with students and staff purchasing drinks and paying with single dollar bills. After three shop periods, the singles were overflowing the register. I had taken a large stack of singles from the first register and was counting out fifty in order to strap them for my daily deposit to the bank. I was standing behind the cashiers, counting the pile of singles, while watching everything that was happening in the store. And as the last of the students for the day were on line, Mr. Connard and his class of twelve students came running into my shop.

Ordinarily, I controlled the bedlam in the store by limiting the number of students in the shop at any given time to three. I had all the students line up in the hallway and let three in, and when one left, I allowed one in. Everyone followed the ShopRite rules, which were posted on a large sign in the hallway, and rule number one was that there was a strict limit of three students in the shop at any given time. Everyone in the school complied. Except, of course, Connard. He wanted his kids back to the gym ASAP and ignored my rules, as he ignored most school rules. So while I was making sure my students were on task, I was forced to keep an eye on his students as well. I did all this, with a large stack of single dollar bills in my hand.

SEEING RED

Seeing another opportunity to be annoying and obnoxious, Connard walked up to me and, raising his voice so all the students would hear, asked, "What are you doing there Gewant, making a Jewish Bankroll?"

His students exploded into laughter! They then started spewing all the racist and anti-Semitic comments they had ever heard, encouraged by Connard's laughter. Instead of stopping them, he made it worse by offering some new slurs that they hadn't heard yet, to which they screamed even louder.

To say 'I saw red' would not come close to how I felt. With my fists and jaw clenched, I got an inch from his nose and growled quietly to him, so no one else heard: "Get the hell out of my shop and never come back in here again, you stupid asshole."

It took every ounce of control I could muster to keep from attacking him, right in my shop, in front of students and staff. It did not matter if I was recorded on the shop cameras knocking him out. I was that infuriated!

"What are you getting so upset about?" he said, mocking me. Minimizing my anger only infuriated me more. "Come on, Gewant. It was only a joke!" However, his sarcastic words and tone showed his true intent.

To which I repeated, "Get out. You and your students are no longer welcome in my shop. If you have a problem with that, call the Principal."

Realizing that I was serious and that he was being forcefully removed, he shouted to his students, "Come on guys... Let's get back to the gym. Nobody in this place has a sense of humor!" He turned and left my shop with his students, just as the dismissal bell rang and my students began to leave.

I noticed how quiet they were as they left the shop. Instead of loudly shouting their goodbyes to me, they clearly saw how upset I was and probably didn't know what to say, so they simply left.

I went into my office, sat and took a breath. I tried to calm myself and understand what had just happened. I knew why I was irritated, but my reaction seemed way over the top. I really wanted to physically attack this fool and it didn't matter if there were students present or not. Granted he was an idiot, but there was more to it.

It would seem that Connard was the first teacher to bring the Don Quixote out in me. He was the first but far from the last. Sitting at my desk, I questioned why Connard had just caused such a reaction in me. So as the last student left the shop and the door clicked shut, I closed my eyes and wondered aloud where that anger had come from.

It's interesting how you can relive your entire life in a split second.

Whether looking back at your childhood through hypnosis or your own recollection, you may come to realize how very powerful memories are at influencing your current state of mind.

BROOKLYN IN THE 50'S

I was born in November of 1949, to a Jewish couple who lived in the Bensonhurst section of Brooklyn, NY. My early years were filled with the joy of my family. My parents, Martin and Charlotte, my grandfather, my baby sister Linnie and I all lived in a two family house owned by the Esposito family. They lived on the first floor and my family lived in the apartment rental on the second floor.

The house we lived in was built in the early 1930's and was typical of homes during that era in Brooklyn. A duplex, brick and mortar, plaster and lath, a small front porch, and large windows overlooking 65th Street.

Usually, there were two owners, one on each side, living in one apartment and renting out the other unit. Sometimes someone owned the entire duplex and rented all four apartments to different families, but in our typical Brooklyn neighborhood, on our typical street, in our typical apartment, the Espositos were the owners of the property and my family and I were their tenants.

OBSERVING DIFFERENCES

I lived in that brick duplex for the first five years of my life. I feel fortunate to have lived in Brooklyn in the early fifties. The neighborhood was like living in the United Nations. Brooklyn was - and still is - a melting pot for immigrants to this country. There are very few places in the world where Jews, Italians, Irish, Asians, Russians etc. can all live in the same neighborhood, peacefully. Observing the differences and similarities between other people and my family began my questioning of long-held stereotypes and prejudice.

My Uncle Bernie, Aunt Clara and Cousin Joyce lived in an apartment house around the corner. My senses were flooded with many new smells, sights and sounds each time I entered their building. The apartment house had marble floors in the entrance and as you walked in, the sound of your footsteps and voices echoed off the thick, plaster walls. We would meet for holidays there and I loved the sensation of entering that building... a microcosm of Brooklyn.

Going up the two flights of stairs to their apartment, I would notice how different the odors were coming from the apartment on the first floor. The smell of Sunday gravy coming from 1B where the D'Napoli family lived made my mouth water. There has always been a debate in Italian households about sauce vs. gravy. In most of the world, Marinara sauce is just that, sauce, but in the Northeast portion of the US, or at least in Brooklyn, Marinara sauce was and always will be called *red gravy*.

As we walked into that wonderful building where so many interesting families lived, I would wonder why upon entering the hallway, my mother turned up her nose. Didn't she find the aromas as appealing as I did? Why did she make that face, which showed contempt and disdain for that family? "Why does she call it gravy," mom would say. "Everyone in America knows it's called Marinara sauce." The D'Napolis seemed so nice to me. My questioning of what I was being taught had just begun.

When their door was open, I always waved at the heavy-set woman who came up to me with such a warm smile. She would call up to my Aunt Clara, in her thick Italian accent, "Clara! You nephews commin' up, but he'sa so tin, I gonna give him some managot, puta some meat onna hiz bones." With a hearty laugh and a loving stroke to the back of my head with her soft hand, I could feel the love from this mother of five. I would ask to go in and play with her son who was my age, but my mother always seemed to have me rush up the stairs.

My family would often get together in Aunt Clara and Uncle Bernie's apartment. Linnie and I would play with our older cousin Joyce who was more like an older sister than a cousin, while my grandfather would watch what he called "that new-fangled contraption" also known as a television. His contempt for anything new did not stop him from sitting and eating peanuts in front of this modern invention, his false teeth clicking away while complaining loudly whenever anyone changed the channel. I would sit on the floor and look around at all of my family instead of the television, until it was time to go home.

My father's business was doing so well that soon we were able to purchase the newest television on the market, which made Dad quite proud. The Espositos, downstairs, had one of the original TVs. It was made of dark maple which was richly detailed, as most of the furniture was in those days. From the rear of their TV, you could see all the wires and tubes which made the picture in the front. Although the box that housed the television was large, the screen itself was only about five inches diagonally. The image was distorted, but it was considerably better than listening to the radio.

JEWISH HOLIDAYS AND MY YOUTH

My father was a big man, who was proud of his Jewish heritage, yet I only recall the family going to temple on the High Holy Days. Mom would make sure my hair was combed perfectly. We would put on our finest clothes and get into our new 1955 Dodge and drive off to temple, about a mile away.

As we were driving, Dad would put on the radio, listening to 57 AM, WMCA, 'The Good Guys'. I thought my Dad was the coolest Dad in the world. We listened to Elvis,

116

Jerry Lee Lewis, Fats Domino and all those new artists singing this new kind of music called Rock and Roll. While some kids' parents were calling this new sound the work of the devil, my Dad was singing along with the radio. I would smell the combination of Old Spice after shave and Chesterfield cigarettes and all I thought was, *When I grow up I want to be just like my ol' man.*

Questioning hypocrisy begins early on this Journey -
The things that your mother teaches you about religion,
sometimes just don't make much sense.

RELIGIOUSLY CONFUSING HYPOCRISIES

Because of Jewish holiday and Sabbath traditions, driving the car on the High Holidays was not allowed. So my mother insisted that my father park the car around the corner, because "How would it look, driving on the High Holy Days?" You can understand my questioning of this confusing situation. We weren't supposed to drive, yet we did. Not to mention that the automobile had only been here for about fifty years, so when was this rule decreed?

Some years we would drive from Brooklyn to Long Island to spend the holiday with Uncle Irving, Aunt June and my three cousins who lived in a brand new suburban development in Oceanside, Long Island. The curving roads were very different from the square shaped 'blocks' of Brooklyn and everything in their neighborhood seemed so new. Even though none of Aunt June's neighbors knew our car - or us for that matter - my mom still insisted that dad park the car around the corner. So, like the religious family we were, we would walk to their house, with a little box of kosher cookies in one hand and a bottle of Kosher Manischewitz wine in the other.

When we got to the door, there was hollering, hugging and kissing, but no one said, "I can't believe it! Irving! Take a look, the Gewants walked all the way from Brooklyn to Long Island! My God, what good Jews! Sit... you all must be exhausted!"

But, no one said anything about it. I supposed that my Long Island relatives assumed that everyone walks on the High Holidays, so we must have started walking a few days ago. The thought that they knew we drove there was very upsetting. How could we be breaking one of God's greatest commandments, especially on the High Holidays? And then lie about it?

That Commandment was just between the Fifth Commandment - 'Thou Shalt Honor Thy Father and Thy Mother' and the Sixth Commandment - 'Thou Shalt Not Kill'. It was the little known, 'Eleventh Commandment' written only for Jewish Brooklynites, which read: 'Thou shalt not drive your 1955 Dodge to Long Island on the Day of Atonement!' It was really Commandment 5 B in the Kabbalah; which, in the King James Version of the bible, was deleted down to ten.

In all seriousness, lying on Yom Kippur was an idea which this kid just couldn't get his head around. As I got older, I just added 'driving on Yom Kippur' to the list of things I had to atone for, which would be the first item on the list for new year.

I knew that lying, in order to adhere to a religious tradition, was more than slightly hypocritical, and this was the beginning of my questioning of all religious rules. A short time later, when I was 6, we moved to our own house in the Marine Park section of Brooklyn. Where, as you recall, I became aware of a new member who joined my family for a few months: the old Jewish man in my room who scared the bajesus out of me.

If God wants us to be happy,
then why is the result of religious decrees so often just the opposite?
Do you think that is the way She (or He) designed it?
But then... Why?

MEETING DREW

After a very tiring moving day, an even more frightening night and a breakfast of Cheerios and milk, I left the house to explore my new neighborhood. I began to walk down the street, just as a boy my age left his own house and began to walk in my direction.

"Hi, I'm Drew. What's your name? Are you new here?" he said as we met midway between our two homes. We were both six years old. I had a sister. He had two sisters and two brothers.

The similarities and differences didn't stop there. We both had two supportive parents, we were both new to the neighborhood, and we had just learned how to ride our blue Schwinn bikes. We liked toys, cap guns, baseball cards, the Yankees, watching TV, playing tag and stickball.

But... I was Jewish and he was an Italian Roman Catholic.

Our similarities well outweighed our differences, and within five minutes, we were the best of friends. Life was so simple then. We spent all our waking hours together that summer. I met his family and he met mine.

One morning in July, Drew excitedly said to me, "I asked my mom and she said if your mom says it's okay, you can eat dinner at my house!" My smile said it all as we turned toward my house and ran at full speed up the steps and into my house, simultaneously pleading with my mother to allow me to eat at Drew's. My mother just nodded and asked me to come into the kitchen for a second.

My mother looked to see that we were alone and proceeded to give me some warm loving motherly advice.

"Now listen," as she pulled my arm to get my full attention. "No elbows on the table. Always say 'yes thank you' or 'no thank you'. Be polite. Don't laugh too hard, you know I hate that forced laugh you have. Drew's family cooks with a lot of spices, so the food is hot. Now, no matter what the food tastes like, don't spit it out. That would be very rude.

"Remember you are representing your whole family... Oh, and another thing. Drew and his family are very nice people, but you know they are not Jewish and they may be doing things differently than we do. So whatever you do, don't embarrass us. Now go and have a good time."

Mom gave me a kiss on my head and sent me off to a new adventure. I felt that I was not only representing my family, but the entire Jewish people.

Not too much pressure for a six-year-old to handle.

DINNER AT DREW'S

Drew's house was just down the block and as we were walking there with permission to eat at his house, I had also been given permission to meet and understand new types of people. I had been to his house often: ringing the doorbell, playing in the garage, using the front fender of his mother's Ford station wagon as first base in our stickball games with the older kids, who always picked Drew and me last. But this was the first time I would be a guest in his home.

I had met Mrs. C often, when calling for Drew at the front door or when she called him in for dinner, but eating in his house with his whole family was something I had never experienced.

After a busy day of playing, Drew opened his front door and walked in with me right behind. He stopped in the vestibule, untied his sneakers and placed them on the floor, announcing, "Mommy! Garry's mom said it's OK for him to eat over. When's Daddy coming home?"

I hadn't even thought of meeting Mr. Costello. It seemed this dinner thing was getting more complicated and frightening by the moment. But Drew had some cool new toys, so I took off my PF Flyers and placed them next to his Keds. When entering their house we always had to take off our shoes, and there were many shoes in the foyer, all in neatly organized pairs, and all in size place.

Drew told me that it seemed that his mom was always cleaning and cooking. I figured, with seven mouths to feed, she had to start the cooking early. I would be invited over for dinner a lot that summer, but this was to be our first dinner together and as with everything else, you always remember the first time.

My fear faded quickly as soon as Mrs. C walked up to me. Smiling, she put her hand on my shoulder and said, "I'm glad you could have dinner with us, Garry." I saw love in the eyes of Drew's mother as she looked at her son and me. It was an accepting, loving look, non-judgmental, non-threatening. Just loving.

We were sitting in his living room, playing with the toys that he said he had gotten for Christmas. The word Christmas was alien to me, but I accepted it at face value. The rich aroma coming from the kitchen was one that I also had never experienced before in my life. When asked by my mother later that evening, I couldn't even describe what the smell was like, other than 'real good'.

As we continued playing with Drew's toys, the large wooden front door opened and Drew's father entered the house. He kicked off his shoes, took off his hat and sports jacket, hanging them up in the foyer closet. I had never met Drew's father before and noticed how he was sweating, wiping his forehead with his sleeve while commenting on the summer heat. I also noticed there was suddenly a lot of commotion going on in the house.

When Mr. C came home from work, everything stopped. All the kids ran to the door to kiss their father hello. Even the baby crawled to him in excitement. As the oldest, Drew was first in line to greet his father. I stood there wondering if I should get in line for a kiss or just stand there looking around awkwardly. I chose the latter. Then Mrs. C kissed her husband on the cheek and informed him with a smile that there would be eight for dinner that night.

The first time you do anything new can be a stressful experience; perhaps that's why we always remember our firsts. When you are six and you are meeting your best friend's father for the first time (and according to your mother, having the fate of your family, along with perhaps, the future of the entire Jewish people riding on your next actions), this dinner had just become much more than simply hanging out with my best friend Drew.

Mr. C bent over, picked up the baby who had crawled over to him, tossed him up in the air and kissed him on the cheek as Mrs. C introduced me to her husband. I just did not know what to expect but anticipated it was not going to be good. He looked stern. He looked down at me and said, "And what's your name?"

"Ga ...Garry (gulp) Sir," trying to smile, but probably looking like I needed to go to the bathroom. His face lightened up as he said, "I hope you're hungry, 'Ga...Garry'... Mom doesn't like to see anyone not finishing their dinner."

With that, a large smile came over his face. I smiled back, realizing that he was not as stern as I had thought. As he turned to go upstairs to change for dinner, he lovingly smacked Mrs. C on the backside. As the pink color in Mrs. C's face blossomed into a bright red blush, I couldn't help but notice the smile on her face also blossoming, and realized that this evening might be fun after all.

Drew and I were listening to the radio in his living room. I found 57 am on the radio dial and *You Ain't Nuthin' But a Hound Dog* came blasting out. "That's Elvis," I said, and explained, "My cousin Joyce says she wants to marry him but my Daddy just laughs and says, 'Someday'..."

"Your dad listens to Rock 'n' Roll?" Drew asked with an amazed look on his face, as his mother started to walk toward us from the kitchen, wiping her hands on her apron.

"Why do they call it 'Rock and Roll'?" I asked his mother.

Her answer was not that elaborate. "I think it's because that Elvis Presley character likes to swing his hips around when he sings. If you ask me, he's kind of cute, but if you don't put on Frank Sinatra or Tony Bennett, Dad is going to have a fit." I found out that although Mrs. C liked Rock 'n' Roll, Mr. Costello liked his old fashioned music and during dinner, there was to be NO Rock 'n' Roll that night.

We were called in to eat at 6:30 sharp. All the kids ran for the kitchen, but once again I was feeling lost. Mr. C was at the head of the table, Drew to his right and as a guest, I sat to Mr. C's left. The girls sat next to me in size place, Drew's brother sat next to him, and his baby brother sat in a high chair next to Mrs. C at the end of the table closer to the oven.

As I sat patiently, albeit a little nervously, waiting for Mr. C to serve the family, I couldn't help but notice the difference between the family traditions during supper in our two homes. There were the obvious differences that I had one sister and a Grandpa, while Drew had two sisters and two brothers. There were also those subtle differences, that weren't really addressed: my family and I were Jewish and Drew and his family were Italian, Roman Catholic. Then, there were the differences that you weren't aware of until they became blatantly obvious.

The smell in the kitchen was one of those differences. I had never experienced an aroma like that before and I was having a very difficult time, not salivating. I picked up the fork in anticipation of putting a taste to the smell, when I felt Drew's father's left hand on my forearm. I looked up. He put his right hand up as if to say 'hold on a minute' as he pointed up to the ceiling, but I still didn't know what he was pointing to, or what was happening. I chose to just observe and not ask the question that was on my mind, which would have been, *You want me to go upstairs?*

Then he said, "Garry, would you like to say Grace?" I felt my face get very hot. Feeling like all eyes were on me, which they were. I didn't know what to do, let alone say. *What? Grace? What's that?* I was learning new things but no one explained what the rules were. *Christmas? Grace?* What I'd thought was going to be a lot of fun, very quickly became very confusing and uncomfortable.

I could have jumped up and hugged Drew's mom when she said, "Daddy, this is the first time Garry is eating over. How about we let him say Grace next time? Drew... could you say Grace, please?"

Looking at Drew's father, I took a deep breath and said my own form of Grace... *Thank you Mrs. C, for saving me from... whatever it was you just saved me from.*

GRACE

"Bless us O Lord, for these thy gifts which we are about to receive from thy bounty, through Christ our Lord, AMEN." I sat for a moment in suspended animation. As Drew began to

123

say these words that he called 'Grace', I experienced a feeling that I had never had before. I began to observe this entire family dinner in super slow motion.

"Bless us O Lord…" *Who was Drew talking to?* I thought. Everyone's head was lowered and their eyes were closed! One of his sisters was squeezing her eyes so tightly that it looked as if she were watching a horror movie. Was there something to be frightened of?

"…For these thy gifts…" *Gifts?… What gifts?… Food, yeah… But gifts?* More confusion.

"…Which we are about to receive…" *Is he talking about the dinner we are about to eat? Why not say: For the food we are gonna eat?* I thought.

"…from thy bounty, through Christ, our Lord…"

Who? What? I was one very confused little Jewish kid…

"AMEN…" *I know that one*, I thought. *That means it's over!*

Suddenly we were back in real time. Everyone opened their eyes, took a breath, smiled, and with some relief, I realized that I could do this Grace thing next time: just close my eyes as tightly as Drew's sister MaryAnn did and wait for the Amen.

As a guest in the house, Mr. C served me first, then Mrs. C, then Drew and down the line to the youngest brother. Finally, Mr. C served himself and sat down; I grabbed my fork and knife. I could not wait another second to taste that ambrosia! Nothing my mother made ever smelled like that, and yet it was only chicken. My mother made chicken four ways: baked with Kellogg's bread crumbs, boiled in chicken soup, broiled and of course, 'take-out'. But what was this chicken Mrs. C was cooking? She called it 'Catch-a-Tory'. I never heard of it, but it could have been called 'Catch-a-little-taste-of-heaven', because it tasted better than it smelled and it smelled amazing!

The summer seemed to fly by and soon it was late August. With the first cool, early pre-autumn breeze, we were both about to enter First Grade.

There are times when you may ask the question
– "Why do bad things happen to good people?" –
The answer may simply be that without bad things,
good people would not have anything to compare good from bad.
The bad makes it possible to know the good,
so that you are able to compare, recognize
and appreciate the good things in life.

FIRST GRADE

Some things happened to our friendship and my life during that first week of First Grade that seemed dark, unexpected, and unfortunately all too common.

Drew and I were involved in our schools during that first week in September of 1955. I went to Public School 197 on Kings Highway and Drew went to Good Shepherd, a Catholic elementary school on Nostrand Ave. Toward the end of that first week, things began to settle down as we got into our school life routine.

On that first Friday, after school, I couldn't wait to get home to see Drew. I figured Drew and I could catch up on old times. We hadn't seen each other for a whole week and in kid years, that's a very long time. I rang the doorbell and I heard someone run to open it. The expression on Drew's face went from glee to sadness. I didn't understand why he looked so sad, but I would find out soon enough.

"Hi Garry," he said, looking down at the floor, and looking as if he had just lost his best friend (a feeling I would soon identify with). "I can't play with you any more. I'm sorry, but the priest told us that you killed Christ." And with a saddened look he began to close the door.

I grabbed the door to stop it from closing. "Killed? Who? What? I didn't kill anyone… I don't even know who Christ is! What are you talking about?" My confusion was overwhelming.

"We learned in school today," he said, "that the Jews killed Christ. So I think that means we can't play anymore," as he sadly closed the door.

I slowly took a step down from his porch and began a long walk home. My head was spinning with all kinds of questions, all of which ended with the feeling of not knowing what I'd done to lose my best friend.

What did he mean, when he said I killed Christ? I remembered that name at the end of the prayer his family would always say before dinner, but I hadn't a clue as to who he was. *Why would a school lie and tell him that his best friend killed somebody?* I thought.

As I walked into my house on the verge of tears, my mother met me at the front door. An expression of concern and confusion showed on her face. "What's wrong, honey?" she asked, taking me by the hand and sitting me on the couch, looking deeply into my eyes.

"Mommy, who's Christ?" I asked. Her expression changed from concern to a knowing, as if she had heard this before. She held my hands and took a deep breath.

"Why do you ask, Ga?" she said, leaning closer to me. I told her what had happened, that Drew had said that his teacher told him that the Jews killed Christ, and that he couldn't play with me any longer. She lifted me up and sat me on her lap as I began to cry.

"Why... can't Drew... be my friend?" I asked her between sobs. "And why is his teacher lying about me, Mommy?"

Mom proceeded to inform me that this had happened to her, too, when she was a child. She explained in very basic terms that Jewish people believe in the same God that Christians do, but that Christians believe that God had a son named Jesus Christ. She went on to say that Jesus Christ had been killed a long time ago, and that many churches have blamed the Jewish people ever since. My mother said that she knew this wasn't fair, but it's one of the reasons that Jews should always stick together.

So I supposed that my best friend Drew couldn't associate with a 'Christ Killer'. The explanation answered why he couldn't be my friend any longer, but the bigger question wasn't answered. Why were his teachers telling lies to Drew that we...that I... killed Christ?

MOM AND PREJUDICE

I went to sleep that night feeling profoundly sad and my confusion was getting worse. I was just falling asleep, the sounds from the television set mixing with the sounds of family members and sounds of Brooklyn. It was late and as I lay in my bed, hands clasped behind my head, I watched the lines of lights dancing on the ceiling, as passing cars drove by. Their headlights reflected through the Venetian blinds, sending parallel lines across the ceiling. As they moved, I would turn my head to see where they were going. These lights moved around my small bedroom like the spotlights on a stage, illuminating my shelf and highlighting my jet fighter and my cowboy hat.

In the distance, the sound of a police siren faded into the night.

The Life of Riley was just going off in my parents' bedroom. This was the time my mother would come into my room, tuck me in and give me a kiss goodnight. But this night was different. It was the first night that her son was going to sleep thinking about, and deeply hurt by, the hypocrisy of religions.

She opened my door and softly sat on the side of the bed.

"Mommy, why can't I be friends with Drew? We both want to be friends. Why can't we? It's not fair!"

She leaned over to stroke my forehead, as she did when I was sick. "I know it's unfair, Garry. It's hard to understand, honey, but we are Jewish and everyone hates the Jews." As she continued, I became even more confused and conflicted by her words, and I can't even recall how the conversation ended.

I do remember lying there in the darkness, analyzing what had transpired that day. I thought to myself: *Mothers don't lie, so she must be telling me the truth. So if mom says that we are Jewish and we are, and that everyone hates the Jews, does that mean that everybody hates me? Even if they're nice to me?*

Does Mrs. D'Napoli from Aunt Clara's apartment building hate me, too?

How could that be?

She seems so nice. And why would anyone hate us anyway?

What did we do to make anyone - everyone hate us?

The questioning was just beginning... Mr. and Mrs. C were also so nice! Inviting me over for dinner, including me in family fun... *They hate me too?*

Another car quietly passed my window, reflecting light across my ceiling that came to rest on my 'Howdy Doody' puppet. Howdy stared down at me from his place on my shelf, with his unblinking puppet eyes. His permanent grin, cowboy hat, boots and freckles always made me smile. But not that night.

Times were so simple then. The good guys wore white cowboy hats and rode horses named Trigger. The lawmen wore shining stars on their chests. The good guys were one of 'us' and it felt good to be on their side, the winning side, the right side. Our side.

The bad guys wore black cowboy hats and had five o'clock shadows. They weren't our kind. They didn't dress the same way we did: the right way. They wore dirty leather vests, sweaty shirts and filthy bandanas on their necks. They didn't look the same way we did: the right way. They didn't act the same way: the right way. It was easy to tell the difference between us and them, good and bad, right and wrong.

But that was on TV and in comic books. I suddenly realized, at that young age, that it wasn't up to you which side you're on, as much as, which side you're put on and which side people think you're on. My child's mind could not resolve this conflict. All I could do was focus on my smiling pal, Howdy Doody, until I felt calm enough to roll over, close my eyes, and quiet my mind.

Hatred, bigotry and intolerance are unnatural to our souls. When young children are put in a room together, they will not even notice their differences. I only wish that this beautiful acceptance of others would never fade. But, I suppose that the inevitable hardness and cynicism that comes with dealing with experiences like the one I'd just had, contribute to bias and the pain it causes throughout the generations.

~ ~ ~

It was Friday night.

Tomorrow would be Saturday.

TV shows and pancakes… but no Drew.

Racism - disguised as a proud cultural identity -
can stay with you for a lifetime,
and sometimes, the lifetimes of your children and grandchildren.

PREJUDICE IS A TWO WAY STREET

"We are Jewish... and everyone hates the Jews... That's why it's so important for us Jews to stick together or else..." And as I grew, Mom was always sure to invoke images of crematoria and starving holocaust survivors in my open mind.

I am living proof that the frightening words instilled into the innocent mind of a child may stay with him forever, even though years later I would question their validity. It was not placed there to direct bias toward others. It was placed there because my mother was frightened for me. She did not want me hurt. But as I grew, I realized that all prejudice is wrong, whether directed toward you, or from you toward others, in misguided self-defense.

~ ~ ~

Back in my office in the shop, I opened my eyes. It had only been a few moments, but my subconscious had clearly revealed to me the source of those strong emotions, triggered by Connard's racist attempt at humor, and reinforced by his students' overjoyed participation in those hateful slurs. I had found the catalyst of my anger.

The filth spewed by Connard - and absorbed by his students - had really touched a nerve. It brought me back to the stories my mother had told me about my parents' childhoods, born into poor immigrant families in 1920's Brooklyn.

~ ~ ~

After dating Chris for three years, I'd told my parents that we were serious and I wanted to marry her. I was caught off guard when they both insisted that it was out of the question and that I should break up with her immediately so I could find myself a 'nice Jewish girl.'

My Dad walked out, but my mother stayed and we had a long conversation about why my parents felt the way they did. She went on to describe to me, in detail, their experiences growing up as outsiders in a Christian world. I learned how bias, directed toward them, shaped their perceptions of themselves and others.

My mother's family emigrated from Russia and my father's from Poland. Their existence in the Old Country was illustrated in the play, Fiddler on the Roof, which was the first Broadway play our parents proudly brought my sister and me to see.

Their families immigrated to the United States in the 1880's and 1890's, decades before WW I, and almost 50 years before the Nazi holocaust began. But it wasn't just their families' terror during Polish and Russian pogroms that caused their xenophobia. That may have been the foundation of their fear and distrust, but it was the anti-Semitism that both my parents personally experienced, in America, that cemented the expectation of rejection as a permanent part of both my parents' psyches.

From the time they first married, in 1902, my maternal grandparents would purchase run-down luncheonettes in Irish or Italian neighborhoods, building them up into profitable businesses. Then they would sell the business and move to a new neighborhood to start again, every 3 to 4 years.

But, each time they moved, Mom and her siblings were the outsiders, and were always the only Jews in their new schools. Mom would steal candy from behind her parents' counter and bring handfuls to school to try to buy friends, but the same children who took her candy would laugh at her "smelly Hebe food" in the cafeteria. They would sit together, enjoying laughter along with their cheese sandwiches on white bread, as she, her little sister, and the few other Jewish children sat alone, dejectedly nibbling their hearty salami on rye with a side of pickles.

And the taunting didn't end in the cafeteria. On the playground or on the way home from school, kids ridiculed her mercilessly and relentlessly. They wagged one palm under their chin, representing a Hasidic beard, and chanted "Sheeny, Sheeny, you killed God," as they chased her and my Aunt June, throwing stones.

My grandmother would reinforce in her young daughter's mind the same thought that Mom would pass down to me, many years later, as she explained why I had just lost my best friend, simply because of my ancestry.

~ ~ ~

Growing up I had heard many stories about my father's childhood, growing up in a more culturally diverse neighborhood. Although there were many more Jewish families where he lived than where my mother had, his experiences in the army during WWII shaded his view of 'other people'. You might assume that it was fighting the Nazis during the war and discovering the horrors of the Holocaust that contributed to his distrust of others. But in fact, it was his treatment by other American GI's who caused his deep seated biases and strong distrust of a Christian's sincerity.

Throughout his teens, my father desperately wanted to assimilate into American culture. And due to his strength and athletic talent, he succeeded. He was so proud that his name was inscribed on the wall with the other football captains of New Utrecht High School, and he always pointed out that he was the first Jewish football captain at his school.

It wasn't until I fell in love with a Catholic girl that he confided that he'd taken the nickname Mutt Gewant in high school, in order to avoid using his Yiddish name, Muttel, that his friends and family called him. He rebelled against his Jewish heritage in order to integrate, but after WWII he was racked with guilt over what he considered turning his back on his people.

Dad often reminded my sister and me of a story I knew quite well: how after enlisting in the army, during basic training in Tennessee, he was held down by five or six other soldiers while one searched his scalp trying to find his 'Jew's horns'. This was commonly believed, due to Michelangelo's famous statue of Moses holding the Ten Commandments. The two small 'horns' on Moses' head were meant to convey the spots where God's lightning bolts had struck him, on Mt. Sinai. This was well known to Christians in the 1500's but between errors in translation and the rise of xenophobia in the US during the war, the truth about Moses' horns was no longer conveyed to American churchgoers of the early 1900's.

Dad relayed to us how he was so incensed by their blatant prejudice, he challenged to fight them all. The realist in him worked out that he would fight all eight men, one at a time, two per night, night after night, to prove that Jews weren't the cowards and weaklings they told him his people were.

By the third night, after having knocked out four of the six and successfully proven his bravery and strength, he was finally respected, and accepted, by the men in his barracks. They slapped him on the back, admitting that he was not a 'typical Jew'. (That description has always irked me. Who in this world is a typical anything? Except for perhaps your typical racist?)

Years later, while he was losing his final battle to lung cancer, my father said to me that he had struggled his whole life with the intolerable pain of feeling he let his parents down by not being as 'religious' as they would have wished for. And as he lay dying in Maimonides Hospital and Chris and I visited him, he waved us both over to him. Even though he lacked energy to speak, he took both of our hands and held them together on his chest: his way of finally accepting Chris and our coming marriage.

~ ~ ~

So, hearing those hateful, hurtful words spoken by Connard and his students stirred my own memories of bigotry, separating me from my best friend in First Grade, and separating me from the girl I loved, if I would capitulate to my parents' demands.

My mother had introduced the fear caused by the prejudice directed to her, toward me. My father reinforced the same bias toward Chris, simply because she was not 'one of us'. And Drew was forbidden to play with me, because I was Jewish and he, Catholic.

My experience with Connard brought out three generations' worth of fear and anger, within my own soul.

~ ~ ~

131

Sitting in the quiet of my office, facing this self-realization, I was overcome with a profound sadness. I wondered how we - all of us - could learn to let the past stay in the past and not affect our present, *our Now*.

I thought of my four generations: my grandparents, my parents, my own generation and the generation of my children.

The sadness came from the thought of countless families being subjected to prejudice, going back hundreds of generations, and the weight of their anger. I shook my head, took a deep breath and thought, *My God, what a day.*

As I took that breath and closed my eyes, preparing to leave school, my subconscious had one more memory for me to digest... this time a hopeful one... about my first friend, Drew...

~ ~ ~

After a very troubling night, trying to understand the inexplicable, I woke up early to the delicious smell of pancakes that my mother knew I loved. I got dressed and went downstairs to the kitchen. I loved my mother's pancakes and mom made a huge stack just for me. As I pulled my chair back, we both heard a knock on the front door. It was Drew. And he was smiling!

I was more than happy to let him in. He began to tell me what had transpired, but he was acting as if our conversation had to be a secret, just as my mother walked into the living room to see who was there. I pleaded to have Drew come up to my room and Mom said, "Of course." And with a smile and a touch to his shoulder, said, "I'm very happy to see you, Drew."

We both ran up the stairs to my room, so no religious eyes could see us or ears hear us. We closed the door and sat on my bed.

"My mom said," Drew began in a hushed whisper, with furtive glances around as if the priest might be hiding around the corner, "that even though we go to church, and we're religious and all, I can still play with you. My mommy told me that sometimes you can do things that our priest says you shouldn't."

He had learned from his mother that if you do a sinful thing (*like play with a Jew*, I thought), there was this thing called 'Confession'. "All you have to do is go into this dark little room in the church. On the other side of the wall, there's a priest," he said, happy about finding this loophole in the law. "He slides open a secret door, kind of like a window, and you tell him all the things you did that God says is wrong. Then you ask for forgiveness and you're forgiven. It's pretty easy, right?" I was so confused that I simply nodded, relieved that Mrs. C had figured a way to get past this terrible hurdle that God had put in front of our friendship.

As we went back downstairs, happy to be best friends again, my mother called us into the kitchen. The table was now set for two, with two tall glasses of ice cold chocolate milk, and two stacks of pancakes, which we both smiled at, and then devoured.

~ ~ ~

Ten years later, on October 28, 1965, The Second Vatican Council passed the 'Declaration on the Relation of Church to Non-Christian Religions Promulgated by His Holiness Pope Paul VI'. This declaration announced that the Pope and council decided to change the view of the Roman Catholic Church. It declared that the Romans killed Christ, not the Jewish people. And in that one moment, One Thousand Nine Hundred and Sixty-Five years of history was changed.

But, back in 1955, the whole issue of who killed Christ faded away with the first snow fall, as Drew and I were friends once again.

*Just when you think your life is perfect just
the way it is and you can finally relax,
things happen to make you consider rocking the apple cart again.*

APPRECIATION AND SYNCHRONICITIES

My definition of *Appreciation* is: thanking those people or the powers that be for giving you the opportunity and assistance in finding joy.

It was 7:30 in the morning on the last Sunday in May, 1996. The house was quiet. Aaron was away at college, Amy was sound asleep in her room, and Chris had just left for work at the hospital. Over a hot cup of coffee, while reading the Sunday paper, I again found myself smiling about how differently my life had turned out, and thinking about how very fortunate I was.

I had just earned a Master's Degree in Vocational Education from Rutgers University, and I was also certified as Teacher of the Handicapped, which would allow me to be a teacher, in an academic classroom, teaching students with learning disabilities. My dream had come true and I was incredibly happy and thankful.

Having completed my Master's Degree, I had the entire summer to myself, with no papers to write, no research to do, no deadlines looming over me, no homework to grade, no lesson plans to write. Honestly, I was starting to get a little bored.

As I was skimming through the Sunday Daily Record, an ad caught my eye. It read: 'Learn to be a HYPNOTHERAPIST.' Memories of my experience with Al came back to me immediately. I recalled what he had said: I should incorporate my experience of being hypnotized, to help others. At the time, I was confused by his meaning, but seeing that ad clarified it for me. I had the time, the finances, and certainly the desire - not to mention the curiosity - to learn more about the process that had saved my life.

I tore the ad out of the paper, picked up the phone, and dialed the number.

I was totally expecting to leave a message, considering it was a Sunday. However the director of the school, Dr. Jamie Feldman, answered the phone. We discussed my experience with hypnosis to quit smoking, and he seemed quite passionate about teaching me the art of hypnosis. After speaking with him, I gave him my name and phone number, and told him that I would talk to my wife about the expenses, etc. Then I took the ad, tossed it into my top dresser drawer, and promptly forgot about it.

Again, the same type of synchronicities that led me to seek a hypnotherapist began anew with regard to becoming one. One week later, I opened my dresser drawer and noticed a crumpled piece of newsprint. My initial thought was to throw it out, but for some reason

I hesitated. It was the ad from the Institute of Hypnotherapy! I put it back, thinking again of what Al had told me. I started to see myself as a hypnotherapist, and I even pictured, in my mind's eye, what my office would look like.

My architectural taste has always leaned toward modern, and yet when I sat down to think about what my office might be like, I pictured it in an old building, certainly not the type I would have chosen. I pictured it as an old Victorian house with dark brocade wallpaper and thick varnished mahogany beams. As I continued picturing my office, I saw it furnished with a desk, an old recliner, a file cabinet and a chair. Everything I would need, based on the furnishings I had observed in Al's office years earlier. Yet Al's office was decorated in a contemporary style, nothing like this Victorian image in my mind. I just shook my head, and made a note to follow up on my initial call to Dr. Feldman. Yet when September came and school started up again, I still hadn't taken that initial step. The ad remained in my drawer.

One September morning, a teacher came into my shop and asked if I could keep our conversation private. And of course I said, yes.

Joseph started out hesitantly. "You know Ga, I'm always bustin' you about how much you must miss smoking, every time I light up in front of you. But I've got to admit - I'm really impressed that after you quit, you never went back." There was sincerity in his voice. "Garry I've tried to quit, like twenty times. You always talk about how hypnosis made it easy. Can you tell me what it was like?"

I was eager to help him, knowing how my life had changed for the better. "You tried to quit twenty times? I must have tried a thousand times to beat that addiction! I don't know how hypnosis works, all I know is that after I left his office, I just didn't think about smoking anymore. It was that easy. And I would do it again in a heartbeat. I know it saved my life."

He asked me if I knew a local hypnotist, so I reached for the Yellow Pages and found Dr. Feldman's number. He called and made an appointment. And to his surprise but not mine, Joseph became an ex-smoker in that one session.

The day he told me that it was successful, I was so proud to have been instrumental in helping him quit. And I realized how much I wanted to continue helping people in that way. That evening, after dinner, I walked into my bedroom, opened my drawer, and once again rummaged through all the junk there. Finding the ad, I walked toward the phone, just as it began ringing. That was before caller ID, so with Dr. Feldman's ad in my hand, I answered the phone.

"Hi, is this Garry? This is Dr. Feldman. I'm calling to thank you for your recommendation." By now, I was becoming increasingly comfortable with these weird coincidences. I knew at that moment that we would be setting up my schedule of hypnosis training, and smiled at the way I was seemingly being pushed to become a hypnotherapist.

I would later understand and accept that the profound coincidences in my life were actually synchronicities. And that being in the flow of synchronistic events energizes you.

It eliminates the energy draining questions like, 'Should I or shouldn't I?' The question then becomes, 'When do we start?'

As Dr. Feldman and I spoke, I got all the information I needed, and realized that this was something that I needed to do. Discussing it for the first time with Chris, she agreed that it could be a good investment in a possible future for me.

Hypnosis classes started in early 1998. Meeting new people and being hypnotized frequently allowed me to enter a very deep meditative state very quickly. And Dr. Feldman would often use me as the subject of various hypnotic techniques because of my ability to enter somnambulism so rapidly.

~ ~ ~

A year later, I graduated as a Certified Hypnotherapist, and registered with the International Certification Board, *The National Guild of Hypnotists,* and three other hypnotherapy certification boards. At graduation, Dr. Feldman strongly suggested that the first thing we must do, as newly certified hypnotherapists, is have professional-looking business cards printed and to buy an ad in our local Yellow Pages. He also recommended that we contact a business lawyer to incorporate as a Limited Liability Company (LLC), which is what I did.

He advised that everyone should start out in the living room of their homes. I knew that would be a problem. Although Chris was supportive of what I was doing, having strangers come in and out of our home at all times of the day or evening just wasn't going to work.

In June of 1999 I became certified as an Advanced Clinical Hypnotherapist, yet I still had not hypnotized a single client. Uncertain as to how to proceed, I signed up for advanced classes at many different schools. Dr. Feldman's methods included traditional hypnosis and advanced Parts Therapy. However, I discovered a different approach when I first studied under Paul Aurand at the Holistic Healing Center of New York. Paul Aurand approaches hypnosis from a metaphysical direction. He offered classes in Therapeutic Touch, Empowered Childbirth, Reiki Healing and even Psychic Development. Although I did not believe in mediumship at that time, it certainly piqued my curiosity.

I have found that life is cyclical and many of our life experiences frequently come full circle

- HYP4LIFE -
IMPROVING YOUR LIFE THROUGH HYPNOTHERAPY

Another year passed, and I thoroughly enjoyed all the additional training I'd had. Recalling back to when I was first hypnotized, I wondered if Al had given me a *post hypnotic suggestion* that I would eventually learn hypnosis. And now I knew I was ready to get started.

I took Jaimie's advice and went to a lawyer to start my LLC. I named it: HYP4LIFE - Improving Your Life Through Hypnotherapy, a long name but both descriptive and accurate. I started my business with a Yellow Page ad, a telephone number, and business cards.

My business was now off the ground, but not yet running. After graduating, and participating in dozens of hypnotherapy in-services and continuing education courses, I still had never hypnotized anyone. Unless you're counting students in the hypnotherapy school, a few friends, and some relatives who just wanted to know how it felt to be hypnotized.

I had spoken to many people at the school about my experiences in the various classes, and my first actual hypnosis client was one of the teachers at school. David was probably 350 pounds, and wanted to be hypnotized for weight loss. Since I had no office yet, I decided that my first professional hypnotherapy session would be held in my shop after classes were over.

The session was proceeding better than I had expected. Dave was a good hypnotic subject who fell deeply into hypnosis and, when I brought him out, he had a new sense of motivation and determination to take back control of his life.

As we left my office, I was surprised at his hyperactive energy level. He was acting as if he'd been given an amphetamine instead of a relaxation suggestion! He was talking a mile a minute about how great he felt and how he was going to get back into shape again.

"Garry!" he said excitedly, "I haven't felt this way since I became a teacher, and gained like 200 pounds. That's when my life spiraled downhill! I was into martial arts before gaining all this weight," pointing to his abdomen. "I almost earned a *Black Belt*! Garry! I was in such great shape then, I could kick so high that my knee would touch my forehead!"

I attempted to calm him down because I was getting a little concerned with his enthusiasm. In all my classes, I'd never seen anyone react to hypnosis like this. Suddenly, Dave insisted on proving to me that he still had it. He directed me to stand against the hallway wall, and proceeded to demonstrate an *Axe Kick*, which is a karate kick where your foot goes over your opponent's head and comes down powerfully onto his shoulder. "Garry, watch this. It's one of the most devastating kicks in Karate!"

So there I was, watching my colleague, fresh from my hypnosis session, in the empty hallway of the school, about to demonstrate his infamous Axe Kick. He squared off, putting both fists tightly clenched at his rather wide hips, took a deep breath, planted his left foot squarely in front of him, bellowed a strong karate shout "HaaaaYaaaahhhh," kicked his right foot straight up in the air and (if it hadn't been for his extended abdomen) he may well have touched his forehead with his knee. But we'll never know.

Because unfortunately - to my horror - and in slow motion - the force and momentum of his right leg flying up pulled his planted left foot right off the ground, and he proceeded to do a somersault that landed him squarely on his back with a loud thud.

Fortunately, Dave's padding kept him from being seriously hurt. Except for his ego, which must have been badly damaged, because he began to avoid me, like the plague, after our first (and last) session.

As you can imagine, after that initial experience as a professional hypnotist, my confidence in my ability to do a hypnotic intervention for weight management was severely diminished.

HOW TO GET HYP4LIFE OFF THE GROUND

How was I going to get HYP4LIFE off the ground? I was positive that I could help so many people in so many ways, but how would people know what I could offer them? It had taken so much of my time and expense already, but there were just so many logistical problems with starting this new business.

I didn't have an office, and even if I found one, without a good client base, how would I be able to pay the rent? I hadn't a clue as to how I could make my new business a success.

When I left the school after that first, rather non-stellar, yet unforgettable, hypnotic intervention, I had to admit that I was lacking one important factor for HYP4LIFE to work...

Clients!

So once again, as I was driving home, I spoke out loud to my father. "Dad, what can I do to get hypnosis clients?" And whether I was speaking to my father, or just voicing my concerns out loud, he came into my mind as he always did.

I saw the image of our dinner table, in our old house, when I was young, and I allowed myself to remember...

Dad would always say to the family, over dinner, that the reason why any business does well is because the owner had a 'gimmick'. "It's not enough to know what you're doing, or who you know," he would tell us. "You have to stand out from the crowd. It's not good enough to be average. If you build a better mouse trap, people will beat a path to your door!"

My father was a natural born story teller. Some fathers refused to relay their wartime experiences, but my dad relished telling (and possibly embellishing) his own. One story that he told us often, was about his trip home at the end of WW II.

Advice is always helpful
but you should never doubt the advice
coming from your own inner advisors.

DAD'S GIMMICK

My father started his business, like many other WWII vets, in the 1940's. And business was doing very well. It was perhaps the most economically active and productive period of time in the history of the United States.

Prior to the war, Dad wasn't happy working for someone else. He knew he wanted to own his own business, but the big question was: What kind of business would it be? A gimmick is all well and good, but you need a business, in order to determine what your gimmick would be.

"Ga," Dad would say as he lit up his Chesterfield, looking up into the smoke that he had just exhaled... "Ya gotta have a gimmick." He would tell me about what his life was like in Brooklyn during the 1930's and early 40's, just before WW II began and enlisting in the Army. He was determined to be his own man when he returned, which meant that he would own his own business.

"Garry, after the war, businesses were blossoming like dandelions on our front lawn in early spring. Lots of GI's were starting businesses to service the needs of the thousands of new families, which were also blossoming like dandelions."

Dad explained how Levitt became a millionaire by building homes for GI's in the suburbs of NYC. "Cape Cods were popping up like mushrooms! He even named towns after himself. Garry, Levittown, Long Island is an example of a gimmick. In a nutshell, Levitt's plan was to build affordable homes in suburbia for all those soldiers returning home to start their families. He saw the potential sales of his affordable homes, but instead of building one house at a time, he built houses on a massive scale. And **then** he worried about selling them." Dad sat back and took a deep drag. "Now **that** was a gimmick."

Although my father saw the potential opportunities in the post war economy, he wasn't a builder and 'Gewantown' just didn't sound quite right anyway.

Dad's business first took shape while sitting on the deck of a troop carrier, on the way home to Brooklyn at the end of WW II. He wanted to get married, make a good living, buy his own house, have kids, and have some 'peace and quiet'. He also knew that if he felt that way, an awful lot of other soldiers returning home felt the same.

He was always ready to fight the competition. Whether as the captain of the New Utrecht High School football team, or as a contestant to see who could eat the most Nathan's hot dogs in Coney Island (he won that competition two years in a row), he was always up for a good fight. He would often speak about his war experiences, but the one I heard most frequently was about the way he started his business with his partner Robert.

He met Robert, another Brooklynite, as they were boarding the ship at the beginning of the war, and they would often speak of what the future held in store for them when they returned to the real world. During the war, these conversations were a way to escape from their perilous situation.

However, discussing an imaginary ideal future during wartime turned into serious conversations during the cruise home. The stress of war was over, replaced by a euphoria brought on by the wonderful possibilities of an unlimited future.

Robert felt as strongly as my father did about being his own boss. But a partnership? Now, that was something that could really work. They could pool their money, resources, skills, knowledge and imagination and continue their friendship if they were business partners.

The longer they discussed the subject, one large problem kept rearing its ugly head. The truth was, that although they knew they wanted to be in business together, neither of them had the slightest idea as to what that business could possibly be. That one little question really stopped the whole plan from coming to fruition, and could put their plan for the future in jeopardy. They pondered the problem with as much concentration as Robert Oppenheimer used when inventing the A-bomb. I can almost hear the way the conversations between Dad and Robert went:

"…We'll each buy a house and a new car, of course, paid for by Da Business…"

"…Yeah, and we'll have a lot of people working for us… Bedda yet, we'll hire our relatives so we can trust them not to mess up Da business…"

"…Right! We wouldn't want anyone taking anything from Da business…"

I'm sure the discussions continued long into the night. I am also sure that it must have ended with, "Yeah, but what the hell is 'Da business' gonna be?"

Their discussions about the future became more serious as the ship drew closer to Brooklyn. I suppose they felt the way I did as a student, after spending four years in college, when graduation was almost upon me. I loved college life, yet I was excited and apprehensive about what the next phase of my life would be.

When Dad had boarded the ship back to Brooklyn, he had a secret stowed in his duffel bag: four bottles of Cognac that he had 'found'. He had a wonderful ability to make friends, and one of his best was the Sergeant in charge of the Officers' Mess. So the night before arriving home, Dad and Robert celebrated the end of the war and the beginning of new opportunities, as the first cork was popped and the Cognac started to flow.

The combination of the brandy and the incredible relief of finally arriving home contributed to their merriment. The two men found a spot on the deck, in a corner by a lifeboat, and finished off two bottles of brandy. As they leaned back against the lifeboat, their nightly conversation was different due to the effect of French Cognac on their sobriety.

"Ya know what, Roberd," Dad said as he took the final swig from his bottle, "Dere's gonna be a lot of us GI's landing on the beaches of Brooklyn pretty damned soon." He giggled a little as he looked at the empty Cognac bottle through slightly crossed eyes. The Cognac was doing its job well, and Dad was not feeling any pain. He put the bottle up to his lips once again and allowed the last few drops to run onto his tongue. After turning the bottle upside down and shaking it, he attempted to throw it overboard, but only succeeded in hitting the edge of the lifeboat and bouncing the empty bottle off the top of Robert's head.

"You... my very inebriated friend... are absolutely right," said Robert, rubbing his head, "but you can't throw a bottle to save your life and you 'almost knocked me block off'," spoken in a very interesting mock accent of half English cockney and half Brooklynese.

"Buddy," said Dad, "if I wanned to hit yer head with dat bottle I couldn't-a done it bedda. And I know I'm feeling priddy good right now, but I'm serious! I think we're gonna miss a great opportunity. Let's figure out what we're gonna do when we're back in the States... back in Brooklyn." Robert nodded in agreement and looked up to see Dad take the bottle by the neck and nonchalantly fling it over his left shoulder, over the railing and into the Atlantic Ocean.

Now, perhaps it was the reaction to the brandy, or the relief felt at the end of war, or a combination of everything, but before long there was a symphony of snores coming from the deck of that troop carrier as the sun started to rise behind the stern of the ship to the East.

"When we get home, I feel sorry for all the women!" Robert said, breaking the morning silence and rubbing the sleep from his eyes.

"Mudders, ya bedda lock up yer daughters, 'cause the boys are a commin' home," Dad said, speaking into the crook of his arm as he lay on his stomach on the hard gray metal deck.

They looked around and realized they were all alone in the salty morning breeze. Usually an MP would have tapped them on the foot with his nightstick long ago to send them back to their berths, but it would seem no one really cared, considering they all had only a few hours left in the service.

"I can't wait to have some of Mom's good cookin'. Then I'm taking the subway to Times Square to look for some broads." Although I never knew my grandmother, dad always said she was a great cook.

Looking at Robert, Dad said, "Can you imagine what's gonna be happenin' when all of us guys get home? I know there is gonna to be a whole lotta people gettin' married. And makin' a whole lotta Whoopee."

"Forget the married part. Just gimme the Whoopee part!" Robert and Dad were the players of their day. They laughed, describing the scene in the States in nine months. "There bedda be enough rooms in the hospitals for all the babies that are gonna to be commin'."

"...Yeah! We're gonna be ass deep in babies!" Dad said as he looked up into the early morning sky. "Can you imagine all those kids?"

"Forget 'ass deep in babies', they're gonna be ass deep in crap and dirty diapers! Phew! What's that smell...?" Robert said, squishing up his face. "Oh, it's the wonderful aroma of all the neighborhood babies making more poop that anyone has ever seen!"

And that's when it hit them.

Dad and Robert looked at each other, jaws agape, eyes wide, with a feeling of a new world opening before them. At the same time, as if it were being said by one voice, they looked into each other's eyes and in harmony screamed...

"DIAPERS!"

The question that had been haunting them since the beginning of the war - the question that had been so elusive - was resolved in that split second.

"We'll start a laundry service for soiled diapers!" (This was well before Pampers.) The ideas came hot and heavy...

"We'll need trucks to make deliveries..."

"Pick up the dirty diapers and deliver a package of clean ones."

"We'll need a warehouse for industrial washers and dryers... And conveyer belts to move it all around."

"And an area to store and package clean diapers..."

"Robert – We can't be the only ones who thought of the future need for a diaper service. We'll have a lot of competition, but you know me. I'm always up for a fight!" Dad said, with a clenched fist. We have to be different from every other diaper service. Something that will make all those new mothers want our diaper service instead of all the others."

And that is how my father created a successful business, using a gimmick. *The Original Monogrammed Diaper Service* began in Brooklyn during the spring of 1947. His idea was to sew a cloth tab on each diaper, with the embroidered initials of each customer's child's name. That way, the mothers knew without doubt that the diapers they received every week had never been on any other baby's 'tush'.

The business did well for my father and Robert for over 20 years, until the advent of Pampers and the AFL-CIO drivers' union strike put them out of business.

~ ~ ~

So, like my father, in order to start my new business, I needed a gimmick. But what could it be?

MY GIMMICK

My problem was the same as everyone who wants to open a new business…

The What, When, Why, How, and Where of starting a new business.

The <u>What</u>, was being a hypnotherapist. I was trained and certified, eager to put my newly gained knowledge and skills to good use.

The <u>When</u>, was now.

The <u>Why</u>, was fairly obvious: it was a good business that I was passionate about.

The <u>How</u>, was through advertising. I had already taken a small ad in a local Yellow Page directory and by printing up flyers which I proceeded to pin up in every store, supermarket, strip mall and wall I could find.

But the <u>Where</u> was my most difficult challenge.

What I did have was the Chicken and the Egg Enigma. I needed an office to hypnotize my clients. But I needed clients to afford an office. So, like my father before me, I needed to think outside the box.

There are times to fight for what you want and need,
and then there are those times to admit defeat.
Then there are those wonderful times
when you find that you have helpers that you never knew you had.

HAVE HYPNOSIS WILL TRAVEL

So, like my father, I needed a gimmick. His was placing his client's baby's monograms on their diapers. But a diaper service is very different than a hypnotherapy service (and I didn't have a Robert to share the ideas or the costs with).

So as I was driving home, I felt my father now showing me an image of us watching TV at home on a Saturday night. Dad would let me stay up late to see Paladin, the gentleman gunfighter, defend the weak and downtrodden on the 1950's television show, *Have Gun, Will Travel*. I realized I had just been shown my future.

My gimmick was: *Have Hypnosis Will Travel*. I would go to people's homes with my hypnosis bag of tricks, and solve all their problems, in the convenience of their own homes. Sounded great! I smiled as I planned how to put my idea into action.

ACCEPTING FAILURE

Knowing what to do and being able to do it can be two very different experiences. The concerns I'd had about not having an office for hypnosis disappeared as I put my plan into motion. *Have Hypnosis Will Travel* was formulated in my mind, and I was even planning to put the quote on my card, just as Paladin's card read: *Have Gun, Will Travel*.

My second client was a referral from Dr. Feldman, who called to let me know he'd given my number to a woman who suffered from a simple phobia of injections.

I knew the best hypnotic technique to use would be to regress her to the first time the fear had presented itself. I would then use a different therapy to reframe her perception of a needle, and hopefully her fear would dissipate. When she called, we made an appointment for me to hypnotize her in the 'comfort and safety of her home', which is what I had advertised in my Yellow Page ad.

When I arrived at her home, I knew I was in big trouble as soon as I pressed the doorbell. Instantly, the chimes were drowned out by the commotion caused by her three Jack Russell Terriers which were all barking, jumping and snarling on the other side of the door. My new client opened the door while talking on her phone, and waved me in to have a seat on the couch.

She left me in her living room for what seemed an eternity. When her three dogs finally stopped barking, they looked at each other and began to encircle me. It felt like I was being sized up for lunch.

Long story short, I tried to hypnotize her but, between the phone ringing, the dogs barking, and the kids quarreling, the result for my second client wasn't even as good as my first, which - as you'll recall - was disastrous.

I was just about ready to say that I'd given hypnotherapy my best shot but the hurdles in making it happen were too many and too difficult to circumvent. I had invested time, money, and a root canal into the dream of having my own business, but I'd been denying the obvious: that without a single client, HYP4LIFE was going to shut its doors before it even had a door to open.

But you know what they say about doors, right? *When one door closes another will open.* I never believed any of that stuff. Not back then. It took some time, but I would soon become a true believer.

By December of 2000, I had accepted the fact that HYP4LIFE was not going to be the success I'd envisioned. As usual, Chris and I attended her Christmas party at the hospital where she'd been working for almost ten years. Although I was enjoying the party, I couldn't shake the sadness and frustration that overcame me whenever the thought of HYP4LIFE crossed my mind.

TRICIA

As we were mingling, I saw Tricia, a massage therapist who worked with Chris at the hospital. A few years before, when my back suddenly went into spasm, Chris had suggested that Tricia could help me. As a massage therapist, she could relax my lower back muscles so that my scheduled chiropractic adjustment would be more effective.

I found that Tricia did more than just relax sore or cramped muscles. She had the ability to lighten your disposition, just by sitting and talking with you. She just seemed to know you. Sometimes she even seemed to know what you were thinking.

From our first appointment, as Tricia worked to eliminate the pain in my back, I started to tell her my whole life story. When I realized I was going on and on, I apologized to her for yacking away. To which she replied, "Don't be silly. I guess I'm the kind of person that people feel comfortable and safe with, 'cause everyone seems to confide in me this easily." And I knew it was true.

Tricia was a hard worker. Along with her position at the hospital, she worked as a part time massage therapist at three different chiropractic offices. As we chatted at the Christmas party, she was excited to tell me that she had finally opened her own office. I told her that I was thrilled for her, but also a little envious. I told her that *Have Hypnosis Will Travel*

146

wasn't working out, and I couldn't afford my own office because I had a total of zero clients. I confessed that although I felt I would be a great hypnotherapist, I was going to have give up my dream.

I didn't understand at the time why Tricia simply smiled as if she had just heard an inside joke.

GIVING YOURSELF TO THE UNIVERSE AND OTHER 'NEW AGE' STUFF

"Garry," she said, "you know, when you give yourself up to the Universe, the Universe always takes care of you."

At that point in my journey, I was certainly not at all into that New Age mindset, so I smiled and asked her to explain what she meant.

"Well, like I said, I have my own office now," she told me. "I was so tired of having to travel between the hospital here and to all the chiropractors' offices, so I 'put it out there' to the Universe that I wanted my own office. Soon synchronicities started to happen for me, and now I have my own office in Netcong! And guess what?" There was that smile again. "There is an extra room in the back that I just use to store a bunch of junk. It would be just perfect for you. Why don't you come over and take a look at it?"

When the party was winding down and everyone was getting their coats, Tricia came over to say goodbye to Chris and me. She looked into my eyes with a broad smile and said, "Garry, always remember this: When one door closes, another one is sure to open."

So on the drive home, I spoke with Chris about Tricia's offer. "That sounds great," she said. "But Ga, even if she's going to give you a very reasonable rent, you don't have a single client. That has been the problem from the beginning, and it's the same problem that anyone who's starting a new business has. We just don't have the money."

Ordinarily, left to my own devices, I can become quite ungrounded. Flights of ideas can carry me away, while my rational thoughts are left far behind. I totally rely upon my wife to be able to ground me (which is wonderful for me, but can be very draining for her).

Chris patiently explained, "You're going to need to pay for rent, advertising, office supplies, furniture, and everything else that goes along with opening a new business. All that costs money. And lots of it! Even if your rent is $200 a month - and that's impossibly low - all your other expenses could add up to more than $700 a month. That's an awful lot of new clients."

My problem has always been that I don't like to listen to rational, intelligent facts, so I did what I usually do: I nodded and decided to see what evolves.

Then it occurred to me what Tricia had said: "When one door closes, another opens." And I began to feel a bit hopeful.

However, I also knew that Chris was right. I didn't have any clients, and I had no money to invest. All I had was a gut feeling of what HYP4LIFE *could* be… But now there might be a way to allow my dream to become that reality.

MY OFFICE

I called Tricia that Saturday and made an appointment to meet at her office at 12 noon. I rang the bell and Tricia opened the door into the waiting room, with a broad smile. "Hi Ga, come on in!" As I entered her office, I was hit with an overwhelming feeling of déjà vu, as if I had been there before.

The house had been built for the original doctor of Netcong in the 1890's. It was a huge old Victorian with thick dark brown mahogany beams and crown moldings. Suddenly I realized why it felt like déjà vu. It wasn't déjà vu at all. I was remembering an event that had occurred before I'd even begun my hypnosis training, when I'd pictured what my office would look like. And this office was exactly the way I'd pictured it! But, how could I have known?

The landlord and his family lived in the home and had brought the entire house back to its original Victorian beauty. Tricia welcomed me, and I entered through the antique varnished mahogany and stained-glass door. We walked into the large waiting room, complete with dark beams and old thick wallpaper. Even the pictures Tricia had on the walls were from the Victorian age, and were hung using the original picture molding to eliminate the need to drive nails into the wood lath and plaster walls.

Tricia's entire office was decorated perfectly for the old Victorian home. As I took it all in, I smiled to myself, realizing that I hadn't experienced déjà vu. Perhaps I'd seen it …psychically.

That might have been the first time it occurred to me that I receive information from a source other than my own senses. Even though I knew I'd been hearing my father's voice for years.

Tricia gave me a tour of her office and showed me the two therapy rooms that were located in the back next to the bathroom. Tricia told me that the small room in the back would be perfect for my office and she was absolutely right. It was perfect!

"Well, what you think?" Trish asked, and I said that I loved the office and that it would be perfect for me. But, my concern was that without any clients, I just couldn't afford it. She motioned me to follow her into the waiting room and said, "Let's sit and discuss it."

As we walked toward the waiting room, I felt some conflicting thoughts. Logically, I realized that she couldn't give me the room for free, and yet I sensed that that was pretty much what was about to happen.

Sure enough, she smiled at me in the way I would become used to, a sort of knowing smile as if she were aware of inside information that I wasn't. "I'm only using this room for storage, so how about this? If you have no clients for the month, you don't owe me anything. But I'll take 25% of whatever you do make as your rent when you do start to get clients. Soon you'll be helping me out with my rent, and you'll have a place to let your business grow." I couldn't believe it. I don't know if I even said anything. I just hugged her. I totally accepted her amazingly gracious offer and thanked her for the opportunity.

I could barely control my excitement! And the very next week I had an office.

I furnished it with the old desk that I had since childhood, which was in my son's room, a used recliner that I'd found for $50, and a file cabinet and rolling chair that was left on the curb with a FREE sign on it.

And the next Saturday, I was sitting, smiling, in my office, wondering what the future had in store for me and HYP4LIFE. I also remembered something else that Tricia had said at that Christmas party. "You know, when you give yourself up to the Universe, the Universe always takes care of you…"

I'd never understood that New Age mumbo-jumbo, until that very moment. Especially after she explained to me what had happened to get both of us to this point.

Tricia had thought that a little extra money toward the rent would be great for her, and she'd been wondering how she could increase her income. At that same moment, I'd been trying to resign myself to the fact that I would have to give up the dream of HYP4LIFE because I could never afford an office. Although this was my first introduction to New Age thinking, it would certainly not be the last.

I was just beginning my journey, and it felt fascinating to me. I wanted to learn more about how this 'Universe' we are living in works, and without knowing it, I also put that up to the Universe. And It answered me!

I continued getting directions in the form of synchronicities, some subtle and some strong enough to make my jaw drop, which would become my physical reaction when I would be in the flow of the Universe.

Even though the pressure of paying rent was eliminated thanks to Tricia's generous offer, I was still anxious to have my first real client in my very own office. Unfortunately, as I sat at my desk, overjoyed with the wonderful progress I was having with my new business, there were dark clouds forming over my perfect, heaven-sent teaching position at the high school.

When you ASS-U-ME, you can lose a client for you and me.

LEARNING THE HARD WAY TO NEVER ASSUME

Now, with my new office cleaned and furnished, I was ready for my first real client. I sat in the recliner to get an impression of what it would feel like to be hypnotized, from the perspective of that first client.

Just then, I heard talking in the waiting room and realized that Tricia's current client was leaving. I walked to the front of the office to say hello. Pamela, a smoker, was Tricia's long time massage client. When Tricia introduced me as a hypnotherapist, Pam said she was very interested in quitting smoking. We made an appointment for the next week, and she became my first real client.

As with any new skill in life, the more you practice and experience, the better you become at that endeavor. Although I unquestionably knew that hypnosis could stop someone from smoking, this would be the first time I would put that belief and the skills I'd learned to the test. I certainly needed a successful hypnosis session to regain the confidence I'd lost on my first two clients.

The following week, I walked Pamela into my office, who commented on how cute it was. Initially, we spoke about the addiction of smoking, about my history of smoking and experience of quitting through hypnotherapy, and about the Part of her that kept her smoking. We spoke for an hour, before I even attempted to hypnotize her. The conversation was quite enjoyable for us both. Pam felt comfortable with me and I felt confident that the skills I'd learned could help her quit. Although I must admit I was somewhat nervous.

I decided to start the hypnotic process with *Progressive Relaxation*, the gold standard induction, to bring a person into the *Trance State*. It is the induction that is used most frequently by new hypnotists. I began the normal hypnosis patter, "…Just take a deep breath, feel all the tension and stress of the day fade away. You can be aware of normal sounds around you. The sounds are unimportant, just let them go…"

I recognized all the indications that she was going into trance. I also knew that in order for her session to be the most effective, I had to bring her into a much deeper level.

I recalled from my training that the deepening method I personally enjoyed the most was called *The Elevator to Relaxation* and decided to use it to deepen Pam's level of hypnosis. In this deepening technique, the person visualizes entering an elevator, on the 10th floor, and with each successive floor the elevator descends, they become more relaxed. The elevator door then opens into a beautiful scene where my client would walk out and find a comfortable place to lie down, where the therapy to quit smoking takes place.

Because I love being on a beach in the summer, I assumed everyone must love the beach in the summer. And so, under hypnosis, I directed Pamela into the *Elevator to Relaxation*, where I directed her to hit the "B" button in order to take her into the basement of relaxation, and into the deepest state of hypnosis.

Unfortunately, as a novice, I did not notice the deep frown line form between her eyebrows, when I mentioned an elevator. Initially, she seemed as if she were experiencing a slight discomfort, which due to my inexperience, I ignored. She did seem to settle down as I directed her to feel the elevator begin its slow and comfortable descent.

I had her feel and see the elevator come to rest in the basement of relaxation. And as the door opened, I had her walk out onto the most perfect beach: turquoise water, blue sky, breathing in the warm, salty summer air and feeling the soft, white, powdery sand between your toes…

Abruptly, her eyes flew open. She had the most troubled look on her face and held her chest as if she were having a heart attack.

"Oh… My… God!" she gasped, "I am petrified of elevators, I hate the heat and I never go to the beach! The feeling of sand under my feet makes me crazy… And BETWEEN MY TOES!!! Ohhh, myyyy Gooddd." She literally flew out of the recliner, grabbed her purse and couldn't get out of my office fast enough.

She ran into the parking lot, with me trying to keep up with her, apologizing all the way to her car, as she jumped in, fired it up and sped away.

As I dejectedly walked back to the office, I took a deep breath and said to myself: *Great Ga, another successful hypnotic intervention! You'd better call and apologize to Tricia, right now! She put her reputation on the line, not to mention that this woman, who just ran out of the office as if her hair was on fire, was Tricia's longtime client! GREAT!* As you can see, I can become very sarcastic when I talk to myself.

Tricia had left for the day, wishing us both luck, so I called her cell phone and you cannot believe how relieved I was when, upon relaying the whole story to her, she began to laugh. Her laughter and support eliminated my concerns and frustrations over my lackluster demonstration of hypnotic skills.

She said that I'd just had an excellent learning experience! And I realized just how right she was. I made a mental note to self: *Never assume with a client.* Tricia then said something to me that, although I acknowledged, I didn't understand until years later.

"Garry, sometimes a really difficult experience, like the one you just had, can be more valuable than a hundred perfect hypnosis sessions. As long as you accept it, as a learning experience, this *Life Lesson* that you just had can be invaluable! However, it is your *Free Will* to either learn from it or not. It's now up to you as to what you will do next. Do you stand right back up, shake yourself off and see what you learned from it? What you did right or wrong, and agree not to do it wrong again? Or do you let it break you? Go and wallow in self-pity and take no responsibility for the cause and its effect?" As always, Tricia was exactly right, as I continued to learn so many things from her.

~ ~ ~

Okay, my third client didn't go exactly as I'd hoped or planned. But what I learned was that there are always silver linings in every rain cloud. As long as you learn from the soaking you receive.

And that would be the first and last time I made an assumption with a client. Another Life Lesson learned.

I soon became very comfortable and confident telling prospective smoking clients that hypnosis absolutely works. I used my personal experience in quitting smoking as a perfect example of a successful hypnotic intervention. And soon I was getting a new smoking client every month or so (although I didn't expect any referrals from Pamela). Tricia still had faith in me and her referrals kept coming in.

Tricia's desire to get a little extra income had come true. I was more than happy to share my fees with her, and my desire to have an office had also come true. Now I had no financial problems, thanks to Tricia, who became my strongest advocate, mentor and close friend.

She told everyone she knew about the hypnotherapist sharing her office, and soon HYP4LIFE was just about at the break-even point. The rent, Yellow Page ads, cards, insurance, and phone bills that had been a concern no longer were. Very soon I started producing a small profit, and a small profit certainly beats being in the red. I was thrilled and thankful that another dream had come true.

~ ~ ~

I graduated from the Institute for Hypnotherapy with a man who, like me, had a daytime job. Mark worked as an I.T. guy in a large corporation, whose hobby was setting up websites. I bought www.HYP4LIFE.com and with his assistance, knowledge and skills, I went live with my own website (even though I was clueless as to how it worked.)

Soon my referrals and website started to bring in more new clients than my Yellow Page ad. Starting generally with smoking referrals, my practice began to open up to include people with phobias, students with sports and artistic performance anxiety, and many more.

**When the truth is an 'Absolute Certainty',
you may discover that the truth about 'The Truth'
is that it is merely an OPINION
that is shared by a majority of people (or only by you).
When EVERYONE in the world knew the truth to be
that the world was flat,
it simply took one rebel to turn the whole world A-ROUND.**

WHAT IS A 'TRUTH'?

Let me digress here for a moment. Let's look at a 'fact'.

The Earth is in an orbit around the Sun. PERIOD: A Fact!

There are nine planets including Earth that orbit our sun, which is a star in the Milky Way Galaxy. PERIOD: A Fact!

Oops… Well, recently 'they' demoted Pluto (not the Disney character, the planet), which no longer is a planet.

It's… errr… something else…

"Ok kids. You know that our science books have been here since your parents were students in our school. Right? Well, let's just disregard the former fact, on page 215, about Pluto being a planet."

Get my point?

Can your perception of reality change when viewed through a different set of eyes? And so, introduce to you a 'newer' truth?

And if this newer truth makes more sense to you, and you feel better and happier with this new belief, then your truth can - and should - change.

And isn't that what education, growth and maturity is all about? The awareness and acceptance of new ideas, which then become: ***new truths***.

Until you realize that you are wearing them,
'Yellow Glasses' can ruin your life.
Removing them will make you see yourself
more clearly than ever before.

JOEL'S YELLOW GLASSES

As I've explained, at this point my hypnosis practice was beginning to expand beyond smokers to include clients who suffered with phobias and unwanted behaviors. I would have many clients, from every walk of life, socio-economic level and age, wanting to gain control over these common fears and behaviors, using hypnotherapy as their method for change.

One such client was a young boy named Joel. I had met him some years earlier, when his mother Jane brought his older brother Zach to me, hoping that hypnotherapy could improve his sports performance.

Zachary loved sports and was a strong, natural athlete. He played both Little League and Pee-Wee Football, and excelled at both. However, his preoccupation with winning held him back in both leagues.

We found out fairly quickly that, along with being a natural athlete, he was an excellent hypnotic subject. After working with his subconscious, I presented the concept to him that it was actually playing the sports that he loved, and winning was secondary. With that understanding and acceptance, Zach excelled in both sports.

Jane's younger son, Joel, came along with his older brother for our sessions and patiently stayed in the waiting room while I worked with Zach. I noticed, at that time, that Joel seemed to be a polite, curious, communicative and clearly very happy child. He was content to sit in the waiting room and kept himself occupied using a coloring book and crayons. He idolized his older brother, and it was obvious to me that Zach loved his baby brother very much.

A few years later, I was surprised when Jane called me for help with her younger son, Joel.

During our phone conversation, she described her anguish for her son. "Garry, I'm really worried. Recently, Joel has developed a very concerning response to criticism, and lately it's been getting worse. In both school and at home, he violently hits himself in the head, whenever he makes a mistake. And he keeps muttering 'Stupid… Stupid…' to himself." She'd taken Joel to see a child psychologist, who tested him and found that Joel's IQ was well above average.

154

"How's his relationship with Zach?" I asked, wondering if sibling rivalry could explain his troubling behavior.

"No, just the opposite. They have a wonderful relationship. Zach's a star athlete, on the varsity football and baseball teams, and Joel just loves to spend time with him. By the way Zach sends his regards and thanks. He said it would be awesome if you could help Joel the way you helped him." She also told me that the only time she sees Joel smiling and happy is when he is with Zach.

We made arrangements for Jane to bring Joel to see me the following week.

~ ~ ~

I was sitting in the waiting room when Jane brought Joel into the office. As they entered, I immediately noticed the change in him from when we'd first met. There was a profound sadness in this young boy's eyes. There was no smile, no eye contact at all. He sat dejectedly, looking down with his hands folded in his lap. When his mother or I asked a question of him, his reply was a simple, quiet yes, no, or just a shrug.

I needed to know more from him to determine the best course of action to take. I needed to determine which *hypnosis script* would be the best to use, in order to help him.

A hypnosis script is a pre-written therapeutic guide, which is read verbatim to a hypnotized person. With more experience, a hypnotherapist can rely less on his scripts, and more on his own intuition, directing the perfect words into the subconscious of his hypnotized client.

As we sat in my waiting room, the discussion continued between Joel, Jane, and me, and I knew that I didn't have a single script that would be appropriate for this problem. Yet, I knew what direction I should take with Joel, a direction that was coming from deep inside my own awareness, and not from a pre-made generic hypnosis script.

By this time, I had been in practice for about eight years and as with anything else, I had become confident in my ability to find an answer to a question by simply allowing it to come to me. It always seemed to work. Answers just seemed to pop into my mind.

I asked Joel why he thought his mother brought him to my office, and he shrugged and said that he didn't know. His shrugs and one word answers were not showing me the direction that I needed to go, so I closed my eyes, took a breath and wondered if I was going to be able to help this very troubled child. I had never had a situation like this before and decided to just go with my gut feeling. I call it "shooting from the 'HYP'." So, as the direction I should take popped into my mind, I just went with it.

"Joel, how about this," I said to him. "Let's play a fun game." And for the first time we made eye contact. "I'm going to say what I think you're thinking, and you just tell me if I'm right or not. OK?" He shrugged again, but this time I was getting more eye contact and a small smile. *YES*, I thought. *A start.*

155

I began a roll play of sorts with him, stating out loud, what I felt was in Joel's mind. What I wasn't aware of, at that time, was that I was actually doing my very first psychic reading, but by calling it a game we both felt much more comfortable. And you can't really be wrong if you are only playing.

So, as the game began, I relayed to Joel what I sensed he was thinking. "My mom is bringing me here, 'cause she thinks I'm stupid and this guy," I said, pointing to myself, "can help me learn better or get smarter or something. Mom tells me she doesn't think I'm stupid but inside, I think she does." I continued along these lines, saying what I felt was in Joel's mind. The more I spoke, the more eye contact I received from Joel, with nods and instead of shrugs I even received a verbal yes or two. The more I described what I sensed was in his thoughts, the more accurate I became.

I know from my research and taking hypnosis in-service classes, that feelings can never be right or wrong. They simply **are**. When you accept facts that are inaccurate and assume that they are correct, the feelings that are caused will ultimately be mistaken, and this contributes to an awful lot of internal conflicts.

I leaned a little closer to him and asked, "Joel, has anyone ever said to you that you shouldn't feel sad or angry or bad?" He nodded with a side glance and a smile to his mom. "They say that because they love you and just want you to be happy. And by the way, anyone who tells you that you shouldn't feel the way you do is very, very wrong."

Both Joel and his mother looked at each other and then at me, as I went on to explain. "Facts, that you believe are true, may not be. They may be very wrong, but the feelings you have from believing those incorrect facts are never wrong. They just simply... **Are**. And, the reason why people, like Mommy and Daddy, tell you that you shouldn't feel the way you do, is because they love you and want you to be happy. They're trying to help you but they don't know how. Remember, your feelings can never be wrong. They are just feelings and you really have no control over them. It would be like me telling you that it shouldn't be raining! If it is raining, it is going to rain. If you feel sad, you are going to be sad. And that's why Mommy brought you to see me, to help you get happy again."

I knew I had to find a way to convince this young boy that his feelings were mistaken. Not wrong, simply mistaken. I considered that this concept may be too heavy for a ten-year-old to grasp. And with a smile to Joel and his mom, a metaphorical light bulb went on over my head.

On the stand next to Joel was a table lamp, and you could clearly see its frosted bulb. Glancing at it, I was hit with an epiphany. "Joel, take a look at that lamp." As he looked, I asked, "What color is the light bulb?"

"White?" he replied hesitantly.

"Right! That bulb IS white! And if I told you it was yellow, would you believe me?" He shook his head, no. "Could there be any way that I could convince you that the bulb is really yellow?" Again he looked at it and shook his head.

"Nope, it's white," he replied, and now he was smiling!

"OK. Now for a little fun… Let's say, I had this pair of really cool yellow sunglasses. Have you ever looked through colored sunglasses?" He nodded, yes. "When you look through these yellow sunglasses, what color will everything appear to be?" I asked him.

"Yellow!" he said, with a smile.

"Right again! Now go along with me here, Joel… If I had you wear these cool yellow sunglasses and you looked at this white light," as I pointed to the lamp, "what color would the light appear to you?" He was already ahead of me, nodding before I finished asking the question.

"Yellow!" His answer was immediate, his confidence evident.

"Right again! But if we know the light is really white, why would it seem yellow to you?"

Again, Joel's face lit up with a big broad smile. "Cause the yellow sunglasses makes **everything** look yellow, so the white bulb would look yellow. Right?"

"Great. Yes, the reason why the light, which is really white, looks yellow to you, is because you have those yellow sunglasses on." I began to move an imaginary pair of sunglasses up and down on my nose.

"Yellow… white… yellow… white… Now, of course you know what color the light really is, but the sunglasses make it look different. You know it's really white, because you are aware that it's the sunglasses that are making it seem yellow to you, right? But is there any question in your mind as to what the REAL color of the light is?"

He shook his head, saying, "The light is really white. It only looks yellow 'cause I put on the glasses."

"So no matter what I tell you, you know it's a white light?" He agreed, but gave me a non-verbal look, which said, *And your point is?*

"Joel, WHAT IF…" I leaned forward to make this point very strong, "you didn't know that you had yellow glasses on? What if they were on your face but you weren't aware of them? What would happen?" He sat up a little straighter and cocked his head to the side with a puzzled look. He didn't understand, so I proceeded to explain just how *yellow glasses* work.

"What would happen if one night, when you were asleep, someone snuck these yellow glasses on you? But these glasses weren't regular glasses. They were custom made for your face so you couldn't feel them at all. They were made of a special plastic that's lighter than a feather, and they're even invisible! Remember, they were put on you when you were sound asleep so you could never know you had them on. You would never know that you were wearing the yellow glasses at all. In the morning, when you woke up and looked at that white light, what color would the light bulb seem to you?"

His response was immediate. "Yellow!"

"So, you understand that the reason for your misunderstanding is because you didn't know that you had the glasses on?" Again he nodded enthusiastically in agreement.

I reaffirmed to Joel and Jane how, although feelings are never wrong, the perception of the facts that create those feelings may be in error. I continued, "At some time in your life, someone put a special pair of sunglasses on you. Instead of making you see yellow, they make you see yourself as being stupid, and no matter what anyone said, you would see **and believe** that you were stupid.

"No matter how much your mom says that she thinks that you're smart, you won't believe her because through those glasses you see yourself as stupid. The same way you would look at a white light and swear it's yellow because you didn't know you had the yellow glasses on."

Joel and his mother both sat and stared at me as they processed this new information. I was pleasantly surprised when Joel spoke first.

"I see what you're talking about," he said, first looking at me and then at his mother. They both smiled. "So even if I am smart, I don't think so because of my stupid glasses, right?"

I smiled and nodded with enthusiasm. And when I said, "You know, Joel, those 'stupid glasses' are really just plain stupid," we all had a good laugh. It was delightful, not only to see him laugh, but to see that he understood.

Jane was once again teary-eyed, but now it was from knowing her son was on the road to healing. I asked my young client, "Are you ready to find out who put these stupid glasses on you?" and he almost jumped out of his chair with anticipation.

Joel and I walked down the hallway from the waiting room to my therapy room, while I thought about which process would be best to help him. I smiled to myself and thought, *This is a no-brainer. Parts Therapy, followed by Regression Therapy, is the only way to go.*

After getting him comfortably situated in the large recliner, I excused myself and went back to the waiting room to invite his mother to come back and listen to what Joel was going to say. I find that parents gain a wonderful insight into their children's perceptions of the world, when they hear their child convey unedited feelings while under hypnosis.

~ ~ ~

I learned Parts Therapy at the Institute of Hypnotherapy, where Dr. Feldman has been one of the pioneers in this advanced hypnotherapeutic technique. Utilizing this procedure, he has been able to unlock the subconscious and remove behaviors which have been found to manifest as physically unwanted behaviors. Parts therapy has had outstanding success in eliminating phobias and deep seated trauma.

From his website, www.partstherapy.com, Dr. Feldman describes Parts Therapy in his advanced classes as:

> *Your subconscious is protective and sets up specific 'parts' to deal with trauma or special needs the individual may require. It is the nature of the mind to be subdivided into an indeterminate number of sub-personalities or 'Parts.' The intention of each part is positive or protective for the individual. There are no 'bad' parts and the goal of Parts Therapy is not to eliminate parts, but instead to help find positive roles or behaviors, also called jobs, for them.*

Joel, like most children, was an excellent hypnotic subject. He went into a very relaxed state quickly, and using Parts Therapy, I began the process to help Joel recall the first time he had exhibited his troubling behavior, in order to assist him on the road to find happiness once again.

I knew that once the root cause of the problem was uncovered, Joel would be able to understand that this unwanted behavior was the result of 'yellow glasses'. It would then become much easier for him to put the experience into a proper perspective, and remove those yellow glasses. Then his subconscious would do the rest, and the problem could actually correct itself.

There are teachers who should teach and there are those who shouldn't even be allowed near children, let alone, teach them. When students are taught by toxic teachers, the lessons they learn may haunt them throughout their entire life.

THE EFFECT OF ANOTHER BAD TEACHER

Joel went into somnambulism very quickly as his mother sat on a folding chair next to her son. I knew that the trauma causing his problem couldn't have been inflicted too long ago. After all, he was only ten years old, and had been a happy child when I'd met him four years ago.

I noticed Jane had anticipated what was going to happen; she had a large wad of tissues clutched tightly into a ball in her hand. The look on her face made it seem as if her son was going in for a serious operation. I smiled at her, and made a hand gesture to relax and breathe, which she did with a smile.

Kids don't need a lot of deepening, so I was able to go directly into Parts Therapy and then Regression Therapy. Again, I used these two therapeutic techniques together to uncover the cause of his problem, and then I could reframe his perception of the trauma. I used these two techniques because they could help Joel take back the control that the memory held over him. And when that traumatic memory loses its power, control shifts back to where it belongs... within Joel.

Now, under hypnosis, I asked Joel about the last time he felt the need to hit himself and he replied in a whisper, "This week in English..."

He was in Fifth Grade, and according to his mom everything in school was fine. She was unaware of any bullying toward him, and his Fifth Grade teacher, Ms. M, was wonderful, new to the profession with the motivation of someone who truly loves her job. Jane had told me that he adored Ms. M and often talked about how nice she was. Ms. M called home frequently and was almost as upset with Joel's self-abusive behavior as his mother was.

I certainly knew that the problem didn't stem from his current teacher, who taught the majority of classes throughout the day. I was trying to narrow down where the problem had begun, and why it was most apparent in English class.

There was such hopelessness in Joel's voice as he described how his current teacher seemed so sad when he hit himself. He even mentioned that it was his fault that Ms. M was so sad. That opinion, feeling responsible for the sadness of others, is common with children in Joel's situation.

"Joel, what part of your body do you feel the urge to hit when you answer a question wrong?" He pointed to his forehead. I told him that I wanted him to focus on the feeling just before he wants hits himself.

We began the regression.

"Joel, did you feel that way in Fourth Grade?" He replied with an affirmative nod. "Third Grade?" Again, an affirmative answer. "How about in Second Grade?"…Quiet, and that silence spoke volumes. He became visibly withdrawn as a tear formed and fell from his eye.

I looked at his mother, who I could see was reviewing his entire life at that moment. She would tell me later that Joel's Second Grade teacher was terrible to the majority of her students, showing favoritism toward some and seemingly taking pleasure in verbally abusing others. She said that she and the parents of Joel's classmates complained to the school's administration frequently about this teacher's methodology. I felt comfortable that I'd found the root cause of Joel's problem. Clearly, his Second Grade teacher should have chosen a different profession.

From the expression on Joel's face I knew that he was very deeply into the memory. "Joel… What are you seeing?" I asked him, but he didn't want to respond.

I saw that he was processing the memory: REM behind his eyelids and an angry expression on his face was a promising emotional change in his demeanor. I say this because in his situation of being a victim of a bully or an abusive teacher - and his own self-directed abuse - anger would be a more appropriate and empowering emotion than his usual sadness.

Quietly he said, "It's Mrs. Tristeza, she's making fun of me again. But never Tommy. Tommy and Billy are always picking on me. They are laughing at me, and every time I look at them I feel like crying." He spoke through clenched teeth, showing even more anger. I was also aware that he was speaking in the present tense. This memory was three years old, being described to me as if it were happening at this very moment, another indication to me that the memory was perceived, not in the past, but quite actively in his present life.

"I don't want Mrs. Tristeza to call home, but she says she will. She says I'm not doing my homework, but I did it all. When she's looking at my notebook she laughs, and that makes Tommy and Billy laugh at me too. And then she looks at them and the three of them laugh at me together. We just took our spelling tests. She is holding up Billy's and Tommy's tests with a big red smiley face and 100% on it… I hope I got 100. But now she is looking at my test. She doesn't say anything but she's looking at it and then she looks right at me and everybody knows whose test it is and she just shakes her head and hits herself on her forehead, like she always does when she's looking at something stupid. I want to cry. So instead I just do what she did and I hit myself in the head and she and Tommy and Billy just keep on laughing at me…"

And so a self-abusive behavior was born. From that moment, every time he felt as if he had answered a question wrong or did anything to prove to himself that he was as stupid as his Second Grade teacher had implied, he would hit himself. Perhaps it was his way to smack the memory out of his head.

It also occurred to me that what he was describing may not be true at all. It was quite possible that Mrs. Tristeza did not treat him the way he was describing, and his memory may be totally different than what actually occurred.

But the 'real' truth doesn't matter in these cases. In order to help Joel, I needed to react as if his perception of that scene was the only truth that mattered. I also realized that, at that moment, Mrs. Tristeza had permanently placed a pair of 'yellow glasses' on Joel.

Change a child's negative perceptions of himself,
and you not only change how he views his life,
you just may change his entire future.

JOEL'S REFRAMING

I knew I had to change his perception of that memory. Up until this point he had accepted the abuse that was being directed toward him. I knew that a person's perceptions form his own personal truth and if Joel believed that he was stupid, no one could change his mind. Neither his Fifth Grade teacher, whom he adored, nor his mother who loved him, nor his protective older brother, nor his hypnocounselor. No one could change his perception of his own inadequacies, except Joel himself.

Joel was still in a deep trance, and once again, I simply allowed the direction I needed to go, to come into my mind. "Joel, I want you to see yourself back in your Second Grade class. Now, I want you to picture Mrs. Tristeza standing there, along with Tommy and Billy, just as you remember it, how you felt so sad, you almost cried."

I looked at Jane and smiled, showing her a strong thumbs-up. It was a good thing that she had those tissues because she was putting them to good use.

~ ~ ~

As I became more experienced in hypnotic intervention with clients like Joel, my connection with people, particularly deeply hypnotized clients, seemed to become stronger. At that early stage in my professional development, I wasn't even thinking that a psychic connection with people might be guiding me. I simply thought that I was becoming a more experienced hypnotherapist.

Years later, I would find that we are all psychic. However, many of us are in denial of the natural intuitive abilities we all have.

I was meditating daily and going into hypnosis frequently, and now I realize why my psychic awareness began to grow quickly. It was the 'opening of my third eye', that had closed when I was six years old. It wasn't that I became more psychic, as much as I began to accept the psychic within me. It would be years before I would be giving psychic and mediumship readings, but at that point, I simply began to understand people, particularly my clients, at a different, deeper level. And this inner knowing of my hypnosis clients began with Joel. I seemed to intuitively know the direction that would work best for him, as well as for the clients I would meet in the future.

I began to listen to this intuitive voice, not analyzing who the voice belonged to, but accepting and benefiting from the path it directed me to. Perhaps it would be more accurate to say that my inner voice was guiding me. We always have the free will to ignore these suggestions. But now, I not only started to listen to them, I began to ask for more directions.

~ ~ ~

In what seemed like a split second, I understood how to reframe his perception that had been haunting him both emotionally and physically with each self-inflicted smack to his head. The same way the image of 'yellow glasses' seemingly popped into my mind, the method in which I could reframe Joel's image of himself also seemed to simply pop up.

The thefreedictionary.com defines **reframing** as:

> ... a technique for altering negative or self-defeating thought patterns by deliberately replacing them with positive, constructive self-talk. For example, athletes might reframe negative self-talk following failure in a competition by telling themselves that it was a useful learning experience.

I find that using a reframing technique during a hypnosis session is an amazingly effective tool for powerful positive change. Because there is no analyzing the memory, while Joel was in the altered state, I was able to easily facilitate a positive change.

I realized that I not only had to change his own perception of that memory, I had to take the power away from his tormenters. The best way to do that is by simply encouraging him to forgive them. A difficult life lesson to say the least, for any of us, and I wondered if this ten-year-old possessed the inner strength to forgive.

Joel was still deeply into that seminal memory. His knowledge of the scene was critical. That moment was when his yellow glasses became firmly attached over his young eyes. **He** did not put those yellow glasses on. They were put onto him by his teacher who, let's hope, didn't realize the extent of the trauma she had inflicted.

"Joel..." I began, "again, I want you to be back in that scene just the way it was. Tommy and Billy are there in the class laughing at you. Mrs. Tristeza has just looked at your test and hit herself in the forehead, shaking her head at you and letting the entire class know how stupid she felt you are... Do you have that memory there?" He nodded. "I want you to notice that the scene is beginning to change...

"You hear the door to the hall open, and everyone in the class turns to look at who is coming in. It's hard for you not to smile! Your big brother Zach walks into the room, looking even bigger than he does now. He is twice as big as Tommy and Billy, who see Zach and their mouths drop open. They realize that he knows they were picking on his little brother. As you look at them, they both look petrified. They can't even look at Zach

164

because of the fear that is within them. They are also afraid to look at you, so they just put their heads down and try to hide.

"Mrs. Tristeza stands up and angrily walks up to Zach, ready to yell at him, ready to tell him to leave the room. But as she does, Zach just stares, looking down into her face.

"Then something very interesting happens. Mrs. Tristeza starts to become smaller! She starts to shrink as you look at her. And she doesn't look angry anymore, as much as she looks sorry. She looks like she's going to cry.

"Zach is now staring down at her and says that he wants her to apologize to you, saying that she must tell you the truth now! That she lied to you!"

The expression on Joel's face showed a combination of confusion and relief, with a subtle smile. I believe he was thoroughly enjoying this scene that I presented to him.

I continued, "Now, Mrs. Tristeza, who is even smaller than you are, comes over to you. She tells you that she's sorry, and you know that she really means it. She says that she didn't want to make you feel stupid, and that it was all her fault. She tells you that she has been teaching too long, and she doesn't notice how kids feel anymore, and now she realizes how very wrong she was. She looks into your eyes, and asks if you can possibly forgive her. She says that you are really smart, and that she was the stupid one to make you feel so sad.

"She then tells you that you started to hit your head because of her, and she is so sorry. She says that you shouldn't blame yourself because of her mistakes. And this time, as she says how sorry she is, you realize that the real reason you smack yourself in the head is to get that memory out!

"Now, Zach goes into the corner of the classroom, where Tommy and Billy are hiding. He grabs them by their collars, lifts them up, and carries them like two little dogs to where you are sitting. He tells them to apologize to you now and, right in front of your eyes, Tommy and Billy begin to look even smaller. At the same time, you feel yourself becoming stronger. They look at you and say that they are sorry for bullying you. Zach lets them go and they run into the corner again, hiding from you."

At that point in the reframing process, I realized the importance of forgiveness. The ability to forgive those who have hurt you is a powerful life lesson. I realized that Tommy, Billy and Mrs. Tristeza have been continuously draining this child's energy; hurting him and still abusing him years after they were no longer in his life. Had his mother not dealt with the problem, he could have become an adult with the same deep seated misperceptions.

"Joel," I said, "Mrs. Tristeza, Tommy and Billy are asking you to forgive them. They have apologized, and they really mean it. They are sorry for what they did to you. But it is up to you to forgive them. You don't have to forget what they did but, by forgiving them, you let the pain evaporate away. You no longer have to think about how they mistreated you. They're sorry, and you no longer have to carry the embarrassment of how they made you feel. Their strength and power are in you now. You have the ability to allow all those memories, all those thoughts, all the pain and all the sadness to leave you. But it is up to you. What would you like to do?"

I noticed that he no longer had that melancholy look on his face. Coming from him now, was a gentle smile, as he completely accepted this new version of what had happened that day. He had accepted the apologies from the three bullies. They were now cowering in the corners of the classroom: tiny, their power removed. Joel was able to forgive them and finally begin to heal.

Although Joel wasn't crying, I couldn't say the same for his mom, who was deeply into my box of Kleenex by this time. But those tears were tears of joy, realizing that her son may have just grown up, before her very eyes.

A week later, I received a call from Jane. "Garry, I waited a week because I wanted to tell you emphatically how much Joel's behavior has changed. Everyone at home and in his school has noticed the incredible change in my baby. My husband, family and I want to tell you how much we appreciate all that you have done for us."

Although it was great to hear and be appreciated for the work that I do, there is an indescribable joy that comes from being a part of changing someone's life for the positive. I knew that I had not only contributed to Joel's happiness, but to the happiness of his family.

And I smiled to myself, when I realized that I also effected those people who would meet Joel in the future, and who would get to know him for who he truly is.

When you become comfortable with your intuitive self,
you also become aware of how your life can change positively
by simply listening to and following
the directions that are being shown to you.

A NEW SMOKING CLIENT

Soon my practice would begin to expand to include weight loss, phobias, and stress management, but at that early time in my practice, smokers were still my bread and butter.

I remember one particular smoking client named Peter, whose session permanently changed the way I would hypnotize smokers in the future. Even on the phone, setting up an appointment, I heard the congestion in his lungs, which reminded me of the horrible rattling in my father's chest as he lay in a coma.

Peter had tried to quit multiple times, but always went back. I knew he really wanted to quit, and as we spoke I realized I didn't need to convince him of the importance of quitting smoking. There was desperation and gloom in his voice. "I know I have to quit, but I keep going back. I guess I just have no will power."

He confided to me about a serious conversation with his cardiologist after his heart attack. Seated at Peter's hospital bedside, his doctor told him how very lucky he was, but advised him to draw up his Last Will and Testament. "My doctor said that if I don't quit smoking immediately, my next heart attack would be my last."

He asked if I could help him, and I assured him that I could. We made an appointment for the next week.

During our one and only session, while I was getting all the information needed to facilitate his behavioral change, Peter had to excuse himself to have another cigarette. He was that addicted. I put on my parka and walked outside with him into the bone-chilling February night. I wanted Peter to realize the stupidity of standing out in the freezing cold, doing something which he no longer wanted to do, and that he knew was going to kill him.

Of course, as an ex-smoker, it was all so obvious to me. I knew exactly how he felt and what he was going through. To Peter, smoking was as much a part of his life as breathing.

And as the wind ripped into my face, memories of a very similar February day, years earlier, came into my mind. It hadn't seemed so stupid to me when I was that smoker; when I chain smoked, driving all the way from Staten Island to Long Island, or when I stood outside the hypnotist's office in Long Island smoking my second and third 'last' cigarette.

I also recalled how, when I met Al, I wanted to go outside for one last cigarette even though I had smoked three 'last' ones before I entered his office.

Then, as I stood there in the freezing night's chill with Peter, I was hit with an epiphany: I realized how important closure is for a smoker. For years, I'd wished I had gone outside just before being hypnotized just so I could say goodbye to my old cherished friend, my Marlboro 100 Lights.

Standing there, I smiled to myself, and realized that I should incorporate the need for closure into my process of smoking cessation. I decided that, from then on, I would have every smoker go outside before I hypnotized them, to give a permanent goodbye kiss to their cigarette. And I started right then and there, with Peter.

Peter took out a cigarette, and I recognized his own ritualistic behavior. As he lit it, he immediately began to cough. It was one of those smoker's coughs that sound like it is coming from the bottom of his lungs as he struggled to bring that thick phlegm up into his throat.

Peter seemed embarrassed as he spit the phlegm into the street. "Sorry, Garry," he muttered.

His embarrassment changed to confusion when I replied, "Don't worry about it. But tell me Peter, do you have another cigarette in that pack?"

I'm sure he was now quite conflicted, thinking that he had just caused the hypnotist, who was supposed to help him quit smoking, fall back into the smoking habit. And, although he seemed hesitant, he pulled out his pack of cigarettes, looked into the box and said that he did have one cigarette left. I smiled at him, because the timing and the situation had worked out perfectly.

"That's great, Peter. But you can put the pack back in your pocket for now," I told him, as the wind began to blow harder and colder. Clearly, we both wanted to go inside, but I knew that the cigarette he had just put out was not enough closure for him. It was simply the continuation of his smoking addiction.

And, as we headed back up the three steps to the waiting room, I said just that. Looking at him before opening the door, I said, "You know the cigarette you just smoked shouldn't be your last one." Now he looked at me with even more confusion as we entered my office, where it was nice and warm, and where I could explain.

As we hung our coats and sat, I continued. "Peter, I want you to actually 'break up' with your cigarettes. I want you to take that last cigarette in your pack, look at it and actually talk to it." Now I'm sure at that point he was questioning, both his decision to work with me, and my sanity, but I continued.

"Like a person in a toxic relationship, you've realized that you have had enough, and need to make the breakup clean and permanent. You'll need to give an explanation to your old friend as to why you must say goodbye. You should thank it for the good times and explain that it isn't *it*, the cigarette. It's you. Tell your cigarette that you need to part ways for your health and for your family."

I continued to describe why having closure for his relationship with cigarettes was so necessary. He looked at me, nodding that he understood.

"Peter, the reason I feel closure is so important is that I still, after all these years, miss not smoking that one last cigarette. Yeah, I smoked a bunch of cigarettes before I went into the office to be hypnotized to quit my habit, but I found that just smoking a bunch of cigarettes isn't closure. Closure is actually telling the last cigarette you smoke that it - that one last cigarette - will end your relationship with them forever.

"I want you to breakup with your cigarette as if it were a girlfriend that intends to kill you. I want you to tell it that this will be the last time you will ever see her." We both smiled, sensing the overly dramatic description of this breakup. But I knew he accepted the reality in what I was asking him to do.

He agreed, and I decided to go outside with him. We put our coats back on and went out to brave those biting February winds one last time.

THE SMOKER'S PATH

Standing in the street, I saw him take out that last cigarette, and quietly say goodbye to it. With a nod, he put the cigarette in his mouth and tried to light it, but the wind kept blowing his lighter out, as if even the weather wanted him to quit. Finally, he lit the last cigarette of his life. I watched as the realization came over him that tobacco addiction was controlling his life and he wanted that control back. I felt the change in him, and I felt honored to have been allowed to be part of that change.

Then, as I observed Peter, what seemed to be a switch was thrown in his energy. When he took that last drag, he looked at the cigarette with total contempt and disgust. I just knew he'd quit. It was the way he dropped it on the floor, stepped on it and twisted his foot. He looked at me and without saying a word, I heard, *That's it! I don't want to do this anymore.* I heard it in my head; no words came from his mouth; they seemed to emanate from him.

Back in my office, we took off our coats and shook off the cold. Peter looked at me and said, "That's it! I'm done with smoking, so let's do whatever it is you do, to make sure I don't smoke any longer."

I led him to the back office where he sat in the recliner as I turned on some relaxing music, and began the hypnosis process.

Peter entered hypnosis quickly and I used the 'Elevator Deepener' to bring him into a deeper state. By this time in my career, I had hypnotized dozens of smokers, but this

169

session was going to be different for me, and it changed the process that I've used with smokers ever since.

As Peter went deeper into hypnosis, I saw a path, in my mind, and images began to unfold before me. I described what I was seeing to him, without any editing on my part. I just trusted that these images were specifically meant for him.

"Peter, picture yourself standing on a path. As you turn around and look backwards, you are looking back into your past."

I used the information from our initial talk to describe his past. "As you look behind you, you see your graduation from high school and college; meeting your girlfriend who would become your wife of 35 years; you see your wedding and the birth of your sons and your daughter and their weddings; you see and feel the joy at the birth of your first grandchild." I saw a smile form on his face, and I knew he was totally in the memory I was presenting. "You see yourself recently, holding that little precious baby girl, looking into her eyes which remind you of how much your granddaughter resembles her mother, your daughter." His smile grew broader.

"Now the scene is changing... You see your cardiologist." I snapped my fingers loudly and the change in his facial expression changed with my snap. "You are back in the hospital after your heart attack. Your cardiologist is talking to you and he is looking very solemn. He is all business. He has your chart in his hands and he is shaking his head and you know what he is about to say before he says it..." I noticed the quivering of his chin as a tear formed between the eyelids of his right eye. "He just said to you that your next heart attack will be your last. That you were very lucky this time, but if you don't quit smoking it's pointless to keep coming to his office. He tells you that you should get your 'Last Will and Testament' in order... You now realize how right he was then and you know that you MUST quit..."

"Those were memories of your past, but now you turn, and look at the path that is directly in front of you. You are standing on this path, now, looking straight into your future.

"Directly in front of you, the road forks, left and right. There are signposts next to each fork in this road. The signpost to the left says, *Continue Smoking*. The signpost to the right says, *Become an EX-Smoker*... Now I would love for you to go down the right road and become an ex-smoker but the choice is, of course, yours. But before you make the decision as to which road you will go down, let's travel down each fork, for a while, to see what the future holds in store for you and your family.

"First, let's go down the left road, that says, *Continue Smoking*.

"As you walk down that path, it seems to be all uphill. It is dark and becoming very cold. You notice how difficult it is to walk, and now you stop.

"Ahead, you see a group of people. As you approach them you see that they are close friends. But they don't see you. You sense how sad they are but you don't understand why.

You notice now that your cousins are there and they are crying and again you don't know why. In the center of this group of people stands your immediate family.

"You see your sons and their wives, your sister and brother-in-law; they are supporting your wife who is crying. She is holding tissues to her face, which are soaking up the tears that are running from her eyes.

"And then you see your daughter and son-in-law. She is holding **her** dear daughter - your grandchild - who is crying uncontrollably. In front of them is a coffin. And as you approach them you see why your family is so very distraught...

"You look into the coffin and see that it is **you** lying there. A shell of who you are now. You try to comfort them but they don't hear you...

"You try to touch them but they don't feel you...

"They are crying because they will miss you, but they are also very angry with you for choosing to continue to smoke when all the time you knew what smoking will do... Kill you."

I hadn't a clue as to where this visualization came from, but I could see the powerful effect it was having on Peter. I didn't think that I had ever read it in any book, or in any of my numerous hypnotic scripts, and I was quite impressed with this creative, inspirational visualization, which seemed to come out of thin air. As I saw the tears falling from his eyes, I knew he was being deeply affected by what he was seeing.

I continued, "You know that this is your future as a smoker. But now let's come back to the fork in the road.

"The signpost on the road to the right, says *Become an EX-Smoker*, so let's go down that road.

"This road is so long it reaches to the horizon, and it is springtime. The trees are in full bloom as are the flowers in the fields to the left of the road. The grass is a perfect green as the birds are flying through a deep blue sky. There are some white clouds, which reflect the setting sun with colors of pink and gold.

"You are walking down this path with your family. Your wife has her arm around your waist. Your sons and their wives and your daughter with her husband walk in front of you. You are holding your sleeping granddaughter, whose arms are around your neck with her head on your shoulder. She feels so protected, safe and comfortable in the arms of her Grandpa, and your love for this little child is almost overwhelming." Peter's expression changed from tears to pure joy, as I continued.

"You have now seen both paths and you know that each is a realistic representation of your two possible futures: one as a smoker and one as an ex-smoker. Again the decision is up to you.

"Your doctor has told you that you must quit smoking, and that your next heart attack will be your last. This decision must be made right now. You know that if you decide to continue smoking, you will not be able to see your granddaughter grow, nor will she have her Grandpa to be there and to play with. She will never know the love of her grandfather. So again, I will ask you…

"Which path do you choose to go down?"

This was the first time I used my *Smoker's Path*. And I've used this process with almost every smoker since then. It has always been quite effective to show the Smoker Part the damage it is inflicting on the physical and emotional well-being of the person in whom it resides. I saw the range of emotions that Peter was going through, from the pain of seeing himself in the coffin and his family grieving his loss, to the joy of feeling the hug of his granddaughter, and ending with the resolution to quit smoking.

Peter's mouth began to slowly and quietly form words. "I want… to go down the right road… the one marked *Become an EX-Smoker.*"

I realized that it wasn't necessary to convince him any longer. I had already convinced his Smoker Part to quit. However, I did want to learn more. So, I continued a little longer.

"I am now addressing myself to Peter's Smoker Part, the Part of Peter that has been smoking for all these years. On the count of three I would like that Part to simply say: *I am here.* One… Two… Three." And, in a raspy voice, his Smoker said, "I… am… here."

Peter's Smoker Part told me that he no longer wanted to be called *a Smoker.* "I am hated here," he said in a very quiet, hoarse voice. "They all hate me." When I asked who hated him, I was intrigued by his answer. He said that all the other Parts hated him!

Although I used Parts therapy for the majority of my clients, I had never heard one say that it was 'hated' by the others. For a second, I didn't know how to proceed. And then again, it just occurred to me in what direction this Part should be taken. It also needed closure.

"Peter, I want you to visualize a conference room. There is a long table and chairs in the center, with doors all around the room. Each room has a sign on its door which describes the Part that resides there. Nod, if you are seeing your conference room." He nodded, as I continued. "The door that says *Smoker* is wide open and your Smoker Part is sitting in a chair at the table."

I had him describe his Smoker Part, along with other various Parts, whom I directed to come out to sit at the table. I had Peter picture his Healthy Part take a seat next to his Smoker Part. I then asked if all the Parts were willing to accept the Smoker and offer him help to stay smoke-free. Each Part was willing, as a new Part asked to join. Peter's new Exercise Part offered to go for walks with the Smoker, if he would stay smoke-free.

I asked Peter if he could accept the offers from the others, and he nodded. I was ready to conclude the session on that note, but decided to make one last suggestion. I asked Peter's

Smoker Part if it would be acceptable to him if I could change his name and the sign on his door to read: *EX-Smoker.*

A broad smile came across Peter's face, as he enthusiastically nodded. After a few more moments I brought Peter out of hypnosis, and his energy had completely shifted. He seemed entirely comfortable considering himself as an ex-smoker now. I felt extremely confident that he would become the ex-smoker he, his wife, his children and granddaughter wanted him to be.

In retrospect, the entire description of the Smoker Path and Conference Room that has become such an effective piece of my smoking cessation process, simply came into my mind when I was trying to find a way to convince Peter's Smoker Part to stop its habit. Again, this experience of having things just come to me began happening more and more frequently. I didn't know where it was coming from then, but the answer would become evident to me over the next few years.

I received an email from Peter, six months later, thanking me for saving his life. One of the alternate responsibilities that I had given his new, EX-Smoker Part was to simply go outside for walks, breathing in the air with the image of exercising his cardiovascular system. He relayed to me that he was no longer smoking and had even lost 10 pounds. His cardiologist had given him a clean bill of health, of course with the warning to make sure he stays the ex-smoker that he has become, and keep the weight down. Peter signed the email with a smiley face and a P.S. that said he gave some of my cards to his cardiologist, who wanted more information about me to give to his patients.

~ ~ ~

It's interesting to view the cycles in your life, once you realize that all facets of life are cyclical. Now, when I do a mediumship reading, one of the symbols I perceive is a rollercoaster. When I see this symbol, I am being shown the cycles in life. And like a roller coaster, sometimes you are moving up with excitement, and then there are those times when you feel like you are going to crash. But just like this rollercoaster analogy, you may come very close to rock bottom, but you never truly crash. And soon, things inevitably begin to move up once again. As fast as you go down, you find yourself on the upswing again. As I said: life is cyclical.

And that was exactly what was happening in my own life at that time. My business, which I feared was about to crash and burn, was now on a very positive upswing. And my school life, which had been on the upswing for so long, was about to turn down (but not burn).

When there is smooth sailing for a long time,
you have to remember that everything changes.
Change is the one constant.
So be prepared for the storms
and realize that they will pass and blue skies will return.

THE CLOSING OF MY PERFECT SUPERMARKET

Fifteen years after being hired for the most perfect job, and five years after my hypnotherapy certification, the Director of Special Education and the Superintendent who had hired me, retired. If I wasn't aware of how supportive these two administrators were to my program, it would become clear as soon as I met their replacements.

The high school had always had a reputation as a school for either Special Education students, or as a dumping ground for the students from other high schools who were at risk of dropping out. The students (and many staff members) felt it was amusing, to refer to our school as "slow tech". And our new Superintendent was determined to raise the reputation of the school.

He wanted to change the enrollment of the school, from having almost 50% of its student enrollment in Special Education, to one with perhaps 15%. Prior to this new administration, there were five vocational shops that were open exclusively to students who were classified. The decision was made to close all the Special Education vocational shops, including the Supermarket Careers Program. Although these changes to the school were met with resistance at first, the change in student enrollment had a very positive effect on the school's state ranking.

Fortunately, a few years after being hired I decided to enroll in the Masters of Vocational Education program at Rutgers University. I received a Master of Education degree in 1996, along with a new teaching certification: 'Teacher of the Handicapped'. This allowed me to teach academic subjects to students with learning disabilities. That decision was quite prophetic. Had I not received my Special Education Certification, I would not have been writing this book. Because I would have lost my teaching position along with my shop (and more than likely, my mind).

Fortunately, my Master's certification allowed me to continue teaching at the school, and I became an in-class support teacher, also known as a co-teacher. This concept of Team Teaching is to have both a subject matter and Special Education teacher in the same room, where classified and regular education students could be enrolled in the same classroom. The purpose of *inclusion classrooms* is to eliminate the stigma of classifying a child as 'Learning Disabled'. Although my responsibility in an inclusive classroom was specifically toward the classified students, I viewed all the students in my classes as my students.

Although I was still teaching, I missed being a vocational instructor in the Supermarket Careers Program. And I felt that my students had been robbed of guaranteed gainful employment. I would come home frustrated and angry and Chris had a wonderful way of putting everything into a proper perspective.

She would ask me, "How did today go?" Which of course started me venting. She would easily bring me back to reality by asking, "Hey... remember Tony? You know you can always go back to your old job..." And that's all it took. I've always said, "My worst day teaching is still better than my best day as an Assistant Manager in a supermarket."

And, of course, if my supermarket shop had not closed, I would not have been a co-teacher with Gloria. I would never have had any of those wonderful synchronistic experiences that I shared with Gloria. I would never have felt, and brought through, her Nana. And Gloria and I wouldn't have been able to help Michael's mother have closure with his passing (as you will remember from Life Lesson # 3).

The year the original SCP closed, I learned the serenity prayer and placed a poster of it on my wall in front of my desk. It reads,

> 'God grant me the serenity to accept the things I cannot change;
> the courage to change the things I can
> and the wisdom to know the difference.'

I memorized those words and read them to myself every day. And I do feel that the wisdom in those words helped me make it through that very difficult time.

~ ~ ~

As a side note... What I was not aware of was that the same administrators whose decisions closed the Supermarket Careers Program, had plans to open a new SCP in the future. And although it did take some years, a brand-new SCP opened. A new building was erected housing a gym and three vocational programs for classified students. Its flagship shop? The new and improved Supermarket Careers Program, designed and opened once again, with the great support of Wakefern Corporation and ShopRite Supermarkets. I had the pleasure in my 25th year of teaching to start from scratch in another brand-new perfect Supermarket Careers Program and, just like my varied occupations, my life as a teacher had come full circle, as I ended my teaching career 15 years later, back in the Supermarket Careers Program that I loved.

*Why is it that sometimes, when you are told by
someone how important you are to them,
instead of feeling wonderful, you feel like crying?*

SAYING GOODBYE CAN BE BITTER-SWEET

During the last week of the last school year for the Supermarket Careers Program, with all my students gone, I kept myself busy by boxing up my mementos from the past fifteen years. Pulling out my chair from my office into the classroom, I sat and observed the shop that had been full of groceries, activity and memories. The old shop was vacant now, except for some broken student desks, bare grocery shelves and three empty and unplugged refrigerator cases.

The silence in the shop was palpable. For the last sixteen years, those three refrigeration cases ran 24 hours a day, 365 days a year. The hum from their compressors was like the pumped in music in a supermarket: no one really listens, it was just there. With the refrigerators shut down, the silence made my old shop feel more like a funeral home… which seemed appropriate for the end of my program.

Just before the end of the day, the door to the parking lot opened and a rather distinguished looking tall Hispanic man came in. I didn't recognize him. I knew he was not a faculty member, but there was a smile on his face as he walked toward me. "May I help you?" I asked him.

His smile got broader as he said, "You don't recognize me, do you Mr. G?"

Instantly I knew who he was. His voice had not changed, but his manner and his professional presentation were unrecognizable. "Oh My God! Larry? How are you? It's been years! You look great!"

Now sixteen years later and in his early thirties, standing with me in the old shop, I could see that Larry had become as successful as I knew he would be. Dressed impeccably in a business suit, with broad shoulders and a sense of confidence that he'd never had in school, you couldn't help but be impressed. But it was his smile that made him unrecognizable to me. His teeth were perfect and it made his smile absolutely brilliant.

"How do you like it?" he said, proudly showing me his smile. "This was the first investment I made when I went into business with my uncle. Yup. No more 'Snaggletooth' for me!"

He gave me his business card, telling me that he'd heard the SCP was closing and he felt he had to come to the old shop to tell me how much he appreciated learning from me.

"I cannot imagine what my life would've been like, if it wasn't for having you as my teacher. You stopped the bullies that always put me down and you built up my confidence. There is no way I can thank you enough for what you did for me."

I felt tears welling up in me. To hide them, I laughed and said, "It was my pleasure to have you in my class. You know Larry," I said, with a playful punch to his broad shoulder, "you also did something for me." He looked at me as I said, "I have worn your Christmas tie, the entire month of December, every year since you gave it to me. I love that soda-drinkin' Santa."

It took everything I had to keep from crying. Crying to feel such appreciation from an old student, and crying for the future Larrys who I wouldn't be able to meet and teach.

To this day, Special Education students of mine from those years are still working in stores, and have union positions with good pay, medical coverage, and benefits, because of the shop I designed and ran with them.

The combining of hypnosis and psychic abilities
makes for a very interesting therapeutic experience.

HYPNOSIS, PHOBIAS and PSYCHIC ABILITIES

As I became a more experienced hypnotherapist, the problems and self-doubt associated with inexperience disappeared. My clients began to ask for my business cards, and soon my referral rate began to be my greatest source of new clients. My practice began to expand, as more and more people called about their desire for the elimination of fears. As the number of clients with phobias increased, I found the process of using hypnosis to help them quite fascinating.

The process for the elimination of a phobia begins as an investigation, of sorts, before I ever introduce hypnosis into the session. It is my opinion that hypnotic intervention for the purpose of eliminating a phobia can produce the most powerfully effective (and at times immediate) positive results.

Phobias, which can manifest as anything from a mild discomfort to full blown panic attacks, dominate the awareness of their victims, who constantly dread and anticipate the emergence of its symptoms. Very often, phobias take on a life of their own: compounding, strengthening and sucking the joy, not only from the person's life, but from the lives of their friends and family.

There are many commonalities between people who suffer with phobias. Their fears are very often life-long, tend to become stronger over the years, and often manifest in other areas of their lives. A phobia makes the person feel hopeless and helpless against its power. Victims often feel alone: that no one can understand how their fear consumes them, and that no one takes their fear seriously. Friends and family may even say insensitive things to them like, "Just deal with it," or "You are such a baby." Often their self-respect is terribly impacted. The phobia itself becomes a tangible entity ever present, ready to pounce and steal away what little joy its victim has left.

THE TERRIBLE TAG TEAM

Perhaps the most debilitating commonality between people suffering with a phobia is the tag team of *Anticipatory Anxiety,* paired with a *Self-Fulfilling Prophesy.* I call them a tag team because that is how they work: in tandem. Anticipatory Anxiety, or the feeling that you may have an attack, sets the stage for it to happen, and unfortunately, it almost always comes true. A Self-Fulfilling Prophesy, or the feeling that you know something will happen and it does, completes the misery, which haunts the life of any phobic person.

You get what your mind conceives, and if you conceive the thought that a panic attack is going to happen, it is almost inevitable.

MARY'S CALL: AN ELEVATOR PHOBIA

Mary called me with a huge concern for her daughter. She said that Michelle was thrilled to have been accepted to the college of her choice, but when she discovered that her room was on the 15th floor of the freshman dorm building, she had a powerful panic attack. Until now, Michelle had been coping with her fear of elevators and enclosed spaces by simply avoiding them. Michelle had sought therapy without success, and Mary was hoping that hypnosis could help her daughter. We made an appointment for the following week.

In the office, my first impression was that Michelle was a sweet 18-year-old who reminded me of my own daughter, who had graduated from the same high school. As I normally do, I began the session with introductions and a brief explanation of how I became involved with hypnosis; how hypnosis works; the conscious and sub-conscious mind; etc.

There are many reasons for chatting at the beginning of each session. It allows people to get comfortable with me, and it allows me to decide which of the hundreds of possible hypnotic interventions might be right for each new client. I allow extra time for what may seem like small talk but is, in fact, critical. It allows everyone to become calm and relaxed before we begin the hypnotherapeutic portion of the session.

I have often said that every time I hypnotize someone, he or she is giving me a compliment. I say this because if clients feel uncomfortable with me, for any reason, they would never allow themselves to relax enough to be hypnotized.

My observation that day was that Michelle was very nervous, which is common for someone anticipating hypnosis for the first time. But there was more. I sensed that she wanted this hypnosis session to work so badly that she just wanted to get right to it, immediately. She obviously did not want to chat at all, and I felt that she regarded all this small talk as unnecessary.

I asked Michelle, "Tell me if my hunch was correct." She nodded, and I continued, "Do you feel that you're okay with hypnosis, but you're so desperate for it to work, that you want to rush right into it and get it done, so that you can be 'cured' of this phobia that's ruining your life?"

"That is exactly how I feel!" she exclaimed. "How did you know?"

If I had to answer her question, I might have said that perhaps I was a psychic (although I didn't believe in that sort of thing, back then).

I smiled and said, "You know, Michelle, I hear that same thing from so many of my clients lately. I don't know how or why, but I just seem to 'read' people well, I guess." I shrugged,

179

looking at her. This seemed to do the trick. She took a deep breath, and as she smiled, I felt her anxiousness dissipate.

I explained that I needed some more information about her before we could get started, and now Michelle was more open to our small talk. She described how the fear of enclosed spaces had impacted her life. She relayed to me that she'd had the opportunity to see the taping of the Tyra Banks TV show in NYC, but as soon as she realized that she would have to take an elevator, she couldn't even enter the building.

Here again, I found that her overwhelming phobia caused annoyance to her friends and embarrassment and frustration for her. Even her boyfriend was losing patience with her now, having to adjust his social life to accommodate her fears.

I asked her if she'd always had this fear, and if anyone else in the family had a similar phobia. She said that her fear was present for as long as she could remember, and Mary recalled that Michelle's father had a similar phobia. With a half-smile, Mary suggested that, "Perhaps Michelle got it from her Dad."

I smiled and explained, "Not in the way you mean, Mary. You see, phobias are not genetic or hereditary. They are formed environmentally. It's not Nature it's Nurture."

Intuitively, I sensed that Michelle's fear had been sparked by a panic attack her father had when Michelle was little, and that his fear had become imprinted in the subconscious of her young mind.

As I was noticing so often, this information just seemed to be there, in my mind. But now I was becoming more aware of **how** this information was coming to me. I was becoming more aware of the source.

But I had a job to do, and decided to think about this 'psychic stuff' later.

I told Michelle, "The important point to remember is that we do not attempt to eliminate the memory. Because we can't. But we **can** change the way you perceive the memory and thus, we can eliminate the emotion, in the form of fear, associated with the thing that is frightening you so badly."

Even though she was 18 years old and considered an adult, I felt that Michelle would be more comfortable having her mother present during the session. So the three of us moved from the waiting room to my office, where Michelle sat on my recliner and her mother sat on a nearby chair.

From my conversation with Michelle and her mother, I decided that a combination of four different techniques would probably be most effective. I would access her Claustrophobic Part by having her enter The Conference Room in her mind, and use Parts Therapy to convince her Claustrophobic Part to talk with me. Once that Part was found, I would use Regression Therapy to go back to the very first time this fearful Part was formed. And finally, I would reframe her perception of the fear.

The session began, with relaxing, New Age-type music playing in the background. I used a standard hypnotic induction, and Michelle allowed herself to relax and enter hypnosis. I deepened her trance state by bringing her to her safe place. Michelle was a great hypnotic subject, going very quickly, easily and deeply into hypnosis.

I found her Claustrophobic Part and had it recall her most recent phobic event. I would use those powerful emotions to bring her back to the very first time she'd experienced this fear. The process of recalling a recent time when her fear was easily recalled, will not reveal the *cause* of the fear. A recent event is referred to as a *Subsequent Sensitizing Event* or SSE, which reinforces the fear and becomes more and more powerful with each panic attack. But that was not where I needed to go. Using a different regression technique, I had Michelle recall the very first time she experienced that fear. This is known as the *Initial Sensitizing Event* or ISE, which sets the foundation for the fear to grow.

Through this process, we determined that Michelle's ISE (the very first time she'd experienced the fear of enclosed places) had occurred in Disneyworld, when she was four years old. This was their first visit to Disneyworld, and the family was unaware that the Haunted Mansion began with such a realistic elevator ride. Had they known, Mary told me later, Michelle's father would never have entered the ride.

Michelle recalled that she was being carried in her father's arms, as they waited to enter The Haunted Mansion. Before getting on the ride, visitors stand in a room that is designed to make people feel as if they are in a large elevator, descending to the basement of the mansion.

As the ride began, it seemed to actually be moving downward. Her father reacted to this pseudo-elevator by having a powerful panic attack, running and screaming out of the ride, blasting past people with his little daughter in his arms.

While in that very deep state of hypnosis, Michelle re-experienced the scene from her 18-year-old vantage point. She realized that this experience was the moment she became claustrophobic. And quietly said as the memory was fresh in her awareness: "I never remembered what happened until this very moment. But I totally remember it now!"

Her father (who was, after all, her protector) had demonstrated that elevators were terrifying and dangerous. Something to desperately fear.

While re-experiencing this dramatic repressed memory, Michelle realized exactly how and why this fear was accepted by her four-year-old self. She also understood that this fear she'd had her entire life, was not truly her own. The knowledge and acceptance that her claustrophobia was caused by her father's fear, and not her own, resulted in an immediate shift in her perception of elevators. It became unnecessary to reframe her perception of the memory because simply re-experiencing it had allowed her to see the truth: It was her father's fear, not her own.

Michelle's hypnosis session had been absolutely perfect!

When the session was over, Mary said, "I remember that awful elevator experience! How could I ever forget my husband's terror, and my little girl's sobs? But I never realized that this was the cause of Michelle's fear! How could I have missed it?"

"Mary," I assured her, "the root cause of almost every phobia usually escapes all of us. Don't feel guilty. If the cause of your daughter's fear was obvious and easily remembered, she wouldn't have developed the phobia in the first place. And that is precisely why hypnosis is such a successful therapy."

Michelle then asked, "Garry, how can it be that I remember that experience so clearly now, but I never did before? It seems so strange that I never even had a clue that it happened."

I explained, "Well, Michelle, that's exactly how a repressed memory works. You were a baby, only four years old. Suddenly your protector - your daddy - demonstrated that being in an elevator was something terrifying. It makes sense that a child would never want to remember being so terrified. Right? So, your four-year-old self repressed the memory. But now, your present 18-year-old self has had the memory brought out of the shadows into your clear, adult awareness."

We discussed the session in greater detail because I wanted to know what concerns Michelle still held. For phobic clients who have just experienced hypnotic intervention, the greatest concern they have is the *What-If's*. Specifically, *What-If* this hypnosis session didn't work? When I brought up the What-If concern, both Mary and Michelle agreed that this was actually their greatest concern.

"Michelle, my response to *What-If's* is that you must challenge yourself, and as quickly as possible." My suggestion was to drive directly to the Rockaway Mall and use every elevator in that mall. "By challenging yourself to go into those elevators, you will gain back the control and confidence that you lost so many years ago. And best of all, you will see that you will never again allow fear to control your life."

When they left my office, I felt absolutely confident that Michelle was going to be fear-free and gain back the control that she so desperately needed.

A week later I received an e-mail from Mary, which read:

> Garry, I have to tell you *about the results of your session with Michelle. There is nothing I can say except, thank you so much! As you suggested, when we left your office, we went to the Rockaway Mall for lunch AND to hopefully ride in an elevator. I knew there was an elevator in the Macy's, so we went directly there. I looked at Michelle and I saw that she wasn't nearly as frightened as she had always been, which made me feel very happy and hopeful. It was soooo good to anticipate the positive change you told us would happen, instead of the fear that we both were so used to.*
>
> *The mall was surprisingly empty when we got there and that made us both feel more relieved. I certainly didn't want to inflict more stress on my daughter*

and as we approached the elevator, the self-doubts, the 'WHAT IF'S', that you mentioned started. I simply hoped that my doubts weren't noticed by Michelle. I smiled at her and she smiled back at me. We stood there for a moment in front of the elevator and then she started to laugh! I thought she was crying, but quickly realized the difference between her crying and laughing! I pressed the button. We heard the elevator begin to move down toward us as we both hugged each other.

Garry, it was magical. The doors opened --- we both stepped in, all the time I'm staring at her, and when the doors closed behind us which in the past would have caused her panic attack, she was actually giddy and laughing!!! We both became convulsed simply going to the second floor. When the doors opened, a woman waiting for the elevator with her little daughter saw us laughing and it was contagious! We left and they walked into the elevator, not knowing why we were laughing so hard, but they just joined in on the laughter. It was incredible. We went to eat in the food court and then went into every single elevator in that mall and guess what? Not only did she have absolutely no fear, she was actually laughing again.

Garry, you not only eliminated her fears but you brought smiles, laughter and joy back to our daughter. My husband and I will never be able to repay you!

When a fear has been with you your whole life,
and takes all the joy in your life away,
you may find that it really hasn't been with you your whole life.
Only the part of your life that you can recall.
And when you finally remember when
and where your joy was taken,
you may just get it back... Instantly!

HOW DO PHOBIAS FORM, ANYWAY?

Are you surprised by Michelle's laughter? Actually, it's not uncommon when someone who has suffered through a lifelong phobia, regains their control. Laughter is the indication that they are aware of the change within them, and they are no longer controlled by fear. The laughter is the release when an overwhelming fear is replaced by a newfound sense of control.

Once again, I will remind you that I am neither a psychologist, social worker, nor a mental health practitioner. I am a hypnotherapist, and in NJ, I am considered a Hypnocounselor. That said, the following is my opinion of how phobias form, derived from my own experiences working with many people with similar fears, along with my research on the subject.

I believe that one of the causal factors to having a phobia resides in the wiring of the human brain and central nervous system. The primitive brain stem and adrenal glands, along with other hard wiring in the body, are responsible for our 'fight-or-flight' response.

This automatic response to a perceived threat was vital for the survival of our primitive ancestors. It remains vital and intact to this day, and is essential for people who live in wild, remote areas or who live in dangerous environments. However, for those of us lucky enough to be living in relative comfort and safety, the innate fight-or-flight response now contributes to many of the phobias we experience in these modern times.

~ ~ ~

Picture this...

The year is 45,000 BC. Homo sapiens (the ancestors of modern day humans) and Neanderthals have lived together since approximately 55,000 BC. And you are a boy, living in a clan of Homo sapiens, in what is now modern day Europe. You and your extended family members are successful hunter/gatherers and your clan is growing. Although the men in your tribe are experienced hunters, you are also prey, hunted by other larger predators. Clearly, your species is not the apex predator of your day.

You are not as large or muscular as your closest relative, the Neanderthals. But you both are considerably smaller and weaker than the other predators at that time, whose eyesight was much more acute than yours, as was their sense of hearing and smell. In fact, as a predator, your clan of Homo sapiens was *physically* unprepared to survive during those primitive times.

But you did have one huge advantage over other competitors for basic survival at that time. And that advantage outweighed large claws and sharp teeth: your brain was much larger and more developed than those of competing predators, including the Neanderthals. This one huge advantage has contributed to the human being becoming the apex predator on the planet today.

The advantage of having a larger brain allowed our ancestors to communicate, reason, analyze, learn and - perhaps most importantly - have the ability to pass that knowledge down to the other members of the clan and in particular, the children.

In order to survive, each clan member must have the ability to react instantly to any threat, and the clan needed to work as one cohesive unit. But how do you 'instantly react'? The clans that had their brains 'wired' with the fight-or-flight response dominated the other clans, and this contributed to their survival as the fittest.

As Darwin hypothesized and then proved, their advanced brain allowed them to survive because they were the fittest to survive. So, as their clan thrived, their genes for a larger, more advanced brain were passed down to their progeny and ultimately to modern day man.

Thus, their advanced brains allowed their clan to prosper. But the knowledge of survival is not instinctive; survival and the skills necessary to survive must be learned... and passed on.

So, there you are in a forest, with your clan, hunting small mammals, picking edible plants, etc. You are five years old, walking behind your mother and older brother. Suddenly a large feline - the ancestor of today's tiger - leaps from the brush and pounces on your older brother, attempting to drag him into the thicket. Your tribe reacts as one!

Instantly, the clan's fight-or-flight response explodes into action. Some of the men throw their spears at the tiger, some throw stones, as other men attempt to save your older brother.

At the same instant, your mother's fight-or-flight instinct is activated and she flees! Without thinking, she grabs you, as the other women grab their small ones, and you all run away from the threat. You are now being carried on your mother's shoulder and you see the horrible scene play out in front of your eyes. The image is burned into your mind: the blood, the screams and the fear, all permanently stored in your five-year-old primitive mind.

Another function of the subconscious mind is to store every memory that you have ever had. Whether these memories are happy or sad, curious or horrifying, these memories are permanently stored in your mind. The subconscious mind also wants to protect you from upsetting memories, by repressing them from your conscious mind, or your awareness. But, if the memory is always there, but repressed, how will you remember to react instantly to the sight of another tiger?

In order for you and your tribe to survive, your subconscious mind will trigger the release of adrenaline and many other hormones into your bloodstream, instantly, when the repressed memory is stimulated. This release will instantly throw you into the fight-or-flight response.

In ancient times it worked perfectly to keep you and your clan safe. So, when a tiger is seen, your tribe reacts immediately, instinctively, and as one fighting unit. But you will never remember **why** you must react the way you do. At that moment, the reason you react to the threat is unimportant. Your reaction is instantaneous and completely necessary for your survival and that of your family.

This response is hard wired in our brains right now, from our distant past. However... what was an invaluable, necessary survival mechanism then, is causing phobias... now.

Keep in mind, that the actual cause (the attack upon a clan member) of the fight-or-flight instinct would have been repressed. The horror of witnessing the killing of a loved one would be blocked from the awareness of the young clan member by the mechanisms of his subconscious. However, the reaction to seeing a tiger (the symbol of the horror) would result in an immediate release of adrenalin, and a critical yet unthinking response.

You may say that the young clan member had a useful, necessary and life-long phobia of tigers, without which, he would become some future tiger's lunch.

In modern society, the threat to our survival is much more complex than those of ancient times. Arguably, our modern day society is more civil than that of primitive times, although there are clans in certain parts of the world today that are still surviving by primitive means. Yet their brains are wired the same as you and me. The human brain has evolved, but still, at its core it retains the same wiring that helped our ancestors survive.

~ ~ ~

Our subconscious has many functions, but not all are yet known to us. The subconscious is a protector, a servant, and the storehouse of knowledge, memories, emotions, habits, and much more. Referring again to the caveman analogy, you can see why the function of repressing the horrific memory, while automatically causing a fight-or-flight reaction, was critical to survival. However, in modern day society, where we are not threatened with life or death situations on a daily basis, the function that was essential to the survival of primitive man is now contributing to the manifestation of phobias.

Generally speaking, phobias can form in two ways. In an adult, a phobia can form after a severe trauma, such as a plane crash, war experience, or a life threatening accident. A phobia that starts due to a traumatic experience is understandable. They are usually

186

temporary and will fade with hypnosis, counseling or time. Phobias formed in childhood, like the one Michelle demonstrated, are much more common, devastating and usually require more intense therapy to eliminate. But once the root cause is uncovered from the depths of the subconscious, healing may be instantaneous.

Sometimes, you learn things at workshops
that you didn't sign up for and never ever expected.

MANY LIVES, MANY MASTERS BY DR. BRIAN WEISS

A few years after I became a certified Hypnotherapist, and had my pain-free root canal, Dr. Goodkin told me that I would need some dental work which would have to be done by a Periodontist. He told me that it might be better not to use hypnosis for this procedure, and that I should use Novocain instead, which is what I decided to do.

I was referred to Dr. David Goteiner and when I was in his chair, waiting for the Novocain to take effect, I mentioned that besides my career as a teacher, I was also a hypnotherapist. He smiled saying that he had always been interested in hypnosis. And, when I told him of my Novocain-free root canal, and the effects of self-hypnosis on my mind and body, he said that he would love to discuss my experience after my dental procedure was over.

Before the procedure began, he asked me if I had read Many Lives, Many Masters, a book by Dr. Brian Weiss. He told me that Dr. Weiss was a psychiatrist in Miami who used hypnosis to help his patients resolve their fears. This certainly piqued my interest, until he said that the novel was about Past Life Regression Therapy, whereupon my interest subsided considerably.

An hour later, during the ensuing conversation, I became aware that although I referred to my hypnotic experiences on the mind and body, Dr. Gotiner continually referred to its effect on the mind, body and *spirit*, which was something I was just beginning to consider. I was becoming more curious about ESP and mediumship, by watching a new TV show called *Crossing Over with John Edward*. Yet, I still viewed reincarnation and past lives as a little too far-out, and would certainly be pushing my belief system further than I was comfortable with.

After I left his office, I didn't think much about the book or the piece of paper on which Dr. Gotiner had written the title. But I was surprised that each time I went to throw it away, I hesitated. I had learned by that point to follow my instincts, so I just let that piece of paper sit on my desk.

WORKSHOPS AND SYNCHRONICITIES

A week later, in February 2003, I took another continuing education course for my hypnosis certification. This workshop was held at a large convention center in Edison NJ. The conference rooms were scheduled with all sorts of hypnosis workshops and lectures. The two that I was particularly interested in were about Advanced Parts Therapy and Emotional Freedom Technique (EFT) also known as 'Tapping'.

During the EFT workshop, one of the therapists there and I were discussing different metaphysical uses of hypnotherapy, such as Therapeutic Touch and Reiki Healing, which I had recently been introduced to. When she asked if I had read <u>Many Lives, Many Masters</u> by Dr. Brian Weiss, I instantly remembered the piece of paper that was still sitting on my desk. Smiling to myself, I thought that this could be, perhaps, a synchronicity, a term that Tricia had recently introduced to me in our office.

The workshop ended and we all broke for lunch, where I had a conversation with a different hypnotherapist, who asked, "By the way, Garry, have you read <u>ML,MM</u>?" His question triggered a very animated conversation, not about Dr. Brian Weiss, but about synchronicities.

It was just so interesting that my dentist, the hypnotherapist at the earlier workshop and now this hypnotherapist whom I had just met, all began talking to me about <u>ML,MM</u>. Although I found it a possible synchronicity, I still wasn't convinced to go to my local Barnes and Nobel to buy it. Since being diagnosed with dyslexia in elementary school, and having a difficult time reading in general, I was in no rush to buy any book, even if I was aware of the synchronicities that may have been involved.

And that was the situation I found myself in, with regard to buying and reading <u>Many Lives, Many Masters</u>. I acknowledged the possibility of the synchronicity and I thought I would eventually get the book, but between my teaching duties and my responsibilities as a hypnotherapist, husband and father, the idea of going out of my way to buy it was just something I wasn't ready to do. No, my free time would be spent vegetating in front of the television.

~ ~ ~

At about that time, my daughter Amy was accepted and enrolled at Elon University in North Carolina. All through middle and high school she loved performing in school plays. She always seemed to get the lead role in the musicals, which led her to choose a college where she could major in musical theater.

Both Chris and I love going into Manhattan to see plays. As our family grew, we brought our children with us to see Broadway productions, and Amy would dream of being on the Broadway stage when she grew up.

During the time that she was enrolled at Elon, we would drive down to North Carolina from New Jersey six or seven times a year, to see our daughter on stage, and those four summers she was also hired in summer stock theaters, performing in plays all around the East Coast.

In the summer of 2002, Amy was at the University of Virginia in Charlottesville, cast in the play <u>Carousel</u>. Watching my daughter on the stage was an indescribably prideful experience, and I would sneak in my handheld camcorder to record her, even though it was technically illegal to do so. After we checked into our hotel, Chris and I began to walk around the historic town, and we wandered into one of the many bookstores there. Chris, an avid reader, was looking for her favorite authors, and I found the New Age section to look for books on the subject of hypnotherapy.

As I scanned the bookshelves, I saw a book on Ericksonian hypnosis that I had not read. As I began to pull it out, another book seemingly attached to it, moved off the shelf with it. As I pulled both books off the shelf, one fell into my right hand. The title read <u>Many Lives, Many Masters</u> by Dr. Brian Weiss.

This book, quite literally, fell into my hands! No longer doubting the synchronicity here, I simply smiled as I looked up into the air and thought, *Okay guys, you've got my attention now.* I bought the book, began reading it that night and could not put it down. Chris couldn't believe I'd bought a book to simply read, nor how fast I read it. That book changed my life, as it has changed the lives of millions upon millions of people around the globe.

The reason why Dr. Weiss' book was so powerful to this ex-cynic, was that he had everything to lose and nothing to gain by writing it. Dr. Weiss studied at Columbia University and graduated from the Yale University School of Medicine in 1970, interned in internal medicine at the NYU Medical Center and at Yale for a two-year residency in psychiatry. Ten years later, in 1980, Dr. Weiss was head of the Psychiatry Department at Mount Sinai Medical Center in Miami Beach and began treating Catherine, a 27-year-old woman, for anxiety, depression and phobias.

His book is about the experiences they shared during her therapy sessions. He used hypnosis to help Catherine remember repressed childhood trauma, but what was disclosed, under hypnosis, was 86 past lives, as well as philosophical messages channeled from 'Master Spirits'. Dr. Weiss was amazed when Catherine's anxieties and phobias disappeared with her access to each past life.

Dr. Weiss published <u>Many Lives, Many Masters</u> in 1988, eight years after helping Catherine eliminate her fears and phobias, which allowed her to have a normal life. In interviews, he stated that he began to do more and more past life regressions as a therapy, and although he was concerned that he could have lost his credibility as a psychiatrist along with his license, he felt compelled to write his book.

Now, Dr. Brian Weiss is the world's greatest expert in Past Life Regression Therapy. His commitment to utilizing this radically new approach to mental (and spiritual) health - along with his acceptance of what the ramifications to his personal and professional life would be by publishing this revolutionary book - convinced me to explore yet another New Age belief. I had only recently begun to accept the possibility of mediumship, and now I was expanding my belief system to include reincarnation. To say I was changing would be a gross understatement.

– Another Life Lesson – # 44

Sometimes, the bad things that happen can become important lessons - if you are willing to view them as such.

AARON'S ACCIDENT

It was one of those quiet times in the Supermarket Careers Program shop. The students in other shops had purchased their snacks for their breaks, which my students had prepared, packed out and rung up. Now, all the other students were back in their classrooms and my students had begun their own break, sitting quietly, eating, drinking sodas and carrying on conversations.

Two days earlier, I'd received a call in my shop from my son. Aaron was attending the College of Staten Island to be a Physical Therapist, and was living in Staten Island at his cousin's home.

"Dad, its Aaron." I could hear anxiety and stress in his voice. "I was in an accident." It was the type of phone call that every parent dreads, as a myriad of horrible thoughts flew through my mind.

"Are you OK?...

Is anyone hurt?...

Where are you?...

What happened?...

Are the police there?"

The fear and concern welled up inside of me like a thermonuclear explosion. In my head, the thoughts were flying at a million miles an hour, and seemed to fly spontaneously from my lips.

I thought to myself, *I'll call Chris first, then the office. I'll tell them I have to leave now. I'll bring my students to the library, jump in my car, and I can be in Staten Island in 45 minutes. I'll go right to the hospital - Damn, did I bring my cell phone?* Trying to keep my emotions in check was becoming an exercise in futility, but it all came to a wonderfully calming halt with just a few words from Aaron.

"Dad! Calm down. I'm fine! The car's drivable, it just has a broken headlight."

I took a deep breath and got the whole story. No biggie, a minor fender bender, no tickets issued.

After my blood pressure came down and my heart rate returned to normal, we arranged for Aaron to bring the car to school. One of the perks that comes with being a teacher in a vocational school is having your car repaired at cost.

The plans were set for Aaron to come to school at 10:00 am on Wednesday. I would be between classes and I could walk my son over to the Auto Body shop to have the car repaired. I sat at my desk with my feet up, waiting for Aaron to arrive. The wall clock read 9:31. Resting my eyes, I let my mind drift, the way thoughts tend to drift, where one thought leads to another and another.

I thought of Aaron and how proud I was of him. I thought of our first visit to Disneyworld and how little he was; how he would be so protective of his little sister. I thought of our visit to the Museum of Natural History, in NYC, to see the dinosaurs that he loved so much.

Unexpectedly, my memories changed. I was back in that tunnel in Manhattan, unable to explain how I knew there was a barrel on the roadway. I knew my father's spirit had protected me. It was the same feeling I'd had when my children were born and I heard and felt his love surround me.

Suddenly my thoughts jumped to another image which came to me from out of the blue… *Crossing Over with John Edward*. Now, I was confused. *Where the hell did that come from?* I thought.

At 9:33, I heard the shop door open. It was Millie, a secretary at school whom I'd known for well over 10 years. I suppose that even though you know someone at work, you don't really know them. Sure, you talk about interesting events in your life, like births, weddings, deaths and the like, but when it comes down to the deep things, I feel that people prefer to keep others at arm's length.

That was the relationship I had with Millie: friendly, personal and pleasant. I knew her daughter was a student at the school. I knew she was bi-lingual and was a competent, dedicated school associate. But other than that, I didn't know much about her.

MILLIE'S READING

The Supermarket Careers Program was probably the most popular shop in the school. After all, there were not many classrooms where you had an opportunity to buy a 20 oz. soda, a bag of Doritos, Otis Spunkmeyer chocolate chip cookies, yogurt, ice cream or a dozen other snacks.

Usually, Millie would call me with a shopping list for the secretaries in the Main Office. This day, however, Millie just walked in.

"Hola, Garry. Como estas, hoy?" I responded with "Bien, y tu," as I got up from my desk with a smile.

As I stood, I suddenly felt my father's presence, but I didn't understand why. Although this was at the very beginning of my acceptance of spirit communication, by this time I was comfortable with the physical sensations, the tingling, I felt when he was close. I usually felt his presence warning me of an impending accident.

But this was certainly not a situation that involved danger. There was no reason for my father to warn me or save me. I was in my safe classroom in my safe school talking to someone I felt very comfortable with. However, this time he wasn't warning me. He was pushing me strongly to begin a conversation about New Age topics with Millie!

Not knowing why, I simply complied. Then I felt a strong impulse to ask her about the book <u>Many Lives, Many Masters</u>, and I just went along with the feeling.

"Oh yes!" she said. "I was at a seminar with Dr. Weiss at *Omega* two years ago. Wasn't his book great?"

What! I thought, as Millie waited for a response. *More synchronicities!* Millie had read <u>ML,MM</u> and mentioned Omega. Just the week before, Tricia had mentioned that she was going to a retreat at a place in Rhinebeck NY called *The Omega Institute for Holistic Studies*. Tricia said that it had the feeling of Woodstock in the 1960's and strongly suggested I go there.

As I mentioned the coincidence between her, Tricia and Omega, Millie smiled and laughingly said, "Garry, that's not a coincidence, it's a Sync..." As I nodded enthusiastically and finished the word for her.

"Synchronicity! Yes, I know! That's what Tricia has been telling me." I was finally ready to accept new learnings and the timing, as it always is, was perfect.

We began to discuss Past Life Regressions, the soul and spirituality, when I felt another strong push. This time it was to mention John Edward.

"Millie?" I asked, looking down at my desk. I was wondering how to phrase the question and it just seemed to form by itself. "Have you ever seen the TV show *Crossing Over with John Edward*? I'm looking all over for a real medium, not like those fake ones on the infomercials. I really need to find someone like John Edward. But I'm sure he's not taking any more private clients; guess he's too busy with the TV show." I looked up to see Millie smiling at me warmly.

"Garry," she said quietly, "did you know that **I'm** a medium? I don't usually tell anyone," she confided, as I felt my jaw drop open. Yet *another* synchronicity! Not only did she know a medium, she **was** a medium! To say I was weirded out would be another huge understatement.

193

I was amazed and awed! I had finally found someone I could talk to about all these crazy coincidences that I was beginning to accept as synchronicities. I could tell Millie about my communication with my father, without the fear that she would think I was nuts or laugh at me. I felt such relief when I knew she would understand all these things that I could not bring up with anyone else.

But most importantly, I hoped that somehow Millie might offer me the validation I yearned for. That, just as John Edward did for members of his television audience, my friend Millie might be able to verify for me that my Dad was not really gone, but still watching over and guiding me.

I jumped up and almost knocked her over in my excitement. Putting her hand up, Millie told me that she needed to talk to me but that I should not say anything, just listen. She told me that it was important for me NOT to ask or tell her anything about any specific person, in spirit, and to just answer yes, no, or that I don't know. She said that she needed to sit, in the quiet, for a moment. She took a deep breath as her eyes seemed to go slightly out of focus.

From my point of view, she had entered an altered state of consciousness, similar to - but not - hypnosis. She was staring off in the distance, eyes half closed. It seemed to me that she was listening to something over her left shoulder. This was getting more and more interesting by the moment.

I knew Aaron would be coming in soon, so I left Millie in my office and stepped out to check on my students. They were sitting quietly, taking their break. I knew they would be fine for a few moments, so I walked back into my office to continue our conversation.

I really wanted to tell her about all the weird stuff that was happening in my life; about the man at the foot of my bed when I was five; my father saving my life in the tunnel... Everything!

As I walked back into my office, I saw Millie sitting there quietly, and in front of my eyes, for the first time, I witnessed communication with the spirit world. However, this was not like the spirit communication I'd seen on Television. I knew who this spirit was: I knew this was my father's spirit. And I was spellbound.

I saw the hair on her arm literally stand straight up as I felt the hair on the back of my own neck do the same. Chills literally went up and down my spine! It felt to me as if the temperature in my normally warm office had dropped by twenty degrees.

"I have your father here," Millie told me in a quiet, far away voice. I noticed that she didn't ask me if my father had passed away. She knew he was in spirit!

"He is so strong! He wants to tell you so much." As I was observing her, again, I could not help but notice the similarities between this psychic trance state and the hypnotic state I knew so well. They seemed to be almost identical.

With her eyes nearly closed, Millie started bringing my father through. "First, he says how proud of you, he is."

I so wanted to hear from him, but my cynical side was still going strong. *Oh please,* I thought sarcastically. *Every father is proud of his kids. For me to believe, you're gonna have to do better than that.*

"He's apologizing... for treating you the way he did," she said. "He says he was never able to express love." I felt a tear start to form in my eye, as she continued. "He has had to relearn, on the other side, what love is. He says that you should no longer doubt that it has been him talking to you all these years."

Oh my God! It's what I have been hoping for.

And Millie went on, "He says, he was at your wedding, after he passed into spirit... He was with you and your wife when 'the boy' and 'the girl' were born... He whispered in your ear that they were beautiful... He was there with you recently when you got the 'birdie'?"

Millie explained that she didn't know what he meant by a birdie, but said that it wasn't meant for her; the birdie was meant for me alone.

That was the proof I needed to hear so desperately.

My father had taught me to play golf when I was twelve years old. As I grew up, we would often play together. When his lung cancer started to weaken him, the first thing to go was his golf game. I explained to Millie that I had played golf the previous week. On a par three, I chipped in to get a birdie. In the part of my mind that I had been hearing him for 30 years, I'd heard him say, *Nice birdie, Ga!*

My normal response to sensing my father had always been, in two parts: First, to my father, *Thanks, Dad,* and second, to myself, *That's what he would say, if he were still here.* Now I knew that he truly **was** still here, watching me play golf, the game that he had taught me.

Millie continued to bring through more information, which I happily validated. Too soon she sat back in her chair and said, "He's pulling back." She smiled and repeated how strong my father's spirit was.

I grabbed a tissue from my desk to wipe my eyes. I felt that there was no way to thank her enough. In those few moments she'd healed the thirty-year-old hole in my heart.

The power of Dr. Brian Weiss' book, which would become so instrumental in my spiritual evolution - along with Millie's reading - truly validated my newfound belief in the continuation of consciousness. Once again, my life had changed.

Just then, the back door to the shop opened and my son Aaron walked into my office. Aaron had worked at the school during his college summer breaks, and knew Millie, but I was surprised to see her suddenly return to her altered state.

"He's back," was all she said, as that same faraway look came over her again. My son looked at the both of us as if we were from another planet.

Millie lifted up her hand, motioning to Aaron with her thumb and pinky held up and her other fingers closed, in the *hang loose* gesture that Hawaiian surfers made popular.

Now addressing Aaron, Millie said, "I don't know what this means, but your grandpa is showing this to you and is saying, 'Pay attention to what you are doing'. I don't know what that means, but he is strongly pointing at you," as she showed her 'hang loose' gesture to Aaron again.

"He really wants you to pay attention…" Then she added quietly, "Now he's pulling back again." She took another deep breath and smiled at me. Then she stood up, hugged Aaron and me, and left my shop.

Aaron knew about my metaphysical interests, but always seemed to be uncomfortable with the whole concept, and I always tried to contain my passion about it when talking with him. But, after that situation, I knew an explanation was necessary. So after a brief clarification, I said with a smile, "I guess your grandfather wants you to focus on school more."

"I don't think so," he said. "Dad, I wasn't going to tell you, but I was talking on my cell when I had the accident."

We both sat quietly for a moment, in order to process what had just happened. It hadn't been the Hawaiian *hang-loose* gesture. It was an 'I was on the phone' gesture!

My son and I never really followed up on the experience. We just took his car to the auto body shop to be repaired.

The rest of that school day was a blur. Honestly, all I was thinking of was the questions that were swirling in my mind.

I did not need to be convinced any longer about the ability to connect with *the dead*. John Edward and Millie had totally convinced me. I did not need to be convinced that *the dead* are still around us and watching over us. The fact that Aaron was not going to tell me that he was on his cell phone when the accident happened, and only told me when I received a heads up from my father in the spirit world, was more than enough proof for me.

Now, another two part question formed in my mind. First: *How old were John, Millie and other mediums when they realized their gift? And second: If I truly have been hearing my father in my head for years, perhaps, just perhaps… I might have some latent mediumship abilities also.*

But I dismissed that thought fairly quickly. I had just begun to believe in what mediums do. To consider myself a medium made me feel much too full of myself.

When the dismissal bell rang at the end of the day, I couldn't wait to get to Millie's office to continue our conversation. I also wanted to find more information about this place called Omega. So at that quiet time of the day when all the students had left, I was able to talk with Millie about Omega, Dr. Weiss, her mediumistic abilities... And of course to thank her again for the priceless gift she'd given me.

~ ~ ~

Years later, I would be brought back to this memory. When I was the medium and felt the presence of Nana, a spirit who wanted to contact her granddaughter Gloria. It was almost the same scenario with Millie that had just changed my life. The roles would change, but the joy and healing were the same.

OMEGA

It had taken decades, but I'd finally accepted that there may be occurrences in my life, that I would have viewed as coincidence, that I could now accept as synchronicity. I wasn't quite ready yet to go into the writings of Carl Jung and his Theory of Synchronicities, but I was willing to accept that a higher power seemed to be at work. I could even accept, on faith alone, that a higher power or energy was behind all the synchronicities that had been assisting me, thus far, on my journey.

I remembered the feelings I'd had back at the supermarket, when Renée came running into my office with the Star Ledger ad. I thought of what she'd said at the time: *'Garry! If God made a job for you it would be this teaching position'.* The feeling I had, about applying for this teaching position, was stronger than 'It may be a good idea to apply'. It was a powerful **need** to apply for that teaching job. It is hard to describe the difference between a feeling and a need, but you know it when you are experiencing it. And once again I knew that I **needed** to go to Omega. And that's exactly what I did.

As I left school, I had to really focus on what I was doing. I had almost driven home, but remembered that I had a new hypnosis client that afternoon, and decided to go straight to my office. I'd hoped that Tricia would be in. I had finally accepted and understood all the New Age views of the Universe she'd always spoken to me about. Tricia would always say to me, with her knowing smile, "When you're ready, you'll know it." And what I knew, at that moment, was that I was indeed ready. And I couldn't wait to tell her.

I had an overwhelming feeling of an acceptance, a knowing and a deep feeling of awe. I knew something was happening that I couldn't explain, but I knew it was right. I also knew that Tricia was the only person who would understand and be able to explain to me what was happening.

- Another Life Lesson - # 45

**When the student is ready the teacher (or teachers) will appear,
even when the student is also a teacher.**

BACK AT TRICIA'S OFFICE

I parked my car and ran up the three steps to our office. I couldn't wait to tell her about all the coincidences (which I was now beginning to think of as synchronicities) and how I felt that my life was about to really change. Tricia was sitting in the waiting room as I blasted through the front door looking like I might explode with excitement.

She had a brochure on her lap as I entered the waiting room. "Perfect timing! I just got this brochure in the mail and immediately thought of you and our metaphysical conversations. Sit and look at this…"

I tried to settle down as Tricia handed me the brochure she had been looking at and once again, my jaw dropped open. And for a second I couldn't even speak.

In my hand was the 2003 full color summer brochure from The Omega Institute for Holistic Studies.

Tricia said, "Garry, you won't believe how wonderful this place is! I've gone there many times, and I just know you'll love it and learn so much there!"

All I could do was hold up my hand and ask her to hold on.

The puzzled expression on Tricia's face changed to a knowing smile when I began to explain what had happened with Millie and Aaron and how this was the fourth synchronicity about Omega. When I said 'synchronicity', her smile became a joyous laugh.

While I was rambling on about how this cannot be explained away by simple coincidence, the Omega brochure slipped from my lap, landed on the floor and opened to a full page picture of Dr. Brian Weiss.

Just as my 4:00 client cancelled.

Honestly…You can't make this stuff up!

MY FIRST PAST LIFE REGRESSION

The memory of being in the bookstore in Virginia came flooding back. The feeling was the same as having <u>Many Lives, Many Masters</u> fall into my hands, reinforcing my new found awareness of synchronicities. One set of synchronicities had led me to read

ML,MM. And now a new set seemed to be directing me to take a week-long workshop with its author.

My reaction was also the same. I looked up and thought, *Okay. You have my attention again... I'll go!*

Brian Weiss - perhaps the world's top expert on Past Life Regression Therapy - was leading a weeklong seminar on Past Life Regression Therapy based on his book Many Lives, Many Masters and I fully intended to be there. I would love to say that booking the trip to Omega was as simple as the decision to go. The decision was simple but going would be a little more complicated.

It would be the first time in our married life that I took a vacation by myself. Now, combine that with the incredible changes happening within me, regarding my spiritual beliefs. I'm sure you can understand how concerned Chris and my entire family were when I informed them that I was going to a place in upstate New York, just north of Woodstock, by myself, for a workshop about reincarnation and past life regressions. In retrospect, I think they were all probably much more than a little concerned. After some cajoling and convincing, we came to the understanding that it may be a great learning experience and if nothing else, I might just get 'it' out of my system.

~ ~ ~

As soon as I got home, I tossed the brochure on my desk, picked up the phone with my credit card in hand, and called Omega to book my reservation for the workshop.

It was 4:55 and I fully expected to hear the recording that would inform me that I was too late and to call back the next day, but a young lady answered the phone and could not have been more helpful. She answered all my questions and when I finished the call, I had to sit back and take a breath. I was now registered for Dr. Brian Weiss' week-long Past Life Regression Workshop at Omega scheduled in mid-August of 2003.

I had been on the go since 6:00 am and I was exhausted. What a day! Between my teaching responsibilities, Millie's reading, Aaron's visit, talking to Tricia, registering for Omega, not to mention all the synchronicities that day, I needed to just chill out!

Picking up the Omega brochure, I realized that it had covered a few pieces of the day's mail. And once again, I almost fell off my chair as I was hit with the final synchronicity of that very long day. (Honestly, I don't think I could have handled any others.)

On the top of the pile of letters and bills was a postcard advertisement from The Holistic Healing Center of NY, which read, 'We will be presenting a one day workshop on PAST LIFE REGRESSION THERAPY.'

Shaking my head and for the second and final time that day, I looked up in the air and acknowledged that last synchronicity. I knew I would be attending this one-day workshop as well.

Bear in mind that I did not wholeheartedly go from a hard core cynic to a total believer. I could never do that. I did go, from being that hard core cynic, to being a very healthy skeptic.

Before I would accept this new belief system, I still needed more information. As I began to explore this new world of extrasensory perception, psychics, mediums, healers, etc., I was very sure of one thing: Along with those wonderful, caring, competent and honest practitioners, there must be some who are frauds and thieves who would try to steal your life savings without batting an eye. I knew that I needed to keep that sense of healthy skepticism with my newly accepted beliefs.

DRIVING TO OMEGA

One of the perks about being a teacher is having the summer off. So when I discovered that Dr. Weiss was holding his seminar at Omega, I was ecstatic! I could not have known how that week, in that relaxed and nurturing environment, would change me. Omega was a 3 hour drive from my home and it gave me some time to think.

Driving up Rt. 80, to Rt. 287, to the NY Thruway brought back pleasant memories of my family driving from the congestion of Brooklyn to the paradise of the Catskill Mountains of New York each summer.

I always find memories fascinating. How the smell of patchouli oil can instantly bring me back to my freshman year in college. How simply hearing a song on the radio can transport me back to 1967, in the middle of the 'Love Generation', listening to Cream and The Doors. I had spent every childhood summer in the Catskill Mountains and between the hotels with family and camp, summer in the Catskills was the reason why I've always loved the summertime.

I have always cherished the memories of how beautiful the Catskill Mountains were during my formative years. And as I drove through those familiar mountains on the way to Omega, it all came back to me, along with more recent memories of my first Past Life Regression.

~ ~ ~

I had been attending classes the Holistic Healing Center of New York for some years and although I was not a believer in many of the New Age classes they offered, I was certainly more open to them than I had been earlier on my journey.

Paul Aurand, the director, offered his Past Life Regression workshop at the perfect time. It was the end of June and school had just ended for the 2003 summer break. I viewed his workshop as a preparatory step for my weeklong workshop with Dr. Weiss. And Paul's class gave me my first opportunity in understanding how to use hypnosis to assist a client, in a regression, to one of their many past lives.

The classes at the HHC usually fill quickly, sometimes with over thirty participants. But for some reason there were only five participants registered for this class. The initial part of the workshop involved a discussion of the belief in past lives, reincarnation, and stories that supported their validity. The second part of the workshop was experiential.

Paul explained how to direct a client into a past life, and emphasized one very important point. He said that, prior to hypnotizing someone for a PLR, we must be aware of 'The Question' we are posing.

The 'The Question' is actually directed to the person's higher self. Their higher self knows every aspect of every life they have had and will block access to a past life that conflicts with the lessons that person came into **this** life to learn.

Paul described going to what he called an *Affect Bridge*, which is where the client is transported back to a life in the past. There are multiple ways to be regressed, using a variety of different affect bridges. One is simply a bridge over the river of time. Another could be an elevator, to transport a person thru time and space, back to a past life.

While being transported back in time, you become aware of your higher self, from whom you ask permission to visit a past life. The reason most people want to visit a past life is to explain a situation in their current life that defies normal explanations. These feelings, of being affected by the past, can present themselves as a strong attraction to a place, culture, or anything that would cause you to question that attraction. But the most popular reason for seeking information from a past life is... Fear.

Just as Catherine's multiple and complex fears and compulsions, in <u>Many Lives, Many Masters</u>, vanished after Dr. Weiss directed her to their root cause, many people seek a Past Life Regressionist for that same purpose.

Paul then described the difference between a 'Group Past Life Regression' and 'Past Life Regression Therapy'. The former is a generic experience, returning to an arbitrary life the person had in the past, simply for the experience. Because of its nature, group hypnosis cannot be individualized.

Past Life Regression Therapy, or PLRT, employs the experience of a past life regression as a therapeutic tool to resolve and reframe an issue in an **individual's** present life.

Paul invited me to be the volunteer subject for the PLR demonstration. And of course I was happy to volunteer for my first Past Life Regression. As he directed me to the chair in front of the class, the other participants moved their chairs closer to have a better view of the procedure.

Although I wanted to observe the PLR process, I have learned that first-hand experience is invaluable for the practitioner. You must know what your client is experiencing in order to connect with them and their experience.

This is why I connect so well with everyone who comes to me to quit smoking. I know from real life experience what quitting smoking is like, so I can empathize with what they are going through. It is the same with past lives (or any other hypnotherapeutic procedure): your technique is dramatically better when you know what your client is experiencing.

"Is there something in your life that you think may be affecting you from a past life?" he asked me. He was forming what "The Question' would be. "It may be an attraction, something you are frightened of or have an aversion to that can't be explained by the experiences you have had in this life?"

It took me a moment to ponder the question. Then I told Paul that I am completely non-competitive, and I had often wondered why. "I love playing racquet ball, but I don't care if I win or not. Other guys I play with are extremely competitive and I actually feel sorry for them. Sometimes when I am winning a game, I don't make shots I can because, it's weird to say, but I don't want to hurt their feelings."

After a short discussion focusing on what exactly I felt, we realized that my discomfort was not centered on competition as much as a desire to never hurt someone. I remembered how terrible I always felt any time I hurt someone physically - even accidentally. Over time, this evolved into even hurting someone's feelings, or beating someone in racquetball or other sports. Although it may sound strange, it made sense to me.

As Paul lowered the lights and put on soothing background music, I prepared myself for a timeless journey. Due to my experience with hypnosis, I only needed to be touched on the shoulder to enter into a deep hypnotic state, which is probably why Paul asked me to volunteer in the first place.

Very quickly I was in the altered state as Paul began his process for a PLR. Having read all of Brian Weiss' books and discussing the procedure earlier with Paul, I had a fairly good idea of what to expect. But as they say: 'Nothing teaches better than experience'.

We started with 'The Question' we had prepared for me to hear at the beginning of the regression. "Can we go back in time, to a life where Garry first felt overly anxious if he physically hurts someone?" It seemed simplistic, but again, it made sense to me.

Paul began my PLR as he had described earlier in class. "Bring yourself to a happy childhood memory." I saw my 4th birthday party in my old house.

"You are now moving to an earlier age; you are 3... 2... 1. You are now in utero in your mother's womb... Ask your higher self for permission to visit the life that is affecting you by..." He repeated 'The Question'. And I didn't receive permission as a verbal or auditory yes or no, it was more of a feeling of simply wanting to continue.

He then brought me to a bridge. "There is now a bridge in front of you. It is not a bridge over a stream; it is a bridge over time. When you cross it you will be in another place at another time." There was a thick fog bank over the river as I approached the crest of the bridge, and as I descended, the fog dissipated.

"Look down… Do you know if you are a man or a woman? What are you wearing on your feet? How are you dressed? What is happening?" Paul asked as he directed me to describe what I was experiencing.

"I am inside a tent," I quietly replied.

"Describe it…"

"It's open on both ends… There is a hot wind blowing through it. I feel very tired. I'm a man… A surgeon. I live in New York City, but I am now in the Union Army. I'm in the Civil War. I'm in a surgical tent. I am standing in thick red mud, which is made of soil and the blood of soldiers." I just seemed to know what I was saying as if it were happening in my present life.

"What is happening around you?"

"I have a surgical saw in my hand which is used for amputations. There is a young soldier on a table in front of me. I hear his screams. There are two men holding him down and a nurse is tightening the tourniquet just below his knee…" I continued to describe, in detail, the horror I was involved in. I knew that if I didn't amputate his leg he would die, but I also knew the amount of torture I was inflicting on this young man.

"Bring yourself to the next significant event in that life." Paul brought me away from the carnage.

"I am back north. It is years later. I am married to my sweetheart in New York." I described how my life had changed, but the memory of the war haunted me throughout my life. I described my life back in New York after the war ended.

"Bring yourself to the next significant event in that life." Paul directed me further and further into that specific lifetime. I continued to describe the life I'd had and with each new memory, the type of man I was became clear.

"We moved southwest to Missouri, on a large farm estate. I am the doctor for the town. I am a respected member of the community. I have three children who I adore and who adore me."

Paul had me move ahead in that life and then directed me further. "…Bring yourself to the last event in that life, before you took your last breath." Paul directed me to experience my death in that life.

"I'm on my horse… there is a rattlesnake on the road. My horse bucks… I am falling off and I feel a terribly sharp pain in my neck… I can't breathe… can't move. There is no more pain and I feel the desire to leave that body."

"Go to the last breath you take in that life."

"I feel myself lift out of my body…"

"Turn and look at what had been your body. What do you see?"

"My horse is running home. I am dead. I can see that I hit my head on a boulder, which broke my neck. I can see my body from above. I was tall and thin with long, grey hair. I am now seeing my family in the parlor of my home. My coffin is in the center of the room. Everyone is there … crying… I try to console them but they are unaware of my presence."

"Become aware of a beautiful white light." Paul began to direct me to the light.

I was drawn into a vortex of white loving light, where I once again became aware of my higher self, who began my life review by showing me all the things, both good and bad, I had done. He brought me back into the tent and allowed me to hear the prayer I had sent him at that time: "If I live through this horror, I will never hurt another human being for as long as I live."

My higher self then relayed to me that I could now understand why I could never hurt anyone. That was the promise I had made to myself, and that memory and promise was so powerful that it bled through, all the way into my current life.

My first PLR also clarified another curious event in my life. Discussing with the group how I felt during the regression, a memory from a decade earlier suddenly entered my mind and I smiled, shaking my head the way you do when you have a profound thought.

Everyone noticed that I had just been hit with a humorous memory and wanted to know why I was now smiling. And I relayed to them a time before I was a teacher, when I worked for a supermarket, and had a spontaneous past life memory from the lifetime I had just visited, while I was awake and at work. I explained that the past life memory came to me when I was wearing a white butcher's coat from the Meat Department, which had been splashed with the blood from a tray of beef…

~ ~ ~

The memory of that first PLR drew to a close just as I approached the highway exit that would take me to Omega. I sighed deeply as I realized how the experiences and the profound insights they formed had changed me. And would allow me to understand the 'future' past lives I would be experiencing over the next week.

Garry with Dr. Brian Weiss, author of <u>Many Lives, Many Masters</u>.
Photo taken at the Omega Institute for Holistic Studies,
Rhinebeck NY - August 2003

When you allow yourself to believe and ask for more 'signposts' (in the form of synchronicities) to be set in front of you, watch your step because you may start to trip over them and become somewhat overwhelmed by how many form.

THE OMEGA EXPERIENCE

The Omega Institute for Holistic Studies is a nonprofit organization, founded in 1977 by Dr. Stephan Rechtschaffen and Elizabeth Lesser. In 1981, Omega moved to the former grounds of Camp Boiberik, a popular Yiddish summer camp. Over the years, the grounds were restored, while maintaining their simplicity. Omega now sits on 250 acres and has more than 100 buildings, including the Sanctuary, the Ram Dass Library and a beautiful lake.

Unfortunately, in 2003 the lake that so many guests used for swimming and canoeing was found to be too high in bacteria and closed. The directors invested in a state of the art water treatment 'Eco Machine'. In October 2010, the Omega Center for Sustainable Living (OCSL) was opened and was one of the first buildings in the world to achieve full certification under the Living Building Challenge. The OCSL demonstrates and teaches what is possible through regenerative design, and has won numerous international awards for excellence. The success of their commitment and investment in sustainable living quickly became evident as the lake that had been closed due to bacterial contaminates was reopened. And now I not only look forward to the workshops at Omega, I look forward to swimming in that perfect lake.

The week long classes at Omega begin on Sunday evenings at 8:30 pm, with an orientation and introduction by the presenters. Dr. Brian Weiss had the Main Hall to handle the 175 or so participants, and his was the largest seminar offered that week.

After the orientation, Brian presented a lecture covering his background and a general description of what we would be participating in that week, along with a discussion of his book. When his lecture concluded, he told the participants to arrive right after breakfast in the morning, so we could get directly into the power of the past life experience, and I couldn't wait to get started!

The next morning, Brian began his first exercise, but it wasn't what I'd expected. He said that he wanted to show everyone, visually, where the people in the room had come from.

Brian asked everyone to stand, and then said, "If you are from the East Coast of the United States, please sit..." I totally expected that 95% of the participants would have been from somewhere on the East Coast. But to my surprise, well over half the audience was still standing. Brian then asked those who were from the rest of the United States, to please have a seat. I was again sure that everyone else would now sit, but there were still many people standing. And I wondered where they could be from, if only those now seated were from the United States.

Addressing the participants who were still standing, Brian said, "If you are from Europe, please raise your hand." I couldn't believe what I was seeing. As ten or fifteen people raised their hands, I realized that my rather long three-hour drive to Omega was nothing compared to these people's flight from Europe.

Once again Brian asked them to sit and there were still more people standing! I heard people all around me whispering exactly how I felt, "Where can these people be from?"

Brian then questioned the remaining participants, "If you are from Mexico, the Caribbean, Central or South America, please raise your hands," and about eight people raised their hands. And yet there were still people standing.

He asked those from Asia to raise their hands, and three people complied. It amazed me. He asked those people to have a seat and now there were three people still standing. Brian asked them where they called home, and they said South Africa. If this were a competition of who travelled furthest to be there, they would have been the champs, hands down.

Brian explained to the now seated audience, "You can see that the interest in reincarnation is not something only for Hindus or Buddhists. It would seem that there are many people interested in it now. As you've just seen, we have people from almost every continent on the planet represented here now. And you can rest assured that you are in for a very interesting week."

As all the conversations subsided in anticipation of what was going to happen next, Brian said, "Considering we are going to be here for a week, we should get to know each other. I'd like each of you to stand for a moment and just give your name, where you are from, and a brief statement as to why you came to this workshop."

In the very front row, a woman stood up, introducing herself as Sarah from Florida. She described herself as a hypnotherapist and psychic medium, and said she wanted to learn more about past life regression.

As Sarah introduced herself, I felt the unmistakable physical signs of the presence of my father once again. The tingling on the back of my neck and the hair on my arms standing up, all told me my father was close. He was now telling me, 'Go to her. Go to Sarah and talk to her!'

I was somewhat uncomfortable, not knowing what I would say to her, but this place was so open I felt that going up to someone who was a complete stranger and asking her about psychic mediumship would be totally acceptable. And I made the decision that sometime during the day, probably when we took our first break, I would talk with Sarah.

As the first row finished introducing themselves and the second and the third, I saw that I would be next. I stood up and introduced myself as a hypnotherapist and Special Education high school teacher from NJ and that, like everyone else, I was there to learn Past Life Regression Therapy from Dr. Weiss.

By the time all the introductions were done, it was almost lunch time so Brian let us all take a quick break. I took the opportunity to walk to the front of the group and introduced myself to Sarah. To my amazement she looked at me and said, "Hi Garry!"

How did she know my name! She wasn't even looking back at me when I introduced myself as a Hypnotherapist from New Jersey!

WOW! Maybe she's the real thing, I thought: *a psychic who knows your name just by talking to you!* Sarah saw my shocked expression and smiled. She seemed to be reading my mind again. After all, she was a psychic. So, of course, she could read my mind!

Again, she smiled at me, as she pointed to my chest. When I looked down I realized why she had been smiling. I had my 'HI my name is GARRY' name tag glued to my shirt!

As we began talking, she looked at me with an interesting smile on her face. She turned her head to the left as if someone there were speaking to her. I noticed the similarities between her seemingly distracted demeanor and Millie's when she had given me my first reading.

I pulled up a chair and said, "I heard you say you're a psychic medium?" She nodded, still seemingly distracted. Her attention was to her left as I continued. "I have been watching the TV show, *Crossing Over with John Edwards*, and I'm very curious about psychic mediumship in general."

Again Sarah's smile shined brightly. "Yes. I understand," she said, nodding but not to me: to whoever was talking to her from her left side. "Your dad's here, and says he wants to talk to you too."

Suddenly, this whole thing was getting to be a little too much. It had only been a month or two since my attitude toward this New Age belief had changed from being a hard core cynic, who looked at mediumship as Mumbo-Jumbo garbage, to a belief in that same Mumbo-Jumbo.

My first real reading had been with Millie and it had eased my skepticism, but now I felt as if I were jumping into the deep end of the pool, without a life preserver. I now found myself at Omega with a group of people who believed in reincarnation, and some claimed to have the ability to communicate with the dead.

Well, it was a good thing that I was sitting. Brian was right when he said it was going to be an interesting week.

I could accept that Millie had sensed my father, because Aaron was going to be coming to class, and my dad needed to give his grandson a message. That made sense to me. I was not yet a true believer (that wouldn't happen for another year), but I was definitely opening up to the possibility of mediumship, although I still had a lot of doubt.

I began a quick review of what had just happened… As Sarah stood to introduce herself to everyone, I felt my father tell me to go and talk to her. Then, with no direction from me - except questioning her about mediumship - she told me that my father was communicating with her and that he wanted to talk to me **too.**

The fact that she said he wanted to talk to me 'too' was more validation for me that she was, in fact, communicating with my father. I pulled the chair closer to her. "OK, I am very new to this," I said. "I've only recently accepted that our loved ones, who've passed, can communicate with us."

Sarah knew that I was about to give her information about what had happened to me and about my father, so she put her hand up to stop me from telling her anything more, just as Millie had done.

She told me that she had already scheduled a reading to do that day at lunch, but that if I wanted, she would be happy to give me a reading the next day. Until then, she couldn't talk to me about my background, but after our reading, we could share any information.

All I could say was, "Sure… Great… Thanks…"

I didn't quite understand what had just happened, but I was pumped. "Oh, by the way," Sarah said, as I began walking back to my seat, "before you go to sleep tonight, ask your father a question that I'll try to answer for you tomorrow."

I really didn't know what to say, but if all this happened before lunch on the first day of class, OMG! What did the rest of the week have in store for me?

After the break, Brian gave us the schedule for the rest of the week, saying that it was tentative because there are so many variables in his workshops that each one is different and unique - even though they are basically the same workshop.

When we broke for lunch, we were told that we would experience our first PLR, in a group setting, when we came back. You could feel the excitement in the air as we walked back to the cafeteria where we would be served breakfast, lunch and dinner for the next five days.

The grounds of the Omega campus are another reason why I have gone back almost every year since the summer of 2003. We walked through the garden paths, to the cafeteria, past the vegetable gardens, birds, chipmunks and butterflies. It is, was and always will be a magical place. The cafeteria is located in a very large building with a huge wrap around covered porch overlooking the great lawn, and seats well over 300 people. As you enter the dining area, two buffet tables in the center divide the building in half with tables and chairs on the left and right. Large fans in the ceiling circulated the warm summer air on that perfect day.

The menu at Omega took some getting used to. In 2003, all meals served in the cafeteria were strictly vegetarian. However, scrambled eggs were available for breakfast, and I realized that they would be the closest thing to meat I would have for the entire week. When I asked one of the kids working there about the menu, I was told that the café, which was open all day, served a great cheeseburger. So, I knew I could rely on the fact that in the café that evening, there would be a hot, juicy cheeseburger made just for the carnivore in me.

Although we had an hour and a half for lunch, I wolfed down my salad and a peanut butter and jelly sandwich and was back in the main hall in less than 45 minutes, along with the majority of the participants. As we all settled in, I introduced myself to some of the people sitting in my row as we eagerly awaited our first past life experience.

I happily described my experience of having a PLR with Paul Aurand, and was surprised to find that only one person in the group had ever been hypnotized, and not a single person had experienced a PLR. As Dr. Weiss came on stage to thunderous applause, I wondered what these people, with no knowledge of hypnosis, would experience. Or if they would have any experience at all.

*When you see yourself as something
so alien to your self-perception that you must look away,
you realize how much you have evolved from then to now.*

MY FIRST PLR IN A GROUP SETTING

As Brian began his induction into hypnosis for the group, I was aware of the difference between my first private PLR and the group PLR which had just begun. During my PLR with Paul Aurand, I was able to describe the images I was sensing to him as I became aware of them. Because Paul knew what I was perceiving, he was able to direct me to the next event at the perfect time. Clearly, a private PLR is much more effective as a therapy than a group PLR. And that is why a private past life regression session is considered Past Life Regression *Therapy*.

Now, as Brian began his group regression, I had the advantage of being able to enter a deep hypnotic state almost instantly.

As most participants were just beginning to take a deep breath, I was already in deep hypnosis. I was aware that Brian had to deepen the group and I just allowed my higher self to 'bring me to a life in the past that can bring me a better understanding of my spiritual self.'

Dr. Weiss couldn't know the depth of hypnosis each of the 175 participants were entering. So he had to anticipate where each person's level was. In group hypnosis, the hypnotist must gear the group as an average. I was already in my regression while many people were barely able to allow their eyes to close.

I found myself at the affect bridge. I knew why Dr. Weiss was directing the group so slowly, but I decided to simply allow my higher self to direct me to the life I needed to visit and that is exactly what occurred.

As I heard Brian direct the group to relax, I had already crossed the affect bridge to a life in my past. I was surprised as to the surroundings I saw as I descended the bridge. I was also somewhat confused by the perspective of what I was experiencing. I was switching between being associated with my body (seeing through my own eyes) and being dissociated (seeing myself as a participant in the scene being played out in front of me). It was like acting in a movie and watching it at the same time.

I knew this place. It was a city in the late 1800's. There were tall stone apartment buildings; the streets were made of cobblestones. Horses pulled old carts and people were buying and selling products from these carts. I was also very aware of the smoke in the air and that it was hard to breath. It seemed that the city had acrid smoke bellowing from all of the thousands of chimneys there. It was winter and very cold. I noticed how many people were warming themselves in front of metal drums as flames leapt out from them.

I then looked down at my clothes. I was dressed warmly in a black coat that seemed much heavier and cleaner that those of the other people in the street. I knew I was 'above' them.

I was aware that I was a small boy walking through the streets with my father. I knew we were Jewish. I had *payos*, the side curls that male orthodox Jews grow from childhood. I looked up at my father walking beside me, with his long beard and traditional garb of orthodox Hasidim. I am aware of orthodox culture in this life, and this knowledge allowed me to understand who and where I was in that life.

I knew I was the only son of a Jewish banker.

As we walked down the street, I felt that my father was different than other people; not only non-Jews but also other Jewish people, who all seemed to hold my father in high regard. They were nodding acknowledgement and shaking his hand. He was clearly respected and loved by those around us.

Without being directed, I moved to the next significant event in that life, as Brian had everyone begin to move across their affect bridge. I was now in my late 20's. I was in the University and had left my traditions behind. I was clean shaven and for all intent and purposes I was like everyone else on the street. I also knew that my father had died and I had inherited all of his wealth, including his bank.

While Brian had everyone begin to observe themselves in their past life, I had moved on. I was now the owner of the bank. I was obese and proud of my girth. It meant, to anyone seeing me, that I was wealthy. People were starving in WW I Germany and I survived through the war and depression that followed by being a shrewd businessman. And being heartless: if there were a person that the Nazi caricature of 'the Jew' was based upon, it would have been me.

As I observed, I was disgusted by how cruel and callous I was to people. And not just toward the people I dealt with through my business affairs; I even treated my family in the same manner. I began to cry as I witnessed my voraciousness. I knew I identified myself as a German first and Jewish as a distant second.

Brian had everyone go to the next significant event in their life and I went to Kristallnacht, the 'Night of Broken Glass' November 9, 1938. The night was named for the shards of broken glass that littered the streets after Jewish-owned stores, buildings, and synagogues had their windows smashed. There was also unspeakable violence against innocent people. Homes were broken into, people beaten and dragged into the streets, many were murdered. It was more violent than just broken glass windowpanes.

Again, I was already aware of the history of WW I and II, but I'd never dreamed that I'd see it through the eyes of my own last incarnation. I realized, in the back of my mind, that I was re-experiencing my most recent past life before reincarnating into the person I am today.

I moved forward in time once again. I left my family behind as I took what money I could grab and hid in the attic of an apartment building I owned. I was starving and paid dearly for a small loaf of moldy bread.

An ex-employee of mine turned me into the Gestapo, who laughed as they kicked and threw me into a flatbed truck that delivered me and a group of others to a train station, from where I was sent to the concentration camp known as Buchenwald. Upon arrival, I was deemed too weak to work, separated from the others and in a group of 20 other men, shot.

The death scene I experienced was quite different from my last. In this past life, I had no funeral. Although I did have a burial, it was in a mass grave, shared with other Jews, Gypsies, Communists, homosexuals and political prisoners. And yet I saw that same white light and was more than happy to leave that life, which explained a lot about my current life experiences.

I had the same feelings, sights and emotions I'd had in my first past life experience. I was aware of the presence of my higher self again, who began my instantaneous life review. Although the experience was similar, the review of who I had been in that life could not have been more different.

Suddenly I realized why I have always been hesitant to tell people (in this life) that I am Jewish.

And now it seemed as clear as Kristallnacht. I felt a combination of shame and fear. Shame over the way I'd acted and treated others in that life, and fear that if anyone knew I was Jewish, I might be discovered again and sent to my death. Could this have been why, years earlier, I had been so incensed by Connard, that anti-Semitic teacher in my school? The insight I received from that past life regression was more than enlightening.

~ ~ ~

After that first group regression, we took a 15 minute break, which I spent by myself outside trying to shake off the melancholy I felt from that life review. But very quickly, my melancholy changed to the happiness you get from a deeper understanding of yourself, which comes with a powerful past life regression.

After the break, we settled into a question and answer period. Brian had three young helpers from Omega with microphones, who stood on the left, right and back of the room. There were so many questions, these three kids were kept busy by running all around the big hall.

I was constantly raising my hand. My mind was so full of questions, but they were being answered before I could ask them. One of the questions I was able to ask Brian, when the mike finally came to me, was: "How do you know if your subconscious mind is not just producing metaphors? In other words, Brian, how do you know if a past life experience is real and not imaginary?" My question indicated that after all my acceptance, I still harbored a good amount of skepticism. And it would seem that there were many other healthy sceptics with me there, judging from the large number of nods coming from the audience.

Brian smiled and said, "If my patient leaves my office with a better understanding of who he truly is, being better able to cope with everyday stressors and having joy come back into his life, does it make a difference whether it's real or imaginary?"

The answer to that question was obvious to me. It doesn't matter whether it's real or imaginary if the results for his patients (and my clients) are as dramatic as Catherine's were in Many Lives, Many Masters.

Then with a smile, Dr. Weiss added, "But past lives are very real. We all do have past lives and future lives, and we are all living on this planet for the education of our souls." That statement was the first time I realized that fact, that truth: we are all here on Earth, in the physical world, to learn - from each human life we experience - present, past or future.

During that week at Omega, we all participated in many Past Life Regressions, some in one large group with Brian, and some when we broke up into small groups and participated in past life regressions with each other.

As that first full day's exercises were coming to a close, there continued to be numerous questions from the class. However, it surprised me that the majority of questions concerned hypnosis, as opposed to the participants' experiences with their past life regressions.

Again, I raised my hand and this time a microphone came to me quickly. "Brian, I would think you would have to hypnotize someone extremely deeply to be able to access past lives?" And again Brian's response was sincere and profound.

"In Many Lives, Many Masters, Catherine was plagued in her everyday life by her past lives." The entire audience was nodding. "Her past lives were right at the surface. She was not even in hypnosis, and yet the memories of her past lives surfaced continually. Hypnosis is a powerful tool to access past lives, but your past lives are as close as a thought, so you don't really need to hypnotize your client that deeply."

As the questions continued, it seemed many people were more confused about hypnosis than about past lives. I realized that they could not appreciate the past life experience given to them by Brian Weiss himself, if they continued to have doubts or questions about hypnosis. I knew that many were much too focused on the process (hypnosis) instead of the experience (a past life regression).

So at the end of our first (very) full day at Omega, before we broke for dinner, I stood up with the microphone and made an announcement to the group.

"Brian, everybody seems to be having a lot of questions about hypnosis," I said, now addressing the audience: "If you are questioning your ability to be hypnotized or would like to know how it feels to be hypnotized, in order to have a deeper appreciation for Brian's past life regressions, come and see me after dinner. I am a hypnotherapist and I'll make sure you understand what hypnosis is."

During the week, classes at Omega end at 5 o'clock, when we all go to dinner. Evenings are spent in conversations all around the campus and in the café, and that's where I found myself directing small groups of people into hypnosis. They just wanted to know what it was like to be hypnotized, and I was very happy to oblige them. I continued to lead these small groups for the next two days, until everyone's questions about their ability to go into hypnosis had been answered.

~ ~ ~

What a first day! I was so involved with the day's activities and the hypnosis sessions in the café, I didn't think until that evening about my second mediumship reading, scheduled with Sarah the next day. That night, as I got into bed, I remembered that Sarah wanted me to ask my father a question. So before I rolled over to go to sleep, with my hands clasped behind my head, staring at the ceiling in my dark dormitory room, I spoke with my father.

Dad, I need proof, I thought. *I need to know that it has been you talking to me all these years and not just my imagination.* It wasn't so much a question as a statement. If Sarah could validate for me that it wasn't my imagination - that it has, in fact, been my father speaking with me since he had passed; that he really wasn't gone and was still able to communicate with me - my life would be dramatically changed, once again!

REIKI HEALING - BEFORE AND AFTER

In the morning of the second day, Brian announced to the group that if anyone was interested in receiving Reiki Healing, there was a group of Reiki Masters from Central America, in the back of the room, who would be happy to *share* Reiki with us. Turning, I saw four people sitting in chairs, seemingly hypnotized, with a Reiki Master standing behind each of them, doing various 'things'. Some were whisking the air around their recipients. However, the majority were simply standing with their hands placed on the person's shoulders, and it looked rather soothing.

I had never put any thought or credibility into New Age ideas, let alone Reiki. I hadn't even heard about Reiki until it was mentioned in one of my earlier hypnosis courses at the Holistic Healing Center of NY, well before my Past Life Regression class with Paul Aurand.

That particular class covered 'Ericksonian Hypnosis.' Milton Erickson was considered one of the pioneers in the field of Hypnotherapy. The class had about 15 practitioners and I noticed, during the introductions, that several hypnotherapists had introduced themselves as Reiki Masters. I wasn't aware of Reiki, so I assumed, who would know more about the subject, than a Master?

At that time, I was also becoming more open to New Age practices, and so decided to see what this Reiki business was all about. I asked one of the Reiki Master/Hypnotists to explain for me what Reiki was, and she began one of the longest and most confusing explanations I have ever tried to follow.

Some highlights: "…Reiki … a form of energy healing… direct application of 'Chi' … strengthening the clients' aura… Chinese mystics… underlying force of the Universe… the Universe is made of energy … affected by thought… we create our own reality …"

After politely listening (for what seemed like an hour), I felt as if I'd just endured a lesson about 'the Force' with Yoda from Star Wars, and I was praying for Darth Vader to come down from the Death Star to put me out of my misery. I was reconsidering my recent acceptance of these New Age beliefs and thought that continuing as a hard core cynic would definitely be preferable to listening to this sort of stuff.

The Reiki Master then told me that talking and describing Reiki is one thing, but experiencing it, "…well that is something quite different."

Now, keep in mind that although I am always open to experience new things, all I wanted at that time was a brief description of what this Reiki was. Her rambling, confusing explanation really had me feeling tense. Nonetheless, I agreed to have her 'do' Reiki on me.

She started to do the same actions that I was now observing in the back of Dr. Weiss' workshop. She said that she was "wiping away the negative energy that I see in your aura."

Needless to say, my cynical attitude completely blocked any perceived positive affect that her Reiki attempt could have had. For me, the long drawn-out explanation had resulted in a bad headache… And produced the complete opposite of an open mind.

I would learn to appreciate and benefit from Reiki healing energy. But at that time, I was not only resistant to it, but I was hoping that my buddy, Darth, would come down with his heavy breathing and red light saber to put an end to the New Age torture I was being subjected to.

> *As a side note… I would later go to this same Hypnotherapist/Reiki Master to learn this ancient and beneficial healing modality. I would receive my own Master ranking in Reiki. And I must say that I feel somewhat ashamed of myself for the cynical view I had of this healing art.*

Now years later, in the back of the Omega workshop, I was considerably more accepting of energy work (but still, years would pass before I would study Reiki). As we broke for lunch, I walked to the back of the room, and one of the Reiki Masters, without a word, gestured for me to sit in her empty chair, which I was happy to do.

As I sat, she gently placed her hands on my shoulders. It felt as if they were on fire. The warmth I felt generating from her hands was not just a physical warmth, but felt as if it came from her very soul. This warm and tingling feeling I was experiencing was running up and down my spine accompanied by a wonderful buzzing feeling in my scalp. This was completely different than the Reiki experience I'd previously endured.

As I sat, I was quite aware that people were leaving, talking and mingling as they left for lunch. I really didn't want the session to stop, as I felt her hands gently pull back from my shoulders. Then, with her hands now on my arms, she whispered in my ear, "God bless you," in a strong Hispanic accent.

I thanked her, stood, and asked her name and where she was from. Anna told me that she was from Costa Rica, and that she had come all the way to Omega to learn from Brian Weiss. She said that she'd travelled to Omega with her partner Marina, another Reiki Master, who she confided was much more advanced than she.

We both left for lunch, and that evening she and her partner joined one of the group hypnosis sessions I led in the café. They had no trouble entering a very deep hypnotic state, and I knew that they would be appreciating the group PLR sessions that they had come so far to experience.

*When you look back upon profoundly life changing experiences,
you realize that they were totally unexpected -
which may be the reason
why they were so very profound in the first place.*

SARAH AND MY FATHER

As soon as I walked into the cafeteria, I saw Sarah sitting at a table. She waved to me and pointed to the chair next to her. I placed my knapsack on the chair, and proceeded to the salad bar to prepare my lunch.

With my salad and a peanut butter and jelly sandwich in hand, I sat at the table. Before I could say anything, Sarah asked for me to refrain from telling her anything about my family. She told me that it wasn't because she didn't want to know, but that it would affect the reading that we would be doing after lunch.

At that point I was aware of the procedures and protocols needed for an accurate mediumship reading, by watching *Crossing Over with John Edward* religiously, and remembering the instructions that Millie had given me, which were all very similar. We finished our meal and walked outside, sitting on two Adirondack chairs on the front lawn.

Sarah began by explaining to me that she, the medium, would be the reader and that I would be the sitter. She reminded me not to tell her anything, even who I wanted to speak with, and that she had no control over who might come through. She told me that whatever she received from *spirit* she would relate to me and that hopefully I would understand it. Then she asked me if I had any questions. I simply shook my head.

Sarah took a deep breath, rubbing her hands together, and with a smile said, "OK, let's begin."

"I have your father here..." she said without looking for any validation from me as she described him. "He says he was a very proud man in life. He is showing me a Jewish skull cap, which is my symbol for someone who is Jewish. He's now showing me two children - a boy and a girl." She then looked at me and asked if that made sense to me and of course I said that it did.

"Good! He's coming through now with apologies to you, saying that he never knew how to show love or affection, and that he is so proud of you for the man that you have become." Sarah had been looking to her left, not looking at me for any type of cue. Now she turned to me and asked again if that made sense and I simply nodded as I attempted to hold back my tears.

She continued relaying to me the information she said was coming from my father and everything that she said made perfect sense. She continued describing our relationship; his relationship with my mother and sister; saying that smoking was the cause of his death; how I had picked up that habit after he had died but that there was a powerful reason and purpose for it. This made absolutely perfect sense to me. After all, if I hadn't started smoking, I never would have needed to be hypnotized and would never have become a hypnotherapist. Instead of nodding, now I was saying "YES... YES... YES..."

Sarah became silent for a moment but continued looking to her left, not at me. I was certain she was listening to my father. And with a smile, she continued, "He is showing me playing golf with you when you were little; he is showing me that he taught you how to play golf. Is that true?" Again I nodded.

"He's saying he was a very difficult teacher and that he's sorry for being so tough on you. And that he is so appreciative that as you got older you enjoyed playing golf with him as much as he enjoyed playing golf with you. He's pointing to the time when you 'birdied' a par three 'in' the mountains..."

Now, I couldn't speak, and she handed me a handful of tissues. The tears were not tears of sadness, but of joy. Each new fact she presented, proved to me beyond the shadow of doubt that she was in direct contact with my father. The doubt that I'd always had, in regard to whether it was my imagination or real communication with my Dad, faded into belief.

Again I saw communication between Sarah and my father happening before my eyes. As with Millie, I looked at her as if she were in a hypnotic state, yet I realized that it wasn't hypnosis, but a completely different type of altered state.

To say I was curious would be another huge understatement. I wanted to know more about this communication that made me feel so wonderful inside. Years of loss, years of pain of not having my father with me, having my children who never knew the love of either grandfather, dissipated with each and every new piece of evidence she presented.

Sarah took another deep breath and looked at me, as if this next piece of evidence was more important than the others.

"He's telling me now, that you had asked him one day who had taught him how to play golf and he said his brother, your uncle. And that your father had to caddie for his older brother until he beat him at golf. And that the game he remembers the most was the one where he beat his brother and no longer had to caddie for him."

Sarah had to stop to allow me to regain my composure. This was something my father had told me, one day when I was 12 years old, while he was teaching me to play golf. It was something in passing, something unimportant to anyone else, but I remembered it. This was something that could not have been guessed or fabricated; this information came directly from my father, undoubtedly.

After my tears stopped, she told me that my father was pulling back. She explained that it takes energy on his part to communicate, and his energy was pulling back, but that he would never pull back from me.

After a few moments, Sarah asked, "Garry, did you ask your father a question last night?" I said that I had, but it was more of a statement than a question. She assured me that it would be fine, and that I should just think of it, without saying it out loud. And that's what I did.

Dad, I need proof, I thought. *I need to know that it has been you all these years talking to me.* Once again I saw the communication happening between the two, my father and Sarah. She looked confused by the response she was receiving, yet she still smiled.

Sarah shrugged as she looked at me and said, "I just have to give you what he just showed me." She began with a slight smirk, "He says, you have everything you need now! What more do you want? A kick in the ass?'"

I couldn't believe my ears! That answer to my question/statement was an actual quote that he would say to me when I was not accepting an obvious answer he'd given me.

After a few more tissues, I thanked her from the bottom of my heart for changing my life. And at that point, sitting in the shade of a 200-year-old maple tree, on the front lawn with Sarah at Omega, my spiritual evolution truly began. The direction my life was now heading in had changed, and had never been so clear.

Your Ego is a necessity to function in this world.
But when it becomes overly self-protective and cautious
you may have to put it in check.

"YOU KNOW YOU ARE A STRONG PSYCHIC"

After two days of PLR therapy during the day, group hypnosis in the evenings, Reiki sessions and the mediumship reading that convinced me of the truth concerning the continuation of consciousness, I was spent!

Excited… Thrilled… Totally involved… Overjoyed… Ecstatic…
But spent, nonetheless.

During breakfast that Wednesday, I noticed Marina, who'd participated in one of my hypnosis groups, sitting at another table, and she must have noticed my lack of energy. She smiled and moved her breakfast to my table.

Marina was a chemical engineer from Poland who had moved to Costa Rica to follow her spiritual path. During introductions on that first day, Marina said that she was a massage therapist, psychic, medium, energy healer and Reiki Master. When I made the announcement about my willingness to hypnotize anyone, Marina had asked me if Anna and she could join our group, and I welcomed both of them to have a seat.

Over breakfast that third morning, Marina asked if she could do *Craniosacral Reiki* with me as a repayment for hypnotizing her on Tuesday evening. She said that she saw me giving so much of my energy to so many people, and that she could clearly see that my energy was down (and she was quite correct). She told me that she wanted to replenish my energy. Of course, I said yes. I was certainly eager to experience Reiki again.

I'd received Reiki from her partner Anna that Tuesday, and it was exhilarating, so this new form of Reiki sounded great to me. I was totally accepting and eager to experience whatever it was that was going to take place, although I had no idea of what it was or how it would affect me.

After the morning exercises, the class broke for lunch, and Marina put a yoga mat on the ground. As everyone left the building, she asked me to lie down. She lifted my head and held it in her lap. As I closed my eyes, I truly felt as if I were lifting off the ground. The experience was so intense that I almost opened my eyes, to see if I were really floating. I felt as if Marina's fingers had penetrated in through my skull and that she was not only touching my skull but my soul. I couldn't tell you how long we were there but when she had me open my eyes, I just could not thank her enough. I felt amazing! I didn't know what she did or how it worked. All I knew was that my energy seemed to have doubled.

As we left the building, walking to the cafeteria, she looked at me and said, "You know you are a very strong psychic, but you are in so much denial! You will have an experience very soon that will prove to you just how strong you really are."

I knew she had an amazing gift, I felt great, and I sensed that she was a powerful psychic, but... me: a psychic? I wasn't convinced.

I thanked her for a wonderful Reiki experience, but in my mind, although I was trying very hard not to, I was saying to myself, "Yeah, right, me a strong psychic...Whatever."

Once again, that voice from my father was there, "Doubt, doubt, doubt. When are you going to believe, Ga? What more proof will you need to stop doubting and start believing and learning and growing?"

I was there already, I just didn't know it... yet.

DANNY

Danny had come to Omega from Scotland. Like Marina, he had come from across the globe to experience this seminar with Brian Weiss. We had spoken a few times prior to that night and he was anxious to be put into a deep hypnotic state to experience a past life.

Danny asked if I thought I could hypnotize him and I said that I was sure I could, although he said that he doubted it. When I asked if he had ever experienced hypnosis before, he informed me that he had been a subject for a stage hypnotist and enjoyed the state of hypnosis very much.

The percentage of hypnotizable people in a given population (for those of you who are into statistics) works out to be a perfect bell shaped curve: 10 percent in the sample group are extremely easy to hypnotize and 10 percent are extremely difficult to hypnotize. The other 80% fall evenly between.

A stage hypnotist can identify those who are easily hypnotized by using various hypnosis tests. These tests can eliminate 90 percent of the audience, so he can bring up on stage only those people who can be hypnotized, literally with the snap of a finger.

A person who has already experienced hypnosis is almost always a good hypnotic subject. However, in the group of highly motivated people at Omega, I assumed the percentage of easily hypnotizable people was more like 99.9 % and doubted that Danny would be in that .01% of difficult subjects. He had been hypnotized before and had even been brought up on stage. Everything he said made me assume that Danny would be a 'snap' to hypnotize. But once again, you know what they say about 'when you assume.'

That evening in the café, I had just gotten six people together who wanted to experience hypnosis and saw Danny speaking with one of them. I asked if he would like to join in, as I knew that he wanted to be hypnotized individually.

With regard to people who are difficult to hypnotize, I find that the second time they attempt hypnosis, the better and easier they go into trance. I assumed Danny would be one of the easier ones. He agreed and I proceeded to guide the group into hypnosis.

During the process of hypnotherapy, the hypnotist must be able to gauge the depth of trance his subjects are in. This can be accomplished in a variety of ways. One method is by 'using a convincer'. A convincer, also known as a 'post hypnotic suggestion', is a suggestion given to a hypnotized subject that is totally accepted by the person and upon awakening convinces the participant that they were truly hypnotized.

This suggestion may be "Try to open your eyes… You will find that you cannot." or "As I hold out your arm, you will find that you cannot put it down. It is locked in place." If the subject cannot open his eyes or put his arm down, he demonstrates to the hypnotist that he is, in fact, hypnotized.

But more importantly, when the person comes out of hypnosis, **he** is convinced that he was hypnotized. If he doubts that he was in hypnosis, the hypnotist simply asks, "If you weren't hypnotized, why were you not able to open your eyes or lower your arm when I asked you to?"

I decided to use the 'Stiff Arm' technique with this group by lifting each subject's right arm perpendicular to their body, and make the suggestion that it is frozen in place. I would be able to judge the depth of their trance by pressing down on their arms and feeling the resistance. The more the arm refuses to go down, the deeper the level of hypnosis the person is in.

As usual, I noticed that some people were going into trance more easily and deeply than others, which is normal and expected.

At this point, all seven subjects had raised their right arms. I gave the suggestion, "Your right arm is like a steel bar, and it cannot be lowered." As I checked the resistance in each subject's arm, I noted how deeply all were hypnotized... with the single exception of Danny. He was by far the most resistant to being hypnotized.

Danny's arm was hardly staying up at all. He even opened his eyes at one point. Opening one's eyes during a hypnotic induction can be an indication of a few things. It may be a control issue: 'You can't tell me what to do'; or a rapport issue: 'I just don't trust this weirdo'; or a fear issue: 'If I let myself go, I don't know what I'll say or do,' etc. I didn't think it was any of these issues, but I needed to wait until the group was conscious and ask Danny directly.

After the group experienced the hypnotic state, I brought them back to consciousness and the discussion was very positive about their hypnotic experience. Again, the reason for these group sessions was to make sure people would be able to appreciate Brian Weiss's work. For many of them, it was the first time experiencing hypnosis, and they were excitedly talking about their perception of it.

Danny, who had told me that he didn't think he could be hypnotized, was leading the conversation! He was telling everyone about the time he was taken on stage as the subject of a stage hypnotist.

If you speak to any hypnotist, they will tell you that someone who has been hypnotized - particularly if he has been on stage - will prove to be the easiest to hypnotize. The reason is simple: people who have had the experience love to be hypnotized again.

There are many misconceptions about hypnosis, and many can be attributed directly to stage hypnosis: "You're not going to make ME cluck like a chicken," is the comment I've heard most often.

One common misconception is that the hypnotist is controlling the group. The truth is that the participants **choose** to 'cluck like a chicken'. Given a few drinks, without even being hypnotized, these people might just be on the bar quacking, barking or dancing! However, if the hypnotist told them to do anything that went against their better judgment, they would immediately come out of hypnosis.

I knew that if a stage hypnotist had Danny on stage, he must be a great subject. His discussion with the other people confused me further. He was telling them that he had been hypnotized many times and that he loved the feeling. He told them that he had had two other past life regressions and how incredible they were!

I briefly felt that perhaps I did something wrong or that I didn't know the technique needed to hypnotize him. But, that just couldn't be. He wanted to be hypnotized! He was practiced at being hypnotized! He meditated daily! Everything he was saying, told me that he should be the easiest of all the people there.

Then why was he not going into trance? There was more here than meets the eye. Now I had a challenge… and I do love a good challenge.

As the group was discussing their experience, I said to Danny: "Danny, why, if you have gone into hypnosis so easily in the past, do you think you didn't go into it, at all, in this group now?"

As he started to speak, many of the people were surprised that he wasn't hypnotized and that I knew it. After I explained to them the procedures I took, Danny seemed to gain more confidence in my abilities. It seemed to be important to him, that I was very competent in the 'art' of hypnosis (and it is really an art). Shortly, I would find out why.

The question I asked Danny stopped all the talk in the group. Others who had been observing the group session joined to hear Danny's answer, who appeared to be a little embarrassed at first, but then seemed to want to tell his story.

He explained to the group, "Well, as I said I am quite comfortable being hypnotized." He went on to relay his experience with what he described as a totally incompetent hypnotist whom he went to for a past life regression.

"I'd had past life regressions before and heard that there was a woman in London who was doing them, so I went to see her, even though she charged a lot of money. Straight away, I felt very uncomfortable in there. She was off in a certain way. I couldn't put my finger on it but I just knew something was wrong.

"I sat in her chair and being the 'great hypnotic subject' that I know I am, I went into a very deep state of hypnosis very quickly. She went on to tell me what my past life was without my having to say anything at all. She said that I'd been a knight in Old England and that I had been killed by a spear to my chest.

"She proceeded to poke my chest where she said I'd been stabbed. The pain I experienced from that touch was excruciating! I felt as if a spear had been thrust into me! I had that pain in my chest for over a month.

"And the worst of it was that I know that it was not my past life. It was a past life that she imagined I'd had. I was infuriated! How dare she do that to someone! Since that experience I have not let anyone hypnotize me. I can't even meditate without thinking of that incompetent witch!"

*When you are experienced, practiced and confident at what you do,
you can put yourself in a situation where
you must prove your worth.
It is at those times the person you impress
the most, may just be yourself.*

BACK DOOR HYPNOSIS WITH DANNY

I knew, after hearing his story, that I couldn't tell him that I was going to hypnotize him... He wouldn't allow it. Yet I was confident that I could help him. I simply needed to convince him that you don't stop a helpful ability like self-hypnosis, just because of one bad experience with an incompetent practitioner.

I decided to try a backdoor approach. Known as covert hypnosis, this is when someone is hypnotized without actually realizing it.

EMTs are taught this procedure, for example, with an automobile accident victim. It is a very subtle approach where you never even mention hypnosis. You simply speak softly yet firmly, and direct their thinking to something other than the injured part of their body.

Danny was like an accident victim. The difference was that in a car accident, the victim has an injured body part; Danny's injury was to his sub-conscience and his ability to access it through hypnotherapy.

The damage that was done by this hypnotist, who imposed her perception of what his past life was, caused him to distrust all other hypnotists. Now she may have been a talented hypnotist and psychic, and her opinion about his previous life may even have been accurate. However, if it was Danny's belief that he had never experienced a life and death as a knight, and that, due to the pain she inflicted that lasted so long afterward, he could no longer trust any hypnotist... He couldn't be hypnotized any longer. And that simply was his truth.

I knew I couldn't convince him that he was mistaken. I had to change his mind and his perception of his experience, without the only tool that I knew would be able to work: namely, hypnosis.

I told Danny that I understood how angry he could be at her and that I wouldn't even try to hypnotize him. "I know and you know that you are in control of your life and your ability to be hypnotized, and if you don't want to give up that control, that's fine.

"But I think I can help get you past this problem and all I want you to do is close your eyes and listen to me and answer some questions. I won't 'hypnotize' you," using my fingers to make air quotes. He agreed and in front of about 10 or 15 people, I proceeded to do a sub-conscious intervention.

I knew I couldn't do a formal induction. As soon as I would start with the 'Your eyes are getting heavy' stuff he would become resistant. But how could I reach his subconscious without using hypnosis?

I simply decided to let my Hypnotherapist Part show me the way. I couldn't go and sit somewhere and write out a script or plan of what to do. I didn't have the time. This had to be spontaneous hypnotherapy and I simply allowed it to happen.

I set up two chairs opposite each other and had him sit across from me. I told him again that we were not doing hypnosis, and that I just wanted him to answer my questions and listen to me for a few moments, with his eyes closed. I explained that closing his eyes would eliminate the distractions around him.

I asked him to picture the best experience he had ever had with hypnosis: "A time when you realized how great that feeling of total relaxation was." He relayed the time that he was on stage with a stage hypnotist.

"It was my first experience with hypnosis, and I knew what was happening. I knew I was doing some strange things on stage but I really didn't care! Afterwards, I felt great... I've been hypnotized often since then, but that was the best time." He still had his eyes closed, which was a good indication that he was actually going into hypnosis.

I said, "Good! Now I want you to take that memory and place it on the side. I want you to be able to remember it again in a moment." He nodded. I then asked him to tell me about the experience with the incompetent quack of a hypnotist.

As Danny was relaying his experience with her, I noticed the beginning signs of hypnosis coming over his face. His eyes started to have REMs as his whole body became very still: more unmistakable signs of deep hypnosis.

He continued to describe the method she used for his disastrous past life regression, and I realized that I needed a way to convince Danny of the difference between a good and bad hypnotist. He had discarded the wonderful ability of being able to go deeply into a healthy and beneficial state of hypnosis because of his perception of a single bad experience with one poor practitioner.

I needed a metaphor to use to show him - rather than explain - what had happened. If he were able to view what had occurred from a separate and fresh perspective, I felt that his resistance to entering the altered state would disappear.

I have found that the use of analogies and metaphors are wonderful educational tools. By involving the person's imagination, the negative emotional connection with a bad experience can be lessened or eliminated as their analytical thinking processes allow a calmer and more logical view of the negative experience, and so healing can begin.

227

Once again, it simply hit me! The perfect analogy for him simply popped into my head. I hadn't a clue where it came from, but as I had become comfortable doing, I just allowed the thought to direct me as I was directing Danny.

"Now, Danny," I said to him, "I want you to take that bad experience and put it on the other side, so that you can retrieve it later." He agreed by slowly nodding and again I noticed that he was already in deep hypnosis.

I also realized why Danny had been chosen by the stage hypnotist. Danny was not only in the top ten percent of the population who can almost instantaneously enter a hypnotic state; he may have been in the top ONE percent.

"Danny," I continued, "I want you to picture this in your mind..." As I spoke, images began to pop into my head, as if they were coming from my own memory.

"You are driving your car down a road..." (I pictured him in a Mercedes.) "It starts to act funny, not running properly. As you are driving, you see an auto repair shop and pull in. You explain the problem to the owner, who takes the car in, and works on it for an hour.

"You pay him and leave, assuming that the car is now fine, but it is as bad as it was before! When you return to the garage and explain that the problem still exists, the owner of the repair shop says that there is nothing wrong with your car. He insists it is all in your mind, and refuses to give you your money back.

"You leave flabbergasted! You continue down the road, hoping that you can make it to the next garage, which was fortunately only a few blocks away. You pull your car into that garage and explain to the owner what had just happened in the first garage. He says he'd be happy to look at it.

"You pop open the hood, and as he looks in, he laughs! Calls the previous mechanic an idiot, adjusts two wires, and asks you to start the car. The car starts instantly and runs PERFECTLY! He refuses to take your money, but says to you that when your car is really broken, you should bring it back to him and then he will charge you."

"Danny," I asked, "wouldn't you go back to that second mechanic if your car needs more work?" He slowly nodded.

By this time I could see that Danny was now deeply hypnotized as I continued. "Now Danny, I want you to simply substitute the image of the first mechanic with the image, in your mind, of the hypnotist in London. You wouldn't throw away your car because of a bad mechanic. Why would you throw away a skill like self-hypnosis and the joy you get from going into hypnosis, because of an incompetent hypnotist?"

I went on to reinforce the fact that, if he feels comfortable with a hypnotist, he can allow himself the enjoyment of being hypnotized. BUT at any time a hypnotist says anything that he would have a problem with, "your conscious mind will react by bringing you right out of hypnosis."

This gave him back the control he had lost to the 'witch'. In fact, he had not lost the ability to go into hypnosis, as demonstrated by his deep state of trance right there in the café. It was his perception: his belief that he could no longer be hypnotized.

I have learned over the years that what your perception is… IS your reality; your truth.

The problem with having your mind blown often and powerfully,
within a short period of time, is that you may become overwhelmed
by how incomprehensible what is happening to you seems.
But remember:
You are never given anything that you are
not fully capable of handling.

DANNY'S CONVINCER AND MARINA'S SMILE

Danny had entered into hypnosis. Once he felt comfortable with me and the similarities I shared with the stage hypnotist who had initially hypnotized him, his resistance disappeared and his natural abilities came right back as he entered somnambulism.

I wanted to prove to him that he could once again be hypnotized, and decided to employ a convincer. I used the same Stiff Arm convincer that he had failed at so badly in the group session, just a half an hour earlier.

I held his arm out and told him, "Your arm is like a steel bar... It cannot come down. Even if I press on it, it bounces back." His arm was as solid as a rock!

People nearby were very impressed, and so was I. Actually, I couldn't believe that I'd thought of such a great analogy off the top of my head.

I slowly brought Danny out of hypnosis, but upon opening his eyes, I was concerned because of the puzzled look on his face. That was when I looked around and noticed, for the first time, how many people had come over to observe my hypnotic technique.

It wasn't Past Life Regression. It wasn't spiritual in the least. I had not used any visualizations of souls, spirits or the like. I had simply performed a very straight forward age regression, which had worked out extremely well.

It felt good to have given all those people a demonstration of the almost magical healing benefits of hypnotherapy. It was a pretty good ego booster also, to have impressed so many people. Actually, I was still surprised by how easily I'd come up with that 'bad mechanic' analogy. *Gosh*, I thought to myself, *that went PERFECTLY!*

When a person emerges from deep hypnosis, it usually takes a few moments for them to come back to full consciousness. I attributed the puzzled look on Danny's face to the fact that he had just been in a deep state of hypnosis, and I assumed that he would be fine in a few minutes.

There was still a large group of people discussing what they had just observed. The discussions seemed to focus on the dangers of a 'bad' past life regression; how I was able to hypnotize Danny covertly; and the fact that he was now once again able to be hypnotized.

As I was discussing this with a few of the six original participants in the hypnosis group, Danny caught my eye. Since we were the focus of all these discussions, when he started to ask me a question, everyone quieted down to listen. No one, especially me, could have expected what Danny was about to say.

"Garry, I need to ask you something." Danny said as everyone listened for the question. "How did you know about the car?"

I didn't quite understand his question and responded, "I needed to get you to understand that it was an issue of one poor practitioner, not an issue with hypnosis. The analogy simply popped into my mind..."

"No, you don't understand," Danny insisted. "How did you know about my car?" I admitted that I didn't understand what he meant, so he clarified his question.

"Garry - What you said to me, about my car? How it started acting up, and going to a garage, and having an argument, and going to another garage...

"The whole story happened just the way you described it. From the car running rough, to the argument... Even the way the second mechanic laughed and called the first one an idiot. And not taking payment! He even said to bring the car back when there was something really wrong with it. Just the way you said it!

"That just happened this last month! But how could you have known that?"

I couldn't answer. Once again, my mouth just dropped open (which would become the normal expression on my face that entire week at Omega).

I asked him what the make of his car was. And when he said, "I have a Mercedes," I got chills from head to toe. All the hair on my arms stood straight up! Then I heard a woman say behind me, "Wow, I guess Garry must be psychic! He read Danny's mind!"

I had to sit and process what had just happened. I found my way to the back corner of the café, fell into one of the plush high backed chairs, and closed my eyes.

I couldn't speak, there were so many thoughts running through my mind at the same time. I needed to focus on what had occurred. How had the car analogy come to me? I'd known that I needed an analogy in order to help Danny; one that could prove to Danny that he shouldn't throw hypnosis away just because of a bad practitioner. That was when the image of a Mercedes mechanic came to me.

It came into my mind simply as a thought would: the perfect analogy to compare a good and bad practitioner, along with the image of Danny driving a Mercedes... just a thought, like any other...

I wasn't 'trying to be psychic'. I was trying to be a good, imaginative hypnotherapist. But I had to agree with the woman who'd said, "Garry must be a psychic."

I told myself that it just couldn't be that easy. Yes, I've been feeling my father's spirit all these years, but I always tried to rationalize his presence away, using logic to deny the possibility that I was psychic and perhaps - just perhaps - a medium.

Once again, sitting there with my eyes closed, I became aware of the presence of my father. This time in my mind's eye I saw him smiling and shaking his head back and forth, "always doubting, always doubting."

He was smiling, in the loving way I remembered him. I pictured him in my mind's eye and, as I opened my eyes, Marina was standing directly in front of me - exactly where I had pictured my father standing - with a big smile on her face.

"Do you still doubt?" she asked.

She had been standing behind me through it all, watching me with Danny. I couldn't answer, but the bewildered look on my face said it all.

"As I said to you before, you are a very strong psychic. There are Spirit Guides all around you. They are your protectors and teachers.

"Once you stop your doubting, they will assist you to advance. But, you must want to expand your awareness. And the work must be for a higher purpose: not for self, but for those who seek you out. I smile because they are saying, and I am seeing, that your 'third eye' is beginning to re-open.

"Enjoy your journey, Garry. Our journey here from our home in Costa Rica is nothing, compared to the journey you are about to embark upon..."

I sat in that chair and remembered how, for so many years, I had denied anything considered New Age. I'd completely dismissed the concept or existence of God, psychic abilities, souls, spirits, etc.

In particular, I'd always dismissed anyone who claimed to be able to talk to a Spirit. There were commercials on television from a group of so-called psychics which reinforced my attitude, which was: this entire field, and everything and everyone associated with it, is a sham designed to take advantage of bereaved people. These vulnerable people, who just wanted to communicate with their loved ones, were easily taken advantage of and became the victims of 'psychic' con-artists.

It was the midpoint of my week at Omega. I felt the power of that week in more than just the concepts being taught by Dr. Weiss; I felt a profound change within my being, within the essence of who I was.

This change clearly started with my acceptance that my father is not gone, and has been communicating with me since his death. All my experiences since losing him culminated at that point. I was now a believer, with an open mind where it had been shut, closed and locked before.

I have always been a very curious person. When I find something that piques my interest and curiosity, I am driven to find out more about it. Now, not only did I believe in all those New Age teachings, but I was being told that I am 'a very strong psychic', by people whom I knew to be very strong psychics themselves.

I smiled at Marina, stood up and said, "OK, you've convinced me. I really do believe now." And I really did.

She gave me a hug and told me, "It will be difficult and challenging, this journey that you are about to begin. But it will be very much worth the trip!"

We went to the Café's food counter, where she picked up the salad to-go she had ordered, said goodnight, and retired to her room. I ordered a cheeseburger, and took it to a small table in a quiet corner. I needed some alone time to process everything that had just happened.

I sat at a table for two... about to allow the meat eater in me to partake of a real meal... and just as I took the first bite, someone pulled back the chair across from me and sat down.

It was Sarah. She said she'd heard about what I'd been doing and said that a lot of people were really appreciative of all the work I was doing for them.

I knew that I was not just doing it for others; I was also doing it for the joy I received from the giving.

Sarah told me that she had been busy, too, doing a lot of past life regressions with people. She'd found that she had a knack for it.

I knew she had an incredible knack as a medium and asked her how long she had been doing mediumship. I expected an answer like, "Oh my whole life," but when she said "Oh... about five years," I couldn't believe it. It seemed like she'd been doing this forever!

A hundred questions came to my mind, all at the same time. The number one question was: how does someone learn to become a medium?

Before I could ask her, she offered to do a past life regression with me, and with my mouth full of half chewed cheeseburger, I nodded enthusiastically. But I so wanted to ask her how she learned mediumship!

She told me she knew I needed privacy right now, which I accepted because, again, I knew she was psychic. She 'read' me very well and she was right. She stood up and, as she was walking away, turned and said, "Garry, you do know that you are a very gifted psychic and a medium too, right?"

Fortunately I had just swallowed, or my mouthful of cheeseburger would have flown out of my mouth.

"Yes, I've been told that recently," I said. "Do you know Marina?"

"No. Why?"

"So you don't know what just happened up here?" She shook her head questioningly as I just smiled, saying, "Oh never mind. When are we going to do my past life?"

We arranged to meet the next day. I knew my questions about how one learns mediumship would definitely be answered before I left Omega on Friday.

When you become emotional for no particular reason,
looking deeply into your soul can help explain why.
But if the cause of the emotion is buried so deep and so far away,
you may need to seek out someone who can
help you access those reasons,
in the form of past memories from further
back than you may have thought.

OUR YOSEMITE VACATION AND MY PLR

There is a story I'd like to share with you, at this point, before we continue to explore that first Omega conference, in 2003.

It was 1996. My family had never been to the West Coast and we decided that our vacation for that year would be flying to San Francisco, renting a car and driving to Yosemite.

Aaron was in college and Amy was a junior in high school. I'd been working as a teacher for about six years and we were all very excited to start our adventure. This was during my cynical stage, when I had no belief in God and considered myself a Darwinist and an agnostic.

When we arrived in San Francisco we did all the normal tourist attractions: the Golden Gate Bridge, Alcatraz Island, the wharf, Lombard Street, and Chinatown. We then rented a brand-new '96 Jeep Grand Cherokee and drove to Yosemite.

It was 73° and breezy in San Francisco when we left and 98° when we arrived at the Ahwahnee Hotel in Yosemite. The strangest thing happened, though. When I got out of that air-conditioned car, the smell of the redwood forest literally took my breath away. Visually the area was breath taking. But the effect on me was surprisingly intense.

One of the reasons I'd majored in art and wanted to become a photographer was because of the work of Ansel Adams, who was renowned for his photographs of Yosemite. As long as I can remember I've loved his work, and always had books of his photographs on my shelves. As we were exploring the redwood forest on that very first day at Yosemite, I couldn't understand the intensity of the feelings I was having. As I said, at that time in my life I was still that hard-core cynic, no belief in God, no belief in the soul and certainly no belief in reincarnation.

I stopped and confided to Chris that I felt as though I had been there before. To which she laughingly said, "Ga... You've never been west of Pennsylvania in your life. You know you've never been here before!"

Now, although she stated the obvious - which we both knew to be fact - I still couldn't understand why, after years of wanting to be there, I felt such an overwhelming melancholy.

On our second day in that heavenly place, we decided to drive to El Capitan, one of the most popular, inspiring and photographed spots in Yosemite. It's a popular destination for mountain climbers, who start at the base and bivouac on that sheer cliff face, climbing for days before reaching its summit.

As we arrived at El Capitan, parked and got out, I found myself humming the Joanie Mitchell song <u>Yellow Taxi</u>, particularly the line: "They paved paradise and put up a parking lot." But that wasn't the reason for the deep, deep sadness I just couldn't shake.

The family walked in the direction the arrow pointed, and as we came out of a group of preserved redwood trees, there to our left, in all its magnificence, was El Capitan.

My 19-year-old son said, "What's the big deal? It's a big mountain. Where are we going now?" Then he looked at me with a very curious expression on his face as he noticed tears streaming from my eyes.

Chris noticed the same thing, and suggested to the kids that they should leave Daddy alone and walk back to the car.

When they were gone, she looked at me and asked, "Garry - are you okay?"

"I don't know," I replied, and not knowing why I was feeling so down, in a place that I had wanted to visit for years, just increased my confusion. I didn't understand why I was so depressed. But the feeling became much more powerful whenever I thought about leaving.

I was haunted by one thought: *I will never return to see this place again, in this life.* All week long, I was haunted by thoughts that I had been there before and that I would never be there again... *in this life.* I had been looking forward to visiting Yosemite for so many years. Now that I was there I should be loving each and every moment. Why then was I so distraught?

I wouldn't find the answer to this question until many years later, on the morning of Thursday, August 7th 2003; the next day at Omega.

~ ~ ~

Over breakfast, that next morning, I discussed my experience on vacation at Yosemite with Sarah and Barbara, a psychologist from Pennsylvania. And on the walk to Brian's workshop we agreed that using that memory might be a good starting point for our next PLR exercise.

During that morning exercise, Brian broke us up into groups of three and Barbara, Sarah and I agreed to work together. The groups were designed to have a past life regressionist, a client and a recorder, whose purpose was to take notes to give to the client. We decided that Sarah would take the role of the regressionist, Barbara the recorder, and I would be the client. We were all looking forward to and curious about what information was about to be uncovered.

Normally during a private session, there is a certain amount of time that is devoted to the actual induction of hypnosis of the client, well before the regression, in order to eliminate the client's natural doubts and concerns about being hypnotized. However, during this week the majority of people went into hypnosis almost instantly because we were being hypnotized so frequently.

The technique we used to hypnotize each other during that week was quite easy. The regressionist would say, "Are you ready?" and when the client nodded yes, the regressionist simply snapped his fingers and the client dropped instantly into a deep state of hypnosis. Rarely is it ever that easy, but then again, this was Omega, and everyone there was hypnotized so often that they seemed to be walking around in the altered state constantly.

Our group went to the corner of the building and settled in to begin my regression. I didn't even need to be asked: I simply reclined back on the mat, took a breath, closed my eyes... and I was hypnotized.

"Bring yourself to the past life that affected your current life during your vacation in Yosemite," Sarah suggested softly. Instantly, I was standing in front of the stone bridge. There was a familiar thick fog over the river, and as I was directed, I began to cross the bridge. At the crest, without being told, I looked down and knew I was a young boy. I began to descend from the bridge, and noticed the fog dissipating.

During the regression, there were times that I was observing myself as if I were watching myself in a movie; I was dissociated from the situation. At other times, I was seeing through my own eyes, totally experiencing what was transpiring as if it were happening in real time.

My first observation as I stepped away from the bridge, into that time, was how lush the foliage was. The trees were just as tall and magnificent in that life as now, except there were so many more! The colors were also so much deeper. But my perception of smell surprised me. As I inhaled, I was brought back to my experience, in this life, as I exited the Jeep in Yosemite. And as I exhaled, I was transported back a century and a half to a life in the wilderness.

"Look down at your feet and see what you are wearing. Are you are a boy or a girl?" Sarah's voice seemed louder. I was no longer at the workshop in Omega. I was in Yosemite.

"I'm a small boy." I found it difficult to speak, as if I were using my vocal cords for the first time.

I was looking down at my feet. "I am wearing moccasins; my clothes are made from deerskin that my mother prepared for me." I don't know how I knew it, I just did. My voice was still very low, as I was becoming acclimated to speech. I was so relaxed, it took a concerted effort on my part to communicate.

"Describe your surroundings," Sarah directed me, and I began to describe the log tepees we lived in.

It was interesting: I had never pictured tepees made of logs, and in all the television shows and movies I'd ever seen, they were made of animal hides. These were made of logs. I continued looking at my surroundings and my family.

Sara moved me to the next significant event in that life. Now I saw myself as an adolescent, learning from my father the songs about our ancestors.

She asked me my name and immediately the name 'Chingachgook' came into my mind... and just as instantly my logical mind took over, as I almost came out of hypnosis.

Chingachgook!? I thought. *He was the last of the Mohicans. They were on the East Coast, not in Yosemite. You are such an idiot!*

Fortunately, Sarah saw the change in me and realized that I was coming out of hypnosis. She did some deepening techniques, telling me that my name, in that life, was unimportant. She had realized that I was searching my conscious mind to find an Indian name, and unfortunately I was not able to recall my Indian name at that time.

She then brought me to the next significant event in that young boy's life. I had been learning from my father the ways of my ancestors, as taught to him by his father. I knew that chiefs in the tribe were not elected as the 'chiefs' are in our society. You became a chief as you became older, more experienced, and became a father. Responsibilities were shared by all the elders, who were respected and revered by everyone in the tribe.

I was once again reliving the experience as if seeing through my own eyes, as my father was demonstrating how to make and set the traps to catch small animals for food and fur. We were working our way quietly through the brush, when I heard a twig snap to our right.

I could already discern the difference in the sounds of snapping twigs. I knew that this was a larger animal, not a rabbit, as it had weight behind it. As I turned to see what was there, I expected to see a large deer, or perhaps a small bear.

Since my father and I had not been hunting, I did not have my bow prepared. I knew that by the time I pulled an arrow from my quiver, drew my bow and prepared to shoot, the prey - whatever it was - would have vanished before I could release my arrow. I knew that my father would tell me to always be ready with an arrow. As I turned, I expected to see the deer vanish into the thicket. But I was unprepared and shocked by what I saw.

Staring at us was a white man with the skin of a raccoon on his head.

My father and I looked at each other. In our culture, the top of your head was a place of honor, as the headdress of eagle feathers he wore.

A headdress of eagle feathers was a sign of honor to the eagle. No one would put the hide of a raccoon on his head, as a place of honor for a lowly raccoon. Looking at this creature, with a raccoon skin on his head, made me want to laugh, but there was no humor in this man.

I saw this white man draw his musket. I had been told about this weapon, but had never seen or heard one.

My mind split: I was looking at what was transpiring through the eyes of that young Native American, aware of my existence in that past life and, at the same instant, I knew from my current life's experience, that this musket was a single shot, muzzle loaded rifle.

That young boy had heard about a stick that spit fire from its end, and the death that followed. The explosion terrified me, but not nearly as much as seeing my father being thrown off his feet, his chest and back ripped open...

And so much blood.

My father gasped for breath, blood gurgling from his chest. His gasping stopped almost immediately, as his eyes rolled back. I knew he was dead.

My awareness was now drawn to the man who had just taken my father's life. This white man was now nervously preparing his weapon, his attention divided between reloading and watching my movements. He seemed so very busy, and yet somehow I was in slow motion.

My motion was effortless as I closed the gap between us. I saw him raising the weapon again. I didn't hear the explosion from the end of the stick, or the pressure of the air as the metal ball blew past my left ear. I felt, more than heard, the guttural scream coming from my throat.

That was the first time I had seen fear in another human, and it was caused by me. With my knife in my left hand and tomahawk in my right I was on him before he realized he was dead.

The noise, the gun shots, and my screams raised the attention of other white men in the vicinity.

I heard voices of many men, in a language I'd never heard before. They were coming up the hill toward me, and felt my heart pounding; my breathing changed from slow and rhythmic to panting, as I lay on the mat at the workshop.

Then another loud explosion came from behind me. The branch to my right disintegrated, and shards of wood cut into my face.

This was my home and I knew exactly where I was and how to escape. I knew every cave and stream for miles around, and with that knowledge I was able to escape. I knew they would be following me and I didn't want them anywhere near my people.

I also knew they would not hesitate to kill my entire tribe, so I ran in the opposite direction of safety, to the high mountains. I was able to make it just below the tree line, where I knew I could move much faster.

I was only 16 years old. I knew that, because my father had told me that this would be my sixteenth winter, and I must be prepared for it.

Although I could survive on my own with the training I'd received from him and the other elders, I did not have the tools, weapons, food or clothing available to me that I would at my home. As I ran from these invaders, I knew I was neither equipped nor capable of surviving on the top of the mountain on my own.

I ran until the next day, but I was not prepared for the cold that came. I knew I needed to get down from the mountain's crest. As I was running through freezing rivers, I also knew I was becoming hypothermic.

Sarah now directed me to the last moments my soul was in that body. I was directed to my death scene.

I had gotten back below the tree line and I was no longer being pursued, but the cold rain now turned much colder. As the wind started to blow even harder, hail was now stinging my face.

Shivering, I found a sheltered spot under a large redwood tree and pulled the leaf litter over me as a blanket. I was freezing! Curled up under the leaves to stay warm, I could no longer move my hands, yet as my shivering stopped, a peaceful sleep came over me.

The hail was now a heavy snow that blanketed the area. In my thoughts, as I took my last breath, was that I would never see another spring here in this land that I so cherished.

MY REFRAMING

Sarah had my soul lift from that body.

As I gently floated above that young Native American, whom my soul had inhabited for such a short period of years, 'I' observed what had been 'me'. I felt a disassociation from the shell that I had been housed in, and I felt… free.

My corpse seemed so frail: thin, blue, half-buried in leaves, and curled up in the fetal position. As I looked down at what had been my body, I knew that this was not who I was. Although I had a sense of being in a body, I was confused. I knew that I, my physical body, had died. It was below me on the ground, on the earth. It was no longer a part of me, nor I, it...

Yet I was aware that I still inhabited what felt like a human body.

And that new body was no longer cold, no longer frightened. There was no more pain. Some years later, after many classes and much research, I understood that what I was experiencing was called my 'etheric' body: not physical, but pure energy.

I then became aware of a warm, bright light coming from just above the tree line. At the same time, I felt more than heard the most beautiful rhythmic music. It was not the rhythmic sounds of the drums I was aware of. It resonated with energy. The only way to describe it is as 'music', but it was vibrating within me.

Now as that loving white light approached me, I was drawn toward it... I felt myself moving quickly through what seemed to be a tunnel of light.

Sarah quietly spoke. "You are becoming aware of a person in that light, who will cross you over, to transition you into that light." But instead of becoming aware of one person, I saw two shapes, two men.

In front of me were two angelic light beings. As I looked at them, they combined into one. And I realized that they were both my father. My father from that life and my father from this life had shared the same soul, and I was their son in both lifetimes.

As I came closer to the energy that was the singular soul of both my fathers, I felt the same warmth and joy as when Millie gave me my first reading and Sarah had given me my second the prior day. But this experience was much more powerful. I witnessed both my fathers reflected back to me as one soul, and I basked in that gentle, loving light. As I embraced the soul energy of my fathers, the scene morphed and I was standing once again on a warm late August afternoon, in a valley. I looked around me and I saw and smelled the huge Redwood trees of Yosemite and looked up to see El Capitan once again.

Sarah had me take a deep breath and helped me realize that – almost 200 years later - I would return. I did come back to that same location, just in a different body. My soul's journey from that life was honored, as I was finally able to rest, surrounded once more by the incredible beauty of the landscape that I had loved in two lifetimes, and by the souls of my loved ones, both in-carnate and dis-carnate.

Sometimes, conversations you have with yourself on a long drive
can clarify your thinking and allow you to believe,
which just may lead you to make a leap, which
may be viewed as a Leap of Faith.

MORE LEARNINGS

I now understood why I'd reacted the way I did years ago, on our family trip to Yosemite. I had returned to that beloved place that, as a young Native American, I thought I would never see again. For my soul it was quite an emotionally charged location. But I understood that although the young man died in the mountains overlooking Yosemite, years later his soul would return to the valley he loved, and see it again through the eyes of a different body: mine.

I also realized why I'd always been drawn to the photographic works of Ansel Adams. I was looking at my ancient home through his portraits. But now everything made such sense to me.

Sarah asked me if I was ready to return to this life. I looked once again into the eyes of the soul of my two fathers, and as we hugged, I knew it was time for my soul to return.

Sarah began her de-hypnosis process. "With another deep breath, you say 'See you soon' to your fathers as you feel a tug to return to this life. As I count from one to five, you feel yourself returning. On the count of five your eyes will open; feeling wonderful ..."

She continued to bring me back to consciousness. My eyes slowly opened and focused, and I was back, lying on a mat on the floor of the main hall, with the other 175 Omega participants.

Suddenly, I became aware of the noise in the room. It was as if someone turned the volume control from one to ten! Everyone was mingling and talking, and it took a moment to refocus. I realized that as I was coming out of hypnosis, both Sarah and Barbara were watching me intently.

"Are you OK?" Barbara asked. I nodded and felt the need to stand and stretch. I was surprised to feel so tight and sore. I knew that when in hypnosis, a person will experience time distortion. What feels like ten minutes may, in reality, be an hour. I would have guessed that my regression had lasted for fifteen minutes, but I was curious to see if I was experiencing the same time distortion that my clients describe to me.

"How long was I under for? It felt like fifteen minutes."

Barbara and Sarah looked at each other and smiled, and Sarah said, "How about an hour and fifteen!" I just shook my head. This was my first experience as the subject of a PLR Therapy session as taught by Dr. Brian Weiss, and I was overwhelmed by the results.

To be honest with you, I don't recall lunch that Thursday, or any of the afternoon exercises following my Past Life Regression Therapy session that morning. What I do recall is a feeling of an utter, complete, and total exhaustion.

There was a lot to process after those first four days, and after dinner I just went to my room and crashed. It was the first time I could remember going to bed before 7 o'clock, but I really needed it. Breakfast at Omega starts at 7 in the morning; I set my alarm for 6:00 am, so I could take a shower, pack up my stuff and be ready to leave.

When the alarm went off I felt wonderful, and realized I'd really needed that sleep. I showered, packed up my clothes and bedding, loading it all into my car just as the doors to the cafeteria opened for breakfast. It was the last day of the Past Life Regression workshop which would be over by noon, although the cafeteria would be open for anyone who wanted a little more time to 'schmooze.'

Breakfast was filled with the exchange of telephone numbers, email addresses and lots of hugs. I made myself a bowl of cereal and was looking for a table when someone threw an arm around my shoulders and in a loud New Jersey accent roared, "Dude! What an amazing week. How was your Past Life with Sarah? Mine was friggin'-awesome! And where were you last night? The café wasn't the same without the *Garry Hypnosis Show!*"

Nathan laughed, and we found a table where we could share breakfast before the closing activities. We recalled how we'd met that first day at Omega, during introductions. Although we had been strangers, by now our relationship felt more like old friends.

On that first day, after I introduced myself, the man sitting directly to my left spoke next. He introduced himself saying, "My name is Nathan, and I came here because I want to learn everything I can from Dr. Weiss." He then turned to look at me, smiled and added, "Coincidentally, I live about five miles away from Garry... How cool is that! This might be one of those 'synchro-somethin'-or-others!'" We both smiled and shook our heads.

That was the beginning of our friendship. Along with the love of Brian's books, we also had a lot in common, not the least of which would be a new-found belief and understanding of synchro-somethin'-or-others.

Nathan and I enjoyed breakfast together. As we laughed and reminisced about our life-changing week, he said, "Hey, do you know that there's a Spiritualist church near us, in Sparta NJ?"

"Nah, I'm not really interested in organized religions."

"Yeah, but you might be interested in this one," he explained. "A Spiritualist church is different. They believe in the Continuation of Consciousness. It's a non-denominational church, Garry. They accept all religions, and even atheists are comfortable there. And you know what will really blow your mind? They have psychics and mediums giving readings right there at the church!"

"Nate, are you kidding me? I've been wondering how to meet some psychics or mediums, outside of these workshops, for a long time now!"

"Then this is the perfect place for you, Ga. I just found out about it. They give psychic and mediumship readings there, just like they do here. And guess what? They're starting a basic psychic development class next month. Ya wanna come with me? It's called the ISD."

"ISD? What's that stand for?" I asked.

"It's the Institute for Spiritual Development, in Sparta. Wadda ya say, are you in?" I told him that I would love to, and we shook on it.

Suddenly we realized that we were alone in the cafeteria, so we ran to the main hall and were the last ones in for Brian's final exercise for the week. It wasn't as much an exercise as an explanation of how to incorporate Past Life Regression Therapy into our practices.

I appreciated that final lecture for two reasons:

One - I needed to understand the business aspect of becoming a Past Life Regressionist; and

Two - If there was going to be any more hypnosis on the day's agenda, I was sure that my head would have imploded.

In any event, I had already decided that I would be incorporating Past Life Regression Therapy into my practice.

The morning lecture was over all too quickly, and before I knew it, we were all saying our goodbyes. The queue to say goodbye and thanks to Brian was extremely long; fortunately, I was one of the first people on line.

With my original copy of <u>Many Lives, Many Masters</u> in my hand along with two of his recent books, I shook his hand and thanked him for the most amazing week of my life.

As Dr. Weiss was signing my books, he thanked me for the work that I had done that week. I looked at him in surprise, and he explained that he'd been told by many people about my hypnosis demonstrations in the café, and said that this was a very giving thing to do, and again thanked me.

Brian Weiss, without question, is one of the warmest, kindest and oldest souls I have ever had the pleasure to meet in this life (or, I'm sure, in all my others).

~ ~ ~

I decided to have lunch when the workshop ended. I saw Pete at a table, and joined him in the nearly empty cafeteria. Pete was a truck driver who drove all the way from Texas to take Brian's workshop. We had shared some conversations during the week, and over lunch that last day, our conversation turned to religion.

He was born into an Evangelical Christian family and I was Jewish, but we both came to the same conclusion, as we got older, that religion promotes a 'mine is better than yours' mentality.

Pete assumed, from our discussions, that I had done extensive reading on the subject. When I told him that I had never read anything about religion or even vaguely New Age-ish, he was quite surprised. Pete thought my views were exactly in line with those of Neale Donald Walsch, the author of Conversations with God (CWG). And he simply suggested that I really should read his work.

Now, bear in mind that the only books I had been purchasing - other than books on hypnotherapy - were those written by Brian Weiss. I thanked Pete, shook his hand, said goodbye, turned around and went straight back to the Omega bookstore.

~ ~ ~

And then, as the final mind-blowing experience of the week, I found myself purchasing not just one, but all three of the Conversations with God series.

As I stood on line, I began questioning why I was rushing to purchase them. This was something I had never done: just go out and buy some books, on the suggestion of a stranger and without really thinking hard about it first. Due to my lifelong dyslexia, I had always avoided reading books, unless I'd researched them and concluded their value would be worth the challenge.

I said to myself, *Garry, this is not you.* I realized that I was this 'new' me, whom I was just beginning to understand and become acquainted with. I was aware of all the changes that had been happening within me over the past few years, and I was a bit concerned about my future. Particularly regarding the relationship I had with my family.

And whether that thought was prophetic or not, life was going to be anything but normal for me when I did get home.

A WEEK OF INSIGHTS AND LEARNING

I tossed the three Conversations with God books onto the passenger seat of my car and started the engine, looked around the parking lot and immediately shut it right down.

I was reminded of the world's oldest active sports car race in endurance racing, the 24 Hours of Le Mans. I witnessed the most chaotic group of drivers trying to work their way out of the Omega 'parking lot'. Well, you can't really call it a parking lot. More like a muddy hay field flattened down by 300 cars. Instead of competing with them, which as you know is not really my style, I decided to wait a while before leaving.

So, having a good 15 minutes of down-time, I began to read the dust cover of <u>CWG Book 1</u>. I learned that Neale Donald Walsch was an angry writer, for various reasons. One evening, while sitting in front of his legal pad, Walsch began to write down questions that had been troubling him for years. He addressed these questions directly to God. Mr. Walsch found that his pen seemed to be automatically writing down the answers to the questions he posed.

The result of this 'transcription from God' was his first three books, which were now sitting on the passenger seat of my car. I discovered that all three books were basically a question and answer journal to and from God. And my initial reaction was quite negative.

Once again, I wondered why I had so impulsively purchased these books. Before attending his workshop, I had easily read and thoroughly enjoyed all the books written by Dr. Weiss. But I would find that reading <u>Conversations with God</u> was going to be considerably slower. It wasn't that my dyslexia became worse - it didn't. And it wasn't that <u>CWG</u> was a particularly difficult read. What slowed my reading down was the work itself.

I couldn't believe that I hadn't gone with my gut feeling and just put the books back on the shelf. I became even angrier with myself when I realized that - before spending almost a hundred dollars on these books - I should have read at least one dust jacket. Had I done that, I would have returned them all to the shelf. Finally, I felt that the author must be fairly presumptuous, to claim that God Himself was answering his questions!

That anger lasted until I had gotten home and finished reading the first few pages of his first book.

Even after my experiences at Omega, I was still an agnostic. But upon reading the questions Walsch asked of God, the answers resonated with me so strongly, I believed that if there were a God, the answers to the questions posed to Him would be exactly what I had just read!

Another reason why all three <u>Conversations with God</u> books were such a slow read for me was that almost every question posed was a question I had asked myself. And what was even more mind-boggling was that the questions AND answers were directly related to things happening in my life, at that very moment!

Each time I read an answer, I had to close the book and put it down. I couldn't contemplate how that question, and its answer, could refer so absolutely perfectly and pertinently to what was happening at that very moment in my life.

A Universal Math lesson...
Three Coincidences Equal One Synchronicity.
I have found that synchronicities come in threes (or more):
The first is simply an experience...
The second could be just a coincidence, or it could
be the beginning of a synchronicity...
A third or fourth supposed coincidence IS a
synchronicity - a 'purposeful coincidence' -
And if it is purposeful, that means that someone or something
wants to wake you up, nudge you, or warn you.
But one thing is for sure about synchronicities:
They can certainly grab your attention!

BACK TO THE DRIVE HOME

After the Omega conference, and with the <u>Conversations with God</u> series beside me on the passenger seat, a 3 hour drive home was something I really needed, just to unwind. And when a rest stop gave me the opportunity, I pulled into the McDonalds for a Quarter Pounder with Cheese. I craved a taste of fast food to replace all the healthy salads I'd just consumed at Omega.

Deep in thought, I walked toward the Golden Arches, beginning to review that incredibly life-changing week, and how changed I had become in that short period of time. I was fascinated by the interesting happenstances that directed me to that point in my life.

I thought of how I was clearly directed to be at Omega: my introduction to <u>Many Lives, Many Masters,</u> by three different people; having that book fall into my hands; feeling my deceased father prompting me to talk to Millie, who told me about Omega; having Tricia hand me a brochure from Omega that fell and opened to a photo of Dr. Brian Weiss. And of course all the mind-boggling experiences at Omega.

I realized that one of the most powerful and obvious lessons concerned synchronicity. And although I had contemplated its reality prior to the conference, if I wasn't 100% convinced by now, I sure was close.

There is a New Age proverb that states, "THERE IS NO SUCH THING AS COINCIDENCE," as a hard and fast rule, implying that each and every coincidence is equally fraught with meaning. I now believe that view to be wrong. Things often do randomly coincide, without any deeper meaning. But I've learned how to distinguish mere happenstance from synchronicity.

As I've said, a synchronicity is a purposeful coincidence, a signpost. I now look for three different interconnected coincidences before I will consider them as a synchronicity. When I do feel that these coincidences are synchronistic, I focus on what has been happening in my life, to discover what this synchronicity would be pushing me toward, away from, or calling my attention to. These synchronicities remain in my awareness and give me the sense that I am on my correct path.

It took some years before I accepted, as a personal truth, *who* was sending these purposeful coincidences to me as a suggestion, a nudge, or a wake-up call.

Sitting there at the fast-food table with a mouth full of cheeseburger deliciousness, I thanked those who'd sent me these signposts and nudges in the form of synchronicities. But who, you may wonder, was I thanking?

My father...? My Spirit Guides...? Angels...? Perhaps all of them? I sat there wondering, too. And I really wanted to know, because I simply wanted to thank them.

I intuitively knew that it was unimportant to *them*, whether or not I knew their identity. They are here to help us whether we are accepting of their help, unaware of their assistance, or even if we outright reject it. Their help is constant, and they require nothing in return.

MY BIG SISTER - COUSIN JOYCIE

Sitting at that rest stop, I realized that I needed to share my experiences of the past week. Unfortunately, there were only two people in my family who showed any interest in my new found passions. In fact, I felt most of my immediate family were concerned that I was becoming overly obsessed with all this New Age mumbo jumbo. (And I knew that feeling just might be justified.)

So I sat back, thinking about the past week:

Yosemite...

My death...

Seeing my fathers in the light ...

And, of course, the insight I gleaned through the experience of that PLR.

It was my sister Lynn and cousin Joyce who shared my new, New Age ideas. We were all members of the Love Generation of the 60's and 70's. Joycie was a Beatnik in her twenties, and Linnie and I were teens as the Hippies began to roam Haight Ashbury. Joyce and Linnie have always had strong mediumistic abilities but as you know, my childhood experience with the ghost in my room turned me off to those types of beliefs. And like me, they had always been uncomfortable with their psychic abilities.

Linnie and I always felt that Joyce was much more than a cousin to us. She was more like our older sister. As I looked at my phone, I felt it was important to call Joyce and share my past life experience with her. And as I dialed the phone, I had the distinct feeling that I was about to experience the last synchronicity of the week.

I called Joycie, and began to share my past life in Yosemite with her. As I was telling her of that life, my father, my love of the land, El Capitan, and my passing at the hands of white men, I noticed Joyce was unusually quiet.

Generally, Joycie's style is to be loudly involved in our metaphysical conversations, excitedly sharing our now mutual beliefs. But, as I shared my past life experiences as a young Native American so long ago, she was atypically silent. As I began to describe my death and feeling Dad in the light, Joyce loudly interrupted me.

"Wait, wait!" she bust out. "Garry, you're not driving, right? Good, 'cause this is weirding me out! It's something that I've never told anyone, because it was so confusing to me. But now it makes so much sense..."

What my cousin proceeded to tell me sent a shiver down my spine, as she began to describe two experiences in her life, separated by decades, which had been drawn out of the recesses of her memory by **my** unexpected description of my PLR.

"I know I never told you about what happened to me when Freddy and I went to Yosemite some years ago. It bothered me so much, but I couldn't tell anyone what happened, because it was so confusing and upsetting to me. I couldn't even explain it to myself. Until this very minute!"

I knew that she and her husband had gone on a cross country trip, and wondered why if something important had happened there, she hadn't confided in me. She never shared her experience there, other than having Freddy show us his photos.

"I know now that it really started when I was six years old, in First Grade. I have always been confused by what happened then and how upset I felt. After all, I was only six. I didn't even know what Yosemite was. But when a boy in the class brought in photos from his family vacation for 'Show and Tell,' and said that they were from Yosemite, I exploded! I screamed at him... 'I HATE YOSEMITE! I hate the word Yosemite! I'll NEVER go there. Don't show me those pictures 'cause I'll rip them up...' I hated the sight of every picture that poor boy held up. But that was a long-lost memory until Fred and I went on vacation."

Joycie paused to catch her breath and try to gather her thoughts. "We decided to explore the west. And I couldn't wait to go," she continued, "until the day he announced that we would be visiting Yosemite."

"You know, Garry, I couldn't understand my immediate reaction. It wasn't even a rational feeling. I suddenly became irate. I complained all the way up the mountain. I hated the climb. I hated the curving road. I wanted to be anywhere else in the world. I asked him

249

to turn back, to take me to a shopping mall! He looked at me like I'd lost my mind. The only way I could understand my anger and desire to turn back, was that I'd had enough mountain views to last the rest of my life, and I was desperate to be somewhere else. And right this minute!"

Joyce was speaking so quickly, it was hard to make sense of her words, but she continued more calmly, "Garry, I was so confused and conflicted as the car continued up that snaking road. Every time Freddy said 'Yosemite', I actually got angrier! Even then, I knew it makes no sense at all. But I realize now that the thought of Yosemite brought back all the same feelings I now remembered having, way back in First Grade!

"But I still didn't know why I was so angry. It made no sense to me at all. Especially since I'd so loved the Grand Canyon and the amazing energy in that land.

"Fred had never, in all the years we'd been together, seen me like that. Everything there was beautiful but the anger in me exploded as soon as we got to the top and saw the view of Half Dome and El Capitan. I got out of the car and screamed to Freddy to get me the hell out of this place. He really thought I went crazy... And so did I."

"I would have too," I said with a laugh.

"But now, as you were describing your past life regression, Garry, all those memories came rushing back to me, as you were talking! And I am positive that my anger when I was six - and again when I was on vacation - came from a past life I had with you!" And finally, Joyce fell silent.

"Garry... Right now as I'm talking with you... I remember what happened!

"When Fred and I left Yosemite, driving the hour and a half down the mountain to the hotel, I kept trying to understand my temper tantrum. Freddy noticed how sullen I was and asked several times if I was OK.

"I told him that I was so confused, and told him what had happened in First Grade. Fred was very understanding, and his kindness made me realize that, along with the irrational anger, I was also very frightened. Even though I knew there was nothing to be frightened of," as her voice trailed off in thought.

"I soon became totally withdrawn, feeling completely powerless over the swirling emotions that were overwhelming me." Joyce paused again. "I think Fred was really concerned about my mental health," she joked in an attempt to lighten the mood. "But in all seriousness, so was I. I really thought I was having a nervous breakdown, but it was the not knowing why, that really concerned me.

"That's the reason why we have never told anyone about my melt down. Long story - short, I settled down when we left Yosemite, and I have never felt that way again. I would just try to tune out anything that called my attention to the subject of Yosemite. And now by telling me your experience, I want to tell you what is coming to me about why I was frightened and angry. And it's CRAZY!"

It would seem that I was about to do my very first PLR therapy session, on a cell phone with my cousin, from the McDonalds on the NYS Thruway. If it sounds bizarre, it really was!

I asked my cousin to get a cold drink, sit in a comfortable chair, and think calmly about what Yosemite reminded her of, without any fear or anxiety. When she told me she was comfortable, I began to guide her with specific questions, helping to direct her ever deeper into that past life.

Right there, on the phone with me, she began to experience spontaneous memories of living in Yosemite long, long ago, when a close member of her tribe and his young son went trapping. She remembered how, when they didn't return, some of her tribe went to search for them. Those on the search party were attacked and decimated in a battle with white soldiers. Those same soldiers ambushed the village that night, systematically killing our whole tribe... Just as **my** life was coming to an end, frozen under the leaf litter.

No wonder she was angry!

We both came to the same conclusion: that my cousin Joyce and I had been close relatives in that lifetime, as well as this one. It made complete sense to us, as we looked back at the relationship we'd shared growing up, and how we had always seemed like so much more than mere cousins. A stronger connection bound us, and now we understood its timeless roots.

When you finally accept that synchronicities are a reality,
they become one of the most interesting
teachers you could ever have.

LEARNING THROUGH SYNCHRONICITY

Back at home, my life was anything but metaphysical. It was physical: Earth bound. Chores, mowing the lawn, chopping wood to prepare for fall, and all the things I had looked forward to, took a different turn. After the week spent at Omega, I wanted more and I wanted it NOW!

I was like a kid in a candy store, impudent, needy, impatient and oh so demanding. I was also very frustrated. I'd had a taste of the metaphysical side of life and I wanted more because it tasted that good. And like a kid, if a little tasted good, a lot more would be better. If it sounds a little like an addiction, you'd be right.

I went to my local Barnes and Nobel to find a book about psychics or mediumship and was terribly disappointed with the limited selection I'd found. Even though I had started to read Conversations with God: Book 1 and had Books Two and Three waiting on my shelf, I was anxiously anticipating the next books I'd buy. Not finding a single book of interest, I left that Barnes and Nobel, frustrated by the realization that I was going to have a difficult time finding the books I wanted.

Driving home, my thoughts returned to my last day at Omega, and how I wanted to keep Spirituality in my life. Then I recalled the conversation I'd had with Nathan, about that metaphysical church that was offering psychic development classes, and I found it very difficult to control my enthusiasm. I just couldn't wait for this new metaphysical experience to begin. And just like that kid in the candy store, I was having tantrums, over wanting MORE and wanting them NOW!

~ ~ ~

A week later, I was back at school, and became aware of a new synchronicity that was strongly drawing my attention. Although I wanted to read every book I could on the subject, I could not ignore the power of this new synchronicity. And fortunately for me, my family and my mental health, I followed where it led me.

It seemed that over a two day period, every time I turned around, the message to *slow down* was hitting me squarely in the chest. The expression, "Rome wasn't built in a day," came to me multiple times in those two days. "Take your time," was said to me in three different classes on the first day. And as I had become accustomed to, I reflected on this new synchronicity. I realized that I was being shown that the steps along this journey, by necessity, had to be baby steps.

When I got home on that second day, I realized that I needed to lower my level of excitement, and although I wanted to drag everyone I knew down my path toward enlightenment, I accepted that I needed to chill out and process what was happening to me. The synchronistic suggestions coming to me to chill out and slow the heck down were probably good advice, and I decided to take them. So instead of reading the rest of the first <u>Conversations with God </u>book, I decided to allow the old me to just chill out by watching my old love, the TV set.

So that night I put on one of the home improvement shows I'd always enjoyed and found one that I had recorded on my VCR. The show was like many others, and half way through I began to fall asleep, until the voice of the carpenter said something that woke me right up. I heard the expert mention to the home owner, "I know you are anxious to get this renovation done, but remember Rome wasn't built in a day, and if you want your home to stand the test of time, we need to take our time and do this foundation the right way."

I jumped up and rewound what I'd just heard to affirm that I wasn't dreaming and what I'd just heard was for real. And when I played it again, I just shook my head. I smiled, grasping that I was now being shown the latest synchronistic event. But this one had been recorded a month earlier and I had to laugh that choosing that particular moment to watch that show was the last and perhaps the most powerful synchronicity of the string.

I found it infuriating because, at that time, my desire to understand what had happened to me at Omega was so intense. I also understood that this phase of my journey was *foundational*. In order for my spiritual house to stand permanently, I accepted that the foundation that house was to be built upon needed to be strong, secure and solid. I accepted that the only way my spiritual growth could continue would be by devoting time, effort, money and education to it.

I also realized that my spiritual evolution, this journey from atheism to spirituality that I'd found myself upon, began to speed up with my acceptance of synchronistic experiences. However, although my spiritual growth had begun at the Christmas party with Trisha, it was not until that recent drive home from Omega that my journey went into second gear and began to pick up speed, from a standstill to the ludicrously blazing light speed of… *Baby Steps*.

~ ~ ~

I thought of the 'old me': cynical of anything that couldn't be proven with the five senses. I thought of the 'future me': anxious about what would happen to me, my wife and my family if I embarked on this new path. Wondering if I should buy more metaphysical books and take psychic development classes or not. Just asking the question got an immediate response in my mind of *Yes*.

I wondered where I would be in the future and, although I felt concerned, I knew my life would be more complete if I followed this spiritual path. And I realized that it didn't matter if I became aware of my journey when I was six years young, looking at a ghost in my old bedroom, or 54 years old in a workshop at Omega.

The 'present me' was being surprisingly realistic and objective, considering what the three of 'us' (my past, present and future selves) had gone through that week. Those three parts of me seemed to be playing very well together. I was looking objectively at the 'old me', realizing that he was able to build a very satisfying, happy and productive life for my family.

I realized that I didn't have to go down this metaphysical path; it was my own choice and I chose to take it. After all, we all do have free will.

I could have simply shrugged and ignored the synchronicities that nudged me to attend the Omega conference. I could have looked at the brochure in Trish's office and said, "How weird is that! I just heard about this place: Omega," and tossed the brochure on the coffee table. I could have shrugged and ignored the myriad synchronicities, but something convinced me to follow them; which eventually led me to this opportunity to contemplate what my future held.

I could have ignored the signposts, and I would have been very happy. I could have ignored the suggestions, and continued my life as a teacher and part-time hypnotherapist. I would have been a very happy man, completely satisfied, with a wonderful life. But instead, I chose the path that I find myself on presently. My life could have continued exactly as it had, except for an interesting metaphysical week-long experience. But it didn't. I **chose** to pursue my metaphysical growth, with a passion and determination that some people called an addiction.

~ ~ ~

Although it took me three months to finish all of the Conversations with God books, I couldn't wait to see if Neale Donald Walsch had written any others. Now, keep in mind, I was still unaware of Amazon (other than the South American river). Until one day in school, I mentioned to another teacher about the difficulty I was having getting specific books at my local book store. She walked over to my computer, sat down, opened Amazon. com, and along with its website, opened up a brand-new world to me.

I signed up, pulled out my business credit card, got my password and discovered how easy it is to access a wealth of New Age knowledge.

I was consuming metaphysical books at a rate of one a week, and at times I was reading two books at the same time. I found that my dyslexia had vanished. (And to my chagrin, most of the spendable income from HYP4LIFE was disappearing too: going directly to my Amazon account!)

Reading the CWG series led me to books like Seat of the Soul by Gary Zukav and The Power of Now by Eckert Tolle. What surprised me as I was reading all these new books, was that their theories did not feel new to me. They seemed to just reinforce what I already intuitively knew. They weren't introducing me to new concepts or knowledge, as much as they reminded me of what I always knew but had temporarily forgotten.

I became an Amazon junkie and was ordering ten books at a time. Along with metaphysical and religious theology, I was buying every book written by all the published mediums, New Age thinkers and hypnotherapists. When I came home from school and found an Amazon cardboard box on my porch, the 'kid in the candy store' turned into a five-year-old under the Christmas tree on Christmas morning.

I'd open the box, take out all the books, and line them up on my bookshelf, which was filling up quickly. I would stand there looking at the new books and ask the question out loud to them: "Which one of you is calling me?" Then I would take my pointer finger and scan it back and forth over the titles. (Perhaps I was expecting one to fall off the shelf as <u>Many Lives. Many Masters</u> had, years before.)

I did this when there was no one else in the room, and sharing this with you now makes me wonder if you are thinking that perhaps I had gone off the deep end. You would not be the only one who shared **that** opinion.

However, my brief - if not bizarre - conversation with my books always seemed to work out well. Just as the <u>Conversations with God</u> series always answered a question I was having, at the exact moment I was having it, so too was the choice of book I was led to read.

I was eagerly looking forward to my next Amazon delivery, knowing I had ordered the next book in the <u>CWG</u> series, <u>Friendship with God: An Uncommon Dialogue</u>, and I already knew it would be my next read.

When it arrived, I placed it on my desk and fit the other books in what limited space I had remaining on my bookshelves. I sat down, anxious to start the next book in my spiritual education, but I was distracted by thoughts of Omega, so instead of beginning the next book in the series I loved, I opened my computer.

As a lark, I Googled - Neale Donald Walsch - and learned that he would be at Omega that autumn. Smiling, I called Omega to reserve a seat for another weekend workshop, this time with Neale Donald Walsch.

Garry with Neale Donald Walsch, Author of <u>Conversations with God</u> Series
Photo taken at the Omega Institute for Holistic Studies,
Rhinebeck NY - Autumn 2008

There is belief and then there is belief at a different level.
A stronger, deeper level.
You can conceptually have belief, but
when you believe at a core level
– true belief – you also learn what it means to have faith.

THE INSTITUTE FOR SPIRITUAL DEVELOPMENT

In September of 2003 I heard from Nathan, the neighbor who sat next to me on that first day at Omega. He called to ask if I was still interested in participating in the psychic development classes being held at an interesting metaphysical Church nearby. I was now comfortable with mediumship, but a metaphysical church where the belief was 'Spiritualism'? Well, this was another new concept for me. So now with my recently acquired computer skills, I Googled both 'Metaphysics' and 'Spiritualism' and discovered an organized religion that I could possibly believe in.

In researching the Institute for Spiritual Development, I found their "Mission statement" and "Vision" completely to my liking. (From their website - www.isdsparta.org)

> *"Our Mission:*
>
> *We are a Metaphysical Church that honors and celebrates each soul. Our community provides an unconditionally loving and healing environment that affirms and encourages all seekers on their spiritual journey.*
>
> *Our Vision:*
>
> *We believe that all great religions and philosophies contain within them the spark of truth and wisdom that can inspire within us a more complete understanding of our place in the Universe. Aided by this belief, we seek to provide a supportive environment through Sunday services, spiritual healing, fellowship and education.*
>
> *About the Institute:*
>
> *The Institute is a non-profit organization dedicated to the service of your growing awareness, and to fostering an environment in which each individual may be stimulated to pursue his or her own true spiritual unfoldment uninhibited by dogmatic concerns. To arouse a process of joyous living, creative genius, cooperation, health, prosperity, and universal service is to arouse the spiritual heart of the organization.*

Believing that the search for your truth embodies a personal examination
of all philosophies and religions, the Institute Experience seeks to provide
the focal point for that search and a nurturing environment in which the
evolution of your spiritual progression may be realized."

This was a 'church' that I could call my own. Non-denominational, meant they were open to and accepting of all (or no) organized religions. Believing in the continuation of consciousness, meant that they believed in reincarnation, past lives and connecting with spirits. And they were actually holding classes that could further my own psychic development!

I was sold! *"Where do I sign up?"*

The ISD is housed in a traditional old church with a big white steeple, on Sparta Avenue in Sparta NJ. I called and made a reservation for their entry-level, beginner's psychic development class, which started that Thursday and continued every Thursday evening for the next two months.

Nathan and I met, drove in together, and caught up with what had happened in both our lives since meeting at Omega a few weeks before. For Nathan it would be just for the experience, and he wasn't interested in taking a second class. For me it was an introduction to a completely new way of thinking, feeling, knowing and living, which continues to this very day.

MY FIRST PSYCHIC DEVELOPMENT CLASS

Nathan and I pulled into the parking lot and were surprised by how many cars were already there. That first class began with an explanation of and introduction to our own psychic/intuitive selves.

While waiting for the class to begin, we shared our experiences at Omega with some of the people who were taking the class. I shouldn't have been surprised by how many were familiar with Omega; after all, this was a Spiritualist Church. And when we told them we had met at Brian Weiss' Past Life Regression workshop, many of them were curious as to what our experience was like. Very quickly I became relaxed and comfortable with all these new people who shared my new found beliefs.

The psychic development class was run by two women who were ordained reverends and professional mediums: Reverends Diane and Christine. The class had twenty participants, and we sat in a circle, as Diane and Chris described what the workshop would be like.

They explained that these classes were designed to introduce and have us participate in exercises to expand our basic understanding of our latent psychic abilities. We were told that the class would also be geared toward expanding what mediumship abilities we all may have. Interestingly, I'd found the exact workshop I'd been looking for, without any effort on my part.

BECOMING 'RELIGIOUS'

On the second Thursday class, both Chris and Diane suggested that I continue my spiritual exploration by coming to their Spiritualist Service at the ISD on Sunday morning. I was so excited about what I was learning and the interesting people I was meeting, that I told Chris (my wife) that I was going to explore what this religion had to offer. I excitedly described what I had learned at the first two classes and asked her if she wanted to go with me to a service. I was surprised and saddened when she declined saying that she just didn't find anything fascinating about my new interests.

So, three days later, I went to my first Spiritualist Sunday service, and was happily surprised that I actually found a religion that I could believe in.

A Spiritualist service is similar to many other religious services. There was singing from a hymnal, a homily that was given that Sunday by Diane, announcements and coming events and classes, a time for donations to the church, and refreshments were served following the service. But there were some very interesting parts of the service that I was drawn to and I hadn't expected.

Two commonalities between all Spiritualist Sunday services, which make them so appealing to me, include Reiki type healing performed by trained spiritual healers, as well as psychic readings. The psychic and mediumship readings are delivered at the conclusion of the service by psychics and mediums who have been tutored, evaluated and approved by the church. Basically, the ISD church provided a continuation of spiritual education I'd been introduced to at Omega that summer.

At the beginning of every Sunday service, the entire congregation reads the "Declaration of Principles," from page one of the hymnals. Each time I read them, I find I resonate with them a little more. I'd like to share them with you and I think you may find them as truthful and powerful as I have over the past 15 years.

DECLARATION OF PRINCIPLES

We believe in Infinite Intelligence.

We believe that Infinite Intelligence expresses Itself in all existence
and in humanity as a manifestation of divine love.

We affirm the unity of all life, everywhere.

We believe in communion with all planes of existence,
and that meaningful communication flows from this connection.

We affirm the divine right of each individual to seek the Truth
in accordance with their consciousness, and that living
in harmony with that Truth defines true spirituality.

We affirm that spiritual unfoldment is progressive and unending,
and that the doorway to reformation is never closed against any soul.

We believe that the highest morality is contained in the mandate: |
"Do onto others as you would have them do unto you"

We affirm the personal responsibility of the individual,
and that we choose our happiness or unhappiness
as we apply the Laws of the Universe.

We affirm that all life is eternal, and that the existence and
personal identity of the individual continue
after the change called death.

We believe the ultimate expression of God in our life is unconditional
love of our neighbors and ourselves.

We accept that the living gifts of Prophecy and Healing,
reported in all Sacred Scripture, are an affirmation of Divine Spirit
working through us.

At the end of the service, and after a meditation, everyone stood, put their arms on each other's shoulders and sang the same song which is always the last one of every service: Let There Be Peace on Earth by Sy Miller and Jill Jackson.

When we finished that closing song, everyone hugged each other, said their goodbyes and began to walk toward the hospitality room for coffee. I was at the end of the pew next to the wall, so instead of walking in front of people I just stood in the pew and allowed the congregants to pass by. I was unaware that I was about to experience the last of the string of mind blowing synchronicities which had started months earlier.

As I stood waiting for everyone to file out of the nave, I noticed the last person in the aisle was a very large man walking out with his wife. And as he passed me, I almost bumped into the woman who was exiting behind him, and whom I never saw until I almost knocked her down. Before I could say "Oops, excuse me," my jaw dropped open as I came face to face with Tricia!

At first I must have looked stunned, like when you see someone from work in the supermarket and you say to yourself, *I know this person, but from where?* That confusion lasted for a second and a half, until she laughed and smacked me playfully on my arm.

"Garry! What are you doing here? I didn't know you heard about the ISD," Tricia said with a hug. "I've been meaning to tell you about the spiritual services here for a while. But you got here on your own, without me. This is just too cool!" She took a breath, smiling broadly. "And you do know exactly what this is. Right?"

"Uh huh," I said. "A synchronicity."

And with another hug and kiss goodbye, Tricia said, "Not just a synchronicity. A very powerful one! One that will stay with you your whole life. And I am so happy, grateful and proud to be a part of it."

ONE EXERCISE STUCK OUT IN MY MIND

Webster.com defines a cynic as:

> "... *A person who has negative opinions about other people and about the things people do; a person who believes that people are selfish and are only interested in helping themselves...*"

I look at the difference between skeptics and cynics as: a skeptic needs strong proof to believe, while a cynic believes that no proof could ever be good enough, because he has already made up his mind to be totally closed to any new possibility.

~ ~ ~

When we entered the church on the fourth week of the PD class, we found the chairs arranged in two concentric circles, 10 on the inside facing outward and 10 on the outside, facing inward. Reverends Diane and Chris separated the twenty of us into two groups of ten. We were told that this exercise had one group acting as the psychics and the other as the sitters, and after this first part of the exercise concluded, we would switch roles so we could all experience this exercise from both perspectives.

"This exercise is designed to eliminate the temptation to guess and make assumptions about your sitter," Chris told us as we all eagerly awaited our instructions. "We call that *doing a cold reading*. And although there are people presenting themselves as psychics and mediums, and can be very convincing to a sitter by doing these cold readings, they are neither psychics nor mediums. They are frauds. A cold reading is the method that fraudulent psychic readers employ to steal money from gullible or bereaved people.

"Unfortunately," she continued, "cynics believe that **all** psychics are quacks who intend to rip people off." Which was exactly the way I'd thought, prior to becoming open to new possibilities and explanations. When I stopped my cynicism, I became a healthy skeptic and then eventually I was able to become a true believer.

They explained that this exercise was designed to aide us in eliminating the effect of our egos on our psychic development, which we were told could keep a beginning student from advancing.

Both reverends directed specific students to sit in the inner circle, which left ten students standing. I was chosen to be in the seated group who were going to be the psychic readers for the first round. The remaining ten students were told that they would be read by the psychics, and that they would be the psychic readers for the second exercise. They were directed to another room, where they would be given the directions for sitters.

When the sitters left with Diane, we the readers were told how this exercise would work, as Chris walked around the circle handing each of us a blindfold. We were told that by making it impossible to see our sitter, we couldn't make assumptions about them: about their age, ethnicity, or anything about them at all. We would be totally unable to look for their reactions to our psychic impressions. We were then told that we wouldn't even be able to hear their voices! The sitters would be directed to sit in front of us in complete silence. The only communication was going to be done by touch.

So, after some interesting comments voicing our concerns about our discomfort with the idea of being blindfolded, we realized what a wonderful learning opportunity this exercise could offer. There could be no expectations, assumptions nor 'cold readings' on our part if we were blindfolded and couldn't even hear our sitter's voice. We were told that this exercise would eliminate our ego from interfering with our reading. Which it did, incredibly well.

As Chris was giving us our directions, in the other room, the sitters were given their instructions by Diane. "Each of you must be completely silent from the moment you re-enter the room. I will point each of you to the chair where you will sit and be read. The reason for this is because your psychic will be blindfolded and by being very quiet, they cannot know who they are reading. Anonymity is essential for this exercise to work effectively. Questions or evidence posed to you by your psychic will be by touch."

As everyone was raising their hands, looking fairly confused, she continued, "I know you have a lot of questions, so let me clarify how you can answer by touch. You will communicate with your psychic by a touch of your index finger to the knee of your reader. Once for yes, twice for no and three times for 'I don't know' or 'I need more information.' Any questions?" And soon, our sitters with no questions were ready to be read silently.

Back in our room, we went through a very quick meditation, after which Chris and Diane directed our 'awareness' to the person who would be sitting in the chair across from us. Then with blindfolds firmly in place, we heard the sitters all coming in, in silence. I was surprised at how excited I was to begin.

Logically, I knew I couldn't identify who the person was who would be sitting across from me. With repeated directions to our sitters about communicating only by touch, we were asked to give our sitter whatever information we received, without evaluating that information. We would then wait for an answer in the form of a tap on our knee.

That was the first time I understood the importance of the expression, 'Give what you get.' I had heard that expression in every single class on psychic or mediumship development that I have ever taken.

As my sitter sat across from me, Diane announced that we should begin to relay to our sitters whatever information we were receiving. I immediately 'saw' a man with grey hair and I felt that he wanted to talk to his son. This was both exciting and confusing, and I immediately doubted what I was receiving. But instead of allowing myself to doubt, I decided to do exactly as I'd been directed to by Diane and Chris. I somehow 'knew' that this man was also in the military. I 'saw' green army fatigues and 'heard' the word "Korea" and then "World War II." I then 'saw' the Eiffel Tower! The images of the army fatigues and of the Eiffel Tower seemed as if they were my own memories as opposed to actually seeing them with my own eyes.

I decided that I wouldn't try to understand what I was perceiving and that I would simply give what I was getting. And that is exactly what I did. I said just loudly enough for my sitter to hear me, "I am aware of a man who is related to you, and I feel he is your father." I felt one tap on my knee indicating a yes. And as soon as I felt the touch, I knew the person sitting across from me was John, another participant! I asked him, "Are you John?" But I received no response and heard someone walk over. I heard whispering and then I felt another yes tap.

A thousand questions formed in my mind in a nanosecond... *How did I know it was John without seeing him and only by a touch to my knee? How did I get two yesses, if I didn't even know who I was talking to? Could I possibly be a medium?* The image of Marina at Omega came quickly to mind, answering my questions - "*Garry you are a medium!*" - And, perhaps she was right.

With that second yes, I felt this man in spirit showing me World War II images. I described each image I sensed, and got one tap on the knee. I was getting an affirmative tap for every single image that came to me! I couldn't believe the accuracy of the information I was receiving. This was my fourth exercise, and I felt I was becoming stronger and more accurate with each new one.

Eventually we would learn how very effective this blindfold exercise was, and I have used the same exercise often in the psychic development classes that I've presented.

Before long I had taken every class they offered, including beginner and advanced mediumship classes. I signed up to be a healer at the church and along with the Reiki certification I'd recently received, I became a card-carrying healer at the ISD.

During one of the advanced mediumship classes, Reverend Chris came to me and invited me to 'give messages' during Sunday service. What she was asking me to do was to be one of the three 'Message Bearers', readers who would stand up at the end of the Sunday service, and give three separate people a mediumship reading, in front of the entire congregation. Just the thought of it made me incredibly nervous. I thanked her very much for her confidence in me, but told her that I was just not ready yet, to which she smiled and said, "You will be soon enough." And she was right.

I became a member of the church and at classes and Sunday services, we would all share metaphysical experiences. One that everyone liked to hear was how new members, like me, had found the ISD. They knew that I'd gone to Omega frequently and that I was a hypnotist, who studied Past Life Regression Therapy under Dr. Brian Weiss. I was asked if I could present a PLR workshop, modeled after those taught by Dr. Weiss, at the ISD and, of course, I was thrilled to do it.

The stress I felt about doing a mediumship reading at their Sunday service, in front of the entire congregation, was too much for me at that time... but leading a group PLR workshop that I had learned from Brian was something I was most definitely up for.

Before long, I was presenting regularly scheduled workshops on PLR along with various hypnosis workshops. And soon enough, Reverend Chris was proven right, as I delivering mediumship messages at the ISD. Clearly, I went full bore into my metaphysical pursuits.

~ ~ ~

One of the first things I learned at the ISD was that the expression "psychic medium" is a redundant term. In my first basic psychic development class I learned that everyone is psychic to various degrees. You can call it intuition or, as police officers like to describe it as their 'Spidey Sense.' Everyone has psychic abilities but although opinions differ, I also believe that everyone also has mediumistic abilities. I believe that you are actually your own best medium. But you probably doubt that you are speaking to your loved ones in spirit, just as I had questioned my connection with my father, for most of my life.

What I have also learned is that - although we can all sense things psychically, including the ability of sensing our own loved ones in the spirit world - not everyone wants to take the time and effort to develop their intuitive abilities.

During the following years, I participated in multiple mediumship classes at Omega and the ISD, along with many other Spiritualist churches in NY and NJ. I consider myself to be extremely fortunate to have been able to work with and learn from some of the world's most renowned mediums.

~ ~ ~

In his third book - Messages from the Masters; Tapping Into The Power Of Love - Dr. Brian Weiss writes:

Spirits, as well as people, are of many levels. Those of the lower levels can transmit misleading or even harmful messages, usually to people with limited mediumistic abilities or lack of proper spiritual development. Spirits of higher levels seem to be accessible only to those people with higher spiritual development and/or those with proper intent, those without ulterior motive for self-gain at the expense of others.

When you meet a seer or wise teacher whose motive is to help others to understand, to heal other people's hearts and to assist them on their spiritual path, a profound shift in your consciousness can occur. The world will seem different, filled with unseen helpers and bathed in a loving Energy that refreshes and renews your soul.

You yourself may spontaneously experience other life-transforming events. Dreams, déjà vu experiences, clairvoyant episodes, and other paranormal occurrences (including Near Death Experiences) can induce a permanent awakening to the true nature of reality. Meditation can increase the likelihood that one or more of these experiences may happen.

But we humans tend to forget, or at least to rationalize and minimize, any experience we consider "improbable" or "extraordinary." Moreover, we allow our "logical" minds to subtract the spiritual meaning from the experience. Someone once said that what we call coincidences are really God's fingerprints.

I believe that the above quote from Dr. Weiss' third book was an accurate description of what was happening to me.

There are three commonalities shared by great teachers. They:
1 – Demonstrate a passion for and a detailed
knowledge of their subject;
2 – Demonstrate a passion for and knowledge of teaching; and
3 – Have the desire and the ability to DO both.

JOHN HOLLAND

The summer after I was certified as a Past Life Regressionist, I returned to Omega for another workshop. I'd first met world-renowned medium John Holland in September of 2004 at the 'Soul Survival Weekend', along with medium Suzane Northrup, Dr. Raymond Mooney, author of <u>Life After Lives</u> and, of course, Dr. Brian Weiss.

John Holland is an International Medium from the Boston area. I realized another synchronicity when, two weeks before this workshop, I was pleasantly surprised to see him on a television show called *Mediums: We See Dead People* where a half-dozen famous mediums - one of whom was John - were interviewed and were able to demonstrate their mediumistic abilities.

John Holland was taken blindfolded into two different buildings in New York City. He had never been to these buildings, and he proceeded to describe important events that had happened in those buildings in the past. A historian was present in order to validate the information that John received, and was surprised at the incredible accuracy of his readings. You should watch it if you get the chance. It still may be on You-Tube.

'The Soul Survival Weekend' was like a metaphysical smorgasbord. Mediums John Holland and Suzanne Northrup were conducting psychic development exercises and mediumship demonstrations. Dr. Raymond Moody presented his life-long work covering <u>Life Between Lives</u> (<u>LBL</u>), an explanation of what the soul experiences between incarnations. And of course, Dr. Brian Weiss presented his lifelong work covering Past Life Regression Therapy.

Many of the exercises during that weekend workshop were devoted to increasing the participants' psychic and/or mediumship abilities. I had been going to the Institute for Spiritual Development for basic psychic development workshops, and I was pleasantly surprised at how accurate my readings had become. I thought that perhaps being back at Omega would increase my confidence and ability to connect psychically with complete strangers, and I also realized how much I had already learned from those courses at the ISD.

At the beginning of the workshop, all four presenters were on stage for the Q&A segment. I was able to ask John Holland a question that had been plaguing me.

"John," I asked, "when I'm doing a psychic development exercise, I keep trying to figure out if the images in my mind are coming **from** me or **to** me."

I saw a lot of nods in the audience and knew that a lot of people in the workshop understood what I was asking.

THE 'FROM ME, TO ME' CONUNDRUM

John Holland's answer was direct, succinct and to the point.

"Practice... practice... and more practice," he said with a warm smile. You could hear the collective exhale of the participants, anticipating and hoping for a much longer explanation of this common dilemma. His three word response of 'practice, practice, practice' may have been brief but it was also the most accurate he could have offered.

John and all the other tutors whose classes I've taken say that the more you practice developing your psychic ability, the more comfortable and confident you become with the subtle differences between your thoughts and the impressions coming from outside.

He also told us that this 'From Me, To Me' dilemma was one of the most frequently asked questions in any psychic development class.

I often think back to those early days in my basic psychic development classes. I was surprised, when I gave a piece of information to a fellow participant which was validated and accurate, knowing that I didn't just guess at it. I was simply awed by the process.

'Being awed' is not a term I use lightly. But it is the best way I know to describe how I felt, not only in those early classes, but even now. When I know that the information that I have relayed to someone comes from their loved ones in spirit, and they are able to validate that information, I always feel humbled, amazed and awed, by simply being a part of the process.

To be a medium is to be standing between two worlds. One foot clearly grounded in the here and now: in the present, physical, mundane, earthbound here and now. The other foot is planted in the light, and it is in that light where all life, all power and pure love is. That light is our true home.

During that workshop, Brian Weiss said, "We are not human beings having a spiritual experience. Rather, we are spiritual beings having a human experience." Of course, he always gives credit for that quote to the various people over the years who have stated its essence in various ways.

I often re-enrolled in many of the same psychic development classes, at the ISD and elsewhere, in order to follow the advice that John had given us, to 'practice, practice, practice'. In search of even more opportunities for practice, I began to tell people at school that I would give them a mediumship reading after school or on our lunch break. The more readings I gave, the more my confidence grew. I also began participating in psychic fairs at the ISD, and soon after that, the 'From Me, To Me' conundrum seemed to fade away.

BACK AT OMEGA FOR FUN, FOOD AND FOR HAVING MY MIND BLOWN... AGAIN!

The following summer of 2005, I was back at Omega, this time to participate in John Holland's 'Develop your Psychic Potential' weekend workshop. It proved to be another incredibly powerful weekend, but not in the way I had anticipated.

By this time, I was very comfortable attending Omega workshops. It was like summer camp for old hippies like me. John Holland's workshop was designed to build upon and expand the psychic abilities of the participants who, like me, had already taken basic psychic development classes and wanted to advance further. After participating in his workshop the prior year, I knew John would be my next tutor.

The schedule for this weekend workshop was the same as the 'Soul Survival Weekend' workshop the prior year.

The arrival time was between 4 and 7 pm on Friday; dinner was from 6:00 - 7:15 and the evening classes began at 7:30 pm and lasted until 10 pm.

I arrived early that Friday and after I checked in, I had an hour before dinner and decided to meditate in my room. (I had learned to set aside a half hour a day to meditate, since this was stressed in so many metaphysical workshops I'd attended.)

Initially I felt that meditation was the same as hypnosis, but with my intention to connect with the energy of discarnate people, I became very aware of the differences between meditation and hypnosis.

If you observe two people - one in hypnosis and the other in meditation - you will notice that they both present themselves almost identically. In either state, the person seems to be asleep. But what is happening in their separate consciousness is dramatically different.

There is nothing that a person in hypnosis has to do except listen to the directions and suggestions of the hypnotist, and allow the images being described to form in the mind. Sometimes he will be asked to describe what he is sensing, but the experience he is having is always **from** him alone: the hypnotized subject.

When you are meditating, for the purpose of connecting with a discarnate soul, all the images - whether through seeing, hearing or feeling - are coming **to** you: from spirit. However, if those images come from your own assumptions, you are thinking. And if you are thinking, by definition, it is neither psychic nor mediumship: it's **from** your thoughts. And our assumptions about a sitter are so much stronger than the subtle energies of their discarnate loved ones, that important information and messages can easily be lost.

As I lay on my bunk, I began my meditative process with the intake of a deep cleansing breath. As I let it out, I visualized my personal spiritual sanctuary. I entered through its heavy wooden doors and walked to the chair that has always been there for me. I became aware of information that was coming **to** me that I knew was NOT **from** me.

I was 'told', during my meditation, that mediums do not just work for their sitters. I was told that a medium is actually working for the souls, in spirit, connected with his sitters.

I would come to realize, in the future, that it is the people in spirit who we mediums truly work for. The answer is really quite simple: without mediums, it is incredibly difficult for these souls to get their messages of love and support through to their loved ones, who are still struggling, here on Earth.

I've learned this through personal experience. We are all our own best medium, but we all have such strong doubt, due to society's denial of the continuity of consciousness. We may sense the presence of our loved ones, but we can't believe it because we have been programmed to accept that death of the physical body also terminates its persona.

I let my thoughts project that I understood this important message I had just received. I stated (in my mind) that the reason I was at this workshop and all the other workshops I had attended, was to be a better medium: *I want to be as helpful as I can for both those in spirit and their loved ones still here on Earth.*

I had lost track of the time and when my eyes opened I realized I now only had 15 minutes for dinner. I ran to the dining hall, wolfed something down, and walked to the main hall where John Holland would hold his workshop.

As I entered the hall I was surprised to see how many people were there already, nearly filling the chairs that were set up in a large horseshoe facing the stage. The workshop had almost a hundred participants and they all seemed to be there, seated by 7:45. And like me, eager to start.

LEARNING HOW TO ASK FOR DIRECTIONS

By this time, I had also become comfortable talking to my Spirit Guides. Whether I believed they were listening to me, or if they even existed, was something I was still unsure of. But, I had had enough experiences that suggested their existence. I made it a point to talk to them and then determine if they had been listening to me, by what the results might be.

At workshops, whether at Omega, the ISD or at a class to continue my hypnosis training, I would walk into a room full of strangers and would say (in thought) to my Guides: *OK gang, I want [such and such], so who do I need to talk to...* I was finding how very accommodating my Guides could be. Whether they were actually listening to me and then following through with what I requested, was at the time still unclear to me. Obviously, at that time I still had some doubt.

It would seem that my Spirit Guides were willing and able to successfully accomplish the tasks I asked of them, as long as I was willing to follow my intuitive feelings, following through with what was suggested to me. But, as I said, I still had some doubts... but not for long.

Their suggestions always came in the form of synchronicities. Now with my acceptance of my own psychic and mediumship abilities and being open to synchronicities, my questions as to whom I needed to talk to, at various classes, was being answered quickly and powerfully.

So as we all settled in for John's workshop, I realized I never discovered who I was meant to talk to. What I normally do is scan everyone in the audience. I could see everyone in the semi-circle of chairs and could feel the excitement in the room build, as we all eagerly looked forward to seeing John. So, once again, I asked my Guides, as I took a deep breath, to be introduced to someone who could help me become a better medium.

With that goal in mind, I put that thought out to the Universe, as the doors to the workshop closed and the last participants filed into the large room.

I took a breath and leaned forward, turning my head to the right just as a man my age leaned forward and turned his head toward me. We made eye contact, smiled at each other, faced forward and leaned back...

Although I had become accustomed to doing this sort of thing, I was nonetheless surprised by the immediacy of the response. Were my Guides directing me to talk to this guy? I decided that, on our first break, I would go and talk to him.

The next instant, an attractive blond woman walked out on stage. She checked her microphone, introduced herself as Gretchen, John's assistant, and began the orientation to John's class. As she was informing us about what the weekend had in store, I wondered what it would be like to be John Holland's assistant. I knew it must be amazing.

After Gretchen finished her orientation, she introduced John, who came out to a roaring ovation. He announced to the group that although he knew that we were all here to develop our own psychic potential, he would do one reading during the weekend. He asked the group if they would like him to do one mediumship reading right then and there, as a demonstration of what we would be learning that weekend, and the crowd went wild. Everyone there was hoping that John would give them a reading. The odds were about 100 to 1. John scanned the room, pointed to a woman to my right and asked her if he could come to her. Of course she agreed and John proceeded to demonstrate how to present an amazingly accurate reading.

At the end of the reading and after the subsequent discussion, Gretchen announced that we would be taking a quick 15 minute break. As she went backstage, I immediately got up and went to talk to the man that I'd had been 'directed' to see.

As everyone stood and stretched, we both walked directly to each other as if it were planned that we should meet. It seemed as if we had known each other for years. And then the synchronicities began...

By counting synchronicities you bring your mind's focus on them.
Then you see the power they have to direct your life in the way
you were wishing and hoping for but never, in your wildest dreams,
thought could actually come true.

COUNTING SYNCHRONICITIES

After shaking hands and introducing ourselves, Dennis and I realized that we had a great many things in common. Considering the way I was 'introduced' to him, I felt that our meeting might be synchronistic in nature. And once I feel the energy of a synchronicity begin, I start to take note, and count them. If it is truly a synchronicity, they will add up quickly; otherwise I simply mark it up to a simple one time coincidence.

As Dennis and I spoke to each other, I quickly began to count.

- The 1st, a commonality: Just something in common, not even a coincidence yet. We were both here, at John Holland's workshop.

- The 2nd, a simple coincidence: We were the same age. Again, as Yoda might say, "Two coincidences, do not, a synchronicity, make."

- The 3rd coincidence, or perhaps the start of a simple synchronicity: We both grew up in Brooklyn, less than two miles away from one another.

- The 4th and 5th synchronicities: We were both introduced to Metaphysics late in life, and we'd both become very passionate about the subject. (Now it was becoming interesting...)

We agreed that it was great to be back at Omega, and shared how many times we had both been there, while laughing about the food and being a couple of old hippies back up by Woodstock again.

As we discovered more about each other, Dennis asked me about my first visit to Omega. I explained how I had initially come to Omega to take Brian Weiss' Past Life Regression workshop, and that along with being a Special Education high school teacher I was also a hypnotherapist, a PLR therapist and now a novice medium.

Dennis started laughing and shook his head, saying that this was such an interesting synchronicity.

- The 6th synchronicity: He mentioned synchronicity while I had already begun to count them.

He told me that he had just been online researching past life regressions in order to find a past life regressionist, and pointed to me. He smiled, shrugged and looked up to the ceiling.

Now it was my turn to laugh. I told Dennis that when I become aware of a synchronicity I do exactly what he had just done: shrug, smile, look up and thank whoever had just set it up.

- The 7th synchronicity: He was seeking a past life regressionist... and here I was!

The number continued to grow all night, but after seven, I just stopped counting. I knew that I was in a very powerful synchronistic flow and decided, rather than counting them, I would just focus on discovering where they were directing me.

We both agreed that there was much more to our meeting than met the eye. Along with mediumship and Metaphysics in general, our conversation also included how being directed by synchronicities can work out so well.

In my mind, I saw how this synchronicity had formed through both of our requests: his, to find a past life regressionist and mine to find someone who could help me become a better medium. To this day it still boggles my mind, how our Guides can do what they do. And that they never stop helping us, in this life, our past lives and even our future lives!

I understood that his request was answered. As we made arrangements for his PLR, Dennis may not have been aware that he had sent a specific request to his Guides. But they answered, whether he addressed the request to them, or just to the Universe.

I wondered, and eagerly looked forward to discovering, how my Guides were going to answer my own request.

After I thought I couldn't be more blown away by the way things turned out, I was about to be blown into the stratosphere, as John Holland's assistant walked out from behind the curtain, jumped down from the stage, and began to walk in our direction.

We both watched Gretchen approach. She was smiling at us both, as if we were all old friends. As I returned her smile, she walked right up to Dennis, threw her arms around him and gave him a big kiss! I guess I must have looked pretty shocked, because they both looked at me and began to laugh, as Dennis introduced me to his girlfriend, Gretchen.

I had just questioned, in my mind, how my request was going to be answered, and in the next instant I was being introduced to Gretchen - John Holland's assistant!

You cannot make this stuff up!

When your mind gets blown,
sometimes the first thing that stops working is your mouth.

GETTING MY MOUTH TO WORK AGAIN

I must have looked shell-shocked, because although my mouth was moving I couldn't seem to form any words. My head was spinning with what had just happened. Even now I am awed by the way synchronicities form. Two complete strangers put out their respective requests to their Guides. One requested to learn more about past life regressions and experience one, and the other to simply find someone to help him become a better medium... Mind boggling!

Yes, we looked at each other, knowingly smiled and sat back; but that didn't make a synchronicity. We met, spoke and discovered that we had many interesting similarities. Yes, but that could still have been coincidental. After all, we were at Omega at a mediumship class; of course we would have many similarities. Every participant in the class did.

I was speechless. What could I say? I was having difficulty understanding it myself, let alone trying to explain it to complete strangers!

'Boggled' didn't come close to the adjective I needed to describe my state of mind at that moment. There is not an adjective in the English language that could adequately describe it.

When I finally got my wits together, I explained why I was at such a loss for words. I explained what had just happened, excitedly describing the synchronicities, the Guides, Dennis' future PLR, my mediumship; I was talking so fast, I had to stop to catch my breath. Gretchen and Dennis just looked at each other, laughed, nodded and shrugged, as if to say this was a common occurrence in their life with John Holland. Certainly it was anything but common for me! Just then, Gretchen looked at her watch and ran to the stage.

"After this last exercise is over," Dennis said, "why don't you hang out for a while? John, Gretchen and I are going to the café for a burger. Wanna join us?"

I couldn't say "Sure!" fast enough.

Gretchen came out on stage with a microphone, as I sat back down, trying to get my jaw to close so I didn't look like I was in the shock that I was in...

You really, really cannot make **this** stuff up!

I was so excited by what had just happened that, honestly, I don't remember what we did for the next exercise. What I do remember was, John handing the microphone to Gretchen as she announced that this would be the end of the evening's exercises, and that they would see us all bright and early in the morning.

As people began mingling, I went back to talk with Dennis once again. We both assumed that Gretchen would be busy in the back working out whatever details she and John needed to take care of.

Almost everyone had left the building when John and Gretchen came out, and there were a few people that had John's books that he was very happy to sign. Smiling and laughing with two women who had waited for him, he waved acknowledgement to Dennis, and once again I just shook my head, being in that awesome synchronistic flow of energy.

And soon there was no one left in the building except John, Gretchen, Dennis and me. I was introduced to John as we all walked up the hill to the café for some hamburgers. The vegan menu at Omega is healthy but for carnivores like John, Gretchen, Dennis and me nothing beats a good burger.

Now you must appreciate the heady feeling I had, after I picked up my plate and sat at the table with John Holland. I noticed how many people were looking at us, as I smiled to myself, knowing that it would've been me wondering who the two lucky guys were, eating with John and Gretchen. So, John, Gretchen and Dennis were having a light conversation and in my mind I thought, *Don't interrupt them, that's John Holland.*

I was sitting there just taking it all in, which was atypically quiet for me, considering how much I do like to talk. But I just sat there with my hamburger in my hands, basically staring across the table at 'The' John Holland, while Gretchen, Dennis and John continued their conversation. I was quite content to just listen to them and happy to be at the same table.

Suddenly, John put his hamburger onto his plate, looked questioningly at me and said, "...What?"

My reaction was simply a dumbfounded look. John sat back, smiled at me and said, "Garry, I'm a guy just like you... I eat burgers and like to meet and talk to new people. But if you don't stop staring at me, I'm not going to be able to eat my burger... And I hate cold burgers." Both Dennis and Gretchen began to laugh as I simply nodded and accepted the truth of his statement.

Now with the ice broken, I went on to talk about synchronicity and how my Guides had so quickly and easily arranged for me to be sitting here. "I asked for help with my mediumship and look how they delivered! I'm sitting here with John Holland!"

Finally I took a breath and a bite of my now ice-cold burger, which still tasted great. Soon, the whole table was involved in an animated discussion of Metaphysics.

John finished his last bite, smiled and gave me advice that I think about to this day.

"Garry, be careful what you wish for because you just might get it. Once you let that genie" (developing my mediumship ability and understanding of Metaphysics) "out of the bottle, there is no way you can put it back in."

When John gave me that advice I already knew that the genie was out and I had no intention, nor ability, to put her back in. I was able to stop being awestruck, and was able to relax and join in the conversation. Very quickly, I found out just how funny John could be. We sat, talked and laughed until 11 o'clock, when the café closed.

We said our good-nights, and I realized that John Holland was not only an amazing world class medium and teacher, he was also a world class nice guy... Not your normal combination.

~ ~ ~

The next morning I was up early for breakfast and as I was eating my cereal, banana and coffee, Dennis came over. He placed his breakfast down on the table and we jumped right back into our conversation from the prior evening. I realized that I hadn't exaggerated my excitement over the synchronicities between the two of us because, although he was also comfortable with the process and believed in synchronicity, he too was impressed with what had occurred.

That breakfast conversation covered the gamut of metaphysical experiences. We both agreed that synchronicities had brought us together and knew that our friendship would grow. Which it has.

I was eager to start the mediumship exercises John had in store for us, and I was also curious to see if I would notice any additional synchronicities. Our animated conversation continued all the way from the dining hall to the building where John would conduct his workshop. As Dennis and I entered the Main Hall, we noticed that all of the participants also seemed to be there early.

The chairs were now divided into rows in front of the stage. Dennis and I sat as Gretchen walked out on stage and introduced John, who jumped from the stage and began to walk around the room, forming a closer connection with all the participants.

Then John said something that I was not aware of, or really prepared to think about. "You may find that your decision to go down this spiritual path may cause you to lose some friends and family."

I thought at the time that this was a pretty harsh statement, considering I was just beginning to explore my own psychic abilities. I couldn't understand how, by enthusiastically exploring this new aspect of my life, I could negatively affect anyone.

I suppose that I should not have been surprised about how prophetic that statement was. After all, John is a psychic as well as an amazingly gifted medium.

Soon, John began to describe what was to be our first exercise, which he called 'psychometry'. As he described what the exercise would entail, I smiled, knowing that I had already done the same exercise at the ISD. I could say that I was relieved, because once again my ego was becoming involved in the process, and like many other metaphysical teachers I have worked with over the years, John was helping us disengage from our egos. Again, the process of letting your ego go is critical for anyone beginning their psychic development.

Psychometry is often the first exercise in any psychic development class. The participants are broken into groups of two who do not know each other. After an initial meditation, one person is designated as the psychic and the other as the sitter.

The sitter is asked to give a personal item, such as a ring, that can be held in the hand of their partner. The psychic is told to hold the item and describe to the sitter any impression, thought or feeling emanating from that item.

The sitter's responsibility is to validate, for the psychic, any information that is accurate. The problem with having your ego standing in the way of this exercise is that your ego wants you to do the reading perfectly, and that usually makes you evaluate your sitter using your five senses instead of your five intuitive senses.

The rest of the weekend was filled with lectures and exercises covering various metaphysical topics including chakras, color, the 'Claire' senses, etc. As the workshop drew to a close, John expanded upon his advice to me with everyone there about how our lives may be quite different after choosing to go down the path that I have been exploring ever since.

~ ~ ~

That October, John Holland presented another workshop for psychic development, in Boston, and I drove the eight hours for another lesson from this master teacher and medium.

And although the workshop expanded upon what I had been taught at Omega, I also realized that the warning about losing friends and family and the difficulty of going down this spiritual path had, in fact, already been proven quite true.

My family knew me as an atheistic and compassionate person who would come home from work to vegetate on the couch watching television. They were not comfortable that within a very short amount of time my beliefs, my attitude and my personality had drastically changed from being atheistic to believing in such New Age beliefs as past life regressions, psychics, mediums, hands-on energy healing and the belief in a higher power.

I also realized I couldn't keep driving up to Boston. So a few weeks after that October workshop, I called Gretchen to ask her opinion of what I should do next regarding my personal psychic development.

Once again the timing could not have been more perfect, because when I called her, she was driving with John. He asked me if I lived anywhere near Pompton Lakes NJ, and suggested that I visit a different Spiritualist church called *The Journey Within*, whose founder was an incredibly gifted medium and teacher by the name of Janet Nohavec. I thanked him and followed through with his suggestion.

So now along with writing the book you are reading, working as a Special Education high school teacher, a hypnotherapist, and a past life regressionist, I was still taking classes at Omega and at the ISD. I became a certified Reiki practitioner, an ISD healer and reader, and began to take advanced mediumship classes at *The Journey Within* Church with some of the most renowned teachers of mediumship in the world.

You can also understand how John's statement to me, that I may be losing friends and family, and how once you open up this bottle you can never get that genie back into it, was true.

The roller coaster that my life was about to become had already begun.

I tightened up the seatbelt and grabbed the lap bar as the ride began to speed up.

The fights you have with those you love and who love you are frequently driven by fear.

MY SPIRITUAL INTERVENTION

In August of 2003, after arriving home from Brian Weiss' workshop, I was a changed man. And this change did not go unnoticed. Everyone who knew me - family, friends and co-workers - could see how profoundly different I was.

I was no longer the 'Old Garry'. I was no longer vegetating in front of the TV. I was constantly reading and talking incessantly about the things I used to scoff at. I was so involved with these new and exciting beliefs, I was unaware of the concern my family was having about me, particularly about my mental health.

It was a Friday in October, after my workshop in Boston, when I came home to find my whole family sitting around the kitchen table. I asked what the celebration was about and was told, "Dad, sit down, we need to talk." My wife, daughter, son and his fiancée Kristie were sitting at the kitchen table looking very concerned.

Initially I was alarmed that something dreadful had happened to someone in the family. But it took only a moment to realize that the family member that this dreadful thing was happening to... was me!

My family seemed to be having an intervention on me. I knew this mediation couldn't be a drug or alcohol intervention. And after voicing their concerns, I realized that their major worry for me came from witnessing this obvious and powerful change in me since my return from Omega. I realized that I was in the middle of a 'Spiritual Intervention'.

Now, through 20/20 hindsight, it is clear to me that their concerns were for my future. They feared that I would have profound remorse if I continued on with what they perceived as flights of fancy. That fear and alarm was initiated and reinforced by the obvious behavioral changes I was exhibiting, and I can't say that they were exaggerating their apprehensions.

The saying 'Hindsight is always 20/20' is very true in my case. I became quite defensive. I dismissed my family's worries as an overactive attempt to control me. Fortunately for my family, but more importantly for me, I came to realize that the comparison to a severe drug addiction was fairly accurate.

When I returned from Omega, I was like a wide-eyed, bushy-tailed, Energizer Bunny on speed. But I was not running on electricity, alcohol or illicit drugs. I was high on - and perhaps overdosing on - a seemingly healthy drug called Metaphysics.

On this drug, I not only saw a new and exciting path for my life, I decided to drag my entire family down **my** path, whether they wanted to or not. It never even occur to me that my family might not be interested in sharing my new found belief and passion in Metaphysics. I had made the decision to devote every waking moment, incessantly discussing every metaphysical topic that fascinated me, with the assumption (there's that damn ASS-U-ME word again) that they would be just as interested in **my** new beliefs as I was... And I was clearly very wrong!

It took a while, but I realized how I was alienating the people I loved. I also realized that what I was doing - forcing my new beliefs on others - was exactly the opposite of what Metaphysics and Spiritualism (the belief in Metaphysics) is all about. My family was truly frightened, and justifiably so, that I was going through a serious mid-life crisis. But instead of looking for younger women, or drinking, or drugging, or buying a Corvette, I was being attracted to my own spiritual side. So I thought, *What could possibly be wrong with that?* Remembering the advice from John Holland was very helpful in putting this new facet of my life into a proper perspective. Although it did take two fairly difficult years.

After convincing my family that I wasn't going to be flying off to an ashram in Oregon to follow the teachings of Neale Donald Walsh, things began to settle down.

And my family began to accept this new me.

They were not going down my path and I accepted they all had their own journeys to experience, as I had mine. I will always be thankful for the relationship Chris and I formed over those difficult years. And even more thankful that she never threw up her hands and said that she was tired of fighting. I have realized that she could have pushed for a divorce, which in my obsessed (addictive) state I might have allowed.

Had that happened, I know you would not be reading this book because it would never have been written.

What I was viewing as an anchor holding me down in that turbulent time was, in fact, my being grounded. Without Chris, I would have floated away into the stratosphere of metaphysical beliefs with no knowledge of how being balanced in this life is essential for our soul's growth. I would also never have known the joy of being a grandfather. Clearly, I would have been a grandfather, but I would have been floating around in a metaphysical stupor. I would have been oblivious to the indescribable joy of seeing and being an integral part of the growth of the children of my children.

GOOGLING A 'R.O.S.E.' FOR CLARIFICATION

Let me take a quick break here... At the present time on my journey, I'd like to clarify what I've learned by looking back again with a little 20/20 hindsight...

From classes, learning from some of the most knowledgeable tutors in the field of Metaphysics, I think I can condense and clarify what I have learned by making a comparison between two worlds - Living and Spirit - to a Google search of the word ROSE.

Now, I'm sure you're thinking, "Hmmm, that's going to be an interesting comparison," but let me explain.

If you want to know about a rose, you can simply Google, "R. O. S. E.," on your computer. Now don't run and open your computer. I did it for you. I googled "R O S E" and got 2,240,000,000 results (in 0.60 seconds, mind you); Two billion, two hundred and forty million snippets of information, and only about a flower. The knowledge of the world at your fingertips! The Web is an amazing, <u>human-made</u> tool.

Not surprisingly, I am sure that if you had the time, and could actually read everything on that Google search, you would know every, single, possible fact about a rose. From planting to cultivating, to pruning and on and on, a computer can answer any question you could ever have about just about anything…

Just go ask Siri. Or Alexa.

After all that research, you could be considered an expert in the field of the rose. So how does the Universe and its complexities relate to a Google search of a rose?

After shedding your body and returning once again to your real home, there is nothing that you don't know. Your essence, your consciousness, combine with the infinite energy of the Universe. It would be like living within the atomic structure of Google. There is nothing about the entirety of the Universe that isn't right there for you. All the knowledge of the Universe is instantaneously available. However, knowing everything there is to know about a rose (or everything else for that matter) as demonstrated in that Google search, could never let you know what a rose is… Physically.

The knowledge of a rose, no matter how in depth it is, could never compare to the fragrance of that rose; or how smelling one can actually relax you; or having the painful, physical experience of having your finger pricked by its thorn; or to experience the physical touch of the softness of that rose's petal.

I began to understand the reason why we are here on this planet. We have an infinite number of lifetimes, in which we combine the experiences of the physical world, learned through our physical senses, with the universal knowledge that we have instant access to when we die.

*Upon shedding our bodies, we return to that place where we truly 'live' between our physical incarnations. And it is in that light that we are able to review **both** worlds.*

The universal knowledge that we have access to, in the spirit world, combines with the knowledge that we have accumulated over a countless number of physical incarnations... Making all the recorded knowledge of human history seem like a Kindergarten primer. Talk about viewing a Google search from a very different perspective! Hmmm.

But again, that **is** only my opinion.

As with anything you do, the more you practice,
the more your experience grows and the better you get -
whether it is working in a supermarket, being a teacher,
or realizing and accepting that you are a medium.

SUE: HELPING ELIMINATE HYDROPHOBIA
WITH A LITTLE HELP FROM ABOVE

Soon after I began taking psychic development classes, I accepted and became comfortable with my own psychic abilities. I realized that it was my intuition that was the source of the change in my method of hypnotherapy which I had been noticing over the past few years.

I began to receive insights from sources other than those of an experienced hypnotherapist. I now understood why, at times, I didn't have to ask a single question of a new client and seemed to know them at a very deep level. And what had confused me in the past became clear with each new PD class I took.

~ ~ ~

Sue was ten minutes early and as she sat, she said that she was praying that this would work. She didn't know what else to do. The more pertinent information I receive from a client, the better insight I have in order to design a hypnotic intervention specifically for them, so I asked her to elaborate.

"I am petrified of going in the water! I have been able to deal really well with my fear. I just don't go in a pool, a lake, the beach or the ocean. I take showers instead of baths. I knew that I could never take a cruise, but that never bothered me."

She was speaking so fast, she barely took a breath, as she continued. "So I felt that I didn't need any help. I dealt with the fear by avoiding water and I was fine. But I now have a major problem and it will ruin my life if I can't fix it.

"I'm a single mom. It has always been just me and Peter, my nine-year-old. But I have been seeing a wonderful man who loves me. He's asked me to marry him and he wants to adopt Peter as his son."

She continued to describe the perfect relationship, but became distraught as she informed me of the huge obstacle that was threatening to ruin her life and that of her son and fiancé.

I gave her some time and a few tissues to dry her eyes, but at that same moment, I became sidetracked by the thought of her father. Although I was listening intently to her, in the back of my mind I strongly felt his presence, which was somewhat distracting. By now, I was quite confident with my ability to use hypnosis to help her and almost as confident that I could help her as a medium. I also knew that her father was a strong spirit communicator, as he relayed to me that he wanted to be involved in this process.

As his daughter and I spoke, I sensed him giving me insight into their relationship, and found it extremely helpful to have this 'inside source' to the cause of her fears. This was not going to be a typical session in any way, shape, or form.

I realized that I was combining two different skill sets. As a hypnocounselor, I use my knowledge and experience in hypnosis to access the part of her that was terrified of water. And as a medium I connected with her father to show me the direction that would be best for his daughter. The end result was a new type of therapy, that I call *Augmented Hypnotherapy*. I've begun to use this eclectic therapeutic technique more frequently, although I never inform my clients that, while I am hypnotizing them, I am also having a conversation with their passed loved ones.

Sue tossed her tissue in the trash, took a deep breath and continued. "My fiancé Sam has a house on Lake Hopatcong, with a dock and a speed boat," she said, as if telling me he had a terminal disease. "He loves his boat. He is on the lake every weekend and all summer long. His friends, who I love, all have boats. Our whole social life is on or near the water. My son loves being there with him and they both go fishing and boating all the time, and they both want me to go out on his boat so badly. I would really love to be out there with them, but as soon as I step foot on the dock, I start to shake. Once Sammy actually had to carry me off the dock! Please, please help me!"

I reassured her that I felt confident hypnosis could help her. Fortunately, she was a good and motivated hypnotic subject, who went into hypnosis easily.

As I have described, I used Parts Therapy to bring out her Fearful Part, the Part of her that was terrified of being in or near the water. It's fascinating how powerfully this procedure works.

I had her visualize being in the conference room in her mind, and in the center of the room was a large table with chairs around it. I asked if she could see it and she slowly nodded her head.

I described the doors that were around this room, and that on each door was a plaque which indicated which Part of her lived within each room. I had her see her 'Daughter' door where the Part of her that dealt with her parents lived, and the 'Mother' door where the Part of her who was a mother to her son lived. She nodded that she understood and pictured the doors, as we proceeded.

She was then directed to find her 'Hydrophobic' Part, which lived in the room that had a sign on the door which read 'Fearful Part'. She acknowledged that she saw it and I asked if she thought I could speak with that Part. Smiling, she nodded yes, and I had the Fearful Part open the door so that she could look into its room, and see her Fearful Part as it walked into the conference room.

I asked Sue to describe her to me. In a very quiet almost childlike voice she began to describe her Hydrophobic Part.

"She is me, when I was six years old." I began a discussion with the six-year-old Phobic Part and asked her if we could go back in time to when the fear first started.

Sue took a deep breath and although she was hypnotized, she looked down with closed eyes and simply nodded yes. I saw her emotions welling up, as tears formed beneath her closed eyelids, which slowly ran down her cheek as her chin began to quiver.

As a hypnotherapist I must be very aware of my clients' emotional state. This is emotional work and I took a tissue from my box of Kleenex at the side of the recliner and quietly said that I was just going to dab her tears away.

"I'm six years old…" she said in a faint almost imperceptible whisper. "It's summer and my parents want me to learn how to swim, so we are going to Lake Hopatcong. They had a lifeguard teach me…" she said quietly.

I noticed her breathing was becoming more rapid and I knew that the memories were coming forward; the memories that she had repressed were being reviewed in her mind. Her eyes were tightly closed, yet I could see her eyes moving left and right as if she were there, seeing it all happening again before her.

Suddenly the hair on the back of my neck stood up, as I became aware once again of her father. I knew that he was observing what was happening and as a father myself I knew how protective this man was. He relayed to me how horrible he felt, that he had allowed his daughter to experience the events she was going to relay to me now and not being able to protect her. He also told me that she felt abandoned by her parents at that point. He was giving me all the information I needed to be able to change her perception of the event and in so doing, eliminate her fear.

She continued, "…We're in the water now. It's deep, up to my neck. The lifeguard is holding me on my stomach. He's telling me to breathe when he says so! He's holding my face under the water. He is turning my head out of the water and yelling: 'BREATH!… HOLD!… BREATH!' He's holding my face underwater and he's only pulling me out when I'm choking!"

With tears again coming from her eyes, she became very still. I knew she was processing what she'd just re-experienced. And then in her own normal voice whispered, "I've never recalled what happened to me until this very moment."

I was very aware of how her description of the memory was in the present tense. Her six-year-old self was describing the scene as if it were spontaneously happening, while her logical adult awareness was observing the memory in real time, which indicated how deeply Sue was hypnotized. I knew that she was reliving the initial cause of her phobia and, by telling me that this was the first time she remembered the incident, I knew she was observing the memory from the perspective of her 'Higher Self'.

I also knew that this would be the perfect time to do her reframing. "Sue, take a deep breath." I touched her shoulder for reinforcement, as she took that deep breath, and I saw her relax.

SUE'S REFRAMING

"You are six years old again, in Lake Hopatcong. You are in the water with the lifeguard who is holding you up. You're coughing and you're frightened. I want you to picture yourself there now!" I snapped my fingers once. I knew she was in the memory by the change in her breathing.

"But now things are beginning to change. The lifeguard doesn't seem as big as he was before. You now see your father standing at the shoreline. Do you see him?" She nodded yes, her chin beginning to quiver.

"Now look at your father's face and see how upset and angry he is with the lifeguard, as he is watching his young daughter being treated this way. He is now running into the water toward you both... Do you see him?"

She nodded. Tears were now streaming from her eyes once again. "Your Dad is now standing in the water with you and the lifeguard. He takes you from the lifeguard and pushes the lifeguard away. You put your arms around his neck and you put your head on his shoulder. You take a breath and feel totally safe once again.

"Your father looks at the lifeguard and says to him that he will never ever touch his daughter again! He says he is going to the director, to tell him that this lifeguard will never teach another kid! The lifeguard now looks even smaller, weaker, as he puts his head down and turns, walking slowly through the water toward the shore."

Again I felt her father communicating with me. I asked him to tell me what he wanted to tell his daughter. As the images came to me, I used them, to change her perception of the swimming lesson.

"Your father is now holding you tightly as he walks back to the shoreline. He is apologizing to you for letting this kid inflict the fear of the water on you. He is saying that he had no idea that the lifeguard had frightened you so."

Through her tears, Sue said, "He doesn't have anything to apologize for. He was the best dad." I heard a quiet 'Thank-you', which I knew came from her father and as quickly as I first heard him, that was how fast I stopped sensing him.

I continued to finalize the reframing: "You are still that six-year-old Sue. But now an interesting feeling comes over you, as you see the adult that you are now, standing at the shore. From the protection of your father's arms, you see the adult woman that she, your six-year-old self will grow up to become, slowly walking into the water toward you.

"She has no fear of the water! In fact, she is enjoying the coolness of the water, on the hot summer's day. She takes her hand and splashes some water on her shoulders and is smiling as she gets closer to you and your dad. She is wearing the bathing suit that you now use to take the sun on your deck, and walks up to you and your father. Dad now places the six-year-old Sue in your arms, the arms of the adult that she will grow to become. The adult Sue now carries the phobic little six-year-old Sue, to the shoreline, and sits on the blanket with her.

"Immediately, there is no one on the beach, except for you and your six-year-old self. You are now the adult, Sue, who is a mother. You hold that little, frightened six-year-old until she feels safe to go in the water... Alone. You are and always will be present when she goes into the water.

"From the blanket, you see the little Sue turn and run into the water. She is splashing and laughing! She had no idea how much fun it is to be in the water. Now see years clicking by, without the fear that has been keeping you from enjoying the water!"

I allowed her to calm and refocus. I closed my eyes, thanked her father for the help and assured him that he had been forgiven for not being there then, because he was sure there for his daughter... Now!

Before I lost my connection with this man, he wanted to relay one more thing to his daughter. And I told her that her father is always with her, but especially when she is in the water, protecting her and always making sure she is safe.

As I was ending the session I wanted to introduce one last thought into her subconscious. "Sue, it is this weekend and you and Peter are on Sam's deck looking at the speedboat. Notice how calm and relaxed you are, and the excitement that your son is showing. He realizes that you have made the decision to enjoy a day on the lake! The weather is perfect. The sky seems to be bluer than you have ever seen. Sam now comes up behind you and puts his arms around you and kisses you on the cheek. You turn and look into his eyes and you realize how much you love him and how very safe you feel with him...'

After the session ended, she thanked me and I told her that the only way she will know for certain that she no longer has a phobia, is to test herself on the boat. She agreed, with the comment, "I'll call you for another appointment if it doesn't work."

That weekend my phone rang and it was Sue. She was on her cell phone and there was so much noise in the background that I could barely hear her.

"Garry?" she yelled into the phone, "I want to thank you for saving my life!" I thought she was exaggerating, but the feeling you get when you realize that an energy-draining phobia is truly eliminated can make a person exaggerate a little. "I am calling from the boat! Me and my new family are on the lake in Sammy's boat! I can't believe it... It is so much fun! Thank you so much!"

~ ~ ~

287

Sometimes while you are doing something you love to do, you learn along with your clients. I stopped doubting my psychic self and eventually my hypnosis skills and techniques combined with my psychic and mediumistic abilities, resulting in some quite interesting hypnosis sessions.

After taking all the classes offered at the Institute for Spiritual Development and knowing I was beginning to incorporate my psychic and mediumship skills into my hypnosis practice, I realized how much more successful my hypnotic interventions were becoming. But more than that, I was becoming more and more fascinated by the way the connections between the two worlds worked. I decided to go back to Omega again when I saw the list of phenomenal mediums who were offering classes there.

PRACTICE, PRACTICE AND MORE PRACTICE

On Monday, July 12, 2010, I had a mediumship reading scheduled with a woman and her thirty-something son. That Friday, I was registered for a weekend workshop with James Van Praagh at Omega. James is a pioneer in the field of mediumship and one of the most celebrated, respected authors and spiritual teachers working today. He has been bringing the subject of 'communication with the dead' into the public eye for the past thirty years. I was excited about the weekend and looked forward to this reading, just as I look forward to every reading I do.

I view a reading with a combination of emotions, from anticipation of the unknown, to dread of being inaccurate.

In my experience, there are minimally three obstacles that mediums create that negatively impact a great reading: their self-doubt, lack of faith, and their ego.

Will I look stupid...?
Am I making this stuff up...?
What if my sitters can't accept the information that I get...?

These internal questions fade with experience. I now realize that these ego issues are the cause of a medium's lack of self-confidence, often tied to the medium's lack of confidence in the spirit world.

Will they be there to give me the information I'm asking for...?
Is anyone out there even listening...?

My doubt in my own ability contributed to my doubt in spirits' ability or desire to communicate with me.

The joy and satisfaction I receive when people leave my office, so much happier than they were when they came in, is hard to describe. When I became more experienced at mediumship readings, the joy of connecting with spirits combined with the happiness of my sitters, and that combination can actually become addictive.

Although I may be repeating myself, the work I do as a medium is more for those who are in spirit than those who are still here and are paying me. I have learned that the work mediums do is perhaps the only way a soul in the spirit world can get information, in the form of a message, to their loved ones here in the physical world. Often, they want closure, just as those who are here do.

Remember that all spirits passionately want to connect with their loved ones, in order to simply send them messages of love, and to let them know that they are happy where they are. And I've learned to never doubt the spirit world.

With John Holland's suggestion that 'practice, practice and more practice' is the best way to improve your mediumistic abilities, I found more opportunities to practice and improve my abilities as a medium. I volunteered my time to be a regular reader at the ISD Psychic Fairs, message circles and their Sunday Service mediumship readings, and I continued to give readings to people at my school.

I soon found I was getting more referrals for private mediumship readings. And not only were the number of readings increasing, so was my self-confidence with my abilities to connect with the spirit world, and my confidence that those in spirt would be able to connect with me.

"AN EDUCATED CONSUMER IS OUR BEST CUSTOMER"

Years ago there was a haberdasher in NY and NJ who had his own gimmick. He was on radio and television with the catch phrase: "... An educated consumer is our best customer." I believe in that statement, not as a gimmick but as the absolute truth. After many classes and lots of practice, I became an educated consumer. Not of clothes, but of Metaphysics.

With more practice as a medium, I began to really understand how 'it' works (at least for me). The 'it' in this case was how psychics and mediums perceive their information. Through analyzing the information I was receiving, I realized that a psychic or medium perceives information from three very different sources, and these sources define the type of reader the psychic and/or medium is.

One source of information that a psychic or medium perceives, comes from the reader's own mind and imagination. This is not ESP. It is purely guessing, which is known as 'cold reading'. This information may be given fraudulently: that is, the reader intentionally manipulates the client. The 'reader' in this case is a fraud. Period.

A reader may be well-intentioned, but unfortunately may be delusional. He or she may truly think that they are connecting with a spirit, but are deluding themselves and their sitters. This type of reader really thinks that they are a psychic or medium, but is sadly mistaken, because the source of the information is still in their own mind.

Many readers, including myself, struggle with this doubt in their own connections with spirit, which was the reason that I'd brought up the 'From Me, To Me' conundrum to John Holland years earlier.

The second area where a reader perceives information is from the sitter him or herself: coming from the sitter's own mind, energy or aura, which is the definition of a psychic reading. Although psychically connecting with another person is certainly psychic, it is not mediumship. In this case, the reader is perceiving information through his 'third eye' located in the middle of the forehead. Again, everyone has a 'third eye': the source of our 'sixth sense'. The sense organ, in the case of our third eye, is in the center of the forehead and lies directly in front of the most misunderstood and underutilized organ in our body...

Our brain.

The third area through which a reader can perceive information is the energy of a spirit's consciousness, which is the definition of mediumship. The medium will perceive information through the same source as a psychic: his third eye. But what he perceives is not from his sitter's energy. It is from the energy of their loved ones who have passed and are always close and around the sitter.

Usually a medium will not maintain eye contact with his sitter while relaying the information coming from the spirit world. This helps minimize the distractions of non-verbal clues coming from sitters, who are so often looking forward to receiving a life-changing message.

As a reader shares more and more readings and gains confidence in his ability and accuracy, he learns how to deal with the 'From Me, To Me' conundrum and how to distinguish between the two. Soon he only focuses on the *To Me*, and can detach from the ego-driven *From Me* thoughts. With that distinction, he begins to gain the confidence he needs to do accurate readings.

I have had great opportunities to see and learn from some world-famous mediums, including Bill Collar, John Edward, John Holland, Simon James, Janet Nohavec, Mavis Pittilla, Brian Robertson, Richard Schoeller, Sharon Siubis, Tony Stockwell, Stella and Steven Upton and James Van Praagh. I have seen them perform mediumship demonstrations in front of hundreds of people, and I have witnessed them 'stick to their guns', and refuse to be shaken by the denial of a sitter to accept the information being offered.

At a mediumship demonstration in southern New Jersey, with an audience of over 1000 people, I saw John Edward stand his ground for a half hour until finally the light went on over the sitter's head and he was able to accept everything that John had offered him.

A novice medium would have folded quickly. There is nothing more devastating to a new reader than to know that he has a good connection with a spirit and his sitter folds his arms over his chest, shaking his head 'no' and giving a look that says, "Is this the best you have?... You **stink**!" That beginning medium must be able to handle rejection and have a thick skin, or he just will not be able to do this work successfully.

This situation is devastating to the confidence of a medium and could easily convince a reader to walk away from mediumship forever. And that was about to happen to me during my scheduled reading on that Monday before leaving for Omega. Unfortunately, I didn't have the confidence of a John Edward and my skin was still fairly thin at that time.

- Another Life Lesson - # 62

*When your ego begins to act like a child
who has had his feelings hurt,
sometimes you need some help to calm him down,
before he overreacts and stops you from
doing the things you love to do.*

THE SITTERS FROM HELL

As I waited for my clients to arrive, I assumed that the anxiety I was feeling must be due to my desire to do the very best I could for both the woman and her adult son. But in reality, the anxiety I felt was centered on the man in spirit whose presence I already felt there with me, before his wife and son arrived.

For me, this man, the woman's husband and the father of her son, was my real client. Although I felt very confident in my ability to connect with him, I also could not shake the apprehensive feeling I had that the reading was not going to be what I (and he) had hoped for.

So on that Monday afternoon, I was ready for a great reading and thought I might even share the experience with James Van Praagh that weekend. Again, I was right... but not quite in the way I had hoped.

As the reading began, I knew I was in trouble. When my two sitters came into the office, the mother looked annoyed at the son, who looked like he'd just stepped off his Harley into a large pile of dog poo.

With a ponytail, beard, tattoos, motorcycle boots and black leather jacket, you didn't need to be psychic to figure out who this guy was.

I said to myself, *It's going to be very difficult **not** to cold read this guy.* Although he may not have driven to my office on a motorcycle, I knew that if the image of a motorcycle rider came to me, it could very well be coming from my assumptions that he was a biker. In other words, the information might be coming FROM me, and that's something I couldn't accept. That thought also caused me a lot of conflict.

I tried very hard to stay focused and allow the information that I needed from spirit to come into my mind, as it usually does. Immediately, I felt the presence of the man I had sensed before my clients arrived. I knew that he had passed in his late 50s from a heart attack; I knew he smoked and that was what caused his heart attack and death.

He was also coming through as very conflicted and I felt that he knew that these two people would not want to have anything to do with him.

Even though I felt confident that the information I was receiving from this man was rock solid, all I got from my two sitters were shrugs. They both just sat there, arms folded, shaking their heads and shrugging. This man in spirit desperately needed to apologize to his family, but as soon as I said "your husband," to the woman, they both stiffened up and turned away from me. They didn't say a word, but they may as well have said, "We don't want anything to do with him." Almost every piece of evidence I brought up, regarding her husband, was minimized and then discarded.

Finally, the son actually said that he really didn't want to hear from his father anyway, and if I could "find somebody else to talk to!" As if it were as easy as picking up my cell phone to disconnect one spirit and call a different spirit...

"Sorry sir, your son doesn't understand how this works... Perhaps, there is someone up there with you that your obnoxious son would prefer to talk to, besides you... Yes, I do know how important it is for you to apologize to him and your wife, but I'm afraid they just don't want to hear from you... Sorry."

I pictured the father slump down on the floor in front of his son, who was refusing to acknowledge anything I was saying, particularly anything with regard to his father.

Obviously, the relationship between the three was problematic at best, and I decided to see if I could connect with someone else. The way I communicate with a spirit is to simply think the words, knowing that a spirit would connect with my mind. I thanked the father for connecting with me and apologized for his family members. I told him that they were just not ready to communicate with him yet, as I felt him sadly pull back.

At the same time the father's energy pulled back, I saw a brown dog lie down at the feet of the son. I could tell the dog was a German shepherd/ black lab mix and then I became aware of a man who passed in his 40s.

This man was definitely a smoker because I felt tightness in my chest and found it difficult to take a breath. (Feeling a spirit's energy that way is called clairsentience: where you feel what the spirit had felt in life.)

I knew he passed from a smoking related disease which felt like lung cancer. I also knew that he shaved his head rather than becoming bald from chemotherapy.

He was showing me a motorcycle, and of course now I was beginning to wonder if the image was coming from me or if the spirit was actually communicating with me: typical of a 'From Me, To Me' situation.

I now, once again, attempted to bring this new information to the son sitting opposite me, explaining that there was a dog lying on the floor. He looked at the floor mockingly as if I were saying there was a real dog on the floor. I refused to allow the son's sarcasm to dissuade me.

I asked him if he knew of a man who died from lung cancer, in his 40's, who smoked cigarettes, shaved his head and drove a Harley motorcycle; all very specific points of information from this new spirit who was coming through to me.

Once again, the son was smirking and rolling his eyes, as his mother just simply stared at the ceiling with her arms folded in front of her.

Finally he said to me, "Yeah, so everybody had a dog! What's HE going to tell me?" as he sneered with more sarcasm.

I started to become defensive and said to him, "OK, did you have a dog that was a German Shepherd and Black Lab mix, growing up?"

I was about to give the son some additional evidence about the motorcyclist who had passed when he said "Yeah... So? Everybody had a dog when I was growing up. And I have a lot of friends who drive bikes," as he pointed to his leather jacket, with the implication that I was cold reading.

"Who also had lung cancer? And had Chemo, and who also shaved his head?" I asked him, as I tried to keep from displaying the frustration and annoyance I was experiencing with them both.

He looked at his watch impatiently and said, "We all smoke and we all have dogs!"

I was giving these two people the very best I could, but they were refusing to accept anything I said and were totally unsatisfied. Not to mention infuriating, dismissive and... well... unbearable.

And that is when I made a huge mistake.

I read them for another hour! Because I truly wanted to work for their husband/father, even though they denied anything I was saying. I refused to listen to my own intuition, which told me to cut the session off, admit that I couldn't get any more information, and stop the session at that point.

Knowing what I know now, I should've stopped that session 15 minutes into it. But then again, that knowledge comes with a great amount of experience.

By this time I was so turned off by my clients that I began to cold read, which is the worst thing a true medium can do. So after a marathon two-hour, miserably depressing session, they left. They did pay for the service... $100.

That evening I received a curt email from the mother, saying how they both felt ripped off by my reading. She went as far as to say that I was a fraud! My reply to her email was to simply request her mailing address so I could sent her a refund, with a note saying that I hoped that at least she no longer felt 'ripped-off'.

That reading made me wonder why I was offering mediumship readings at all. I was that upset. I considered taking down all my blog postings on mediumship, removing all references to psychic and mediumship from my website, and just give up.

I went home that night ready to cancel my weekend at Omega and take down my proverbial mediumship shingle for good.

When mediums first start their practice, readings like that will challenge their resolve. Having sitters who refuse to accept anything that is presented to them is an experience that every single professional medium has had. Any professional medium you speak to about having difficult sitters will be happy to share their experiences with you. More than likely, their experiences are very similar to the one I had just endured.

The challenge for a new medium is to find a way to get past the gut wrenching, demeaning and frustrating experience of trying to work with a difficult sitter. The joy that a medium receives from a wonderful reading known as a 'Wow' reading - when every single piece of information is accepted with gasps, laughter and tears; when the client leaves and before walking out the door hugs you and thanks you for changing their life - can disappear in an instant by having the type of client I'd just sent a full refund.

Fortunately, I have very supportive friends and as soon as I got home I picked up the phone and called one. I spoke with my friend Susan, an excellent medium, who helped me tremendously.

"Garry," she said, "picture a balance scale measuring every single reading you have ever done. On one side sits all the good ones and on the other, all the bad ones. What would this balance scale look like?"

As that image formed in my mind, I saw the scale overwhelmingly heavy with good readings and only a handful of bad ones. I not only saw the good readings, but the faces of the sitters who were so happy with their readings; how their energy changed after their reading; how wonderful I felt after giving them messages; and how I was aware of a feeling of appreciation and gratitude from spirit after the 'Wow' readings. As I have said before, mediums work for those in spirit more than for the sitters who hire us.

That conversation with Susan was just what I needed to get up off the floor and back in the game. Sometimes it seems to be necessary to get shot down occasionally, so that you know how to get up, brush yourself off and keep on keepin' on.

I thanked Susan for showing me the truth in that simple metaphor. I realized that I had allowed those two people to so negativity influence me that I wanted to quit this work that I love to do. I also realized that my ego was hurt and that was why I felt like quitting; it hurts when your self-image and self-perceptions are attacked.

Garry with James Van Praagh, medium, author, producer
and teacher at the beginning of the workshop.
Photo taken at the Omega Institute for Holistic Studies,
Rhinebeck NY - July 2010

JAMES VAN PRAAGH

In the shower, I washed off the negative energy that I had absorbed from that reading, and after a good night's sleep, I woke up looking forward to the upcoming weekend at Omega, where I would participate in a workshop lead by James Van Praagh.

I had read many of his books and I couldn't wait to meet and learn from one of the most renowned mediums on the planet. I hoped to share with him, and the other participants in the workshop, the frustrating experience of trying to give a reading where your sitters refuse to accept anything that you present.

I consider myself extremely fortunate in my metaphysical exploration, living only a quick three hour drive from Omega. So a few days later, I was headed back there for the Van Praagh weekend workshop.

I finally arrived at Omega at 7:30 pm, after a drive from hell. Route 287 North was closed for repair and a 3 hour ride took well over 6 hours.

After unloading my car, I ran to the Main Hall, and made it just as James Van Praagh came out on stage. There were over 125 people seated as James began the workshop by answering questions from the participants. I settled in, hoping to be able to ask him the question that was still preying on my mind.

I was unaware that one of the helpers handling the microphones was standing directly behind me. When James asked if anyone had any questions and I raised my hand, the microphone seemed to magically appear before me.

"James, I had a really frustrating reading recently," I said into the microphone. "I was giving a reading to a woman and her 35-year-old son..." I relayed how no matter what I said - no matter how strongly I knew I had a good link with the spirit of their husband/father - they refused to accept anything. I said that I was aware that all mediums have had experiences with difficult sitters, and wondered how he would handle a situation like that.

His answer to me was understandable and simple, but his follow up about the ego was profound and worth relaying to you.

Van Praagh explained, "All you can do as a medium is to give the information that you are receiving from a spirit, to the sitter, the best you can. If your intention is coming from a place of love, if you are doing this work for all the right reasons, and if your heart is in the right place, that's the best anyone can do. But when your sitter is too closed off to accept what you are relaying, or when they've come to the reading with preconceived ideas, or only want to hear from one specific spirit… there is nothing anyone can do."

He went on to say, "Accept the fact that as a 'working medium', there will be sitters that you will not be able to read. Whether they refuse to accept the spirit you have, or it is difficult to connect with the sitter or his loved ones, when your intuition tells you that the reading is not working, you should terminate it as quickly as possible."

Now, I have gone further. I know that if after ten minutes I haven't made a connection with a spirit, I will apologize for not being able to connect and I refuse to take payment. I cannot, in good conscience, take payment for a service that I was unable to render. Lots of my friends disagree with me, saying that I should be paid for my time, but that's a discussion for another time.

I understood and accepted his basic response, but then he continued…

- Another Life Lesson - # 63

When someone says to you:
"What people think about you is none of YOUR business,"
and you vehemently argue the point,
take a breath and think of what Part of
you so adamantly disagrees...
And then say hello to your EGO.

"WHAT PEOPLE THINK ABOUT YOU..."

"Sometimes," Van Praagh said, "your ego gets in the way and you get upset because the person you are working with doesn't understand that you are a wonderful medium; that you are a loving individual who is doing this work for all the right reasons. They don't see the effort you are putting in, or the energy it takes to do mediumship. They don't know that you were a boy scout and that you love puppy dogs and you go to church every Sunday... They misjudge you..."

He then said something that is worth repeating. Often.

"What people think about you," he said, "...is none of YOUR business!"

Now re-read that statement, because it is simple, true, and something a lot of us would disagree with. It is truly none of your business what people think of you! What **you** think of you is much, much more important for your growth. And, in reality, there is nothing you can do about what other people think about you... It is their problem, not yours!

On Saturday morning, I got up even earlier than my alarm. Took my shower, brushed my teeth and couldn't get to breakfast fast enough. Smiling to myself as I looked around the cafeteria, I realized how much I enjoyed being at Omega once again. With my steaming hot cup of coffee and my bowl of cereal, banana and a slice of watermelon, I sat by myself at a table.

Soon the table filled with people who recognized me from my question the night before. The conversation validated for me that the work we do as mediums is never as simple as understanding and passing along information from one soul to another. It really has a lot to do with understanding yourself.

James Van Praagh's workshop really was a great learning experience, and I met some great people. I had become accustomed to both Omega and taking psychic and mediumship development workshops. However, James brought a different energy to this workshop; his energy was off the wall... Literally!

He had us up on our feet, dancing and singing and running around. As I said, it was a different type of workshop to say the least. Although some of the exercises he described, I had done before, having learned that the best way to improve is through 'practice, practice, practice', I didn't view the exercises as redundant. I relished practicing them in order to hone my mediumship skills. During Friday evening and Saturday's exercises, James was constantly circulating among the participants, observing us and giving helpful suggestions.

~ ~ ~

Right after breakfast on Sunday morning, as we all settled in for the first mediumship exercise of the final day, James announced that he had a plane to catch and that he had to leave at 12:00 sharp. As our last exercise, he wanted to bring some of us up to read for the audience, but because he had to leave exactly at noon, he could only have five participants come up to demonstrate their ability to bring messages from spirit to the entire group.

Talk about pressure! Doing a mediumship demonstration to a group of mediums with James Van Praagh sitting behind you... and he is NOT an easy teacher. A great teacher, yes, but not an easy teacher. He said from the start that he was going to push us right out of our comfort zones, and he sure did! When he said that he was planning to bring up some of us to read for the group, every hand in the room raised up.

"Great!" James said and picked a woman in the front row. He said he had seen her work and wanted to help her with her first public mediumship demonstration. She came up and did he ever push her! He helped her refine the information she was getting so that it was really accurate, but by the time the reading was through, she looked totally exhausted.

After she handed the microphone back to James and stepped down from the stage, I saw a lot of hands that had been waving wildly go down, and some of the hands were actually being sat upon!

I was torn between wanting to challenge myself, and possibly embarrassing myself. I knew that the push I felt to get up and challenge myself by doing a public reading was coming from my 'higher self': my sub-conscious medium self. At the same time my (fragile) ego was trying to frighten me into sitting on the hand that I was now waving at James.

One of the important lessons James taught us that weekend was the detrimental effect of listening to our ego over our intuitive self. He told us that his acronym for EGO was 'Edging God Out'. I had come to that workshop in order to challenge myself, and decided to ignore my ego (although with that decision it just got louder).

As I made the decision to raise my hand and volunteer to be on stage with James Van Praagh, I felt the presence of an older man in spirit, touch my arm. As James was choosing who would be next to read, my hand had a mind of its own! It shot straight up waving like one of my students who had to really, really go to the bathroom. I felt as if the spirit of this older man was standing behind me, controlling my hand! I knew I could be like many of the others and put my hand down and sit on it. But I also knew that I wanted to challenge myself for a number of reasons.

First, I felt very comfortable that I had a strong connection with this man and after all is said and done, we mediums work for them. If he needed this message to get to someone in the audience, I felt it would be my honor, privilege and pleasure to bring his message through.

Secondly, this was the time and place to challenge our comfort zones. James was able to push people, but I had to make the decision to stand up and be vulnerable. In order to be more accurate, I needed to push myself out of my comfort zone. But I was not vulnerable... my E.G.O. was. Everyone there was extremely supportive of one another; there were no concerns about failing at Omega.

I was clearly ready to do this.

Now, James asked the audience who wanted to be the next person to read. My hand shot straight up as he pointed to another medium, from the back of the room, whom he had also observed during earlier exercises.

My hand came down with a feeling of anxiety and frustration. I was anxious to assist this man's spirit connect with his loved one in the audience, and I was frustrated thinking that I may be leaving soon with this poor man's reading left behind. When I was not called for the third reading, knowing that there were only two readings left, I honestly felt that I was not going to be picked... when the strangest thing happened!

I did what Tricia always told me to do. I 'threw it up to the Universe'. I said in my head to whomever was listening - my Spirit Guides; my higher self; the spirit of the old man; God - *If I am going to do this work and the time is right, it will work out.*

I felt a sense of calmness wash over me and I heard, *'You'll be the last one up!'* I don't know who it was that said it to me, but I heard it as clear as day... Then I began to listen to the words that were being said to me in my left ear, where I hear spirits.

'Calm yourself... Prepare yourself...' And again I heard, *'You will be the last one up.'* The calmness I felt continued as James picked the fourth reader from the right side of the audience.

I felt I would be next: no fear; no apprehension; no doubt. When that fourth reader stepped off the stage, handing James the microphone, James had his back to me, looking at a sea of hands all wanting to be the last to read. I knew he couldn't see me from the stage, considering his back was to me. I was sitting to his left as he was looking to the audience from the center to the right. I simply closed my eyes for a second and told whomever was listening to me, *It's up to you guys now.* I really wanted to get up on stage and give a physical voice to this old man who was in my thoughts, but the ability to go on stage was not up to me. It was up to James Van Praagh, and he had a plane to catch.

To my complete and utter amazement, as I opened my eyes I saw him turn around as if I had just yelled his name. And with the microphone in hand, pointed it at me and said, "Garry? Want to do the last reading?"

I can't describe to you what went through my mind in one millisecond!

Me?...Yeah!... Hell Yeah! I want to read! OMG! It really worked! I asked spirit to help and they did exactly what I asked for! They said I would be last one up to read and I am going to be the last reader!

It was happening just as I'd been told it would, and yet I still couldn't believe it was actually happening. Talk about having your mind blown! Once again, the Omega Experience lived up to its reputation. If it hadn't happened to me, I don't know if I would believe it.

This internal conversation was going on inside my head as I walked up to the stage. I shook James' hand, and he handed me the microphone. Then he put his arm around my shoulder and directed me to sit in the large wicker chair in the center of the stage.

OK guy, it's up to you now. I am all ears, talk to me. Who do you want to connect with? What relationship did you have with the person in the audience? How did you die? Give me more information...

James directed me to calm my thoughts and focus on the spirit. I followed his direction and felt James standing behind me.

Then another voice said... *'Holy crap! You better do this right! This is THE James Van Praagh who just called you up on stage here, pal! You better not screw this up, like you did on Monday!'*

Unfortunately, I knew that my E.G.O. had gotten back in the room!

In an instant I pictured myself standing up facing my ego, grabbing him by the scruff of the neck and his belt, kicking the door open, throwing him out the doorway like John Wayne did in every western he ever made... I took control over my ego at that point and gave myself completely to that old man who needed to connect with his loved one somewhere out there in the audience.

I was on stage, sitting in a large wicker chair with James sitting directly behind me, to my left. Again he prompted me to calm myself...to breathe deeply...to allow an image to form...

The reading began.

"I have an older man here," I started...

"Good," said James, "describe him!"

"He is telling me that he drank and that is what contributed to his death." (I felt a pain in my abdomen and knew it was my liver... Cancer.) "He died of cancer of the liver. He is showing me that toward the end of his life he lost a lot of weight. He is a father to a man who is not here, but his wife is..."

"So, this is a woman's father in law?" James questioned.

"Yes. He was an educated man. A professional. A doctor or a lawyer... A tough demanding father... showed no love to his son... her husband..."

I continued with some more evidence with James giving me hints, as what to ask him or how to phrase my questions. I felt that James knew exactly who I was connected to. I knew that two mediums could connect with the same spirit, but this was the first time I experienced that type of connection.

Finally two women raised their hands claiming this man may be for them, one in the front of the group and one in the back. More evidence came through and we were able to narrow down who this spirit was connected to. It was the woman in the back of the room, and she was able to accept everything that had come though, along with the new evidence I had just received.

Her father-in-law wanted me to thank her for being such a wonderful daughter-in-law and wife to his son. She acknowledged by nodding. He had me relate to her specific things that she did for him, before he passed, that even his own daughter wouldn't or couldn't do. With that I could see people giving her tissues as she began to cry.

Then I felt the information now turning to messages, which were short and powerful. I continued looking directly at his daughter-in-law and said, "He says to please relay to his son that he is so very proud of him... That he was never able to show his pride for his son while he was alive... That he was incapable of showing love in life and that alcohol only made his aloofness all the more hardened and at times violent... He says that although he passed three years before his son went back to college, he is aware of how he graduated magna cum laude... And that your husband is a compassionate businessman and he emphasizes the word compassionate.

"He is telling me now that his son has surpassed him in business and in life and that he is an incredible father... He is asking for forgiveness from his whole family... He says that this is the first time he has been able to get through to anyone. He says that he was extremely difficult to live with, and wants to humbly ask you, his daughter-in-law, to pass this information along to your husband, his son."

I felt the link with this man starting to fade, as a microphone went to his daughter-in-law, in the audience. She thanked me for the message and validated everything I had said.

She told us that she had been thinking of her father-in-law all weekend long, and that it was coming up on the anniversary of his death. She validated that she really was the only person he ever felt close to, and that she actually missed him, although her husband had mixed feelings due to the history he had with his father. She said that she had been working on her mediumship abilities, but felt too close and emotionally connected to the family to trust her readings. Then she thanked me for validating what she had been feeling.

I knew that through the openness of his daughter-in-law, the message would finally be delivered to his son, along with the father's acknowledgement that his son had become a better person, man and father than he himself had ever been. Through his son's wife, this spirit was finally able to tell his son that he is proud of the man he has become, and that he truly loves him.

Garry giving his first mediumship "Dem" with James Van Praagh on stage.
Photo taken at the Omega Institute for Holistic Studies,
Rhinebeck NY – Last day of the workshop July 2010

~ ~ ~

Your loved ones, in spirit, know exactly where you will be and what you will be doing... Even before you ever leave your home.

BILL COLLER

In the winter of 2008, I was participating in a mediumship workshop presented by Bill Coller, a third generation medium and spiritualist from Scotland and a tutor at Arthur Findlay College. The following is from their website:

> *The Arthur Findlay College is located in England and offers facilities in the Spiritualist movement as a residential center where students can study Spiritualist philosophy and religious practice, Spiritualist healing and awareness, spiritual and psychic unfolding and kindred disciplines. Courses, lectures and demonstrations are all offered by leading exponents, together with the additional features of a library, museum, lake, magnificent grounds, recreational facilities and full board accommodation.*
> *- www.arthurfindlaycollege.org*

By that time, I had taken many advanced mediumship classes, workshops and seminars and was accustomed to accurate readings from both the medium tutors and the gifted students with whom I had been taking workshops.

I am never blasé about witnessing a great reading, and I'm always amazed by the way our passed loved ones can communicate with us. But I was not prepared for the astonishing demonstration of mediumship that was in store for the participants of this particular development class.

Bill Collar's day-long workshop began with a lecture and various mediumship development exercises. We took our lunch break from noon to 1:00 pm, and I was anxious to continue the class, so I re-entered the church at around 12:45.

As I walked in, I saw Bill sitting in one of the chairs, intently writing in a memo pad. When he finished, he closed the pad and placed it on a small table to the right of the first chair.

There were 16 chairs in a horseshoe for the 16 participants, and Bill sat in front, facing us. After placing his notepad down, he took another chair and placed it in the horseshoe layout.

I assumed that there would be another person joining our class after lunch, but I would have, once again, assumed wrong.

As we started the first exercise of the afternoon, Bill asked us if we were all comfortable with where we were sitting. We were all in the same seats we had originally chosen for the morning session, so we all realized what the extra seat was for. Soon a woman stood up and sat in the newly placed 17th seat; a man stood up to take her vacated seat, and that triggered a five minute game of music-less chairs.

Finally, we were all fairly satisfied that we had shuffled around enough. Bill asked if we were all positive that we no longer wanted to move; the 7th seat from his left was now unoccupied.

Bill asked once again if anyone wanted to move. The man in the 6th seat stood and sat in the seat to his right, which left the 6th seat open. Bill once again asked if anyone wanted to move; we all declined. Yet, again he asked if we were comfortable with our current seats, and after asking a fourth time he said that we were done moving.

There was no way that there could have been any manipulation on his part in arranging the new seating plan. The seats were changed by the participants themselves, and were chosen purely intuitively. No one knew who would be sitting where... including Bill.

Bill smiled and asked the man in the first seat to pick up Bill's memo pad and read what he had written out loud to everyone. As the man looked at what was written, his eyes widened as he said "Holy Shit!" Turning a little red, he apologized and began to read what had been written, by Bill, when he sat alone during our lunch break.

"There will be a man in the 7th seat from my left..." Yes, that was correct.

"This man was adopted at birth..." All eyes went to the man, whose jaw had just dropped open as he nodded yes.

"He has been looking for his birth father for 6 years..." Again the man nodded as more jaws dropped.

"His adoptive parents were supportive, loving and of Italian heritage, but he has always felt he was Irish..." More nods. All jaws were now agape with wonder, awe and amazement.

"He has been married for 4 years and his wife is currently with child and the child is a boy..." Another nod yes, as someone quietly said, "Unbelievable." (I think it may have been me.)

What Bill had written was nearly 100% accurate, and the man who was the recipient of this incredible reading looked like he was in shock.

"Your birth father IS in spirit, and he wants you to know he has been watching over you. He was indeed Irish, but says that it was better that you had never met. He says that he was not a nice man in life."

I had never seen such a demonstration before or since. Bill did not demonstrate his ability as a medium, as much as his confidence in the spirit world, which may be the hardest lesson for a novice medium to learn.

Years later I would enroll in Bill's two-year advanced mediumship course offered at the Inner Spiritual Center in Fairfield NJ.

Simply stated...
The Universe really DOES work in wondrous and mysterious ways!
And when you not only accept it, but request 'its' assistance,
the wonders and mysteries will appear almost instantaneously.

DIFFICULT TIMES CAN PRODUCE THE BEST LESSONS

Two years after opening HYP4LIFE, my business, like many others, experienced a slump. Although my bills were being paid, I knew I needed to get my name out there. I wasn't concerned about paying my office rent to Trish, but other bills often drained my finances.

At that time, the only way to attract new hypnosis clients was through the Yellow Pages, newspaper ads, radio and television. Television was out of the question; however I passed our local radio station every day, and decided to stop in with a flyer for my upcoming Smoking Clinic.

Remembering the advice of my father, I devised another gimmick for my Smoking Clinic. I offered a 'Conditional Guarantee,' which I use to this day. It read, "If for any reason this clinic doesn't work for you, I will double your fee of $75, and give you a $150 discount toward a private smoking hypnosis session."

When I entered the WRNJ radio station, I thought I would just be dropping the flyer off. But one of the salesmen there was curious and decided to go to the clinic to quit his smoking addiction.

At the same time, he convinced me that I could afford radio advertising at the station. I signed up to record two commercials with the remaining money in my advertising budget for that year. Realizing that I could reach more people through the radio than the print media I had been using, I basically doubled down on radio advertising.

I rented a room at the local Comfort Suites and advertised my February "New Year's Resolutions Smoking Clinic." Not only did I advertise on the radio, I was interviewed by their DJ about hypnosis, smoking and my clinic, and I placed a small ad in the local paper.

Keeping in mind that although I had recently opened my website, I was still clueless about the Internet or Google rankings, I invested every penny I had into advertising HYP4LIFE and my Smoking Clinic on WRNJ Radio.

My decision to advertise on the radio paid off handsomely. My clinic was an incredible success. I had over 40 people quit smoking that day. I would love to say that all the participants quit and claim I had a hundred percent success rate, but I am a realist, and to be honest I am quite sure that some of them went back to smoking. However, only two participants would take advantage of the guarantee, and thereafter were successful.

There was a subtle benefit to the advertising on the radio also, not only with new smoking clients at the clinic but with people who had heard me on the radio and clicked on my website. I found that this led to more interesting hypnotic interventions. Smoking Cessation was the mainstay, but now sports performance, academic performance, elimination of phobias and stress management all began to increase. Soon I found that HYP4LIFE was actually starting to show a small profit, despite the additional expense of advertising.

~ ~ ~

I have come to understand and accept that good times can never last forever. Life is constantly changing and that's what life is all about; good or bad times all contribute to the lessons we learn. When you realize that, the bad things aren't really that bad if you view them as a particularly difficult lesson that once learned, never needs repeating and that they - the difficult lessons - help you learn and grow.

On one particular day I had another smoking client scheduled after school. I arrived at the office at 4:00 for his 4:30 appointment, just as Tricia was leaving. Normally every time we met it was always with a big smile, a big hug, and many questions from Trisha asking what's new with HYP4LIFE. But this time I immediately sensed that something was wrong. Whether it was the expression on her face or her lack of an enthusiastic greeting, or I just psychically read her, I knew something was off, and I was right. She sat in one of the large, plush, antique chairs in the waiting room and motioned that I should sit down in the other.

"Ga, we have to talk," she said.

I realized just how very much I hated conversations starting in that manner. "What's up?" I asked.

"I just met with the landlord to pay the rent," she explained, "and he asked me who you are. I told him that you're a friend of mine and you are renting a room from me for hypnotherapy."

I had met the landlord a few times but always in passing. I'd never really said anything to him, and didn't even realize that I was subletting the office.

I took a deep breath as my head just dropped down. I had been thinking about how good things had been going. Perhaps too good, too quickly. I was 'waiting for the other shoe to drop' and it did... drop squarely on the top of my head.

Tricia continued to tell me about her conversation. "He reminded me about a small clause in our lease that I hadn't remembered. Garry, the clause states - no subletting."

Before I could make a suggestion of what we could do, I realized that I hadn't a clue as to what to even suggest.

However, Tricia told me that it was all worked out with the landlord. "I told him that you were staying and we decided upon a raise in my rent. Unfortunately now that my rent has gone up, you and I need to change our agreement."

I would have to start paying her a set rent, not just the 25% of whatever clients I had (which had worked out so perfectly for me, but as it turned out not so perfectly for her).

Trish, always the optimist, told me not to look so defeated. "There's another way to deal with this problem," she said. "I have another friend who is a reflexologist and Reiki Master. She is also looking for an office and said she is very willing to share the office with you! You both can split the rent. You could alternate weekend days and evenings, although you'll have to remove some of your things to make room for her Reiki table."

I had my office set up exactly the way I wanted it. I had my diplomas and degrees on the walls. I had my recliner, desk, chair and file cabinet all exactly where they needed to be. The thought of removing them was something I did not want to do.

"Tricia, I don't want to move out of this office, and I don't want to share it," I said. "I know that it might sound selfish, but I love our office, just the way it is..."

Trish shook her head saying, "It's not being selfish to want to keep what you love. It's completely understandable. But we have to look at the finances."

I reminded her of the Christmas party where we discussed the possibility of my subletting the room and quoted her statement back to her. "Trish, you have convinced me and now I am a believer." I explained to her, "When I've put myself out to the Universe it has actually taken care of me. I just now put myself out there, to whoever is listening, and asked them to send me some new clients. Hopefully, they want me to continue the work that I am doing, and everything will work out fine." I don't think Tricia could have smiled more brightly.

"I will be paying you my rent monthly. Let's work out what will cover your raise and be a reasonable rent that I will be able to afford. There's no need to bring anyone else in to subsidize the raise you just received. I know I will have the money to cover it."

That was the first month that I began to pay a steady consistent rent for my office. And true to form, the Universe has taken care of me ever since. There was never a point where I couldn't make my bills, including the increased rent. There were times when it was tight and times when it was close, but I never had to wonder how I was going to get by.

The Universe did indeed take care of me. I was and am indebted and appreciative to my entire unseen support team.

*When things suddenly look bleak and you
can't seem to find a way out,
remember to ask for help from your spiritual helpers.
Some people call this prayer; some people
say that the belief in prayer is naïve.
I simply say... "Thank-You."*

GETTING 'DIRECTIONS' TO MY NEW OFFICE

Earlier in my psychic development, I was told that forming a 'development circle' was an intrinsic part of every medium's progress. Traditional development circles are formed by a group of psychics and mediums who are committed to expanding their innate psychic abilities by meeting in the same place and time weekly for years. So I asked two other students in my psychic classes if they wanted to meet every Tuesday evening to work on our development as mediums and form our own development circle.

That original psychic development circle - which I called 'Connecting with Loved Ones in Spirit' - became fairly popular. Bill, Jill and I were inviting people into our circle to have a reading from all three of us. We would bring entire family groups in and sit with them, in my office, and connect these families with their passed loved ones. This concept, of having three mediums doing a family group reading, was something new and exciting, and we worked every Tuesday evening for two years.

However, over the years, the three of us have found different directions to go in each of our lives, which is another purpose for a psychic development circle: to explore our own psychic potential.

When Bill and Jill moved on and our weekly psychic development group disbanded, I missed that regularly scheduled connection to the spirit world and wanted to establish a new psychic development circle.

Sometime later, I advertised in a few New Age magazines that I was beginning a psychic development class. And on Tuesday evenings for three months, I held a regularly scheduled class for novices in psychic development.

~ ~ ~

The three month class became very popular, and when it ended, I asked three students if they would be interested in beginning a psychic development circle. After describing what it would entail, they were all very excited to continue their psychic development using a tried and true method: a traditional regularly scheduled psychic development circle.

Every Tuesday evening the four of us would meet to work as a group to develop our own psychic and mediumship abilities. We would sit in a circle in the same seats, open the circle using a contemplation technique known as 'Sitting in the Power' and give readings, both psychic and mediumship, to each other.

At this point in 2013, things, in general, were going wonderfully. Heather, Jamie, Joella and I had worked with each other for over a year before we began to invite sitters into our circle. And as I did with my previous development circle, I called our Tuesday evening group 'Connecting with Loved Ones in Spirit'. We began to invite people to be our sitters, and all four of us gave psychic and mediumship readings to our guests.

From the standpoint of our sitters, especially those people who had never had a mediumship reading before, being read by four mediums at the same time could be a bit overwhelming.

Although things were going very smoothly for me, I was aware of a feeling of dread. Tricia had been taking more and more time off from her massage clients and I was truly missing our conversations. The feeling I had was that I should be looking for a new office, but that was the last thing I would want, so I refused to consider the possibility.

Normally when I was conflicted in that way, Trish would be the first person I would talk to, but it had been two months since our paths had crossed. I would leave my rent check in an envelope by her phone and often noticed that it hadn't been picked up for two or three weeks.

I called her and we spoke. She said she'd been very busy with her family, but she was fine, just needing some 'me' time.

By now I was comfortable accepting and following through on my intuitive feelings, and I was still being strongly pushed to find another office. But as I often do in a conflict between what I feel intuitively and what I am afraid might happen, I ignored my intuition and preferred to use what I have called 'Ostrich Management': I stuck my head in the ground hoping everything would be alright. Until something bit me in the butt. And I was about to be bitten. Hard.

One evening when I was leading my psychic development circle, I introduced Tricia to the 'girls'. Joella already knew her; she had been one of Tricia's massage clients for years. And whenever Tricia was working late on a Tuesday, we would all talk about Metaphysics and mediumship with her. She was extremely supportive of our development circle and would always tell me how wonderful she felt about my growth, as a psychic and a medium.

Then on one Monday morning in early August of 2013, I received a disconcerting phone call from Tricia. "Garry can you come over? We have to talk." The seriousness in her voice along with her words sent a chill down my spine. I knew something was up and I also knew that it pertained to the concern I'd felt over the urgency to look for a new office. Yet I still refused to allow myself to think about that possibility.

As usual, her timing was perfect. I had nothing scheduled, with no clients and Chris was still at work when she called. I was just relaxing at the house and told her I would be there in five minutes.

Entering our office, Tricia was sitting in the waiting room and gestured that I should sit next to her. It felt like 'Déjà vu, all over again', but I knew it wasn't going to be as easy as a raise in rent this time.

"Garry, I'm going to retire," she said.

Although I was relieved that Tricia got right to the purpose of our meeting, I felt my stomach drop as if I were sitting in the front seat of a roller coaster as it plunged over the crest of the first hill.

Where will I go? I can't have people coming to my house late at night... There is no privacy. How am I going to keep HYP4LIFE open and running?

I also had to admit that I'd been feeling this for a while and if I'd only listened to my intuition, I might have been in a new office by now.

Tricia told me that she spoke with the landlord and told him that she would be leaving on October 1st. This meant that I had less than two months to find a new office, and I hadn't a clue as to how I would find one.

I suddenly realized, to my shock, that although I had until October 1st, I only had two weeks before school started, at which point I certainly would be too busy to be looking for an office. My stomach took another drop on that annoying rollercoaster.

Trish looked at me with empathy and sympathy, and said, "I spoke with the landlord and he said you can stay here," which made me feel a little better for a second or two. And again I heard the words I always did in a situation like this: *When you put it out to the Universe, the Universe always takes care of you.*

Trish had told me that in December of 1999. I didn't believe it then, but very quickly I'd learned to trust in its truth.

I told Tricia what I had just heard in my mind. She smiled, put her hand on my shoulder, and told me, in no uncertain terms, that I should not worry, that I would find a place. And soon.

I got up, gave her a shrug and a hug, saying, "It is what it is."

And as we walked to our cars, she reaffirmed what she'd said, looking into my eyes and shaking my arms to get my attention. "Garry, I know you will find your own office."

And I believed her. But even so, all the old concerns and fears came rushing back.

So now I began talking to anyone up there who would listen. As I had previously said to them, *Okay guys. If you want me to do this work, I need a place to do it. Help me out here guys. Please!*

The deadline was approaching quickly. I discussed the situation with the landlord, who told me that he hadn't decided what my rent would be, but he estimated that it would be between $700 and $900 a month... Before informing me, quite off-handedly, that the rent did <u>not</u> include heat, electric or water.

I almost fell off my chair! By my estimate, my cost to keep the office could reach $2000 a month! There would be no way I could afford that.

I was really trying to fight the gloom that was creeping up upon me, when once again I heard, *When you put it out to the Universe, the Universe always takes care of you,* and fought to stay positive. But it was a losing battle.

The combination of losing my office AND not having Tricia's support, friendship and mentorship was a daunting task even for... The Universe!

"Que sera, sera... What will be, will be..." My father used to say that whenever he was faced with a seemingly insurmountable problem. I took a breath, and wondered what to do now. *Que sera, sera,* I thought.

That Tuesday evening, I sat alone in the office that I knew I would have to be leaving soon. Although I truly believed that it would all work out, I couldn't help the melancholy I felt as I looked around the office that I loved.

It was 6:30. I knew that the women in my psychic development circle would be coming in momentarily, and I was preparing to tell them the bad news. Usually they would come in separately, but that evening, they all came through the door at the same time, excitedly talking about something they had just seen outside.

I couldn't help the sadness within me. Considering this was a psychic development circle, I was sure they would sense my sadness and ask what was troubling me, so this was how the teacher in me planned to convert the sadness into a learning experience.

As they came in, I skipped our usual opening meditation and asked them to tune in to how I was feeling. However, all three women were talking so excitedly about something they'd seen, that I don't think they even heard my request to 'tune into my energy'.

"Garry, have you seen what's been done to the Hugh Allen Mansion?" Jamie asked.

"You mean that run-down building around the corner? I rarely drive that way, so I haven't noticed anything different. But there's something more important for us to discuss tonight."

But there was no redirecting their attention. Joella and Heather joined Jamie in explaining how someone had renovated it, and how beautiful the run-down historic building looked now.

Again, I suggested that we discuss the old building's renovation later, because right now I had some more important news to share with them. But they were on a mission. One that could not be stopped.

"No, Garry, you don't understand," Joella insisted. "There's a sign in front of the building that says they have office space for rent!"

Chaos ensued as the three women interrupted each other in an attempt to impress me with their shared vision. It seemed that each one insisted they all 'saw' us holding our circle in that old historic building.

As they continued talking about their vision of us holding a séance in the mansion, I held up my hand.

"Hold on... Hold on," I said. "Have any of you talked with Tricia recently?"

They all said that they hadn't. Then their attention turned serious as they noticed my expression and finally realized something negative was happening.

Joella was the first to inquire, "Garry? What's wrong?"

"I was going to start the circle by having you all tune into my energy, so you could tell me what you feel is happening with me. But with your focus already on this mansion, this may be even more interesting."

As they seated themselves and became more centered, I asked them, "So none of you are aware that Tricia is retiring?"

They were all stunned, and at that moment I became aware that I was now in the middle of a very powerful synchronicity. We had to stop and regroup, to understand what had just happened, and again, I began counting the synchronicities.

> 1 - No one knew that Tricia was retiring.
> 2 - They were all unaware that the day before I had been told I needed to find a new office.
> 3 - They all met and drove to the office together, which is something they had never done.
> 4 - As they drove by the Hugh Alan Mansion, which they'd all driven by frequently, they all became aware of the completed renovation, the sign saying 'Office for Rent' and agreed that it would be a perfect office for me. They even 'saw' us having our circle there.

5 - They had driven by that building through its renovation, every Tuesday for the past six months, but never once discussed it or mentioned it to me... until that day.

All this occurred just one day after I found out that I would be in need of a new office and asked the Universe for assistance! This synchronicity was so profound because it not only showed the unlikely arbitrary events that led to that moment; it also answered my request of the Universe so clearly that it took my breath away!

Talk about one door closing and another literally opening! And as I have become quite accustomed to doing, I looked up to the ceiling, shook my head in the profoundness of the moment, and whispered, "Thank you," to whatever energy was there listening and following through with my request for help.

I knew I had less than two weeks before school started, which would severely limit the time I had to find an office and furnish it. But the sense of urgency had been lifted. I drove by the renovated mansion and left a voicemail to make an appointment to see the new office.

That Wednesday, I had a 5 o'clock hypnosis appointment and entered the office at 4:30, preparing for my client but anxious to get a return phone call from the new landlord. I was also very aware of how fast time was flying by. The next week would be Labor Day and then the start of a new school year. I needed to determine if the new office would work out. If it didn't, I had no backup plan.

At 4:45 I had an intuitive feeling that my 5:00 appointment wasn't going to show up, so I checked my messages and found that he had, indeed, cancelled. I smiled to myself as I do when I sense something that proves true, just as my cell phone rang with the number I had called the previous day.

It was the mansion's landlord, who wanted to know when I would like to come down to see the office. I told her I could be there in five minutes. Once again I found myself looking up at the ceiling, quietly thanking my Guides for continuing this amazing synchronicity.

As I locked the door to my office, I decided to walk the two blocks to what would become my new office. I realized the profundity of the process that I now truly believed in. Again it was proven to me that our Guides are always around us, always watching out for us, and always responding to our requests for help.

As I walked the two blocks to the Hugh Allen Mansion, I also knew that my request for help was just part of this ongoing synchronicity. I no longer doubted this relationship with my Guides. Doubt had been replaced by acceptance and appreciation. I now had faith in something that can't be proven by logic or the five senses.

I met the landlord, and we walked up the four steps to the large front porch. Although the office was old, it was freshly painted. There wasn't a level line in the entire house. Each room was like a set from a Tim Burton movie. The two original windows were anything but square, but they were 10 foot tall with the original leaded glass amazingly preserved and beautiful in their antiquity.

Before I even walked into the office I knew it would be mine, the same way 23 years earlier I knew that I would be teaching at my school; it was a knowing that I had become quite accustomed to.

When the tour was over I asked what the rent would be. It was considerably higher than I had been giving to Tricia, yet it would be affordable. But when I was told that the rent included heat, electricity and water, I just smiled, looked into the perfect blue August sky, and said with a smile, "I'll take it!"

Over the next two weeks with the help of my wife, my son, Heather, Jamie, and Joella, I was able to have my office furnished and ready for my first client.

~ ~ ~

I was quite happy in my new office and thought that I'd be happy there forever.

Then early one Sunday morning in August of 2017, eight months after I retired from teaching, and four years after I moved into my new office, I was surprised by a really strong desire to be at the Institute for Spiritual Development. And as you know, I have learned by now to follow my gut feeling, so I left to attend the Sunday morning service at the ISD.

I'm always very busy through the summer, and it had been almost two months since I'd been there last. As I parked my car, I saw and waved at Reverend Chris in the parking lot. When our eyes met, I felt a wave of appreciation for this woman who had been so instrumental in my spiritual education, and had been the co-teacher of the first psychic development class I'd ever attended, way back in 2003.

After a big hug, Reverend Chris shook me by the arms and said, "I knew you'd be here this morning! Listen, I'm the homilist for the service today, so I must rush, but do you have a minute after service? I have to talk to you about something." She smiled broadly when I said I would wait for her, and she ran off saying, "Great! See you later. Thanks!"

Now I understood why I'd been drawn to the ISD that morning. But I was left to wonder what she might want to discuss with me.

After service ended and everyone was in the hospitality room, enjoying coffee, tea, snacks and conversation, Reverend Chris walked me over to one of the four newly renovated offices.

"Garry, I realize that your hypnosis office is in Netcong, but I have an offer I'd like you to think about. You know that we've recently renovated the building, right? Well, this is one of the newly built offices we've added." She gestured with her arm, inviting me to take a look at the immaculate space.

"Garry, the ISD Board and I would like to offer this office to you. We have planned these offices because we knew that we would be able to offer so much more to everyone who comes here. We now offer massage therapy, spiritual healing, as well as psychic and mediumship readings, all available right here, under our new roof. We have this room available and we love working with you, and it would be wonderful to have you here. You would allow us to offer hypnotherapy as a wonderful healing modality at the church, and you can use the office for your own hypnotherapy clients or to have a quiet place to work on your books. What do you think, Garry? Are you interested?"

I thought about it for a second and then realized that this was the reason for that gut feeling I'd had, to come to the ISD that morning. But I didn't have to think too long. I realized that if I accepted Chris's offer, I would be *coming home*. I had been missing Tricia for the last four years, and now I had the opportunity to come full circle, back to the source of her Spiritualist beliefs.

I thought about that very first Sunday service I'd attended at the ISD, and how I - quite literally - bumped into Tricia. I recalled how she'd told me that this was where she had learned about her belief in the soul... A belief I now so strongly share.

I knew that if I accepted the offer, I'd be back home where it all started. So I looked at Reverend Chris and said, "I think that would be amazing!"

~ ~ ~

As I have said, life is cyclical. So just as my first book is about to be published, here I am, making plans to 'move home' to the ISD, where it all began and where I would begin my second book.

THE END OF THE BOOK
But not the Journey...

There is something 'special' about becoming a father.
Although that statement seems clearly obvious,
becoming a grandfather gave a new meaning to the word: 'special'.

A FATHER'S LOVE

There is a joke in our family, that I love Amy more than I love Aaron, but since Chris loves Aaron more than Amy... it's a wash in the love department. However, that type of teasing isn't as funny as it is inaccurate.

As a father, I've come to realize that there is a difference between the love I have for my son and my daughter. That love is, was, and will always be just as equal and strong for both - just different.

There are roles we all play in life. As Aaron's father, I view that my role is a teacher: to share with him what I've learned in life, to help him on *his* journey. I have always known that my role as Amy's father was as a protector. But, the differences between these two roles are slight and are frequently interchangeable. As parents, I believe, the purpose of these roles we play is to prepare and assist our children on their life's paths.

I love my family with every ounce of my being, but we all love in different ways. Love is not a substance that can be put on a scale and weighed. You can't quantify love as if it's a pound of ground beef that you can divide up or short change. Love **is**... what it **is**.

Since Aaron was born, I have used every opportunity to teach him a lesson. Not in the negative connotation that the phrase carries, but in the best sense of the concept: that of teaching your child.

After reviewing what I'd learned at Omega regarding my past life in Yosemite, I wondered if my desire to teach Aaron everything I've learned in this life was a reflection of my Native American culture, during that lifetime.

Is that why it has been so important to me that I carefully guide my son? And as with all sons, there were many times when he was resistant to my advice. But, as we both grew, I was indescribably proud of him through every stage of life as I watched him become the man he is today. Along with love and pride, I have a surprising sense of comfort, which comes with the knowledge that he will be self-sufficient and that he and his family will be able to survive and thrive after I'm gone. And I have wondered if that need for comfort with my children's future is also a residual feelings from that same past life memory.

Now I see my son in a different light. I see him as a father, husband and provider: the man I always hoped he would be. And I am proud to say that he has succeeded in all three areas, far beyond my expectations.

A 'SPECIAL TREAT' CALLED: ELYSE

Amy and Keith were married in the summer of 2008. Six years later, I was daydreaming on the drive home from school. The next year would be my 25th at the school, and for the first time I considered retirement.

With that thought, I took a deep breath, shook myself out of my reverie, and noticed the bumper sticker on the car in front of me. It read:

'Grandchildren are the reward for not killing your kids!'

I smiled and thought how funny and true that statement was. Instantly, my thoughts went to Amy. I didn't think it was prophetic, I just saw the obvious connection between that bumper sticker and my married daughter. I laughed at the thought, *How are you going to handle being a grandpa for the fourth time?* I knew that I absolutely loved being a grandpa to Aaron and Kristie's three kids: Meghan, Paige and Cole. And I realized just how much I was looking forward to seeing my daughter, one day, with her first child.

When I arrived home that afternoon, Chris was on the phone with Amy, who suggested that if we wanted, we could meet at Applebee's for dinner. As always, I was more than happy to go out with 'the kids'.

Both cars pulled into the parking lot at the same time and as we were walking toward each other, I sensed something different about Amy. I just couldn't put my finger on it. She was walking toward us with a smile, but she always meets us with a big smile, so it wasn't that. She was dressed for a dinner out, so it wasn't that, either. Her hair style and make-up were the same; but still, she seemed different to me.

I was brought back to my drive home that afternoon and wondered if I had sensed that my daughter would soon be having a baby. As we stood in front of the entrance, the feeling changed into a *knowing*. I was now quite sure that she was pregnant, but I kept that feeling to myself.

Although at that time I was a 'professional' medium (a person who is paid for a service, would be considered a professional), I had given up on 'reading' anyone in my family. In particular, I'd had a less than stellar history of predicting the gender of the babies in our family. Since our first grandchild, I have kept any prediction strictly confidential, if only for the purpose of self-protection. The male members of my extended family just love to tease me over the mistakes I've made in the past, so I no longer give them any more ammunition.

As the four of us settled into the booth and ordered dinner, I knew Amy was bursting to tell us something, and I was more and more certain that I knew what it was. Chris wasn't aware of my feelings, and I decided not to say anything, other than, "I'm starving!" And after the waiter said he'd be back with our drinks, Amy smiled and cleared her throat, as if to prepare for an announcement.

"So, guys," she said with a glance and a smile to Keith, who also had a big grin on his face, "how do you both feel about being grandparents again?" Chris and I knew how much they wanted to become parents. And after all the hugging and kissing settled down, we had an animated conversation about how she'd informed Keith, and the plans they had for the future, as they prepared for parenthood.

And now I saw my daughter in a different light.

~ ~ ~

Six months later, when Amy looked as if she were about ready to give birth at any moment, I asked her if she would be interested in *hypnobirthing*. With a shrug, she said, "Sure. Why not?" So we made a plan for the expectant couple to come to the house for a barbecue, where Amy and I would go downstairs and I could introduce her to hypnobirthing.

I had used the process with Aaron's sister-in-law for the birth of her first child, and she was very pleased with the results. She even mentioned how relaxed she'd felt in hypnosis and suggested to Amy that it would be a good idea to take advantage of having her 'daddy' hypnotize her.

As Amy sat in the plush chair in the den and took a breath, I started the hypnotic induction. "Just take a relaxing breath... You can be aware of normal sounds around you; ignore them..."

I saw that instead of allowing hypnosis to take her to that relaxed state, she was clearly trying to control the smile on her face before it turned into a laugh. But as I continued, she lost control and started giggling.

"Dad, thank you for trying, but in my eyes, you're not a hypnotherapist - you're my Daddy! I love you, but as soon as you start that hypnosis stuff, I turn back into your little girl and I can't stop laughing." She stood up, kissed me on the cheek and whispered, "I love you, Daddy."

So much for trying to hypnotize Amy. In fact, I've never been able to hypnotize any of my family members. But I know that as long as I am taking a breath, I will be a protector for my daughter and a teacher for my son, as I have now continued those important roles, with their children.

~ ~ ~

Very soon we were at the maternity ward of Morristown Hospital. And as I met my fourth grandchild, I looked at my wife and exclaimed, "Oh my God, Elyse is a clone of Amy!" And it would seem that just like her Mom, Elyse was verbal from the age of a week! Her giggling and cooing just tickled my heart.

Over the next two years, I could not deny how much my new grandchild reminded me of my daughter. After Elyse's second birthday, Chris and I pulled out our old family photo albums to compare Amy's first two years' worth of photos to those of Elyse, and they could have been the same baby. At two years old, she was speaking in full sentences with totally appropriate facial expressions… for an adult.

When I say that she's a clone of my daughter, including how she'd made her mother crazy, I'm not kidding! But that didn't happen with Amy until she was in high school! Elyse is the cutest child but, for a three-year-old, she can do some serious 'button pushing' with her mommy.

We frequently go to Amy and Keith's home for dinner, and Keith is an incredible chef. After dinner, if Elyse is well behaved, Keith or Amy say to her: "Leesy, you are being very good! Would you like a 'special treat'?" Which always makes Elyse laugh and applaud while nodding yes. Elyse loves Skittles and there is a mason jar full of the multi-colored candy on the counter for some positive reinforcement of good manners.

But there is something about that question – The expression 'special treat' always makes me smile because I have always looked at my daughter and granddaughter, as my very own *special treats*.

Watching Elyse grow, Amy and I are in total agreement that the expression *The Terrible Two's* is totally inaccurate, and that the description should be, *The Terrific Two's* and the *Terrible Three's*. Although, in confidence, I think my youngest granddaughter is terrific all the time. But she can be a real handful for her mother, much as Amy had been for Chris.

LET'S PLAY 'WHISPER'

I retired in January of 2017, and I was now babysitting all four grandkids a lot, particularly my youngest: four-year-old Cole and three-year-old Elyse. I love the laughter-filled memories that are created for them and for me.

Over the past twelve years, I've become fairly proficient as a puppeteer. I'd used an old sock as a quasi-puppet with our older grandkids and would have stimulating conversations between Meghan and Paige and 'Lambchop', the baby lamb (with no credit to Shari Lewis, the inventor of that sock puppet, which I clearly plagiarized). As they grew out of the Grandpa Puppet Show stage and Cole was more interested cars, trucks and guy things than listening to Grandpa's silly puppet accents, I retired Lambchop.

Now, Elyse loves her stuffed animals, and everyone knows it. There are at least a hundred living in the menagerie in her bedroom. And when she comes to our home, she must come with at least twenty of her furry playmates, in their own carrying case.

Another aspect of my youngest grandchild is that Elyse is perhaps the most observant child I have ever seen. Nothing gets by her. And she remembers EVERYTHING! She'll remind me if I forget things, like: "Grandpa! Nana says to light a candle when you cook an egg, 'cause the house stinks!" With an expression on her face that clearly reflects her Nana's attitude: a hand on her hip with a sideways 'stink-eyed' glance at me... Really!

My little three-year-old Leesy also will never leave the house without her purse over her shoulder. And insists that Amy's small Coach clutch is for her because: "It's too little for a mommy, but it's just right for me." I'm sure that Elyse is the only kid in her nursery school with a mauve Coach purse... 'To die for!' as her mother describes the clutch that has now been commandeered by her impeccably dressed daughter.

One day, while babysitting, I recalled that I had retired Lambchop to the bottom of our toy chest. Leesy wanted to know what I was looking for as I was rummaging through it, until I dusted off my old white sock with the eyes and mouth drawn with a Sharpie. And instantly Lambchop was back from retirement and on stage once again, playing to a brand new audience of one.

Leesy knows where everything is in my house and whenever she visited, would run to the toy chest for my puppet. It became our thing. I would let Lambchop whisper in my ear and tell Leesy what she said to me. Everything was working fine until one day she looked at my old puppet that I described as Lambchop the lamb, and said to me with a frown: "Grandpa! THAT," pointing to the old sock, "is not a lamb... It's a sock!" with a look eerily reminiscent of the looks I get from both her mother and her Nana. She calmly picked up her own favorite stuffed lamb and said, "Grandpa. THIS... is a lamb," extending the appropriate puppet to me.

I was having a hard time controlling the laughter, which became impossible to control, when she picked up my dirty, ten-year-old sock, and walked it into the kitchen, where she proceeded to throw it in the trash.

Now, laughing so hard that I was barely able to breathe, she walked up to me, handed me her *real* lamb, and said: "What is my Lammy saying?"

With an opportunity to make Elyse laugh, I used the skills and techniques I'd developed with Meghan and Paige to entertain my Leesy. And soon each time she came into the house, we would line up all the stuffed animals that came to visit Nana and Grandpa, and each one would whisper something to me that I would relay to my granddaughter. I don't think anyone knew how fluent I had become in *stuffed-anamaleze*. But the joy and laughter it brought her, was surpassed by the joy and laughter she continually brings me.

I also know that these past years with my four grandchildren have been the most joyous of my life.

PICTURING MY GRANDSON

It was the autumn of 2005, two years after Aaron and Kristie were married. I had been teaching for fifteen years and it was two years after my introduction to Metaphysics. I was teaching during the day, and when I wasn't hypnotizing clients, I was taking psychic and mediumship classes in the evening. I was also clearly obsessed with my new found spiritual beliefs and psychic abilities.

At one metaphysical class, the topic of dreams was discussed and we were told that it would be an interesting learning experience to start a dream journal. And with a new marble notebook that I had purchased for all the classes I was taking, I started it, that very night.

At 3:00 am, I had a dream that I had a grandson. Bleary eyed, I took that brand new journal into the bathroom, and in the bright light, scribbled down the memories of that dream.

I woke up in the morning and as I was getting ready to leave for school, I went back to my night stand and read what I had jotted down. I entered the date and time of the dream and titled it <u>My Grandson</u>, the first entry in the first of many dream journals over the years.

Dreams are curious. And remembering them, is more so. As you recall what you had dreamt, the images often go in reverse. One image is recalled as the previous image comes to mind. As the last memory of the dream came to mind, I pictured my grandson as a combination of my son and myself. He looked like Aaron, but wore glasses just like mine. He was wiry and full of energy as his father was at the age I pictured him, about four years old. In the last memory before I woke up, we were both sitting in the booth of a restaurant having breakfast. Just him and me.

And I woke up.

Now re-reading my journal entry, before leaving my house, I thought, *Hmmm, I wonder if Aaron and Kristie are expecting.* And with that thought, I was convinced that whenever that blessed event might happen, I was going to have a grandson.

The next night, when Chris and I had finished dinner, the doorbell rang unexpectedly...

*There is a joy and wonderment
in seeing the growth in your children;
and sometimes the "seeing" may come at unexpected times.*

MEETING MEGHAN

I had been in the delivery room with my wife for the birth of both our kids. When we were about to have our first child, we would often visit my mother in Brooklyn.

Unlike previous generations, when we - The Love Generation - became parents, it was a new and exciting practice for fathers to be in the delivery room with their wives. When I told my mother that we were taking *Lamaze* natural childbirth classes together so we both could experience childbirth, and that I would be right there in the delivery room for the birth of her first grandchild, she was clearly less than supportive.

Those who fought in WW II - The Greatest Generation - were the first to give birth in hospitals with anesthesia, and the American medical profession recommended that mothers be sedated so deeply that they were unable to participate in the birth. This was seen as wonderful medical progress in the 1940's, through the 70's. But for many of us approaching parenthood in the 1970's and 80's, experiencing natural childbirth, with a supportive father at his wife's side, completely involved in his infant's birth, was the new Gold Standard in becoming a family.

My Mom was never known for keeping her opinions to herself. She was positive that Chris would choose to be 'put out' when the time came, but she was determined to change our minds regarding expectant Dads in the delivery room. And try she did, as she freely voiced all of her concerns and misconceptions about men being involved with the birth of their children.

She would tell us the endearing stories of how all the men in the family would hang out in the waiting room, smoking cigars and doing male bonding things while my cousins, sister and I were being born.

All through Chris' first pregnancy, Mom loved to relive the night she went into labor with me (and she re-told that story every time she had a chance, during anyone's pregnancy...)

"Chris, it was just like my favorite *I Love Lucy* episode. When Desi Jr. was born? You have seen it? Right?" Not waiting for Chris to answer she continued. "It was just like that for Morty and me, the night Garry was born!

"It was a Saturday night, and all our family was sitting on chairs around the TV set at Uncle Bernie's apartment. This was four years after the war. 1949, you understand, and

Dad was working so hard at his business, and we were just about to buy our own TV. So right in the middle of *Your Show of Shows*, I go into labor!

"Well! It was chaos! Morty running to get the car... You know, I spent ten days in the hospital... Uncle Irv running down the stairs with my suitcase... Aunt Junie carrying my purse and my makeup case... Uncle Bernie making jokes... Grandpa warning me to hold the railing... And Aunt Clara trying to herd us all down the stairs as quickly and safely as possible..."

And as the quintessential Jewish mother she was, she continued, "You see, kids, that's the way childbirth should be. The men pacing in the waiting room, the mom-to-be put out of it with medication... Chris! Why suffer? This is the 20th Century, darling! Take the anesthesia. Let the doctors take care of it. Have sweet dreams, and wake up with a baby in your arms!

"Which reminds me. Kids! What is this nonsense about fathers in the delivery room?!? Listen, Chris... You don't have to have Garry there, just because he **thinks** he has to! This is terrible! Dangerous... for the marriage, I mean.

"What man could ever look at his wife the same way again? All that disgusting stuff... I don't even want to THINK about it! After that, I'm warning you... Now, I'm not a witch, but I'm ALWAYS right... After that... Well, how can I put it? Do I have to draw you a picture? It's all over. The romance is over. A husband won't see his wife the same way... How could he?"

She took a breath for a second to look at both our faces, and realized that neither of us shared her view of childbirth. I was smirking, shaking my head, knowing that my mother was never going to stop her attempt to change our minds. Which she continued right up to my phone call to her that we were off to the hospital.

"Ach, what can I do with you? Your generation! You just don't listen. Well, I tried my hardest. No one can say I didn't try. There's just no reasoning with you two..."

Chris and I tried to explain to her that that may have been the norm for **her** generation, but **our** generation viewed childbirth as the most beautiful experience two people could share.

And as an aside, with a smile and a wink at Chris, I said to my mother, "Well, considering I caused this..." putting my hand on her 7-month-pregnant belly, "I really should be there to support her... Not to mention that I want Chris and I to be the first people to know if we are the parents of a little boy or a little girl."

Although she accepted our decision, Mom was still very much of the 1940's mindset. I assured her that the relationship between Chris and I would be fine, even though I would be in the delivery room to participate in all that would be involved in the birth of our child. (Now, I can't imagine a father not wanting to be there.)

And in 1977 Chris and I were the first people to know that we had a son. From childhood on, Aaron has heard my stories of being a first time father, and my inexperience with the midnight feedings and diaper changes. He would laugh at what I went through, knowing that he was the cause of all my exasperation.

~ ~ ~

Twenty-six years later, Aaron married his girlfriend Kristie, and they would frequently come over to our home for dinner. One evening, when Chris and I had just finished dinner, the doorbell rang unexpectedly.

At the door were Aaron and Kristie, who walked into the kitchen and asked us if we wanted to see an interesting photograph. Kristie handed me a fuzzy, black and white photo. Looking at it from all angles, I had no idea what it was and handed it to Chris. And I became even more confused when, with one look, Chris screamed and started hugging and kissing Kristie!

After the hugging and screaming settled down, they all looked at me - who looked and felt clearly out of the loop - until Chris explained, "Ga! It's a sonogram... This is the first photograph of our grandchild!"

Now totally **in** the loop, I started jumping, hugging and screaming along with everyone else.

That night after everyone left, I went into my bedroom and took out the dream journal that I'd started three days earlier. I opened it to that first entry titled <u>My Grandson</u>, and as I read it, I was sure that I was going to have a grandson.

Like most families, when a pregnancy is announced it seems that everyone becomes a psychic. Whether it's reading tea leaves, or threading a needle to hang over the belly of the poor expectant woman, everyone wants to know the baby's gender and many freely offer their opinions. Some folks ask the older members of the family, who have proven over the years to be more accurate in the gender guessing game than a 50/50 game of chance...

And some actually go to a psychic.

At that time in my life, I was still overly preoccupied with my new metaphysical beliefs and due to the excitement I felt about these discoveries, I wanted everyone to understand how very cool they were. I started to tell everyone about my dream and how sure I was that I was going to have a grand-**son**! It wasn't that I preferred a boy over a girl. It was more important for me to believe in my perceived ability to see my grandson in that dream... And then the next day I find that I was going to be a grandfather. It was an easy jump, to think that this coincidence or synchronicity was making me feel confident enough in my new found abilities to tell everyone I knew that this baby was going to be a boy.

Well, that was all a number of my in-laws needed for some (less-than) good natured fun, at my expense. Many were anything but supportive of my new belief, and I was too caught up in that belief to curtail my opinion, that I presented so naïvely as an absolute certainty.

I also learned through that experience, that some Life Lessons come at the expense of being wrong, some come with embarrassment, some come with being the subject of good-natured teasing. And some come with all that and more.

~ ~ ~

Seven months later on May 13, 2005, I received a call from Chris as I was signing out in the school's main office. Everyone in the school was excitedly waiting for the news about my first grandchild.

So when my cell phone rang all eyes looked at me, as I heard Chris say, "She's going to the hospital! She's having contractions. Get home quick!" I announced to everyone that this was the phone call I'd been waiting for, and I would let them know pretty soon… That I had a grandson.

Chris and I entered the maternity waiting room at around 5 o'clock and joined Kristie's parents and my daughter Amy, who were already there waiting for news. As we sat, there was laughter, casual conversation, yawning… and a lot of expectation. After three hours, Aaron came into the waiting room and said that the contractions had stopped, and the doctors weren't going to induce labor until midnight. He told us to go home, get some sleep, and be ready to return at around 2:00 am.

Although we would only get a few hours of sleep, our own beds were considerably more comfortable than trying to nap on waiting room chairs. So we all left Morristown Hospital at around 9:00 pm, knowing Kristie was not going to deliver any time soon.

By the time we got home, brushed our teeth and got into bed, it was already 10:30. After an exciting although anticlimactic day, I must confess that going to sleep sounded like the perfect thing to do. Just as I felt the first snore exit my nose and reverberate through the bedroom, the phone rang at 11:35. Somehow, it seemed considerably louder than normal. Before I could get the "O" out of "Hell-o", a frantic Aaron yelled, "She's fully dilated and the doctor told her to push!! GET BACK HERE NOW!!... Click."

The scene that ensued would have made Lucy, Desi, and my mother proud. Chris, Amy, and I all bumping into each other, running all around, finally jumping into the car and taking off back to Morristown. On the way back, we were all just so excited! It was such a wonderful time for all of us, to welcome in a new member to our family, and we were relishing every single moment of it.

By 2:00 am the relishing was over and we were desperate to know what was happening with Kristie. No one had come into the waiting room to update us since we'd arrived.

Chris said, "OK. I'm going in to find out what's going on!"

But before she reached the door, a delivery nurse entered the waiting room and said, "Would you like to go in and see her?"

My thoughts were swirling, distracted and confused.

What? Between contractions? What's going on...?

We'd been waiting for two and a half hours and no one came out to tell us what's going on...?

How's Kristie? Where's Aaron? Is she going to need a C-section...?

As the nurse led us down the brightly lit hallway, Chris, Amy, and I - along with Kristie's parents - all had the same perplexed look on our faces. When Aaron and Kristie had gone for all her pre-natal examinations, they told all the nurses and doctors not to tell them what sex the baby was. So, when the nurse opened the door, Kristie was very calmly sitting in her bed looking peaceful, smiling and blissful, eating a dish of ice cream. Now our confusion only grew!

Kristie said to the nurse, "They don't know if the baby's a girl or a boy yet so let it be a surprise to them, too!"

I looked at Chris and everyone else and then back at Kristie. "You had the baby already?"

Kristie looked shocked as she asked, "You mean no one told you?"

We just shouted, "See ya later," to Kristie and followed the nurse down the maternity ward corridor, like little ducklings following their mother, all the way to the nursery... where Aaron was standing, cradling his newborn.

You could feel the anticipation in the sanitized, antiseptic, hospital air. The excitement was obvious, and the concern and fear of not knowing how Kristie and the baby were, was gone.

We had seen Kristie, in her hospital bed, with the excitement and joy of having just given birth; we knew that both mother and child were fine. The concerns of a C-section, the fears of the possible complications inherent in childbirth had all disappeared with Kristie's smile from her hospital bed. The broad smile and the twinkle in her eyes, said it all. All that was left was the big question: *A boy or a girl?*

Standing with everyone in the hallway, the memory of my dream came back to me. And with a private internal smile to myself, I looked forward to meeting my grandson.

I stood behind everyone, taking it all in. Memories of the births of our own two children came quickly to mind. As we approached the glass windows, I saw my son, holding his child, as the doctor said, "So... are you guys ready to see your little princess?"

My daughter just jumped straight up in the air, "OH... MY... GOD! A girl!! That is SOOO wonderful!" as her hands covered her mouth to keep her from screaming louder. I saw Ken and Ginny, Kristie's parents, with their arms around each other. I stood behind Chris with my hands on her shoulders, as we watched our son and our new granddaughter.

Aaron was holding his daughter and seemed to be moving her arms and legs with studied concentration. I looked at Chris questioningly, knowing that, as a nurse, she would understand what Aaron was doing to his newborn. With love and pride in every word, Chris whispered to me that Aaron (now a Physical Therapist) was checking his daughter's reflexes. Soon, he looked up with a smile, and winked at Chris. She turned and whispered to me that the baby was perfect.

THE METAMORPHOSIS

As I stood watching my son holding his newborn, not yet two hours old, a subtle metamorphosis took place. Not in Aaron, because he had been preparing for this moment for much longer than nine months.

The metamorphosis I mentioned was not in Aaron. It was within me. At the instant I saw my son with his tiny baby, I changed. My perception of Aaron changed. MY *yellow glasses* became obvious to me. My perception of what a father, son and grandfather should be, had been viewed through my personal yellow glasses and, as in all cases of 'Yellow Glassitus', once the glasses are removed, the wearer's view of the world is changed immediately and permanently. Once they were removed, the metamorphosis within me was as inevitable as the pride I felt when I witnessed my son become a father.

It wasn't the abrupt change that occurs in the children of friends, who you hadn't seen in a while. How their once gangly, pre-adolescent son suddenly has an Adam's apple, a mustache and has grown six inches and forty pounds since the last time you'd seen him. Those kinds of changes are powerful and obvious.

This was the subtle change you see in family members, while viewing a photo album. As you flip through the cellophane covered pages of the old photographs, noting with nostalgia how tiny the kids were; feeling the slight grin that forms as you muse over the memories of those early days in your family's life. With the turn of each page, like the years themselves, evolving... Recalling the physical changes documented by the camera over so many years makes you sit back, with a deep breath, and smile.

It is good to reminisce.

But in that split second, I saw my son evolve from a five pound nine ounce baby boy, to a toddler, to an adolescent, to a young adult, to a man. No longer my forgetful kid, no longer the teenager who played video games instead of doing his homework, no longer a young married man. In that one second he became the man I'd always known he'd become... A man and a father in the very best sense of the word. And, indeed, he has proven to be the incredible father I knew he would be.

The next day as we all visited the new family, I was able to hold my granddaughter for the first time. Looking at tiny Meghan, I realized the difference between being a father, and a grandfather. The concerns and fears I'd had when her father was her age - 12 hours old - were not present. There were no concerns. All there was, was joy.

As I held my first grandchild, in my mind I silently said to her, *Thank-you Meghan, for joining our family. I am looking forward to being your grandpa.* Her eyes opened for just a second. She looked directly into mine. And smiled.

No one was aware of this conversation, the look, or her smile. Had they been aware of my private thoughts, they would have told me that a newborn can't see, and certainly was not able to smile. They would tell me she was reacting to the stimulus of being moved from one relative to another. And that babies who have gas look just like they are smiling. So I never told anyone. But I knew that my day-old granddaughter and I had a little secret.

I knew she heard me. I knew she smiled, to tell me that she was happy to be in our family too, and was looking forward to being my granddaughter. I wondered who the soul in that little body had been during her most recent incarnation. Was she my father or mother? Had we perhaps shared past lives together?

But it was a moot point. Because whomever Meghan had been in a past life, I could not love her any more than I do in this lifetime. Two years later, my ability to love doubled when I met her baby sister, Paige. (And I am blessed to say that I have had the love and joy of being a grandpa quadrupled since first meeting Meghan that day.)

Although I was disappointed and embarrassed with my psychic in-abilities, especially when everyone in the family reminded me how emphatic I'd been that Meghan was going to be a boy, I was beyond thrilled with that sweet, precious gift: Our Meghan.

COLE

Two years after Meghan was born, in 2007, Paige joined her older sister in our family. And in September of 2012, I finally met my grandson: Cole.

Every Wednesday since Meghan was born, Chris babysat our grandchildren. And now, with both Meghan and Paige in elementary school, Cole was the only grandchild she babysat for during the day.

In late 2016, with retirement coming on the first of the year, I decided that it would be a great memory for Cole (and for me), if we made a habit of going to breakfast every Wednesday morning. I told Chris my thoughts and said that I would pick him up on Wednesdays and take him to the local Panera for breakfast. She thought it was a great idea and appreciated being able to sleep a little later on Wednesdays.

And on that first Wednesday of my retirement, I went to pick up my grandson for breakfast. It became the first of many Wednesdays we would spend together.

We drove to the Panera restaurant in the Trade Zone, the closest mall to us in Flanders, and got out of the car. The mall was built on the top of an elevated section of Flanders, and the wind howls there even on the calmest of days.

We ran in through the double doors, laughing and shaking off the cold while taking off our coats and tossing them in a booth. Panera was fairly empty and there was no one on line as the girl behind the counter greeted us with a smile as warm as the restaurant itself. I tossed Cole up in the air and carried him over to the glass display case with the muffins and huge cookies. I asked Cole to tell her what he wanted for breakfast. As he was deciding, with his thumb and index finger pinching his chin, showing how deep in thought he was, she looked at me and smiled at the cute couple she was serving: a grandpa and his adorable four-year-old grandson. I couldn't deny I had a wonderful sense of joy, pride and love in the experience.

He ordered his chocolate chip muffin top and chocolate milk, I ordered my power breakfast and coffee, as I became aware of a familiar feeling of déjà vu. I carried the tray as we walked to the booth with our breakfast which would become *our* booth.

We pushed our coats over and sat, and I smiled as I cut up his muffin top. Cole had just gotten glasses, and they looked very similar to mine. As he took a triangular shaped piece of muffin and popped it in his mouth, he gave me a big, one-tooth-missing smile (he'd his left incisor tooth extracted after a fall).

I'd been to this Panera many times, sometimes with the whole family, but that morning, it seemed different to me. I smiled as I watched Cole use his four fingers, covered in sticky chocolate chip muffin, to push his glasses up on the bridge of his nose. Looking at his smeared lenses brought back a memory.

And then I realized why I was experiencing déjà vu. The feeling wasn't déjà vu at all. As with other experiences like the one I was having, I understood why it seemed so familiar.

It was the dream I'd had, 12 years earlier, months before I became a grandfather. I had seen this moment in time, when I would be sitting in a booth in a restaurant, with my grandson - eyes twinkling behind his glasses - who wouldn't be born for another seven years.

And as I recalled the dream, I found myself looking at Cole in a far off way. The way you look when you are daydreaming. As I refocused my eyes back on Cole, a big smile formed on his little face and he stuck out his tongue at me and did a raspberry, the way I always did to him. I laughed out loud and said, "You are such a goofy kid." To which, his smile got bigger as he simply nodded yes, giggled and slipped under the table.

As he popped his head up, I thought to myself how incredibly fortunate and happy I was at that moment.

Education is a two way street... As you teach, you also learn.
As you observe the growth in those you love,
you also feel growth within yourself.

LEARNING WITH MEGHAN

As I've said, when Meghan and Paige were small, my wife and I had the joy of babysitting every Wednesday. Chris would drive to our son's home where she would pick up our granddaughters. I was at school, but would leave immediately after classes were done, to rush home so I could get a few hours with my girls.

All too soon, Meghan was in Second Grade and Paige was in Kindergarten. Wednesdays became my day to work with Meghan on her homework, and as I always did with my students, I tried to make learning as much fun as possible. We would always laugh and learn at the same time. I'd sit back and smile as I saw her little fingers fly over the keyboard of our home computer. One day she pulled up her online English homework and we worked on it together. Her homework that day was to read some paragraphs and then answer the on-line questions. She looked at me and said, "Grandpa, how about I read a paragraph and you read a paragraph?" I answered with a smile, as I was thinking of how I could make this fun.

Her homework assignment was reading about life in Australia. As I read my paragraph, I attempted to use an Australian accent, which was really bad but made my Meghan laugh. Her Nana yelled down to us to stop playing around because dinner was almost ready and Meghan had to finish her homework before we took the girls home.

As we read the paragraphs to each other, Meghan was picking up a fairly good Australian accent herself, and we laughed quietly at our little joke. Just before she finished writing the answers, she stopped, took a deep breath and looked at me in a questioning way. Which made me look right back at her, asking, "What?"

Meghan took another deep breath, still smiling at me, looked at me with her perfectly blue eyes, and said, "I love you, Grandpa."

It was one of those moments that define what grandparenting is all about. Words could not accurately describe how I felt, other than 'beaming'.

At that moment, the thought hit me, that when I am no longer here and my little Meghan has a family with children of her own, she might seek out a medium like me. Perhaps he might even be a grandfather himself, and could relate to the information that I would be sending him... The same way I relay the information I get from grandfatherly spirits who want to connect with their granddaughters, who have grown and now have families of their own. Just as I had passed on messages to Gloria from her Nana, years before.

I would be able to communicate with my grandchildren through this medium. I would bring the image to the medium, of him sitting with his own granddaughter at their computer desk, laughing and learning. I would send him the image of his granddaughter putting her head on his shoulder, saying, "Grandpa, I love you."

I would have him say to Meghan, "Your grandpa is here and he's showing me how much fun you two had; when he was helping you with your homework; and how you laughed together using silly Australian accents until your Nana yelled down for you to stop; and how you told him, 'I love you, Grandpa'."

I would then send him a message for her that was more than a simple "He loves you." I would help him send the message to her that I am still here with her. Although it will be in the far future, I imagine my granddaughter's eyes well with tears, as she realizes that I am not really gone... never really gone... But simply, watching her and her own family grow from a different vantage point.

As you get older, you can see and be thrilled by
the growth in the young ones you love.
But as you get older it seems that your
own growth is quite minimal.
Until someone much older than you
shows you how much they love and are thrilled
by just how much <u>you've</u> grown.

GROWING WITH PAIGE

It was a perfect Wednesday in the fall of 2008. The temperature was in the 60's, sunny with a gentle breeze. As I pulled up, Chris was playing with Meghan, drawing pictures on the blacktop with bright blue chalk, as Paige sat on a blanket next to them. I parked in the street and briskly walked toward them, laughing as little Paige smiled at me and extended her arms for me to pick her up.

Paige was a year old and had just started to walk by herself, with the classic and comical movements of a toddler: arms outstretched, wobbling side to side. At home, I would walk around following behind her, prepared to catch her if she began to fall, closing doors to stairways, gently guiding her to safe areas of the house. As she navigated her way around the house, I always marveled at the way intelligence grows in a child.

At that time, Aaron and I both had goatees: his was dark brown, mine almost all grey. As I held Paige, she would touch my beard, while looking at her father's. I realized that she was noticing the differences and similarities of the people around her. As she was growing physically, she was growing intellectually.

Now I walked up to her, lifted her from the blanket, and stood her up on the blacktop of our driveway, using my index finger as a support until she felt confident enough to walk by herself. I followed behind, smiling the way grandparents smile at the children of their children; marveling at the intelligence beginning to blossom in their minds, and the strength growing in their little bodies. At that time, Paige was walking like a drunken sailor, bending over trying to pick up a twig and falling face first on the grass, laughing as I picked her up.

She began to walk toward the street, with me immediately behind. Instead of picking her up (which was my first inclination), I chose to walk behind her, observing, protecting and allowing her to explore. As she moved further away from the house, she turned to look for her Nana and sister, who were very much occupied drawing stick figures on the blacktop. Turning to see me and feeling more confident and curious, Paige turned and began to walk more quickly toward the street.

With one foot on the grass and one on the blacktop, she lost her balance and once again, instead of picking her up, I simply put my hand out to allow her to take my hand for support. She reached up, and with all five tiny fingers, grabbed my pinky tightly. Balance regained and confidence restored, she continued down the drive with me to her right, offering a helpful pinky each time she needed it.

She stopped at the street with me close behind. As she stepped off the driveway onto the street, she once again lost her balance. Without looking for me, her hand went up behind her shoulder and took hold of my pinky. I smiled, because she didn't need to look for my hand. She just reached up for it, on faith alone. She just knew I would be there for her. And I was!

Now, walking confidently down the street, she eventually releasing her grip on my finger, never looking for me but knowing I was there. I marveled at the way everything excited her. "Disss" she said pointing to a bird. In her young life her vocabulary was limited to "Disss" and "Daaa", but she definitely had a way of communicating with us.

We continued down the street, Paige in front, exploring, me behind in the role of a loving protector and observer... and in my own way a student in the way little souls grow. In my head, I thanked the immortal soul in that little body, for choosing to join our family. I wondered if hers was the soul of one of my grandmothers whom I had never known. I thought about how our lives would be; our relationship; our time together on the planet; if we had shared past lives together. (I intuitively knew the answer without asking.) My mediumship experiences were far from my mind as I played and walked with Paige, just enjoying being present in the moment.

Then, I became aware of a presence... That little voice in my head, coming from my left ear, from that place where I connect with spirits. I was very comfortable with that voice and that feeling, although I didn't expect to feel the presence of a spirit at that moment. It just came from out of the blue. However, I have learned not to ignore it or think it is my imagination as I used to. I now listen. Always.

What I heard made me pause. I had become comfortable with the difference between the 'From Me, To Me's of the past. This voice/thought was most definitely not from me, and as I always do, I honored it. But what was confusing me was that, although I felt it the same way I feel a spirit of a passed loved one, I knew that this time it wasn't a spirit that I was feeling. Something else... Perhaps a Spirit Guide or even an archangel? Whatever it was, it had my complete attention.

I knew that this spirit energy was female: the way women in spirit feel to me. But this energy was different than those spirits who want to communicate through me, to their loved ones who are still here. This spirit was simply talking to me. She also felt like a teacher or guide.

It occurred to me that she very well might be one of my own Spirit Guides, as she said to me, *'That is what We do as We observe you.'* As I have become comfortable doing, I asked for clarification, and this gentle, quiet voice came back - showing me more than telling me - that in spirit our loved ones, Spirit Guides, angels, are still with us... loving us, protecting us, helping to direct us so we can continue to do what we came here to do... Learn!

I either realized or was shown that the way I feel toward my granddaughter is the same way the souls of our loved ones and our Guides feel about us. Sometimes we look and ask for a hand to help. Sometimes we reach up, simply on faith that they will be there and grab a hold of a spiritual pinky. Just as my granddaughter reached up on faith alone, knowing that my pinky would be there for her.

I now accepted that this communication was indeed coming from one of my Spirit Guides, and as soon as I acknowledged that, in my thoughts she mentioned that Paige has more faith in me than I have in my Guide, herself. Sending me the image of what I already knew: that I would always be there for my grandchildren, as my Guides would always be there for me, whether I believed in them or not. She also helped me understand this Truth: when we accept that our Guides will be with us always, positive change can happen instantly.

Then again, that voice said to me with a spiritual smile, *'We, as you, are like a grandparent, lovingly watching our grandchildren grow...'* And with a shrug, she gently sent the words to me...

'Sometimes our grandchildren listen, sometimes they don't... Did you think it would be different in spirit than it is on Earth?'

Yes, I thought. But that last statement did make me smile.

That loving spirit let me know that it was proud and overjoyed with the little baby steps I was taking, just as I was proud and overjoyed by the baby steps my granddaughter was taking. I picked up Paige in my arms and tossed her in the air and she squealed with delight and wrapped her arms around my neck as if to say, "Thank you Grandpa for playing with me... for watching out for me... for being there for me." The same life lesson and the same way I was feeling about my Guides and protectors.

I thanked the spirit as I always do as she was pulling back. Although I lost my connection with her, I still felt her, in the joy and happiness of being a proud grandfather and feeling the love reflected back to me from that familiar, loving soul I saw in Paige's eyes.

*Once you find an answer to a question, it is
quickly replaced by another question,
and so you will never be without a question...
And because it is in our nature, humans always question.
However, as soon as we think we have an answer to one,
it is rarely replaced with another.
It is usually replaced with many more!*

LEARNING FROM LIFE

In his third book - **Messages From The Masters - Tapping Into The Power Of Love** - Dr. Brian Weiss wrote:

In this one-room schoolhouse we called the Earth, we do not learn all of our lessons simultaneously. For example, we may have already mastered the course in compassion and charity, but we may only be beginners when it comes to patience or forgiveness. We may be graduate students in faith and hope, but kindergartners in anger and non-violence.

Similarly, we may carry over skills and talents learned in earlier incarnations, skills we have mastered, yet we may be novices in other areas. We have among us many who have mastered certain courses and skills, and they are here to share their knowledge with us, the students. In other areas, our roles may reverse.

Thus we are all teachers and we are all students, and we must share our knowledge with each other.

Many physicians have chosen to be doctors in order to manifest their healing abilities, to help and to teach others. Conversely a wise physician will always be open to learning from his or her patients. The patient might be able to teach the physician about love, about courage, about inner peace, or any of the other lessons we are here to learn. Both physician and patient benefit.

I've come to understand that we are all students on a journey of education. The purpose of this educational process (as Dr. Weiss would say) is to learn as much as we can about the very complex subject of Humanity, at this school called Earth.

Some of us pass with flying colors. Some of us squeak by just happy to get out in one piece. Some of us fail and some of us fail miserably. There is no Hell for them, for there is no such thing as Hell. They fail just like in school, but in this school called Earth, there is no political passing. There is no 'teaching to the test'. There is no cheating. If you fail like

337

Adolph Hitler and all the other tyrants throughout history, you just get left back to take the course over again... until you get it right.

I've also learned, on my journey, that we don't live on Earth alone. I'm not talking about family, friends, acquaintances or strangers. I'm talking about *spirit helpers*: our Team. The goal of our Team is to help us survive, live, succeed, learn, grow and be happy. If we succeed in learning all we have come to Earth to learn, we are at the top of our class. But that seems a bit judgmental. There are no levels of learning in our School. We all help each other and find joy in our growth AND in every other soul's growth.

Whether in this life or the next, we come here to learn who we truly are: who and what our souls truly are. And it is the mission of our Team to assist us on our Journey: our Spiritual Evolution. What they - our loved ones and Guides - **cannot** do is force us to do anything. They can and do offer suggestions. They nudge us. They guide us. They warn us, all in the form of synchronicities. But when it comes to making a choice for us, they can do nothing.

"FREE WILL," to quote Gene Roddenberry - creator of *Star Trek* - "is the **Prime Directive**." No Guide, angel or loved one can override our free will. If life on Earth is truly for our education, having our Spirit Guides or teachers tell us in which direction we **must** go, would be as if they gave us the answers to a very difficult and important test. They just cannot do it. That would be cheating!

So as you continue your own education on Earth, working on your advanced degree on the subject of 'Being Human', look for those synchronicities. Feel the *nudges*. When you are trying to do something as difficult as quitting smoking, and four different people in your life tell you about hypnosis, acknowledge the *nudge*, and seek out a hypnotist.

Realize that if you think, *If God could make a job specifically for me, it would be this one*, know that He actually **did**, and jump at the opportunity being offered to you.

Look for the suggestions and synchronicities in books like <u>Many Lives, Many Masters</u>, as they will literally fall into your hands. And follow up on the information within the book.

Once you understand the way our Guides, helpers and loved ones send us help, you will realize how that help was, is, and always will be constantly there... simply waiting for you to listen to their suggestions. I have learned many lessons so far on my journey. Another Life Lesson is that you never stop learning, here on Earth or anywhere else your soul may find itself. But once again...

That's just my opinion.

And as for me,

MY JOURNEY CONTINUES...

ACKNOWLEDGEMENTS

I want to thank so many people:

My family:

- Chris - Thank-you for accepting and understanding the changes I have gone through and keeping me grounded. Believe me when I say that I know how hard (headed) I can be. Without your presence in my life I would have not known the love of family.
- Aaron, Amy, their spouses Kristie and Keith and my grandchildren - who make me smile every single day -
- Meghan, Paige, Cole and Elyse; I love you all soooo much!
- My cousin / big sister Joyce.
- All my cousins, in-laws, nieces and nephews. With a special thanks to Melissa and Rose for the support and suggestions.

My friends at the Institute for Spiritual Development, and Inner Spiritual Center.

My fellow metaphysical explorers:

- Tricia, thank-you my friend, teacher, mentor and guide, without you there would have been no book; I would not have embarked on this metaphysical journey.
- Bill, Heather, Jamie, Jill, Joella, and Susan for the support and being there from the start.

The authors and teachers in my life - Thank you all for your life's work -

- Bill Collar,
- John Edward,
- John Holland,
- Simon James,
- Janet Nohavec,
- Mavis Pittilla,
- Brian Robertson,
- Richard Schoeller,
- Dr. Gary E. Schwartz
- Sharon Siubis,
- Tony Stockwell,
- Eckhart Tolle,
- James Van Praagh,
- Neale Donald Walsch
- Dr. Brian Weiss.

And last but never least…

A huge thank-you (truly there are no words capable of expressing my love and appreciation) to and for my baby sister - Linnie: Retired English teacher and the incredible Editor - par excellence - of this book (notice the proper use of a colon; you see, you really **are** never too old to learn ;)